AF184005

ICSA Study Text

Company Law

ICSA Study Text

Company Law

Lee Roach

icsa

The Governance Institute

First published 2019
Published by ICSA Publishing Ltd
Saffron House
6–10 Kirby Street
London EC1N 8TS

Typeset by Paul Barrett Book Production, Cambridge

British Cataloguing in Publication Data
A catalogue record for this book is available from the British Library.

ISBN 9781860727474

Contents

How to use this study text

This study text has been developed to support the Company Law module of the ICSA's qualifying programme and includes a range of navigational, self-testing and illustrative features to help you get the most out of the support materials.

The text is divided into three main sections:

- introductory material
- the text itself
- reference material.

The sections below show you how to find your way around the text and make the most of its features.

Introductory material

The introductory section includes a full contents list and the aims and learning outcomes of the qualification, as well as a list of acronyms and abbreviations.

The text itself

Each part opens with a list of the chapters to follow, an overview of what will be covered and learning outcomes for the part.

Every chapter opens with a list of the topics covered and an introduction specific to that chapter.

Chapters are structured to allow students to break the content down into manageable sections for study. Each chapter ends with a summary of key content to reinforce understanding.

Features

The text is enhanced by a range of illustrative and self-testing features to assist understanding and to help you prepare for the examination. You will find answers to the 'Test yourself' questions towards the end of this text. Each feature is presented in a standard format, so that you will become familiar with how to use them in your study.

These features are identified by a series of icons.

The text also includes tables, figures and other illustrations as relevant.

Reference material

The text contains a range of additional guidance and reference material, including a glossary of key terms and a comprehensive index.

Stop and think

Test yourself

Case law

Case study

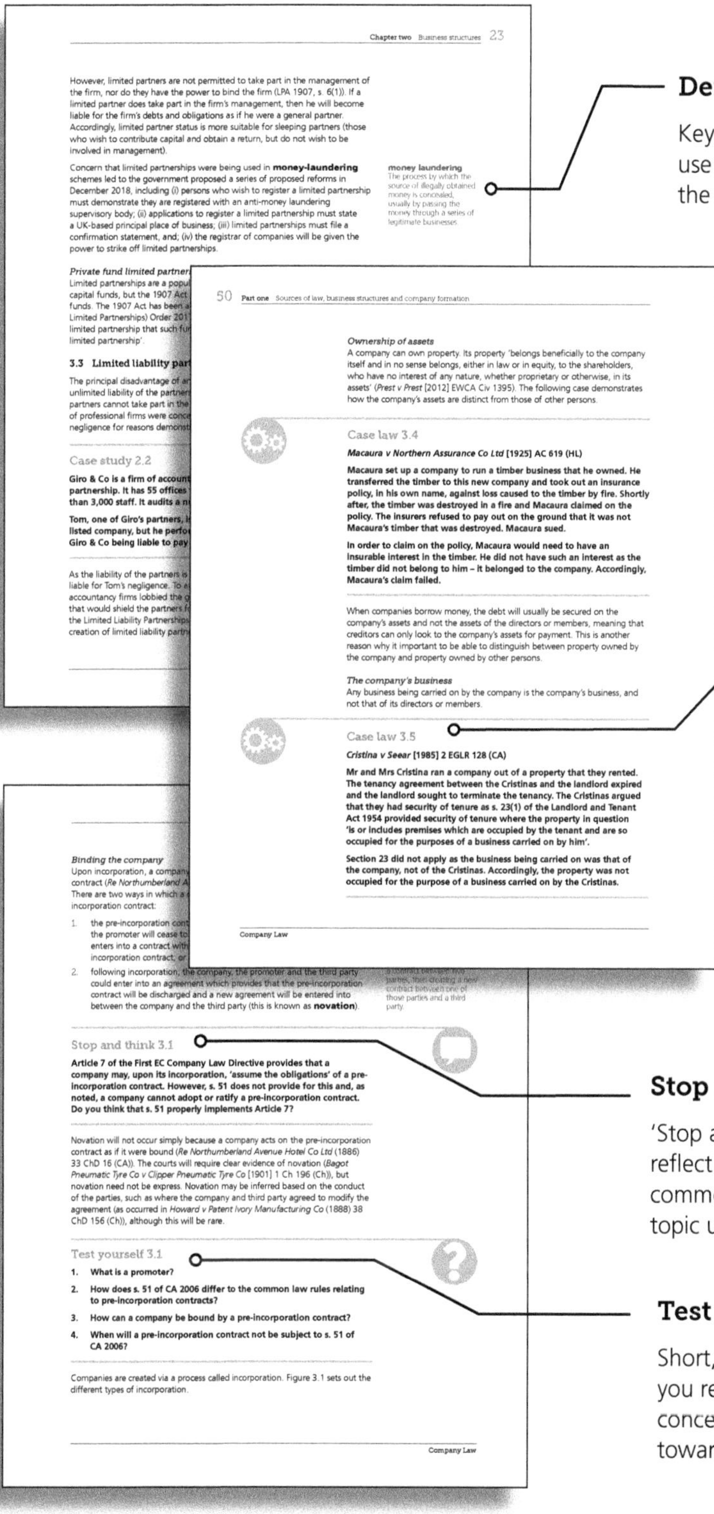
Chapter two Business structures 23

However, limited partners are not permitted to take part in the management of the firm, nor do they have the power to bind the firm (LPA 1907, s. 6(1)). If a limited partner does take part in the firm's management, then he will become liable for the firm's debts and obligations as if he were a general partner. Accordingly, limited partner status is more suitable for sleeping partners (those who wish to contribute capital and obtain a return, but do not wish to be involved in management).

Concern that limited partnerships were being used in **money-laundering** schemes led to the government proposed a series of proposed reforms in December 2018, including (i) persons who wish to register a limited partnership must demonstrate they are registered with an anti-money laundering supervisory body; (ii) applications to register a limited partnership must state a UK-based principal place of business; (iii) limited partnerships must file a confirmation statement, and; (iv) the registrar of companies will be given the power to strike off limited partnerships.

money laundering The process by which the source of illegally obtained money is concealed, usually by passing the money through a series of legitimate businesses.

50 Part one Sources of law, business structures and company formation

Ownership of assets
A company can own property. Its property 'belongs beneficially to the company itself and in no sense belongs, either in law or in equity, to the shareholders, who have no interest of any nature, whether proprietary or otherwise, in its assets' (*Prest v Prest* [2012] EWCA Civ 1395). The following case demonstrates how the company's assets are distinct from those of other persons.

Case law 3.4
***Macaura v Northern Assurance Co Ltd* [1925] AC 619 (HL)**
Macaura set up a company to run a timber business that he owned. He transferred the timber to this new company and took out an insurance policy, in his own name, against loss caused to the timber by fire. Shortly after, the timber was destroyed in a fire and Macaura claimed on the policy. The insurers refused to pay out on the ground that it was not Macaura's timber that was destroyed. Macaura sued.
In order to claim on the policy, Macaura would need to have an insurable interest in the timber. He did not have such an interest as the timber did not belong to him – it belonged to the company. Accordingly, Macaura's claim failed.

When companies borrow money, the debt will usually be secured on the company's assets and not the assets of the directors or members, meaning that creditors can only look to the company's assets for payment. This is another reason why it important to be able to distinguish between property owned by the company and property owned by other persons.

The company's business
Any business being carried on by the company is the company's business, and not that of its directors or members.

Case law 3.5
***Cristina v Seear* [1985] 2 EGLR 128 (CA)**
Mr and Mrs Cristina ran a company out of a property that they rented. The tenancy agreement between the Cristinas and the landlord expired and the landlord sought to terminate the tenancy. The Cristinas argued that they had security of tenure as s. 23(1) of the Landlord and Tenant Act 1954 provided security of tenure where the property in question 'is or includes premises which are occupied by the tenant and are so occupied for the purposes of a business carried on by him'.
Section 23 did not apply as the business being carried on was that of the company, not of the Cristinas. Accordingly, the property was not occupied for the purpose of a business carried on by the Cristinas.

Company Law

Stop and think 3.1
Article 7 of the First EC Company Law Directive provides that a company may, upon its incorporation, 'assume the obligations' of a pre-incorporation contract. However, s. 51 does not provide for this and, as noted, a company cannot adopt or ratify a pre-incorporation contract. Do you think that s. 51 properly implements Article 7?

Novation will not occur simply because a company acts on the pre-incorporation contract as if it were bound (*Re Northumberland Avenue Hotel Co Ltd* (1886) 33 ChD 16 (CA)). The courts will require clear evidence of novation (*Bagot Pneumatic Tyre Co v Clipper Pneumatic Tyre Co* [1901] 1 Ch 196 (Ch)), but novation need not be express. Novation may be inferred based on the conduct of the parties, such as where the company and third party agreed to modify the agreement (as occurred in *Howard v Patent Ivory Manufacturing Co* (1888) 38 ChD 156 (Ch)), although this will be rare.

Test yourself 3.1
1. **What is a promoter?**
2. **How does s. 51 of CA 2006 differ to the common law rules relating to pre-incorporation contracts?**
3. **How can a company be bound by a pre-incorporation contract?**
4. **When will a pre-incorporation contract not be subject to s. 51 of CA 2006?**

Companies are created via a process called incorporation. Figure 3.1 sets out the different types of incorporation.

Company Law

Definitions

Key terms are highlighted in bold on first use and defined in the page margins and the end of book glossary.

Case law

Summaries of landmark cases and judgements allow you to link theory to real-world examples.

Stop and think

'Stop and think' boxes encourage you to reflect on how your own experiences or common business scenarios relate to the topic under discussion.

Test yourself

Short, revision-style questions to help you recap on key information and core concepts. Answers are to be found towards the end of the text.

About the Author

Dr Lee Roach is a Senior Lecturer in Law at the University of Portsmouth. He has nearly twenty years' teaching experience lecturing in company law and corporate governance, and has written numerous textbooks including *Card & James' Business Law* (4th edn, OUP 2016), *Company Law Concentrate* (5th edn, OUP 2018), *Commercial Law* (3rd edn, OUP 2019), and *Company Law* (OUP 2019). He is also a co-author of ICSA's *Foundation Programme* study text and is a member of ICSA's Law Review Group.

Acronyms and abbreviations

ACCA	Association of Chartered Certified Accountants
AGM	annual general meeting
BEIS	Department for Business, Energy and Industrial Strategy
CA 2006	Companies Act 2006
CARD	Consolidated Admission and Reporting Directive
CDDA 1986	Company Directors Disqualification Act 1986
CEO	chief executive officer
CIC	community interest company
CIO	charitable incorporated organisation
CJA 1993	Criminal Justice Act 1993
CPR	Civil Procedure Rules
CVA	company voluntary arrangement
DTRs	Disclosure Guidance and Transparency Rules
EC	European Community
ECHR	European Convention on Human Rights
EEA	European Economic Area
EEC	European Economic Community
EGM	extraordinary general meeting
EU	European Union
FCA	Financial Conduct Authority
FRC	Financial Reporting Council
FSA 2012	Financial Services Act 2012
FSMA 2000	Financial Services and Markets Act 2000
GLO	group litigation order
HMRC	Her Majesty's Revenue and Customs
IA 1986	Insolvency Act 1986
ICAEW	Institute of Chartered Accountants in England and Wales
ICAS	Institute of Chartered Accountants in Scotland
IPO	initial public offering
IR 2016	Insolvency (England and Wales) Rules 2016
LLP	limited liability partnership
LLPA 2000	Limited Liability Partnerships Act 2000
LP	limited partnership
LPA 1907	Limited Partnerships Act 1907
LR	Listing Rule
LSE	London Stock Exchange

Ltd	Limited
MAR	Market Abuse Regulation
NED	non-executive director
PA 1890	Partnership Act 1890
PAYE	Pay As You Earn
PIE	public interest entity
plc	public limited company
PSC	people/person with significant control
SBEEA 2015	Small Business, Enterprise and Employment Act 2015
SE	*Societas Europaea*
SI	statutory instrument
TFEU	Treaty on the Functioning of the European Union
UKLA	UK Listing Authority
USR 2001	Uncertificated Securities Regulations 2001

Part one

Sources of law, business structures and company formation

Overview

Part one looks at the various sources of company law, the principal business structures, the process for creating a company and the key features of the company.

Chapter 1 sets out the sources of the rules that regulate companies, notably UK legislation, case law, the company's constitution, contract law, corporate governance codes and reports and EU law.

Chapter 2 looks at the various structures available to those who wish to undertake some form of business activity, notably the sole proprietorship, the partnership, the limited liability partnership, the company and the various forms of mutual organisation.

Chapter 3 discusses how to incorporate a company, the rules relating to a company's separate legal personality and in what instances a company can be liable for the actions of others.

Chapter 4 looks at how companies can become legally bound to others. This includes an examination of how companies enter into contracts, the role of a company's constitution, a company's contractual capacity and the ability of others to enter into contracts on behalf of a company.

At the end of this Part, students will be able to:

- identify the key sources of, and the relationship between, company law and corporate governance principles;
- identify the principal business structures available to those who wish to undertake some form of business activity;
- identify the different types of company and demonstrate the differences between them;
- understand the rules relating to promoters and pre-incorporation contracts;
- understand the various ways in which a company can be created;
- discuss the process by which a company can be incorporated by registration;
- demonstrate the importance of the company having a separate legal personality;
- understand when a company's separate personality will be disregarded;
- consider when a company can be liable for the actions of others;
- identify how a company can enter into contracts;
- demonstrate the importance of the company's constitution;
- consider the extent and limitations upon a company's contractual capacity;
- discuss the authority directors have as agents of the company; and
- demonstrate an awareness of the limitations placed upon the board's authority.

Chapter one

Sources of company law and governance

Contents

1. Introduction

This chapter outlines the UK's company law and corporate governance frameworks by examining the key sources of company law and corporate governance principles. Sources of company law and corporate governance principles are usually separate but there is an increasingly connected relationship between them. In order to obtain a full understanding of certain topics, it is important to look at both the law and best practice recommendations. The appointment of a director provides a good example of this.

Case study 1.1

X-Corp plc is a listed company that wishes to appoint a new director to its board. It must comply with a number of laws during this process. X-Corp will need to ensure that the proposed new director is eligible to act as a director, as the law provides that certain persons (for example, X-Corp's auditor) cannot be appointed as a director. The process for appointing a director is a matter for X-Corp's articles but if the articles are silent on this, case law provides that the power to appoint a director is vested in the company's members. Different laws apply depending on whether the director is appointed by the members or the directors.

The UK Corporate Governance Code also contains material relating to appointing directors, notably by providing that X-Corp should set up a nomination committee. The Code also states that the new director's notice or contract period should be set at one year or less, whereas the Companies Act 2006 provides that any guaranteed term of employment over two years requires member approval.

Finally, in recent years, increasing focus has been placed on board diversity, so larger companies like X-Corp should bear in mind the gender and ethnic makeup of their boards when considering board appointments.

2. Legislation

Legislation is the principal source of company law, with Table 1.1 setting out the main examples of company law legislation.

Acts of Parliament	Subordinate legislation	Rules with legislative backing
◆ Stock Transfer Act 1963 ◆ Companies Act 1985 ◆ Insolvency Act 1986 ◆ Company Directors Disqualification Act 1986 ◆ Criminal Justice Act 1993 ◆ Financial Services and Markets Act 2000 ◆ Companies Act 2006 ◆ Corporate Manslaughter and Corporate Homicide Act 2007 ◆ Financial Services Act 2012 ◆ Enterprise and Regulatory Reform Act 2013 ◆ Small Business, Enterprise and Employment Act 2015	◆ Uncertificated Securities Regulations 2001 ◆ Companies (Model Articles) Regulations 2008 ◆ Small Companies and Groups (Accounts and Directors' Report) Regulations 2008 ◆ Large and Medium-Sized Companies and Groups (Accounts and Reports) Regulations 2008 ◆ Overseas Companies Regulations 2009 ◆ Company, Limited Liability Partnership and Business (Names and Trading Disclosures) Regulations 2015 ◆ Insolvency (England and Wales) Rules 2016 ◆ Register of People with Significant Control Regulations 2016	◆ The City Code on Takeovers and Mergers (The Takeover Code) ◆ The Financial Conduct Authority Handbook

Table 1.1 Key pieces of company law legislation

Acts of Parliament make up the dominant form of company law legislation. As Lord Halsbury LC stated in *Ooregum Gold Mining Co of India Ltd v Roper* [1892] AC 125 (HL), 'a limited company owes its existence to the Act of Parliament, and it is to the Act of Parliament one must refer to see what are its powers, and within what limits it is free to act'.

The Act of Parliament he was referring to is the central Companies Act, around which much company law is based.

2.1 The Companies Act 2006

The UK system of company law has been built around a central Companies Act since 1856. There have been many Companies Acts. The current Companies Act 2006 (CA 2006) is reportedly the lengthiest piece of legislation ever passed by Parliament. The Act is divided into 47 parts, with each part covering a particular area of company law (for example, Part 12 sets out the relevant provisions relating to company secretaries). Since the Act's enactment in November 2006, it has been substantially amended and updated by other Acts of Parliament (notably the Enterprise and Regulatory Reform Act 2013 and the Small Business, Enterprise and Employment Act 2015) and subordinate legislation.

2.2 Other notable Acts of Parliament

Certain company law topics that were once covered under a Companies Act are now covered by their own Act of Parliament. Notable examples include the following.

- **Stock Transfer Act 1963:** establishes rules relating to the transfer of shares.
- **Companies Act 1985:** this Act (the predecessor to the CA 2006) has been largely repealed, but some provisions remain in force (namely the provisions relating to company investigations).
- **Insolvency Act 1986:** this Act is the UK's framework for corporate insolvency law and contains rules on how to wind up a company, as well as providing for a number of mechanisms that seek to rescue financially struggling companies.
- **Company Directors Disqualification Act 1986:** this Act establishes when a director can be disqualified and imposes penalties upon those who act as a director while disqualified.
- **Criminal Justice Act 1993:** Part V of this Act establishes the rules relating to the criminal offence of insider dealing.
- **Financial Services and Markets Act 2000 (FSMA 2000):** this Act establishes a financial regulator, namely the Financial Conduct Authority (FCA), and establishes rules designed to regulate financial services and markets.
- **Corporate Manslaughter and Corporate Homicide Act 2007:** this Act created the offence of corporate manslaughter.

2.3 Subordinate legislation

Subordinate legislation, usually in the form of statutory instruments (SIs), is extremely significant. It has five notable functions.

1. It expands upon the basic rules found within an Act of Parliament. For example, Part 15 of the CA 2006 establishes the broad rules relating to a company's annual reports and accounts, but the detailed rules regarding these reports and accounts are found in the Small Companies and Groups (Accounts and Directors' Report) Regulations 2008 (SI 2008/409) and the Large and Medium-Sized Companies and Groups (Accounts and Reports) Regulations 2008 (SI 2008/410). At the time of writing, over 130 SIs have been passed under the CA 2006, many of which serve to flesh out the Act's provisions.
2. It is used to bring parts of Acts of Parliament into force in the form of Commencement Orders. For example, when the CA 2006 was first enacted, only 29 of its 1,300 sections came into force. The remainder of the Act (apart from a few subsections which are still not in force) was brought into force over the next three years via the passing of eight Commencement Orders.
3. It can be used to amend existing legislation, including (controversially) amending Acts of Parliament.
4. It is often used to implement EU law. For example, the Companies (Shareholders' Rights) Regulations 2009 (SI 2009/1632) implemented the Shareholder Rights Directive.
5. It can empower certain persons or bodies to create law. For example, the Secretary of State for Business, Energy and Industrial Strategy is empowered by the CA 2006 to make regulations that provide for a model set of articles that companies may use, namely the Companies (Model Articles) Regulations 2008 (SI 2008/3229).

2.4 Department for Business, Energy and Industrial Strategy

As noted above, legislation often empowers the Secretary of State for Business, Energy and Industrial Strategy (BEIS) to make law (in the form of subordinate legislation) and to exercise a range of company law powers (for example, the ability to commence disqualification proceedings).

It is worth briefly noting here the role of BEIS. According to its website, BEIS is responsible for (amongst other things) 'leading the government's relationship with business'. It is the government department that is most closely involved in company law and corporate governance reform. At the time of writing, BEIS has engaged in a consultation on company law reform and has published a series of governance reform proposals.

2.5 Rules with legislative backing

Certain rules are not found in legislation, but have legislative backing or are recognised by legislation. Examples of non-legislative rules that are recognised by legislation include:

- the FSMA 2000 empowers the FCA to impose rules (notably the FCA Handbook) on companies that wish to trade their shares on an FCA-regulated stock exchange;
- the CA 2006 empowers the Takeover Panel to make rules (namely the City Code on Takeovers and Mergers) regulating takeovers and mergers; and
- the Financial Reporting Council (which is due to be replaced by a new regulator called the Audit, Reporting and Governance Authority) imposes standards upon auditors relating to the quality and ethics of statutory audit work.

Test yourself 1.1

1. **Name the principal piece of UK company law legislation.**
2. **Why is subordinate legislation such an important source of company law?**
3. **What role does BEIS have in relation to company law?**
4. **Provide three examples of company law rules that have legislative backing.**

3. Case law

Despite the breadth and depth of company law legislation, it is not exhaustive. Case law still constitutes an extremely important source of company law for four reasons.

1. Certain company law topics are largely creations of case law and have little or no legislative involvement. For example, the rules relating to attribution (i.e. whose actions can be attributed to the company) are entirely made by judges.
2. Well-established case law principles may be codified into statute (e.g. the general duties found in ss 171–77 of the CA 2006).
3. Legislation will often empower the courts to grant remedies and, in the case of criminal offences, impose punishments. The scope and application of these remedies and punishments is often determined via case law.
4. Legislative rules need to be interpreted and applied. Statutory rules may be made purposely broad and vague in some cases to afford the courts sufficient flexibility. The role of applying those rules in specific instances will be left to the courts. For example, the most important member remedy is the unfair prejudice petition, but only three sections of the CA 2006 (namely ss. 994–96) are devoted to this remedy. These sections provide no guidance on the application of the law. This task has been left entirely to the courts and a substantial body of case law has developed. In some instances, as in the following case, the statutory provision may be drafted poorly or unclearly and may need to be interpreted by the court to reveal its full effect.

Case law 1.1

***Braymist Ltd v Wise Finance Co Ltd* [2002] EWCA Civ 127**

Sturges entered into a contract on behalf of Braymist Ltd (Braymist), under which Braymist would sell a piece of land to Wise Finance Co Ltd (Wise). However, at the time that this contract was entered into, Braymist was in the process of being incorporated, and so it did not yet exist. Subsequently, Wise refused to complete the sale and the issue was whether a valid contract existed and, if so, who was it between. Section 36C(1) of the Companies Act 1985 (now replaced by s. 51(1) of the CA 2006) provided that if a promoter (which Sturges was) entered into a contract with a third party on behalf of a company at a time when that company had not been formed, then the promoter was personally liable on the contract. From this, it is clear that a contract existed between Sturges and Wise, but it was not clear whether Wise could be held liable on the contract as s. 36C only expressly imposed liability on the promoter.

Arden LJ stated that it was clearly Parliament's intention that s. 36C resulted in the creation of a contract between the promoter (Sturges) and the third party (Wise). A contract could only take effect if both parties were able to enforce it, and so Sturges was able to sue Wise on the contract.

4. The constitution of the company

Despite the bulk of company law legislation and case law, companies are afforded the ability to create their own internal rules (namely via the company's constitution) that determine how the company is run.

For example, the CA 2006 says nothing about who determines the directors' remuneration. This is a matter that companies can decide for themselves by placing their own remuneration rules in their articles. In some cases, statute will even allow companies to use their constitution to exclude or modify statutory rules. For example, s. 561 of the CA 2006 grants a company's shareholders rights of pre-emption, which essentially entitles them to the right of first refusal when a new batch of shares are allotted. Private companies can, however, insert a provision in their articles completely excluding these pre-emption rights (CA 2006, s. 567).

As well as empowering the company and its directors, the constitution can also limit powers. For example, the articles can limit the types of activities that the company, directors or members can engage in. Breach of these limitations can amount to a breach of the *ultra vires* rule, breach of contract, or breach of the directors' duties.

5. Contract

One of the most important sources of law from a day-to-day perspective is contract. Every day, companies enter into contracts with suppliers, directors, shareholders, consumers, clients and many other types of person. These relationships will largely be governed by contract, which allows companies to effectively create legally binding rules.

These contracts are governed by general contract law principles, but company law does establish some specific contractual rules. For example, even though the company is a person, it cannot write a signature 'on the dotted line'. Therefore, special rules have developed regarding how companies enter into contracts (discussed in Chapter 4).

6. Corporate governance codes and reports

The UK's corporate governance system is dominated, not by legal rules, by a series of reports and codes that establish best practice principles and provisions.

These codes and reports will be discussed in more detail in the Corporate Governance module, but a basic exposition of them will be beneficial here, given the notable overlap between company law and corporate governance.

6.1 Codes

The UK was one of the first countries in the world to establish a corporate governance code (the 1992 Cadbury Code). Today, the UK's corporate governance system is dominated by three governance codes, namely:

1. the UK Corporate Governance Code, which is primarily aimed at companies and directors;
2. the UK Stewardship Code, which is aimed at certain large shareholders, known as 'institutional investors'; and
3. the Wates Corporate Governance Principles for Large Private Companies.

The UK Corporate Governance Code

The UK Corporate Governance Code was first published in 2010 (although this was a renamed and updated version of the Combined Code on Corporate Governance, which was first published in 1998).

The Code was updated in 2012, 2014, 2016 and 2018. The 2018 Code applies to accounting periods beginning on or after 1 January 2019, so companies will not start reporting on this Code until 2020. The 2018 update represents the most significant update of the Code to date: it is notably shorter than previous Codes and completely restructures the Code (although parts of the 2016 Code have been moved into the accompanying Guidance on Board Effectiveness).

premium listing
A company whose shares have a premium listing is subject to additional rules and is expected to meet the highest standards of regulation and governance.

The Code consists of a series of broad principles that are backed up by a series of slightly more detailed provisions. The Code states that it applies to companies with a **premium listing**, whether incorporated in the UK or elsewhere, but it also recognises that the guidance contained in the Code will not be suitable for every such company. The introduction to the Code therefore states that '[a]n alternative to complying with a Provision may be justified in particular circumstances based on a range of factors, including the size, complexity, history and ownership structure of the company.'

As a result, the Code operates on a comply or explain basis. The detailed operation of this is set out in the Listing Rules, which provide that companies with a premium listing must state in their annual financial report:

- how the company has applied the Code's principles (Listing Rule (LR) 9.8.6(5)R); and
- a statement as to whether the company has complied with all the relevant provisions of the Code, or a statement identifying:
  - which provisions were not complied with;
  - the period within which they were not complied with; and
  - the reasons for non-compliance (LR 9.8.6(6)R).

This approach means that companies can comply with the Code's provisions where they think it appropriate to do so but can depart from the Code's provisions if there are good reasons for doing so.

One criticism of the Code is its scope. The Code applies to companies with a premium listing, indicating that the UK's corporate governance system has historically focused on the UK's largest public companies. The collapse of BHS Ltd and the subsequent revelations of poor governance in the company led to an increased recognition that governance is not only relevant to large public companies. This led to the development of the Wates Corporate Governance Principles for Large Private Companies.

The Wates Corporate Governance Principles

As part of its 2016 Corporate Governance Review, BEIS invited the Financial Reporting Council (FRC), the Institute of Directors and other interested bodies to develop a voluntary set of principles for larger private companies ('Corporate Governance Reform: The Government Response to the Green Paper Consultation').

In January 2018, an industry group was set up by the government to draw up these principles and, in December 2018, the Wates Corporate Governance Principles for Large Private Companies were published. It sets out six core principles.

1. **Purpose and leadership:** an effective board develops and promotes the purpose of a company, and ensures that its values, strategy and culture align with that purpose.
2. **Board composition:** effective board composition requires an effective chair and a balance of skills, backgrounds, experience and knowledge,

with individual directors having sufficient capacity to make a valuable contribution. The size of a board should be guided by the scale and complexity of the company.

3. **Director responsibilities:** the board and individual directors should have a clear understanding of their accountability and responsibilities. The board's policies and procedures should support effective decision making and independent challenge.
4. **Opportunity and risk:** a board should promote the long-term success of the company by identifying opportunities to create and preserve value, and establishing oversight for the identification and mitigation of risks.
5. **Remuneration:** a board should promote executive remuneration structures aligned to the sustainable long term success of a company, taking into account pay and conditions elsewhere in the company.
6. **Stakeholder relationships and engagement:** directors should foster effective stakeholder relationships aligned to the company's purpose. The board is responsible for overseeing meaningful engagement with stakeholders, including the workforce, and having regard to their views when taking decisions.

Unlike the UK Corporate Governance Code, which operates on a comply or explain basis, the Wates Principles operate on an apply and explain basis as follows.

- A company that adopts the Wates Principles should follow them in a way that is most appropriate for their particular organisation. The board should apply each principle by considering them individually within the context of the company's specific circumstances. The board should then explain, in their own words, how they have addressed the principles in their governance practices. Companies should provide a supporting statement that provides an understanding of how their corporate governance policies and processes operate to achieve the desired outcome for each principle.
- Each principle is accompanied by supporting guidance. The guidance exists to assist companies in explaining their approach to applying each principle, and so it does not need to be reported on (unlike the guidance provisions in the UK Corporate Governance Code).

The Wates Principles can be adopted by those companies required to produce a statement of corporate governance arrangements (discussed in Chapter 14), namely, any company that:

1. has more than 2,000 employees; and/or
2. has a turnover of more than £200 million and a balance sheet total of more than £2 billion.

The rules regarding statements of corporate governance arrangements came into effect on 1 January 2019, so companies can adopt the Wates Principles from that date onwards.

institutional investors
Powerful shareholders such as banks, pension funds and insurance companies that invest significant sums in the stock market on their own behalf and on behalf of their customers/clients.

The UK Stewardship Code

The UK Corporate Governance Code and the Wates Principles are primarily aimed at companies and directors, but shareholders also play an important role in promoting good governance. The 2009 Walker Review noted that, during the financial crisis, large **institutional investors** (notably insurance companies, pension funds and banks) were slow to act and exercised insufficient oversight over the companies they held shares in. Accordingly, the Walker Review recommended that a Stewardship Code be created that would provide best practice guidance and recommendations to institutional investors. The UK Stewardship Code was published in 2010 and was first updated in 2012. At the time of writing, the FRC is consulting on a new Stewardship Code that is due to come into effect in July 2019.

The 2019 Code consists of a series of Principles that are accompanied by Provisions that provide more detail. The UK Stewardship Code, like the UK Corporate Governance Code, operates on a comply or explain basis, so investors may choose not to comply with the Stewardship Code. However, certain investors and fund managers (notably those authorised by the FCA) must comply with the Stewardship Code or explain their reasons for non-compliance.

6.2 Reports

The UK's governance codes are complemented and influenced by a series of reports.

In 1992, the first major UK report on corporate governance was published, namely the Report of the Committee on the Financial Aspects of Corporate Governance (better known as the Cadbury Report). This report laid the foundations of the UK's corporate governance system. Since then, numerous reports have been published on a wide range of governance issues, including:

- the Greenbury Report (1995) on directors' remuneration
- the Turnbull Report (1999) on internal control
- the Smith Report (2003) on audit committees
- the Higgs Report (2003) on the role and effectiveness of non-executive directors
- the Walker Review (2009) on the governance of UK banks during the financial crisis
- Lord Davies' Women on Boards reports (2011–2016) on gender diversity in the boardroom (the Hampton-Alexander Review has taken over from Lord Davies)
- the Parker Review (2017) into ethnic diversity in the boardroom.

These reports often establish recommendations or best practice guidance which, if commanding enough acceptance, often find their way into the corporate governance codes discussed in section 6.1 on page 9.

Test yourself 1.2

1. **Name the principal corporate governance codes that operate in the UK.**
2. **Explain how the 'comply or explain' approach operates, and how it differs to the 'apply and explain' approach.**
3. **What type of company is subject to the UK Corporate Governance Code?**

7. European law

European law has had a major impact upon the UK system of company law. Two sources of European law are discussed here, namely: (i) EU law; and (ii) human rights law under the European Convention on Human Rights.

7.1 European Union law

European Union (EU) law has had a significant impact upon our company law system. The UK is currently in the process of withdrawing from the EU, so the impact of EU law will be affected by this (discussed on page 14). This section looks at the impact EU law has had on our company law system, beginning with the right of establishment.

Right of establishment

One of the key rights contained in the Treaty on the Functioning of the European Union (TFEU) is the right of EU nationals to establish a business anywhere in the EU. Article 49 of TFEU prohibits restrictions on the freedom of establishment, which includes the right to 'set up and manage undertakings, in particular companies or firms... under the conditions laid down for its own nationals by the law of the country where such establishment is effected'.

A UK company that wishes to establish a presence in an EU Member State (or vice versa) currently has three broad options.

1. A UK company could simply set up a subsidiary in that Member State, but there may be justifiable reasons for not wanting to do this (for example, the expense involved or the burden of being subject to that state's legal system).
2. Article 49 provides that prohibitions on restrictions of the right to establishment 'shall also apply to restrictions on the setting-up of agencies, branches or subsidiaries by nationals of any Member State established in the territory of any Member State'. Instead of setting up a subsidiary, a UK company could simply set up a branch in another Member State, and this branch would not be subject to the full force of that state's law (see Case C-212/97 *Centros Ltd v Erhvervs-og Selskabsstyrelsen* [1999] ECR I-1459).

3. A UK company could relocate to another Member State and become subject to the laws of that state.

The harmonisation programme

It is necessary for there to be a degree of harmonisation across the company laws of EU Member States, to facilitate cross-border company activity and for the **right of establishment** to be of benefit.

right of establishment
The right afforded to EU persons to establish a business in another EU Member State.

Article 50(2)(g) of TFEU provides that attaining freedom of establishment involves 'co-ordinating to the necessary extent the safeguards which, for the protection of the interests of members and others, are required by Member States of companies or firms... with a view to making such safeguards equivalent throughout the Union.' To that end, the EU embarked upon a programme that aimed to better harmonise company law across EU member states.

Article 50(1) of TFEU states that freedom of establishment shall be attained 'by means of directives', and so EU company law harmonisation has been attained by the passing of directives. In theory, directives are useful as they allow considerable flexibility – the directives set out broad goals or aims, giving Member State discretion in how those aims are implemented. In practice, however, many company law directives do not offer much flexibility as they are extremely detailed. Some (for example, the Prospectus Directive) impose 'maximum harmonisation'. This means the directive's minimum standards must be implemented but the Member State cannot impose more exacting standards.

To date, the EU has passed 11 harmonisation directives. In 2012, the European Commission recommended that these directives be merged into a single legal instrument and has adopted a proposal that would merge many of the existing company law directives into a single directive.

The UK's withdrawal from the EU

In June 2016, the UK decided via referendum to leave the EU. The process of leaving the EU was triggered in March 2017, meaning that the UK should have left the EU by the 29 March 2019. However, following Parliament rejecting the government's withdrawal agreement, the EU and the UK agreed to delay the UK's withdrawal.

The effects of Brexit on UK company law cannot be stated with certainty at this stage, but some broad points can be made. The UK system of company law is predominantly domestic, but there are significant areas of company law that are EU-derived or exist in their current form in order to comply with EU law. Notable examples include the law relating to:

- cross-border mergers and insolvencies
- the Listing Regime
- the regulation and independence of auditors
- the market abuse regime
- the capital maintenance regime

- takeovers
- shareholders' rights
- corporate transparency.

The European Union (Withdrawal) Act 2018 provides that all directly applicable EU law (such as EU Regulations) will be converted to domestic law upon exit day (s. 3) and all EU-derived law (for example, subordinate legislation that implements EU directives) will be preserved (s. 2).

As a result, the short term effects of Brexit on our system of company law will likely be minimal. Following Brexit, Parliament may decide that it wishes to reform those areas of company law that it was not able to reform due to having to comply with the EU law, so the longer term effects of Brexit may be more significant.

One concern relating to Brexit is the fact that UK companies may lose their **passporting** rights upon the UK leaving the EU. Passporting essentially means that companies engaged in certain areas (notably financial services) that are registered in a European Economic Area (EEA) state are free to do business in any other EEA state without obtaining further authorisation.

passporting
The right of a company registered in an EEA state to do business in another EEA state without obtaining further authorisation.

A company registered in the UK is currently free to do business in any other EEA state but, upon the UK leaving the EEA, UK companies will require authorisation in order to do business in EEA states unless the UK secures some sort of passporting rights as part of a future agreement. This is of particular concern to companies that provide financial services, as London is currently the financial centre of Europe. A number of major financial services companies have stated that they are considering relocating to an EEA state post-Brexit.

7.2 Human rights laws

Despite its title, the European Convention on Human Rights (ECHR) also applies to legal persons, such as companies. Not all human rights are applicable to companies (for example, the prohibition of torture) but the ECHR does often specify that certain rights can apply to companies. For example, Article 1 of the First Protocol of the ECHR states that 'every natural or legal person is entitled to peaceful enjoyment of his possessions.'

Test yourself 1.3

1. **What are the two major sources of European company law?**
2. **What is the 'right of establishment'?**
3. **Why has the EU process of company law harmonisation been largely carried out via directives?**
4. **Name five areas of UK company law that have been heavily influenced by EU law.**

Chapter summary

- The sources of company law are legislation, case law, the constitution of the company, contract law, EU law, and human rights law.
- Legislation is the principal source of company law, with the Companies Act 2006 being the dominant piece of company law legislation.
- The function of subordinate legislation includes:
  - expanding upon rules found in Acts of Parliament;
  - bringing parts of Acts of Parliament into force;
  - amending existing legislation;
  - implementing EU law; and
  - empowering certain persons or bodies to create law.
- Case law is important because:
  - certain areas of law are created by case law;
  - case law principles may end up in legislation;
  - case law sets out the operation and scope of statutory remedies and punishments; and
  - case law provides the interpretation of statutory rules.
- Many rules by which a company is run are created by the company itself via its constitution (notably its articles of association).
- The main sources of corporate governance principles are codes and reports.
- The key corporate governance codes are the UK Corporate Governance Code, the UK Stewardship Code, and the Wates Corporate Governance Principles for Large Private Companies.
- The UK Corporate Governance Code and the UK Stewardship Code operate on a comply or explain basis, meaning companies and persons to whom these Codes apply must comply with these codes or explain their reasons for non-compliance.
- The Wates Corporate Governance Principles for Large Private Companies operate on an apply and explain basis, meaning that companies that adopt the Wates Principles must apply the Code and explain how they have applied it.
- EU law has had a significant effect on the UK system of company law, but the UK has decided to withdraw from the EU.

Chapter two
Business structures

Contents

1. Introduction

This chapter outlines the principal business structures available to a person who wishes to undertake some form of business activity. Although this study text is primarily concerned with the company as a business structure, a full understanding of the advantages and disadvantages of the company can only be obtained if you compare the company to other available business structures.

Four business structures will be discussed in this chapter, namely:

1. the sole proprietorship
2. the various types of partnership
3. the company
4. the mutual organisation

Limited liability partnerships (LLPs) and companies are created via a process known as incorporation, and so are commonly referred to as 'incorporated business structures' (although the relevant statutes refer to them as bodies corporate). Sole proprietorships, ordinary partnerships and limited partnerships are not created by incorporation, and so are known as 'unincorporated business structures'.

2. Sole proprietorships

A sole proprietor is an individual carrying on some form of business activity on their own account (such individuals are also known as self-employed or as independent contractors). There are two types of sole proprietor:

- If the sole proprietor is a professional, they are called a 'sole practitioner'.
- If the sole proprietor is not a professional, they are called a 'sole trader'.

To understand why a person would wish to conduct business through a sole proprietorship, consider the following example.

Case study 2.1

Karen Watson has recently qualified as an accountant and, instead of applying for jobs in an accountancy firm, has decided to set up her own accountancy business. As she has never run her own business before, she is keen to avoid excessive regulation and red tape. At first, she will run the business by herself (as she wants to keep all the profit that the business generates), but may want to take on employees if the business expands sufficiently.

As Karen wishes to run the business by herself, a partnership would not be suitable, leaving a sole proprietorship and a company as viable options. Of these, a sole proprietorship will likely be the most appropriate business structure for Karen for several reasons.

- **Creating and running a sole proprietorship is much more straightforward than creating and running a partnership or company.**
- **Sole proprietors are free to take on employees, although most do not.**
- **As a sole proprietorship has no separate personality, there is no legal distinction between the sole proprietor and the sole proprietorship. Accordingly, the sole proprietor owns all the business's assets and is entitled to all the profit that the business generates. However, the sole proprietor is also liable for all the debts and liabilities of the business. Liability is personal and unlimited, so the sole proprietor's personal assets can be seized in order to satisfy the sole proprietorship's liabilities.**
- **Unlike companies, sole proprietorships are not required to disclose business information to the public, so the business can be run in privacy.**

2.1 Formation and operation

In order to create a sole proprietorship, all that an individual need do is to register themselves as self-employed with Her Majesty's Revenue and Customs (HMRC). They will need to choose a name for the sole proprietorship. Most sole proprietors use some form of their own name (e.g. Watson, Karen Watson, or K Watson). If they choose a name other than their name, then this will be regarded as a 'business name' and will be subject to the prohibitions and limitations discussed in Chapter 3.

Sole proprietorships are subject to much less regulation than partnerships and companies. However, sole proprietors are required to comply with the relevant rules regarding tax, namely:

1. they must file their own tax returns, so must maintain adequate records of all sales and purchases;
2. once the sole proprietorship's revenue reaches a certain amount, the sole proprietor must register for VAT purposes; and
3. if the sole proprietor takes on any employees, they must register with HMRC for Pay As You Earn (PAYE) purposes.

2.2 Finance

Compared to other business structures, sole proprietors may encounter difficulty in relation to raising finance. Partnerships can admit new partners or request finance from existing partners. Companies can sell shares to raise finance. There are several options available if a sole proprietor needs to raise money for the business.

- They could invest their own money into the business, but they run the risk of losing it if the business fails.
- They could obtain a loan. However, as most sole proprietors are small businesses, banks are cautious when lending money – obtaining significant amounts of **debt capital** is usually impossible.
- They could seek investment from outside persons, but such persons would usually demand a share of the profits.
- They could adopt a different business structure – incorporate the business as a company and sell shares, or enter into partnership with someone else.

debt capital
Capital obtained by borrowing from others (also known as loan capital).

2.3 Dissolution

Ending the existence of a sole proprietorship is easy. The sole proprietor simply needs to inform HMRC that they are no longer self-employed. Prior to this, the sole proprietor should tie up any loose ends (collect any debts owed, pay off creditors, lay off employees and so on). Any leftover money belongs to the sole proprietor.

Test yourself 2.1

1. **What is a sole proprietorship?**
2. **What is the difference between a sole practitioner and a sole trader?**
3. **Explain the advantages and disadvantages of running a business through a sole proprietorship.**
4. **How can a sole proprietor raise finance?**

3. Partnerships

A sole proprietorship is of no use where two or more persons wish to engage in business together. For such persons, a partnership may be an appropriate business structure, but a decision will need to be made regarding which type of partnership to choose. There are three different types of partnership:

1. the ordinary partnership (also known as 'general partnerships' or simply 'partnerships')
2. the limited partnership
3. the limited liability partnership (LLP)

The ordinary partnership is by far the most popular.

3.1 Ordinary partnerships

The Partnership Act 1890 (PA 1890) defines a partnership as 'the relation which subsists between persons carrying on a business in common with a view of profit' (PA 1890, s. 1(1)). Several words and phrases within this definition invite further comment.

- The word 'relation' indicates that an ordinary partnership is based upon the relationship between the partners.
- The word 'persons' indicates that (i) a single person cannot form a partnership; and (ii) the partners of a partnership can be natural persons and/or legal person (for example companies or limited liability partnerships).
- The phrase 'carrying on' indicates some form of continuous activity is required, but the courts have stated that a partnership can be set up for a one-off transaction (*George Hall & Sons v Platt* [1954] TLR 331).
- The word 'business' is defined as including 'every trade, occupation or profession' (PA 1890, s. 45).
- The partners must be carrying on the business 'in common'. If this is not the case, it may be the case that no partnership exists.
- The business must be carried on 'with a view of profit', indicating that a partnership cannot be set up for purely altruistic or benevolent purposes. This does not mean that a partnership must make a profit – it merely means that the partners intend to make a profit.

As a partnership is an unincorporated business structure, it follows that every partner is liable jointly with the other partners for all the debts and obligations of the partnership incurred while they are partners (PA 1890, s. 9). If a partner dies, their estate is liable for such debts and obligations (PA 1890, s. 9). The liability of the partners is unlimited.

The relationship between the partners

The relationship between the partners (and their rights and obligations) is usually determined by a partnership agreement. This agreement can be drafted by the partners themselves, but it need not be in writing – it can be oral or implied via the partners' conduct. In order to avoid disputes, the agreement is usually in writing and will take the form of a contract.

However, there is no requirement for a partnership to have a partnership agreement. Where there is no written partnership agreement, then ss. 24 and 25 of PA 1890 set out 10 rules that determine the relationship between the partners and how the partnership is to be run, including:

- the right to an equal share in the partnership's profits;
- the right to take part in the management of the partnership;
- a prohibition on any person being admitted as a partner without the consent of all the other partners; and
- a prohibition on a partner being expelled from the partnership unless all the other partners so agree.

Even if a written partnership agreement does exist, the rules set out in ss. 24 and 25 will form part of the partnership agreement, unless they are inconsistent with or excluded by the partnership agreement. The terms of a partnership agreement can be altered if all the partners consent. This consent can be express or implied (PA 1890, s. 19).

The relationship between the partners and third parties

As the partnership is an unincorporated body, it does not have its own separate legal personality. The PA 1890 puts in place rules regarding the relationship between the partnership and third parties. The two key provisions are ss. 5 and 10. Section 5 primarily deals with the ability of a partner to contractually bind the partnership and his co-partners to a third party, and provides that:

> 'Every partner is an agent of the firm and his other partners for the purpose of the business of the partnership; and the acts of every partner who does any act for carrying on in the usual way business of the kind carried on by the firm of which he is a member bind the firm and his partners, unless the partner so acting has in fact no authority to act for the firm in the particular matter, and the person with whom he is dealing either knows that he has no authority, or does not know or believe him to be a partner.'

If a partner enters into an agreement with a third party, the partnership and the other partners will be bound by that agreement. However, the partnership and the other partners will not be bound if the partner had no authority to enter into the agreement and the third party he dealt with (i) knew that he had no authority; or (ii) did not know or believe him to be a partner.

Section 10 of PA 1890 primarily relates to a partner's criminal or tortious liability and provides that:

> 'Where, by any wrongful act or omission of any partner acting in the ordinary course of the business of the firm, or with the authority of his co-partners, loss or injury is caused to any person not being a partner in the firm, or any penalty is incurred, the firm is liable therefor to the same extent as the partner so acting or omitting to act.'

vicarious liability
Liability imposed upon a person for the acts or omissions of another person.

This means that each partner is **vicariously liable** for the wrongful acts or omissions of another partner, as long as the partner was acting within the ordinary business of the partnership or within his authority. Liability under s. 10 is joint and several, meaning that the claimant can sue each partner in turn, or all the partners at once, until he has recovered the amount of his loss.

Dissolution
A partnership can be dissolved in a number of ways, including the following.

- As a partnership agreement usually takes the form of a contract, the partnership can be dissolved if the partners so agree. This agreement can be express or implied.
- The partnership agreement might provide that the partnership will be dissolved upon the occurrence of a particular event. Sections 32–33 of PA 1890 imply several terms into the partnership agreement that state when a partnership will be dissolved (for example, if a partner dies or is declared bankrupt).
- A partnership will be dissolved if an event occurs that makes it unlawful for the business of the partnership to carry on (PA 1890, s. 34).
- Section 35 of PA 1890 provides that the court can, following an application from a partner, dissolve a partnership in certain cases (for example, where the business of the partnership can only be carried on at a loss or where the court thinks it is just and equitable to dissolve the partnership).
- The relationship between the partners may break down and result in the partnership's dissolution.

3.2 Limited partnerships

Limited partnerships, although not common, do play an important role in certain areas of business (for example, venture capital and equity investment) so it is worth briefly discussing them. It is also important that they are not confused with limited liability partnerships.

Limited partnerships are created under the Limited Partnerships Act 1907 (LPA 1907) and differ from ordinary partnerships in two principal ways. First, their method of creation is different, as limited partnerships are created by registering specified documentation with Companies House (LPA 1907, ss. 5 and 8A). Limited partnerships registered since October 2009 must end their name with the words 'Limited Partnership' or the abbreviation 'LP' (LPA 1907, s. 8B(2)). Although they are created in a similar manner to companies and LLPs, they are not incorporated structures and do not have a corporate personality.

Second, the composition of a limited partnership differs from an ordinary partnership. Whereas an ordinary partnership consists only of general partners whose liability is unlimited, a limited partnership must consist of one or more general partners and one or more limited partners (LPA 1907, s. 1(2)). The general partners will be liable for all the debts and obligations of the limited partnership, whereas the limited partners are only liable for an amount specified in the registration documentation (LPA 1907, s. 8A(2)(d)).

However, limited partners are not permitted to take part in the management of the firm, nor do they have the power to bind the firm (LPA 1907, s. 6(1)). If a limited partner does take part in the firm's management, then he will become liable for the firm's debts and obligations as if he were a general partner. Accordingly, limited partner status is more suitable for sleeping partners (those who wish to contribute capital and obtain a return, but do not wish to be involved in management).

Concern that limited partnerships were being used in **money-laundering** schemes led to the government proposed a series of proposed reforms in December 2018, including (i) persons who wish to register a limited partnership must demonstrate they are registered with an anti-money laundering supervisory body; (ii) applications to register a limited partnership must state a UK-based principal place of business; (iii) limited partnerships must file a confirmation statement, and; (iv) the registrar of companies will be given the power to strike off limited partnerships.

money laundering
The process by which the source of illegally obtained money is concealed, usually by passing the money through a series of legitimate businesses.

Private fund limited partnerships

Limited partnerships are a popular structure for private equity and venture capital funds, but the 1907 Act had not evolved to cater for the needs of these funds. The 1907 Act has been amended by the Legislative Reform (Private Fund Limited Partnerships) Order 2017 (SI 2017/514) to provide a specific form of limited partnership that such funds could use. This is known as a 'private fund limited partnership'.

3.3 Limited liability partnerships

The principal disadvantage of an ordinary partnership is the personal and unlimited liability of the partners. A limited partner's liability is limited, but such partners cannot take part in the firm's management. The partners of a number of professional firms were concerned regarding their liability for professional negligence for reasons demonstrated in the following example.

Case study 2.2

Giro & Co is a firm of accountants that operates via an ordinary partnership. It has 55 offices throughout the UK, 150 partners, and more than 3,000 staff. It audits a number of extremely large UK companies.

Tom, one of Giro's partners, is engaged to audit the accounts of a large listed company, but he performs the audit negligently, which results in Giro & Co being liable to pay £75 million in damages.

As the liability of the partners is joint, all of the other 149 partners could be liable for Tom's negligence. To avoid this exposure to liability, a number of large accountancy firms lobbied the government to create a new form of partnership that would shield the partners from liability. Eventually, Parliament passed the Limited Liability Partnerships Act 2000 (LLPA 2000), which allows for the creation of limited liability partnerships (LLPs).

Comparison to ordinary partnerships and companies

In some respects, LLPs are similar to ordinary partnerships but differ notably in other respects, as Table 2.1 demonstrates.

	Ordinary partnership	Limited liability partnership
Regulating legislation	PA 1890	LLPA 2000 and accompanying subordinate legislation
Governed by which area of law	Partnership law	Company law, unless LLPA 2000 states otherwise
Formation	Formed via an agreement between the partners	Formed by registering specified documents with Companies House
Has corporate personality	No	Yes
Partners known as	Partners	Members
Liability of the partners	Personal and unlimited	The LLP is liable for its debts and liabilities, and the members' liability is limited

Table 2.1 Ordinary partnerships and LLPs

Limited liability partnerships have more in common with companies than with ordinary partnerships. As a result, they are regulated as stringently as companies, meaning that only larger professional firms have tended to adopt LLP status. As of December 2018, there were only 49,736 LLPs registered in the UK (Companies House, Incorporated Companies in the United Kingdom, October to December (2018), Table 1c).

Liability

The key difference between an ordinary partnership and an LLP is in relation to the liability of the partners. Like a company, an LLP is a body corporate (LLPA 2000, s. 1(2)) and so has a separate personality. The LLP is liable for the debts and liabilities of the LLP, and the LLP's members are protected. Section 6(1) of LLPA 2000 provides that every member is an agent of the LLP, meaning that the LLP itself can be vicariously liable for the acts of its members.

This is not to say that the members face no liability. In the event of an LLP being wound up, the members of an LLP are required to contribute such assets as is provided for under LLPA 2000 (LLP 2000, s. 1(4)), with the Act providing that regulations may be passed that provide what the members must contribute in the event of the LLP's winding up (LLPA 2000, s. 14(1)).

Regulation 5 and Schedule 3, para 1 of the Limited Liability Partnerships Regulations 2001 (SI 2001/1090) provide that a modified version of s. 74 of the Insolvency Act 1986 will apply to LLPs. This provides that, when an LLP is wound up, every member is liable to contribute to the LLP such an amount as he has agreed. This agreed amount is usually found in the LLP's partnership agreement.

Test yourself 2.2

1. **What are the three types of partnership that can be created?**
2. **Explain what ss. 5 and 10 of PA 1890 state.**
3. **How does a limited partnership differ to an ordinary partnership?**
4. **Explain the differences between an LLP and an ordinary partnership.**

4. Companies

The company is the most popular business structure in the UK, with companies forming 71.4% of VAT/PAYE business each year (Office of National Statistics, UK Business: Activity, Size and Location 2018 (2018), Figure 2). The remainder of this study text focuses on how companies are regulated. This section will focus on the different types of company that can be created and the differing ways in which companies can be classified.

Companies can be classified as registered or unregistered, with the classification depending on how the company was created. Companies incorporated by royal charter or Act of Parliament are known as unregistered companies, whereas companies incorporated by registration are known as registered companies. These three methods of incorporation are discussed in Chapter 3 but, as registered companies vastly outnumber unregistered companies, this text largely focuses on registered companies (although, in practice, registered and unregistered companies are usually regulated the same way).

When incorporating a company, the promoters will have to make three key decisions. These decisions will determine what type of company they create.

1. Will the company be public or private?
2. Will the company have a share capital?
3. Will the liability of the company's members be limited or unlimited?

The last two questions are irrelevant if the company will be a public company, as public companies must have a share capital and the members' liability must be limited. As a result, there are five different types of company that can be registered under the CA 2006. When completing **Form IN01**, the promoter must tick which company they wish to create:

Form IN01
The application for registration that provides details regarding the company to be incorporated.

- a public company limited by shares
- a private company limited by shares
- a private company limited by guarantee
- a private unlimited company with a share capital
- a private unlimited company without a share capital

4.1 Public and private companies

The definitions of public and private companies found in ss. 4(1) and (2) of the CA 2006 do not really help us understand the differences between them.

- A public company is a company limited by shares, or limited by guarantee and having a share capital, the certificate of incorporation of which states that it is a public company.
- A private company is any company that is not a public company.

Of more use is s. 4(4), which states that Part 20 of the CA 2006 sets out the two major differences between public and private companies.

securities
Shares or debentures (note, this is the CA 2006 definition – other legislation may define the term differently).

1. Private limited companies are prohibited from offering their **securities** to the public at large (CA 2006, s. 755(1)), whereas public companies are free to offer their securities to the public.
2. Public companies must not engage in any business unless they have been issued with a trading certificate. This certificate will only be issued if the company has an authorised minimum share capital (CA 2006, s. 76, discussed in Chapter 11). Conversely, private companies do not require a trading certificate and have no minimum capital requirement (although a private company with a share capital will need at least one share, worth at least 1 penny).

In reality, there are numerous differences between public and private companies. These are set out in Table 2.2.

	Public company	Private company
Required to have a share capital	Yes	No
Liability of members	Must be limited	Limited or unlimited
Can offer to sell securities to the public at large	Yes	No
Can offer securities on a stock exchange	Yes	No
Minimum capital requirement	Yes (£50,000)	No minimum capital requirement
Minimum number of directors	Two	One
Suffix	'plc' or 'public limited company'	'Ltd' or 'Limited'
Required to appoint a company secretary	Yes	No (unless the articles provide otherwise)
Can be classified as micro-entity, small or medium-sized	No	Yes

Table 2.2 The differences between public and private companies

The law regulates public companies much more stringently than private companies. As a result, private company status will be most appropriate for most companies (especially small companies). This is reflected in the fact that over 99% of companies are private.

Quoted, listed and traded companies
Public companies can offer their shares to the public at large. To facilitate this, they can offer their shares on a stock exchange and seek an official listing.

Private companies are not permitted to list their shares (Financial Services and Markets Act (FSMA) 2000, s. 75(3) and FSMA 2000 (Official Listing of Securities) Regulations 2001 (SI 2001/2956), reg 3(a)). Companies that offer their shares on a stock market are often referred to as listed or quoted companies. There is a distinction between these two terms.

- A listed company is a company that has a class of its securities listed on the UK's **Official List** (FCA Handbook, Glossary).
- A quoted company is a company whose share capital (i) has been included on the Official List; or (ii) is officially listed in an EEA state; or (iii) is admitted to dealing on the New York Stock Exchange or NASDAQ (CA 2006, s. 385(2)). A company that is not a quoted company is known as an unquoted company (s. 385(3)).

Official List
The FCA-maintained list of companies that have securities listed on a UK-regulated market.

Case study 2.3

FakeCo plc is the parent company of three other public companies, namely X plc, Y plc and Z plc. The shares of FakeCo are on the official list, so FakeCo is both listed and quoted. The details of its subsidiaries are as follows.

1. **X plc has decided to only offer its shares on the New York Stock Exchange. Accordingly, it is not a listed company, but it is a quoted company.**
2. **Y plc is offering its shares for sale on AIM (discussed on p. 224). AIM is not part of the Official List nor does it fall within the definition of a quoted company, so it is not a listed company and it is unquoted.**
3. **Z plc does not offer any shares to the public, but it has listed debt securities on the Official List. Accordingly, it is a listed company, but as the definition of a quoted company only relates to share capital, it follows that Z plc is unquoted.**

Certain provisions in the CA 2006 apply only to 'traded companies'. These are companies whose shares carry rights to vote at general meetings, and which are admitted to trading on a regulated market in an EEA state by or with the consent of the company (CA 2006, s. 360C). In practice, most listed/quoted companies will also be traded companies.

4.2 Share capital

The promoters of a company will need to decide if the company is to have a share capital or not. If the company is to be public, then the company must have a share capital (CA 2006, s. 4(2)). A private company need not have a share capital, but the vast majority do.

4.3 Limited and unlimited companies

As a company has a corporate personality, it follows that the members are not usually liable for the company's debts and liabilities. However, the law may require that the members are liable to contribute to the company, with the extent of the contribution being determined by whether the members' liability is limited or unlimited.

When creating a company, the promoters will need to decide whether the members' liability will be limited or unlimited. If the company is to be public, then the members' liability must be limited (CA 2006, s. 4(2)). The liability of the members of a private company can be limited or unlimited, although the vast majority of private companies are limited.

Limited companies

Section 3(1) of the CA 2006 provides that a company will be a limited company if 'the liability of its members is limited by its constitution', which begs the following questions:

- When are the members liable?
- What is the liability limitation?

The answers depend on how the members' liability is limited. There are two types of limitation, namely: (i) companies limited by guarantee; and (ii) companies limited by shares.

- If a private limited company does not have a share capital, then the liability of its members will be limited by guarantee. The liability of such members is limited to the amount they have undertaken to contribute in the event of its being wound up (CA 2006, s. 3(3); Insolvency Act 1986 (IA 1986), s. 74(3)). This amount will be stated in the statement of guarantee submitted to Companies House when the company was incorporated and is usually very small (usually £1). Many companies limited by guarantee are not for profit companies or are engaged in some form of community-driven activity, so it is important that the members are not exposed to excessive liability upon liquidation.
- The vast majority of limited companies are limited by shares. The liability of the members of such companies is limited to the amount that is unpaid on their shares (CA 2006, s. 3(2)). Members who have fully paid for their shares are not liable to contribute any more to the company upon its liquidation (IA 1986, s. 74(2)(d)).

The following example demonstrates both forms of limited liability in practice.

Case study 2.4

FakeCo plc has two subsidiaries, namely A Ltd and B Ltd. A Ltd is a company limited by guarantee and the company's statement of guarantee states that the company's members each undertake to contribute £20. Note that they will only be required to contribute this sum in the event of A Ltd being wound up.

B Ltd is a company limited by shares. It has an issued share capital of £50, consisting of 50 £1 shares. 30 of these shares are owned by FakeCo and they have been fully paid up. The remaining 20 shares are held by Simon, a local businessman. When Simon subscribed for the shares, he was offered the opportunity to pay half the price on allotment and the remainder at a later date. He took up this offer and so has only paid £10. Simon's liability is limited to £10 (i.e. the amount remaining unpaid on his shares). This unpaid amount is a debt that B Ltd can call upon whenever it wishes. If this debt were to be outstanding when B Ltd was wound up, the liquidator could recover it from Simon. The liquidator could not recover anything from FakeCo as it has fully paid for its shares.

Unlimited companies

The liability of the members of an unlimited company is, unsurprisingly, unlimited (CA 2006, s. 3(4)). This unlimited liability differs from the unlimited liability of sole proprietors or partners, as sole proprietors and partners can be sued directly for any monies owed or liability.

The creditors of a company cannot usually sue the members as the company has a corporate personality – it is the company itself that they must sue. If the company cannot pay its creditors, a creditor will likely petition the court to have the company wound up. It is at this point that the members will become liable as the liquidator can require the members to contribute to the company's assets. There is no limit on the amount that the creditor can claim (subject to the amount of the debt owed).

Stop and think 2.1

Why would the promoters choose to create a company with unlimited liability? What are the advantages of creating an unlimited company and do these advantages offset the benefit of limited liability?

4.4 Company size

Companies can also be classified in terms of size. The principal significance of this is that certain statutory obligations do not apply to companies of a certain size (for example, a small company is not required to have its accounts audited

(CA 2006, s. 477(1)). The CA 2006 determines company size by reference to (i) turnover; (ii) balance sheet total; and (iii) number of employees.

	Micro-entity (s. 384A)	Small (s. 382(3))	Medium-sized (s. 465(3))	Large
Turnover	Not more than £623,000	Not more than £10.2 million	Not more than £36 million	Any company that is not a micro-entity, small or medium-sized
Balance sheet total	Not more than £316,000	Not more than £5.1 million	Not more than £18 million	
Number of employees	Not more than 10	Not more than 50	Not more than 250	

Public companies and traded companies cannot be classified as micro-entitles, small or medium-sized (ss. 384(2) and 467(2)).

Table 2.3 Company sizes

The application of the above three criteria is as follows. In a company's first financial year, it need only satisfy at least two criteria out of three (ss. 382(1) and (3), 384A(1) and (4) and 465(1) and (3)).

In subsequent years, a company that is classified as a certain size will continue to be classified as that size unless it fails to satisfy at least two criteria in two consecutive financial years (ss. 382(2), 384A(3) and 465(2)).

Case study 2.5

X-Corp Ltd was incorporated in 2014 and the following table shows key facts relating to its size.

Financial year	Turnover	Balance sheet total	Number of employees
2015/16	**£600,000**	**£330,000**	**8**
2016/17	**£610,000**	**£312,000**	**11**
2017/18	**£620,000**	**£320,000**	**11**
2018/19	**£640,000**	**£330,000**	**13**

In 2015/16, X-Corp would be classified as a micro-entity (and also as a small company because micro-entities are also classified as small), as it satisfied two criteria, namely turnover and number of employees. In 2016/17, it would remain a micro-entity as it still satisfied two criteria (albeit not the same two as in 2015/16). In 2017/18, it only satisfied one criteria, but would remain a micro-entity.

In 2018/19, it satisfied no criteria for a micro-entity, and so would cease to be a micro-entity, as it has failed to satisfy at least two criteria in two consecutive financial years. It would therefore be classified as small only.

This is not the only way to classify a company's size. Special groups of companies (known as FTSE 100, 250 and 350 companies) are classified by the size of their market capitalisation (how the investment community tends to measure a company's size). A company's market cap is calculated by multiplying a company's share price by the number of its shares. A company's market cap will fluctuate.

- The largest 100 companies on the London Stock Exchange in terms of market capitalisation constitute the FTSE 100.
- The next 250 companies after the FTSE 100 (i.e. the 101st largest to the 350th largest) constitute the FTSE 250.
- Companies in the FTSE 100 and FTSE 250 collectively form the FTSE 350.

It is important to know if a company is FTSE 100, 250 or 350 as certain laws and governance principles only apply to such companies. For example, the recommendations of the Hampton-Alexander Review on gender diversity in the boardroom largely apply only to FTSE 350 companies.

4.5 Specific company types

Charitable, social and community-focused companies

It is common for a charity to be run via a company limited by guarantee. However, two other business structures exist that are designed for companies that engage in charitable or social activities: community interest companies and charitable incorporated organisations.

Community interest companies (CICs) were established by the Companies (Audit, Investigations and Community Enterprise) Act 2004 as a vehicle for companies that combine a commercial purpose with social, charitable or community-focused activities. CICs are formed in the same manner as standard companies, except that Companies House will send the registration documents to the Regulator of Community Interest Companies. The CIC Regulator will determine if the proposed CIC meets the 'community interest test', namely whether a reasonable person might consider that the company's activities are being carried on for the benefit of the community (Companies (Audit, Investigations and Community Enterprise) Act 2004, s. 35(2)).

CICs are generally subject to the CA 2006, but are also subject to additional rules found in the 2004 Act. For example, CICs must produce an annual 'community interest company report' which states out how the CIC's activities have benefitted the community (Companies (Audit, Investigations and Community Enterprise) Act 2004, s. 34; Community Interest Company Regulations 2005 (SI 2005/1788), reg 26)).

A CIC cannot register as a charity. A company that wishes to be registered as a charity might find it more appropriate to engage in business as a charitable incorporated organisation (CIO). The principal advantage of CIO status relates to regulation and a reduction in bureaucracy. Charitable companies that are not CIOs are subject to general company law and also have to comply with any additional rules relating to charities. CIOs are regulated by the Charities Act 2011 and accompanying subordinate legislation (notably the Charitable Incorporated Organisations (General) Regulations 2012 (SI 2012/3012)). They also only deal with one regulator, the Charity Commission, whereas charitable companies that are not CIOs must deal with the Charity Commission and Companies House.

Overseas companies

A company incorporated outside the UK may wish to do business in the UK. The company could incorporate a UK subsidiary (and many multinational companies do), but it may not wish to set up a subsidiary, in which case it may simply act as a branch or establishment of an 'overseas company'.

An overseas company is a company incorporated outside the UK (CA 2006, s. 1044). If such a company opens a 'branch' or 'establishment' in the UK, it will be required to provide certain information to Companies House regarding the overseas company and the branch or establishment (CA 2006, s .1046; Overseas Companies Regulations 2009 (SI 2009/1801) regs 3–11). Failure to provide this information is a criminal offence (CA 2006, s. 1054).

European companies

For a long time, the EU sought to establish an EU-wide company structure, and this was achieved in 2001 when the Statute for a European Company was passed, which allowed companies in EU Member States to merge to form a *Societas Europaea* (SE). However, SEs have not proven popular, largely because the right of establishment means that EU citizens are free to set up companies in any EU Member State.

In 2008, a proposal was put forward to provide for a smaller form of European company, namely the European private company (*societas privata Europaea*). This proposal was withdrawn in 2014 due to a lack of political agreement. A new proposal was put forward to create a European single-member private company (*Societas Unius Personae*), but this proposal has not been acted upon.

4.6 Re-registration

It may be beneficial for a company to change its legal status due to the needs of its business (for example, a private company may wish to raise additional capital, and so it may wish to re-register as a public company so that it can sell shares to the public).

Part 7 of the CA 2006 allows for most forms of company re-registration, but there are some types of re-registration that cannot be undertaken under Part 7 (e.g. there is no process for a company limited by guarantee to re-register as a company limited by shares). The various forms of re-registration are as follows.

- A private company can re-register as a public company by passing a special resolution, delivering specified documents to Companies House (see

Form RR01), and complying with certain conditions placed upon public companies (e.g. the minimum share capital requirement) (CA 2006, s. 90).

- A public company can re-register as a private limited company (to reduce its regulatory burden) by passing a special resolution and delivering specified documents to Companies House (CA 2006, s. 97, see Form RR02).
- A private limited company can re-register as unlimited if all the members of the company assent to the re-registration, and if specified documents are delivered to Companies House (CA 2006, s. 102(1), see Form RR05).
- An unlimited private company can re-register as a limited company by passing a special resolution and delivering specified documents to Companies House (CA 2006, s. 105(1), see Form RR06).
- A public company can re-register as an unlimited private company with a share capital if all the members of the company assent to the re-registration, and if specified documents are delivered to Companies House (CA 2006, s. 109(1), see Form RR07).

Where relevant, the company may be required to change its name and articles to comply with the requirements of its new status (e.g. change its designation from 'Ltd' to 'plc'). In all cases, a re-registration fee is payable and a new certificate of incorporation will be issued upon re-registration.

Test yourself 2.3

1. **What are the five types of company that can be created under the CA 2006?**
2. **What are the differences between a public and private company?**
3. **In a limited company, to what extent is the members' liability limited?**
4. **What is the difference between a quoted company and a listed company?**
5. **How does the CA 2006 classify companies in terms of size?**
6. **How can a private company re-register as public, and vice versa?**

5. Mutual organisations

Brief mention should be made of a group of organisations referred to as 'mutual organisations'.

The government has defined a mutual organisation as an organisation 'that is owned by, and run for, the benefit of its members, who are actively and directly involved in the business – whether employees, suppliers, or the community or consumers it serves – rather than being owned and controlled by outside investors' (BIS, *A Guide to Mutual Ownership Models* (2011)). Mutual organisations can be set up using standard business structures (such as a partnership, LLP or company), but two specialist structures also exist that can be registered with the FCA under the Co-operative and Community Benefit Societies Act 2014:

- co-operative societies, which are run for the benefit of those members who use its services; and
- community benefit societies, which are run for the benefit of the community, and not just its members.

Other types of mutual organisation include building societies, credit unions (which provide credit services to their members) and friendly societies (which usually provide financial aid to their members during periods of sickness, unemployment or retirement).

Chapter summary

- The principal UK business structures are the sole proprietorship, the partnership and the registered company.
- A sole proprietorship is a sole individual carrying on some form of business activity on his own account. The liability of the sole proprietor is personal and unlimited.
- There are three types of partnership, namely ordinary partnerships, limited partnerships and limited liability partnerships.
- When creating a company, the three key decisions to make are:
  - Will the company be public or private?
  - Will the company have a share capital?
  - Will the liability of the members be limited or unlimited?
- Public companies are so called because they can offer their shares to the public, whereas private companies cannot. Numerous other differences exist between public and private companies. The vast majority of UK companies are private companies.
- Most companies in the UK have a share capital and their members have limited liability, meaning that their liability is limited to the amount unpaid on their shares.
- Companies can change their status by re-registering (e.g. from private to public).

Chapter three

Incorporation and corporate personality

Contents

1. Introduction

This chapter outlines the role, duties and legal liabilities of a company promoter, before going on to look at the process by which a company can be created (incorporation). Corporate personality is discussed, including an examination of the consequences of corporate personality, and the ways in which corporate personality can be disregarded. Finally, the chapter concludes by looking at the various ways in which liability can be imposed upon a company.

2. Promotion and pre-incorporation contracts

Company law is not only concerned with what happens once a company is created – it is also important to regulate the activities of persons in the process of setting up a company. Such persons are known as **promoters** and usually go on to become the company's first directors.

promoter
A person involved in the creation of a company, other than through providing professional services.

2.1 Promotion of the company

It is important to know whether a person is a promoter because promoters owe duties to the unformed company and promoters can be held liable for acts engaged in on behalf of the unformed company.

Despite this, the law has not sought to define what a promoter is (for fear that persons would try to exclude themselves from such a definition). It has instead provided broad guidance regarding who is a promoter. Bowen J in *Whaley Bridge Calico Printing Co v Green* (1880) LR 5 QBD 109 (QB) stated that:

> 'The term promoter is a term not of law, but of business, usefully summing up in a single word a number of business operations familiar to the commercial world by which a company is generally brought into existence.'

'Business operations' would include deciding to set up a company, seeking others to become involved in the company (as directors or members), engaging in preparatory activities (obtaining premises, equipment or capital), and negotiating contracts on behalf of the unformed company.

Not all persons involved in the formation of a company will be promoters. For example, persons involved in the formation of a company by virtue of their professional duties (such as solicitors or accountants who provide advice to the promoters) will not be regarded as promoters (*Re Great Wheal Polgooth Co Ltd* (1883) 53 LJ Ch 42 (Ch)).

Duties of a promoter

A promoter may attempt to improperly benefit themselves (for example, by acquiring assets and then selling them for an extortionate sum to the company they promoted). To combat this, the law provides that promoters occupy a **fiduciary** position in relation to the unformed company. A promoter cannot make a profit out of the company's promotion unless they disclose the nature of the transaction and the profit made. This disclosure will only be valid if the persons to whom disclosure is made are independent (such as an independent board or body of members).

fiduciary
A person who occupies a position of trust in relation to another and owes certain duties to that other person.

Case law 3.1

***Erlanger v New Sombrero Phosphate Co* (1878) LR 3 App Cas 1218 (HL)**

Erlanger headed a syndicate that, for £55,000, acquired certain mining rights. The syndicate incorporated a company to take advantage of the mining rights. Two of the company's five directors spent most of their time abroad, one was the Lord Mayor of London (and so devoted little time to the company), and the remaining two had strong links to Erlanger. Through one of the directors with links to Erlanger, the mining rights were sold to the company for £110,000. Full details of the transaction were not disclosed to the company's members.

The disclosure of the details of the transaction to the directors was insufficient as the key directors were puppets who, according to Lord Blackburn, had not given the transaction the 'intelligent judgment of an independent executive'. Accordingly, the contract for the sale of the mining rights was voidable, allowing the company to rescind the contract and recover the £110,000 paid.

Breach of a promoter's fiduciary duty results in a transaction being voidable, so it can be rescinded by the company. If rescission does not recover the value of the profit or if the right to rescind is lost, then the promoter may be made to account to the company for the profit gained (*Emma Silver Mining Co v Grant* (1879) LR 11 ChD 918 (Ch)).

2.2 Pre-incorporation contracts

Promoters may need to engage in certain preparatory activities prior to the company's incorporation (such as purchasing or renting premises or equipment, hiring workers and so on) which may result in the promoter contracting with third parties. A problem arises if the promoter purports to contract on behalf of a company that has not yet been fully incorporated. This is known as a pre-incorporation contract. Until incorporation is complete, the company will not exist and so will have no **contractual capacity**. The issue here is whether pre-incorporation contracts are valid and, if so, who are the parties to the contract.

contractual capacity The ability to enter into contracts.

A pre-incorporation contract does not bind the company upon its incorporation. Whether the promoter could be liable on the contract has, historically, caused the courts difficulty. *Phonogram Ltd v Lane* [1982] QB 939 (CA) established that the relevant test was to determine the intention of the parties as evidenced in the contract (based on the contract, did the promoter intend to be bound?). Unfortunately, this test is difficult to apply in practice, which resulted in cases turning on minor and technical distinctions, as the following cases demonstrate.

- In *Kelner v Baxter* (1866) LR 2 CP 174, the promoter signed the contract 'on behalf of' the unformed company. It was held that a binding contract existed between the promoter and the third party.
- In *Newborne v Sensolid (Great Britain) Ltd* [1954] 1 QB 45 (CA), the promoter signed the contract using the unformed company's name and added his own signature underneath. It was held that the contract was between the promoter and the unformed company and, as the company had no contractual capacity, no contract existed.

The UK's entry into the European Economic Community (EEC) obliged it to implement Article 7 of the First EC Company Law Directive. The relevant provision is now found in s. 51(1) of the CA 2006, which states:

> 'A contract that purports to be made by or on behalf of a company at a time when the company has not been formed has effect, subject to any agreement to the contrary, as one made with the person purporting to act for the company or as agent for it, and he is personally liable on the contract accordingly.'

Where s. 51(1) applies, a promoter will be personally liable for a pre-incorporation contract, irrespective of how he expresses his signature. This obviously benefits third parties, who will now be able to enforce the contract against the promoter. The issue that arises is whether the promoter can enforce the contract against the third party. Section 51(1) provides that the promoter can be held liable on the contract, but it does not state that the promoter can enforce the contract. Fortunately, the Court of Appeal in *Braymist Ltd v Wise Finance Co Ltd* [2002] EWCA Civ 127 held that a promoter can enforce the contract, but the fact that such clarification was necessary demonstrates a flaw in the drafting of s. 51.

There are several instances where s. 51 does not apply, in which case the common law rules discussed above apply. For example, s. 51 will not apply where:

- a company was bought off the shelf after the contract was entered into, but was in existence at the time the contract was entered into; or
- where the company once existed but has since been dissolved (*Cotronic (UK) Ltd v Dezonie* [1991] BCC 200 (CA)).

Agreements to the contrary

Section 51 operates 'subject to any agreement to the contrary.' A promoter will therefore not be liable on a pre-incorporation contract if there exists an agreement stating that he will not be liable (such as where the pre-incorporation contract expressly states that the promoter is not liable on the contract).

Simply acting as a promoter will not be enough to establish the existence of an agreement (*Phonogram Ltd v Lane* [1982] QB 938 (CA)). The agreement must be explicit or clearly capable of being inferred from the terms of the pre-incorporation contract. The parties must also have intended to exclude the operation of s. 51 from the agreement.

Case law 3.2

***Royal Mail Estates Ltd v Maple Teesdale* [2015] EWHC 1890 (Ch)**

Maple Teesdale (MT) promoted Kensington Gateway Holdings Ltd (Kensington). Royal Mail Estates Ltd (RME) contracted to sell a piece of property to Kensington. The contract provided that the word 'Buyer' referred to Kensington and it was signed 'for and on behalf of the Buyer' followed by 'Maple Teesdale pp Buyer'. When the contract was entered into, Kensington had not been incorporated, but neither RME nor MT knew this. MT decided not to go ahead with the purchase and so RME sued, claiming that under s. 51, MT was personally liable on the contract. Clause 24.1 of the contract stated that 'the benefit of the contract is personal to the Buyer' and MT argued that this constituted an agreement to the contrary. MT applied to have the case summarily dismissed.

The court stated that 'there is only a contrary agreement... if there is found to be an agreement between the parties by which they intended to exclude the [s. 51] effect'. As neither RME nor MT knew that Kensington had not been incorporated at the time of the contract, it followed that they could not have had in mind s. 51 when they agreed the words in clause 24.1. Accordingly, clause 24.1 did not amount to an agreement to the contrary and MT's application was refused.

Binding the company

Upon incorporation, a company cannot adopt or ratify a pre-incorporation contract (*Re Northumberland Avenue Hotel Co Ltd* (1886) 33 ChD 16 (CA)). There are two ways in which a company can become bound by a pre-incorporation contract:

1. the pre-incorporation contract could provide that, upon incorporation, the promoter will cease to be liable under the contract if the company enters into a contract with the third party on the same terms as the pre-incorporation contract; or
2. following incorporation, the company, the promoter and the third party could enter into an agreement which provides that the pre-incorporation contract will be discharged and a new agreement will be entered into between the company and the third party (this is known as **novation**).

novation
A tripartite agreement which involves discharging a contract between two parties, then creating a new contract between one of those parties and a third party.

Stop and think 3.1

Article 7 of the First EC Company Law Directive provides that a company may, upon its incorporation, 'assume the obligations' of a pre-incorporation contract. However, s. 51 does not provide for this and, as noted, a company cannot adopt or ratify a pre-incorporation contract. Do you think that s. 51 properly implements Article 7?

Novation will not occur simply because a company acts on the pre-incorporation contract as if it were bound (*Re Northumberland Avenue Hotel Co Ltd* (1886) 33 ChD 16 (CA)). The courts will require clear evidence of novation (*Bagot Pneumatic Tyre Co v Clipper Pneumatic Tyre Co* [1901] 1 Ch 196 (Ch)), but novation need not be express. Novation may be inferred based on the conduct of the parties, such as where the company and third party agreed to modify the agreement (as occurred in *Howard v Patent Ivory Manufacturing Co* (1888) 38 ChD 156 (Ch)), although this will be rare.

Test yourself 3.1

1. **What is a promoter?**
2. **How does s. 51 of the CA 2006 differ to the common law rules relating to pre-incorporation contracts?**
3. **How can a company be bound by a pre-incorporation contract?**
4. **When will a pre-incorporation contract not be subject to s. 51 of the CA 2006?**

Companies are created via a process called incorporation. Figure 3.1 sets out the different types of incorporation.

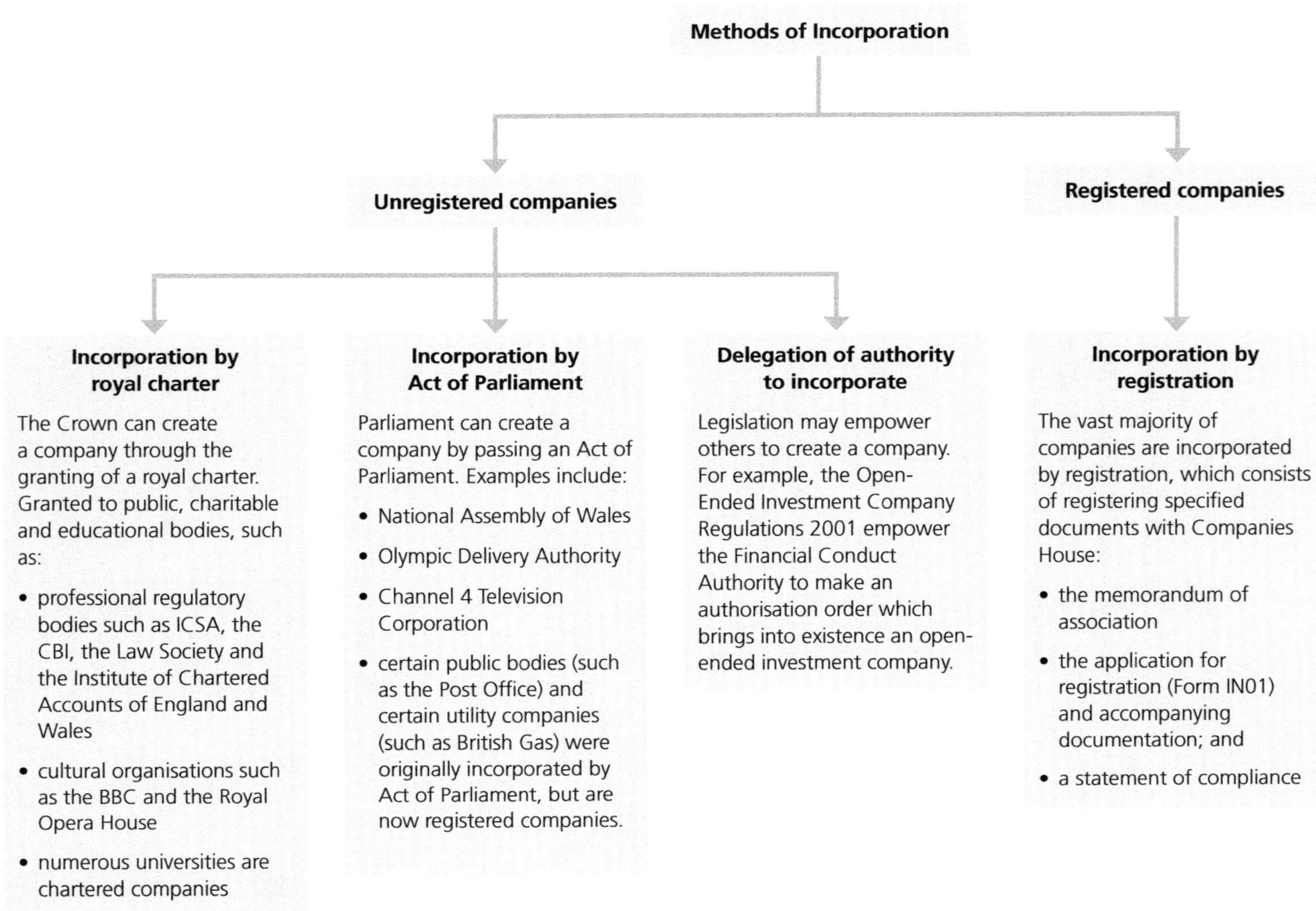

Figure 3.1 Methods of incorporation

3. Incorporation of an unregistered company

Unregistered companies (companies not incorporated by registration) are very rare, but unregistered companies can be notable, so it is worth explaining their creation. By default, the CA 2006 does not apply to unregistered companies (CA 2006, s. 1), but the Secretary of State can pass regulations that extend provisions of the CA 2006 to cover unregistered companies (CA 2006, s. 1043). There are three ways of incorporating an unregistered company.

3.1 Incorporation by royal charter

The Crown has the power to create a 'chartered company' through the granting of a **royal charter**. Around 860 chartered companies currently exist and only a few are created each year (no charters appears to have been granted in 2018). Today, charters are granted exclusively to bodies engaged in charitable, educational or non-profit-making activities. Examples include the Bank of England (1694), the Royal Bank of Scotland (1727), the Law Society (1845), the Institute of Chartered Accountants of England and Wales (1880), the Institute of Chartered Secretaries and Administrators (1902) and the British Broadcasting Corporation (1926).

royal charter
A formal document issued by the Crown or certain persons empowered to act on her behalf.

3.2 Incorporation by Act of Parliament

Parliament can create a company by passing an Act of Parliament, but such companies are rare. The exact nature of the company usually depends on the type of Act.

- Companies created by a **public Act** are usually of national importance and are usually created to serve some public need. For example, the London Olympic Games and Paralympic Games Act 2006 created the Olympic Delivery Authority – the body that was responsible for the organisation of the 2012 London Olympic and Paralympic Games.
- Persons may petition Parliament to pass a **private Act** that will create a company that facilitates that person's commercial dealings. Historically, most so-called 'statutory companies' were created to run newly-privatised industries, but most have since become registered companies under the CA 2006.

public Act
An Act of Parliament that deals with matters of public interest and usually affects the general population.

private Act
An Act of Parliament that affects specified persons, groups of persons, organisations or localities.

3.3 Delegation of authority to incorporate

Legislation may confer upon others the ability to create a company. For example, the Open-Ended Investment Company Regulations 2001 (SI 2001/1288) empower the FCA to make an authorisation order which brings into existence an open-ended investment company.

4. Incorporation of a registered company

The vast majority of newly created companies are incorporated by registration. Persons who wish to incorporate a company by registration must subscribe their names to a memorandum of association and comply with the CA 2006's requirements regarding registration (CA 2006, s. 7(1)).

The incorporation of companies is carried out by Companies House – a body that is sponsored by BEIS and whose functions include: incorporating and dissolving companies; storing information of companies in the register of companies; and making such information available to the public. Virtually all information on the register of companies can be accessed online for free (see https://beta.companieshouse.gov.uk and the Companies House phone app). This information is used by millions of people as a basis for making commercial decisions. It is therefore vital that company secretaries provide accurate information to Companies House when required.

To incorporate a company by registration, the promoters must provide the following registration documents to Companies House (CA 2006, s 9(1):

- the memorandum of association
- the application for registration and accompanying documentation
- the statement of compliance

4.1 The memorandum of association

memorandum of association
A document that provides details of a company at the time of its incorporation.

All companies must have a **memorandum of association** as part of the registration documents (CA 2006, s. 9(1)). Those persons wishing to incorporate a company by registration must subscribe their names to the memorandum (CA 2006, s. 7(1)(a)). Upon incorporation, those persons will become the company's first members (CA 2006, s. 112(1)). The memorandum must state that the subscribers:

- wish to form a company under the CA 2006;
- agree to become members of the company; and
- in the case of a company that is to have a share capital, to take at least one share each (CA 2006, s. 8(1)).

4.2 The application for registration and accompanying documentation

The promoters must complete an application for registration along with the necessary accompanying documentation (CA 2006, s. 9). For many filing activities, Companies House provides standard forms that comply with the relevant statutory requirements and Form IN01 is the standard application for registration form (an extract from this form can be found on the next page).

In accordance with Section 9 of the Companies Act 2006.

IN01
Application to register a company

Companies House

A fee is payable with this form.
Please see 'How to pay' on the last page.

✓ What this form is for
You may use this form to register a private or public company.

✗ What this form is NOT for
You cannot use this form to register a limited liability partnership. To do this, please use form LL IN01. Do not use this form if any individual person with significant control is applying or has applied for protection from having their details disclosed on the public register. Contact enquiries@companieshouse.gov.uk to get a separate form.

For further information, please refer to our guidance at www.gov.uk/companieshouse

Part 1 Company details

A1 Company name

Check if a company name is available by using our name availability search:
www.companieshouse.gov.uk/info

Please show the proposed company name below.

Proposed company name in full ❶

For official use

→ Filling in this form
Please complete in typescript or in bold black capitals.

All fields are mandatory unless specified or indicated by *

❶ Duplicate names
Duplicate names are not permitted. A list of registered names can be found on our website. There are various rules that may affect your choice of name. More information on this is available in our guidance at: www.gov.uk/companieshouse

A2 Company name restrictions ❷

Please tick the box only if the proposed company name contains sensitive or restricted words or expressions that require you to seek comments of a government department or other specified body.

☐ I confirm that the proposed company name contains sensitive or restricted words or expressions and that approval, where appropriate, has been sought of a government department or other specified body and I attach a copy of their response.

❷ Company name restrictions
A list of sensitive or restricted words or expressions that require consent can be found in our guidance at: www.gov.uk/companieshouse

A3 Exemption from name ending with 'Limited' or 'Cyfyngedig' ❸

Please tick the box if you wish to apply for exemption from the requirement to have the name ending with 'Limited', Cyfyngedig' or permitted alternative.

☐ I confirm that the above proposed company meets the conditions for exemption from the requirement to have a name ending with 'Limited', 'Cyfyngedig' or permitted alternative.

❸ Name ending exemption
Only private companies that are limited by guarantee and meet other specific requirements or private companies that are charities are eligible to apply for this. For more details, please go to our website: www.gov.uk/companieshouse

Figure 3.2 Extract from form IN01

The application for registration requires the promoters to provide certain basic information concerning the company, such as: (i) whether the company will be public or private; (ii) whether the liability of the members will be limited or unlimited; and (iii) if liability is to be limited, whether it will be limited by shares or guarantee (CA 2006, s. 9(2)). Section 9 also requires the application to provide the following.

- The proposed name of the company (discussed below).
- The intended address of the company's registered office and whether that office is to be situated in England and Wales (or in Wales), Scotland or Northern Ireland.
- If the proposed company is to have a share capital, a statement of capital and initial shareholdings. The information contained in this statement includes the total number of shares to be taken by the subscribers, details of each subscriber (name, address and so on) and the amount paid up and unpaid on each share (CA 2006, s. 10).
- If the proposed company is to be limited by guarantee, the application must contain a statement of guarantee. This statement must state the name and address of each subscriber to the memorandum, and that each member undertakes that if the company is wound up while he is a member, or within one year after he ceases to be a member, he will contribute to the assets of the company such amount (not exceeding a specified amount) as may be required for:
  - payment of the debts and liabilities of the company contracted before he ceases to be a member;
  - payment of the costs, charges and expenses of winding up; and
  - adjustment of the rights of the contributories among themselves (CA 2006, s. 11).
- The application must contain a statement of the company's proposed officers, which must provide required particulars (name, nationality, date of birth) of the first director(s) of the company and, if applicable, the first company secretary (or joint secretaries) (CA 2006, s. 12(1)).
- The application must contain a statement of significant control, which identifies whether, on incorporation, there will be any persons with significant control (PSC) over the company (CA 2006, s. 12A(1)). Persons with significant control are discussed in Chapter 8.
- Unless the proposed company wishes to adopt the **model articles**, the application for registration must contain a copy of the proposed **articles of association** (discussed in Chapter 4). If no articles are submitted alongside the application, the company will be governed by the relevant model articles (CA 2006, s. 20(1)).
- The application must contain a statement of the company type and its intended business activities.
- If the promoters of a private company elect to keep certain register information on the public register held by Companies House, then Companies House must be informed of this when the registration

model articles
A set of default articles provided by the Companies (Model Articles) Regulations 2008.

articles of association
The internal constitutional rules that regulate a company.

documents are delivered to Companies House (CA 2006, ss. 128B, 167A, 279A and 790X). This election is discussed more on page 275.

The proposed name of the company

The regulation of company names is notable in terms of what words or phrases must and cannot be used. Third parties dealing with a company should know what type of company they are dealing with, and so most companies must include a specified designation at the end of their name to indicate their company type.

- Private limited companies must add the suffix 'ltd' or 'limited' (CA 2006, s. 59(1)).
- Public limited companies must add the suffix 'plc' or 'public limited company' (CA 2006, s. 58(1)).
- Private community interest companies must add the suffix 'cic' or 'community interest company' (Companies (Audit, Investigations and Community Enterprise) Act 2004, s 33(1)).
- Public community interest companies must add the suffix 'community interest public company' or 'community interest plc' (Companies (Audit, Investigations and Community Enterprise) Act 2004, s. 33(3)).

Historically, companies needed to have their names approved prior to incorporation. Today, pre-approval is no longer generally required and companies may use any name, subject to the following prohibitions and limitations.

- A company name must not be registered if, in the opinion of the Secretary of State, it is offensive or if the use of that name would constitute an offence (CA 2006, s. 53).
- Companies House must keep an index of company names (CA 2006, s. 1099(1)). A company cannot have the same name as a company already listed on the index (CA 2006, s. 66(1)). If the Secretary of State is of the opinion that a company's name is the same as, or too similar to, an existing company name, they can direct the company to change its name (CA 2006, s. 67).
- Promoters should take care to ensure that the company's name does not contain any words or phrases that infringe the intellectual property rights of others. Acceptance of a name by Companies House does not mean that the name does not infringe intellectual property rights.
- Section 216 of IA 1986 (discussed in Chapter 18) establishes limitations on using the names of companies that have gone into insolvent liquidation.

In some cases, pre-approval is required and permission will need to be obtained to use certain words and phrases in a company name.

- Approval of the Secretary of State is required if a company name gives the impression that the company is connected with certain governmental bodies (CA 2006, s. 54) or if certain sensitive words or expressions are used (e.g. British, NHS) (CA 2006, s. 55).

- Some words and phrases can only be used if permission is obtained from certain persons (for example, a company that wishes to use the word 'insurance' in its name must obtain a letter of non-objection from the FCA).

The Company, Limited Liability Partnership and Business (Names and Trading Disclosures) Regulations 2015 (SI 2015/17) provide that, upon incorporation, the company must display its registered name at its registered office, any inspection place and any other location where it carries on business (regs 21(1) and 22). Its registered name must be disclosed on the company's website, and on documents such as business letters, cheques and all other forms of business correspondence and documentation (reg 24). Failure to comply with these rules, without reasonable excuse, is a criminal offence (reg 28).

Following incorporation, a company may change its name by either passing a special resolution (CA 2006, ss. 77(1)(a) and 78), or by some other means provided for by its articles (CA 2006, ss. 77(1)(b) and 79). Notice of the change must be given to Companies House (see Form NM01) and the registrar will then issue a new certificate of incorporation (CA 2006, s. 80(3)). The new name has effect from the date of the certificate's issue.

4.3 Statement of compliance

The application for registration must be accompanied by a statement of compliance, which states that the requirements of the CA 2006 as to registration have been complied with (CA 2006, s. 13(1)). Companies House may accept this statement as sufficient evidence of compliance.

4.4 Submission and registration

The registration documents should be submitted to the Registrar of Companies that is responsible for the country in which the registered office is to be based, namely (i) the registrar of companies for England and Wales; (ii) the registrar of companies for Scotland; or (iii) the registrar of companies for Northern Ireland (CA 2006, s. 9(6)).

The registrar will examine the registration documents to make sure they are completed properly and fully. If they are not, the application may be rejected. The registrar can also refuse to register a company if it is formed for an unlawful purpose (see *R v Registrar of Joint Stock Companies* [1931] 2 KB 197 (CA)). Section 7(2) of the CA 2006 prohibits a company being formed for such a purpose. The final step before the documents will be registered is for the promoter to pay the registration fee.

Certificate of incorporation

Following payment of the fee, the registrar will register the registration documents, allocate the company with a registration number and issue a certificate of incorporation (CA 2006, s. 15(1)). This certificate provides that the company has been duly registered under the CA 2006 and provides conclusive evidence that it has complied with the CA 2006's registration requirements (CA 2006, s. 15(4)).

The certificate will state the date of registration. From this date, the company's subscribers become members (and shareholders if applicable), the company's separate personality comes into existence and the company's directors and secretaries will be appointed to their respective offices (CA 2006, s. 16).

Trading certificate

It is a criminal offence for a public company to commence business or exercise borrowing powers until it has been issued with a trading certificate (CA 2006, ss. 761(1) and 767). A public company will need to apply for a trading certificate using Form SH50. Companies House will only issue this certificate if it is satisfied that the company has complied with the additional requirements relating to public companies, namely the minimum capital requirement discussed in Chapter 11 (CA 2006, ss. 761(2) and 762). A public company may be wound up by the court if it has yet to be issued with a trading certificate a year after registration (IA 1986, s. 122(1)(b)).

4.5 'Off-the-shelf' companies

Promoters who lack sufficient knowledge to prepare the registration documents, or who simply do not wish to engage in the effort of preparing such documents, can instead simply purchase an existing company.

Persons (often known as company formation agents) specialise in creating and selling companies. They create companies and then leave them dormant 'on the shelf' until such time as they are purchased. When such a off-the-shelf company is purchased, the agent will transfer the company to the purchaser and notify Companies House of the relevant changes (change of directors, registered office and so on).

The advantage to the purchaser is that they need not engage in the registration process themselves and a company can be obtained very quickly and inexpensively. The disadvantage is that the company's details will have been created by the agent and so may not exactly meet the needs of the purchaser. If the purchaser is willing to spend more money, the agent will create a bespoke company that fits the purchaser's exact needs

Test yourself 3.2

1. **What documentation must be submitted to Companies House to incorporate a company by registration?**
2. **What information does Form IN01 require?**
3. **What limitations and restrictions exist in relation to a company's name?**
4. **Explain the differences between a certificate of incorporation and a trading certificate.**
5. **What is an 'off-the-shelf' company, and what are the advantages and disadvantages of such companies?**

5. Corporate personality

Corporate personality distinguishes a company from most other business organisations (notably sole proprietorships and ordinary partnerships). Corporate personality refers to the fact that a company is a person, and several fundamental consequences flow from this. Here, what corporate personality is, its consequences, and the ways in which it can be disregarded will be discussed. It is important to first discuss the use of certain terminology used in relation to corporate personality.

5.1 Legal and natural persons, and individuals

It is important to understand the differences (and overlaps) between persons and individuals, as statute usually uses these terms to mean different things.

The word 'person' can refer to a natural person (a human being) or a legal person (a body corporate, such as a company or LLP). In legislation, unless the contrary intention appears, the word person includes both natural and legal persons (Interpretation Act 1987, s. 5 and Sch 1, para 1).

The word 'individual' is usually used to refer to natural persons only. It is important to appreciate this distinction, especially when determining upon whom liability can be imposed for a breach of the law, as the following example demonstrates.

Case study 3.1

John is a director of X-Corp plc and his daughter, Kate, is a director of Y-Corp plc. Y-Corp holds a number of shares in X-Corp. John informs Kate that X-Corp has just lost a major client. When this news becomes public, it will cause X-Corp's share price to drop considerably and so John advises Kate that Y-Corp should sell its shares in X-Corp immediately, which Y-Corp does.

Section 52 of the Criminal Justice Act 1993 provides that insider dealing is a criminal offence, but liability can only be imposed upon an individual. From this, it follows that John and Kate could be convicted of insider dealing, but Y-Corp could not.

5.2 The company as a person

A company is a legal person or, to use the language of the CA 2006, it is a 'body corporate' that comes into existence when the company is incorporated (CA 2006, s. 16(1)–(2)). It has many of the same rights and attributes as natural persons. However, as the company is, to quote Marshal CJ in *Trustees of Dartmouth College v Woodward* (1819) 17 US (4 Wheat) 518, 'an artificial being, invisible, intangible, and existing only in operation of law', not all laws can apply to companies. For example, as a company cannot be imprisoned, a company cannot be convicted of an offence for which the only punishment is imprisonment, such as murder (*R v ICR Haulage* [1944] KB 551).

A company's corporate personality results in various consequences.

Nationality, domicile and residence

Like a natural person, a company can have a nationality, domicile and residence.

- A company's nationality is based on the country in which it is registered (*Janson v Driefontein Consolidated Mines Ltd* [1902] AC 484 (HL)). This also determines where a company is domiciled (*Gasque v Inland Revenue Commissioners* [1940] 2 KB 80 (KB)). While a natural person can change their nationality or domicile, a company cannot.
- A company's residence is determined by where a company 'really keeps house and does business' with business being carried out 'where the central management and control actually abides' (*De Beers Consolidated Mines Ltd v Howe* [1906] AC 455 (HL)). In practice, a company's residence is only relevant for the purposes of determining its tax liabilities.

Perpetual succession

As a company has no physical being, it can continue to exist perpetually. The company's directors, members, employees and creditors will change over time, but as the company has no physical existence, it can continue forever.

Contractual capacity

A company can enter into contracts with persons outside the company and also with persons within it, as the following case demonstrates.

Case law 3.3

***Lee v Lee's Air Farming Ltd* [1961] AC 12 (PC)**

Lee was the only director of a company and held 2,999 of its 3,000 shares. He was also employed by the company as a pilot, but was killed when his plane crashed while engaged in company business. Widows of employees killed while on company business were entitled to compensation, but the company argued that Lee's widow was not entitled to compensation on the ground that Lee was synonymous with the company and so his employment contract was in effect entered into with himself. A person cannot enter into a contract with themselves (as an agreement requires two parties), so the insurance company argued that Lee's employment contract was invalid and he was not therefore an employee.

Lee might have been the company's only director and owned almost all its shares, but this did not alter the fact that the company was a separate person. Accordingly, he had not entered into a contract with himself – he contracted with the company and was its employee. Lee's widow was therefore entitled to compensation.

Ownership of assets
A company can own property. Its property 'belongs beneficially to the company itself and in no sense belongs, either in law or in equity, to the shareholders, who have no interest of any nature, whether proprietary or otherwise, in its assets' (*Prest v Prest* [2012] EWCA Civ 1395). The following case demonstrates how the company's assets are distinct from those of other persons.

Case law 3.4

***Macaura v Northern Assurance Co Ltd* [1925] AC 619 (HL)**

Macaura set up a company to run a timber business that he owned. He transferred the timber to this new company and took out an insurance policy, in his own name, against loss caused to the timber by fire. Shortly after, the timber was destroyed in a fire and Macaura claimed on the policy. The insurers refused to pay out on the ground that it was not Macaura's timber that was destroyed. Macaura sued.

In order to claim on the policy, Macaura would need to have an insurable interest in the timber. He did not have such an interest as the timber did not belong to him – it belonged to the company. Accordingly, Macaura's claim failed.

When companies borrow money, the debt will usually be secured on the company's assets and not the assets of the directors or members, meaning that creditors can only look to the company's assets for payment. This is another reason why it important to be able to distinguish between property owned by the company and property owned by other persons.

The company's business
Any business being carried on by the company is the company's business, and not that of its directors or members.

Case law 3.5

***Cristina v Seear* [1985] 2 EGLR 128 (CA)**

Mr and Mrs Cristina ran a company out of a property that they rented. The tenancy agreement between the Cristinas and the landlord expired and the landlord sought to terminate the tenancy. The Cristinas argued that they had security of tenure as s. 23(1) of the Landlord and Tenant Act 1954 provided security of tenure where the property in question 'is or includes premises which are occupied by the tenant and are so occupied for the purposes of a business carried on by him'.

Section 23 did not apply as the business being carried on was that of the company, not of the Cristinas. Accordingly, the property was not occupied for the purpose of a business carried on by the Cristinas.

Commencing and defending legal proceedings

As the company is a person, it can commence legal proceedings if it is wronged or suffers loss due to the actions or omissions of another person (including those within the company). A company can also be sued if it commits a civil wrong and can also be convicted of a criminal offence. However, as the company cannot act on its own and can only act through human actors, special rules have been created in order to determine when a company can be liable (discussed in Chapter 4).

'Human rights'

Companies have 'human rights' under the ECHR, although not all rights can apply to companies (Article 3, which prohibits torture, clearly cannot apply to a company). In some cases, the ECHR expressly provides rights to companies, as is the case with Article 1 of the First Protocol, which states '[e]very natural or legal person is entitled to the peaceful enjoyment of his possessions'. Other provisions do not expressly include companies, but state that the protection is afforded to 'everyone', which would include companies.

5.3 The case of *Salomon*

Understanding the seminal case of *Salomon v A Salomon & Co Ltd* is vital in order to understand why corporate personality is so significant. Many students incorrectly believe that *Salomon* created the concept of corporate personality, but this is not the case. The importance of *Salomon* lies in the fact that it indicates that the courts finally understood the full significance of what corporate personality entails.

Case law 3.6

***Salomon v A Salomon & Co Ltd* [1897] AC 22 (HL)**

Salomon decided to incorporate his bootmaking business. Accordingly, he set up a company and, in order to comply with the then-statutory requirement that all companies have at least seven members, he took one share and his wife and five children each took one share. Salomon transferred his bootmaking business to this new company, in return for which he received an additional 20,000 £1 shares in the company, £10,000 worth of debentures secured by floating charge and a cash payment.

debenture
A document which acknowledges or creates a debt.

Unfortunately, the business soon failed and went into liquidation owing significant sums to several creditors, of which Salomon was one as he was a debenture holder. As Salomon's loan was secured by a floating charge, his debt was paid first. This meant the other creditors (whose debts were unsecured) went unpaid. The liquidator stated that Salomon should be personally liable for the company's debts.

At first instance, the court held that Salomon was liable for the company's debts as the company was his agent. Salomon appealed but his appeal was dismissed, with the Court of Appeal holding that

Salomon was liable because CA 1862 'contemplated the incorporation of seven independent bona fide members, who had a mind and a will of their own, and were not the mere puppets of an individual who, adopting the machinery of the Act, carried on his old business in the same way as before, when he was a sole trader'. Salomon appealed to the House of Lords.

The appeal was allowed and the House held that Salomon was not liable for the company's debts. As to whether the company was an agent of Salomon, Lord Herschell stated:

> **'a company may in every sense be said to carry on business for and on behalf of its shareholders; but this certainly does not in point of law constitute the relation of principal and agent between them or render the shareholders liable to indemnify the company against debts which it incurs.'**

As to the issue of whether the company complied with the requirement to have seven members, Lord Macnaghten stated '[t]here is nothing in the Act requiring that the subscribers to the memorandum should be independent or unconnected, or that they or any one of them should take a substantial interest in the undertaking, or that they should have a mind and will of their own...'

Salomon is a seminal company law case for three reasons:

1. the House recognised that a validly incorporated company could legitimately be used to shield its members from liability for the company's debts;
2. it implicitly recognised the validity of the 'one-person company' (that is, a company run only by one person, with several dormant nominee shareholders) almost a century before it was possible to formally create a one-person company in 1992; and
3. it recognised that a relationship of agency or trusteeship is not established simply because a person holds shares (even all the shares) in a company.

The House in *Salomon* strongly upheld the company's separate personality. However, it is also clear that corporate personality can be abused. It is possible to disregard a company's separate personality and impose liability on directors, members or other relevant persons. This disregarding of a company's corporate personality is often referred to as 'lifting' or 'piercing' the corporate veil. Figure 3.3 sets out the three methods of disregarding corporate personality.

5.4 Disregarding corporate personality under statute

Corporate personality is bestowed upon companies via statute (namely s. 16(2) of the CA 2006), and can be taken away by statute. There are many statutory provisions that disregard a company's corporate personality when a breach of the law occurs, including:

Corporate Personality

At law, a company is a person and has many of the same rights and abilities as a natural person. However, a company's separate personality can be disregarded in three ways.

Statute

As corporate personality is granted by statute, it can be disregarded by statute. Examples include:

- CA 2006, s. 399 (group accounts)
- CA 2006, s. 767 (doing business without a trading certificate)
- CA 2006, s. 993 (fraudulent)
- IA 1986, ss. 213 and 246ZA (fraudulent trading)
- IA 1986, ss. 214 and 246ZB (wrongful trading)
- IA 1986, s. 238 (transaction at an undervalue)
- IA 1986, s. 239 (preferences).

Common Law

Following *Petrodel Resources Ltd v Prest*, the courts can disregard a company's corporate personality:

- where a person is under an existing legal obligation or liability or subject to an existing legal restriction which he deliberately evades or whose enforcement he deliberately frustrates by interposing a company under his control; and
- if other, more conventional, remedies have proved to be of no assistance.

Contract

A company's corporate personality can be disregarded via contract (e.g. where a member or director contractually agrees to be liable for the company's debts or liabilities).

Figure 3.3 Disregarding corporate personality

- if a public company does business or exercises any borrowing powers prior to being issued with a trading certificate, then every officer in default will have committed an offence (CA 2006, s. 767(1)); and
- persons found to have engaged in fraudulent trading will have committed a criminal offence (CA 2006, s. 993), and may be ordered to contribute to the assets of the company (IA 1986, ss. 213 and 246ZA).

Statute may disregard a company's corporate personality not because the law has been breached, but for some other justifiable reason. For example, persons who hold shares in, or have loaned money to, a company that is part of a group of companies will want to know how the entire group is performing. Accordingly, statute provides that parent companies must, in addition to providing their own accounts, also prepare consolidated accounts covering all companies in the group (CA 2006, ss. 399 and 404).

5.5 Disregarding corporate personality under the common law

The courts also have the ability to disregard corporate personality where no statutory authority to do so exists. However, as corporate personality is bestowed upon companies by statute, the courts have always exercised this power cautiously.

For many years, the exact instances where the courts would disregard corporate personality were unclear, but there were two notable instances in which corporate personality could be disregarded.

First, a company's corporate personality could be disregarded where the company was being used to perpetrate a fraud, was a façade or a sham, or was being used to evade some form of legal obligation, as the following case demonstrates.

Case law 3.7

***Gilford Motor Co Ltd v Horne* [1933] Ch 935 (CA)**

Horne's employment contract provided that, if he left the employment of Gilford Motor Co Ltd, he would not solicit any of its clients. Horne's employment was terminated and, at Horne's behest, his wife set up a company that competed with Gilford. It was clear that this company was controlled by Horne. Gilford sued Horne to enforce the restrictive covenant and prevent the new company from soliciting Gilford's clients.

Lord Hanworth MR stated that the company set up by Mrs Horne was 'formed as a device, a stratagem, in order to mask the effective carrying on of a business of [Horne]'. Accordingly, Gilford's action succeeded and the court granted an injunction prohibiting Horne and the new company from soliciting Gilford's clients.

Second, the courts could disregard a company's corporate personality where a relationship of agency existed. In such a relationship, the principal is liable for the acts of their agent. Accordingly, in the following case, the court held that a relationship of agency existed between a parent company and its subsidiary, and so the corporate personality of the subsidiary was disregarded.

Case law 3.8

***Smith, Stone and Knight Ltd v Birmingham Corporation* [1939] 4 All ER 116 (QB)**

Smith, Stone and Knight Ltd (SSK) acquired a waste paper business. It incorporated a subsidiary to run this business, but SSK retained ownership of the business and the land upon which the business

operated. This land was compulsorily purchased by Birmingham Corporation, who planned to compensate the subsidiary for the loss of the land and the disturbance to its business. However, SSK stated that it, not the subsidiary, was entitled to the compensation.

The court held that, due to the level of domination that SSK had over the subsidiary (SSK owned the subsidiary's business, the land upon which it conducted business and it owned 497 of the subsidiary's 502 shares), the subsidiary was an agent of SSK. Accordingly, the subsidiary's corporate personality was disregarded and SSK received the compensation.

The courts were not always consistent in their disregarding of corporate personality and so clarity was required. The Supreme Court has now provided clarity in the case of *Petrodel Resources Ltd v Prest* [2013] UKSC 34. The Supreme Court decision in *Prest* provides much needed clarity, but it does so by adopting a very restrictive approach as to when the courts can disregard corporate personality.

Case law 3.9

***Petrodel Resources Ltd v Prest* [2013] UKSC 34**

A court ordered Mr Prest to pay Mrs Prest £17.5 million as part of a divorce settlement. The problem was that most of Mr Prest's assets were tied up in companies that he solely controlled. Section 24(1)(a) of the Matrimonial Causes Act 1973 empowered the courts to 'order that a party to the marriage shall transfer to the other party... property to which the first mentioned party is entitled'. Mr Prest stated that the s. 24 power could not be used here as he did not own the property in question – it was owned by the companies he controlled.

The High Court disagreed and exercised the s. 24 power by disregarding the corporate personalities of the companies concerned. Mr Prest appealed and the Court of Appeal allowed his appeal, stating that the corporate personalities of the companies could not be disregarded in this way. Mrs Prest appealed.

Mrs Prest's appeal was allowed and the Supreme Court ordered that the assets held by the companies were held on trust for Mrs Prest's benefit. Accordingly, the Court did not need to disregard the companies' corporate personalities and indeed, the Court refused to do so.

The Court did clarify when the courts could disregard corporate personality (although such comments were only *obiter*). Lord Sumption stated that there was only one instance in which the courts could pierce the veil, namely where 'a person is under an existing legal obligation or liability or subject to an existing legal restriction which he deliberately evades or whose enforcement he deliberately frustrates by interposing a company under his control'.

obiter dictum
'A thing said by the way.' A statement made by a judge in a judgment which is not directly relevant to the case, and so is merely of persuasive authority.

Further, a court could only pierce the veil in this instance if 'all other, more conventional, remedies have proved to be no assistance'.

When can the courts disregard corporate personality?

The first point to note is how the Court redefined what disregarding corporate personality means. Lord Sumption stated that disregarding corporate personality refers 'only of those cases which are true exceptions to the rule in *Salomon*... i.e. where a person who owns and controls a company is said in certain circumstances to be identified with it in law by virtue of that ownership and control'.

Lord Sumption was of the opinion that many pre-*Prest* cases did not fall within this definition and so were not true examples of disregarding corporate personality. Instead, he regarded them as examples of what he called the 'concealment principle', which provides that 'the interposition of a company or perhaps several companies so as to conceal the identity of the real actors will not deter the courts from identifying them, assuming that their identity is legally relevant'.

For Lord Sumption, the concealment principle is 'legally banal and does not involve piercing the veil at all'. Instead, all that the court is doing is 'looking behind [the company's corporate personality] to discover the facts which the corporate structure is concealing'.

The only instance when the courts can disregard a company's corporate personality is where the 'evasion principle' applies, namely 'where a person is under an existing legal obligation or liability or subject to an existing legal restriction which he deliberately evades or whose enforcement he deliberately frustrates by interposing a company under his control'. Where the evasion principle applies, the court may 'pierce the corporate veil for the purpose, and only for the purpose, of depriving the company or its controller of the advantage that they would otherwise have obtained by the company's separate legal personality'.

From Lord Sumption's definition of the evasion principle, it can be seen that for the evasion principle to apply and liability to be imposed upon a person (*X*), three conditions need to be met.

1. There must be an existing legal obligation, liability or restriction placed upon *X*. Accordingly, if the obligation is not placed upon *X*, the evasion principle will not apply. Thus, in *Yukong Line Ltd of Korea v Rendsburg Investment Corps of Liberia* [1998] 1 WLR 294 (QB), the company's corporate personality was not disregarded because the obligation in question was placed upon the company that *X* worked for, and not *X* himself.
2. *X* must interpose a company in order to frustrate the obligation, liability or restriction in question. *Gilford Motor Co Ltd v Horne* discussed on page 54 is a good example of how a company was interposed in order to evade a legal restriction.
3. The company being interposed by *X* must be under *X*'s control. Again, *Gilford Motor Co Ltd* provides a good example of this as, although Horne

was not a member or director of the company, he clearly was in control of it.

The satisfaction of these three conditions will mean that the evasion principle applies, but it does not mean that the company's corporate personality will be disregarded. Lord Neuberger stated that a company's corporate personality should only be disregarded 'when all other, more conventional, remedies have proved to be of no assistance …', while Lord Sumption stated that 'if it is not necessary to pierce the corporate veil, it is not appropriate to do so'.

Piercing the veil should be a remedy of last resort. If alternative remedies are available, or if the court can achieve a desired result without piercing the veil, then the veil should not be pierced.

The application of Prest

It should be noted that only two of the seven Justices in *Prest* expressly endorsed the concealment and evasion approach. There was also disagreement as to whether the evasion principle was the only instance in which the veil could be pierced. Clearly, Lords Sumption and Neuberger believed this to be the case, but other Justices (Lords Mance and Clarke) were open to the idea of other instances of piercing the veil, albeit with Lord Mance stating that such instances would be 'novel and very rare'. It is also the case that Lord Sumption's comments were only *obiter*.

It was not certain that future courts would follow the approach established by Lord Sumption in *Prest*. Unsurprisingly, however, post-*Prest* cases have unanimously adopted the approach set out by Lord Sumption. For example, in the following case, the court used the concealment principle to justify disregarding a company's corporate personality.

Case law 3.10

***Wood v Baker* [2015] EWHC 2536 (Ch)**

A bankruptcy order was made against Baker and he was required to disclose to his trustees in bankruptcy details of any property acquired or increases in income (IA 1986, s. 33). An HMRC investigation resulted in several of Baker's associates being arrested on suspicion of fraud and money laundering. These associates revealed that Baker had used a series of companies he controlled to place assets out of the reach of his trustees in bankruptcy. Accordingly, Baker's trustees in bankruptcy applied to the court for an order freezing the assets of these companies.

The Court stated Baker had 'demonstrated a way of working which involves interposing front men, or front companies, between his trustees and his business affairs…' These companies were clearly interposed in order to avoid the obligations he owed to his trustees in bankruptcy, which was a clear example of the evasion principle in action. Accordingly, the court order was granted and the corporate personalities of the various companies were disregarded and their assets frozen.

Following *Prest*, it is rare for a company's corporate personality to be disregarded. Instead, the courts have sought to achieve a similar result by using more conventional legal means. Indeed, there were indications that such an approach was evident prior to *Prest*. For example, in the following case, the court utilised the concept of the duty of care to impose liability on a parent company for injuries sustained to an employee of its subsidiary.

Case law 3.11

***Chandler v Cape Industries plc* [2012] EWCA Civ 525**

Between 1959 and 1962, Chandler was an employee of Cape Building Products Ltd (CBP), a subsidiary of Cape plc. In 2007, Chandler discovered that he had contracted asbestosis due to being exposed to asbestos while working for CBP. He sought to obtain compensation, but CBP had been dissolved many years before. Accordingly, Chandler commenced proceedings against CBP's parent, Cape plc.

Cape was ordered to pay damages to Chandler. However, the court 'emphatically' rejected any suggestion that the imposition of liability on Cape plc involved a piercing of the corporate veil. Instead, the court held that Cape owed a duty of care to Chandler, which it had breached. Arden LJ stated that such a duty could be imposed where:

- **the businesses of the parent and subsidiary are in a relevant respect the same;**
- **the parent has, or ought to have, superior knowledge on some relevant aspect of health and safety in the particular industry;**
- **the subsidiary's system of work is unsafe as the parent company knew, or ought to have known; and**
- **the parent knew or ought to have foreseen that the subsidiary or its employees would rely on its using that superior knowledge for the employees' protection.**

The above circumstances were present here and so Cape plc had assumed a responsibility to Chandler, and so it was ordered to pay him damages.

5.6 Circumventing corporate personality via contract

Corporate personality shields those behind the corporate veil from liability. However, such persons may contract out of this protection and render themselves personally liable. This often occurs where creditors lend money to smaller companies. Such creditors will often seek to ensure repayment of the loan by requiring the directors or members (who are often the same persons) to guarantee the loan.

Test yourself 3.3

1. **What is the difference between a person and an individual?**
2. **Explain the key consequences of a company having a corporate personality.**
3. **In *Salomon*, how did the House of Lords disagree with the High Court and Court of Appeal?**
4. **Why is *Salomon* considered to be such a seminal case?**
5. **When will the courts disregard a company's corporate personality?**
6. **What are the three conditions required for the evasion principle to apply?**

6. Corporate liability

As a company is a person, it can be liable for civil wrongs and convicted of crimes. However, the fact that the company can only act through human intermediaries (directors, employees, agents and so on) presents a problem in terms of imposing liability. Who should be liable – the company or those persons who engage in unlawful acts on its behalf? The law has devised four forms of liability to determine upon whom liability should be placed.

6.1 Personal liability

Establishing who is liable is not usually a problem, as the law (especially statute) will expressly impose personal liability upon a person for an unlawful act. For example, many provisions of the CA 2006 expressly state who is to be liable for their breach. However, this is not always the case and so the courts will often have to determine upon whom liability should be placed. How they do this depends upon the type of liability in question.

Civil liability

As a company has contractual capacity, it can be liable for breach of contract. As a company requires others to act on its behalf, a related issue is whether such persons can also be contractually liable. By applying principles of agency law (discussed in Chapter 4), the company will usually be contractually liable for the acts of those who act on its behalf.

The imposition of tortious liability usually also results in liability being placed on the company, as the company is normally vicariously liable (discussed in Chapter 4) for the acts of its directors, employees and agents. However, there may be some instances where imposing liability upon the company will be of no aid (such as where it has been dissolved) and so the issue is whether liability be imposed on those who committed the tort.

In *C Evans & Sons Ltd v Spritebrand Ltd* [1985] 1 WLR 317 (CA), the court established that a director who commits a tort when acting for the company will not be liable. In order to impose liability on the director, it will need to be established that (i) he engaged in the tort, not in his capacity as a director, but in some personal capacity (see e.g. *Standard Chartered Bank v Pakistan National Shipping Corp (No 2)* [2002] UKHL 43); and (ii) he had satisfied the requirements of the tort. As the following case demonstrates, this is not easy to establish, especially if the tort in question requires establishing that the director owed a duty of care.

Case law 3.12

Williams v Natural Life Health Foods Ltd **[1998] 1 WLR 830 (HL)**

The claimants were considering acquiring a franchise in the defendant company's business, and so an employee of the company sent them favourable projections regarding the franchise's projected financial performance. These projections were negligently produced. When the claimants acquired a franchise, its performance was much worse than projected. The claimants sought to sue the defendant company but it was subsequently liquidated, so they sued Mistlin, the company's sole director and majority shareholder, on the ground that the projections constituted a negligent misstatement.

negligent misstatement
A statement negligently made where the statement maker owes a duty to another person and that person has suffered loss due to the statement.

Mistlin was not liable. In order to establish liability for negligent misstatement, the claimants would need to show that Mistlin assumed a responsibility towards them when making the statement. Mistlin had never dealt directly with the claimants and so the court held that '[t]here were no exchanges or conduct crossing the line which could have conveyed to the [claimants] that Mr. Mistlin was willing to assume personal responsibility to them'.

Criminal liability

A company can be found personally guilty of a criminal offence, although there are some offences that a company cannot be convicted of (such as a crime for which the only punishment is imprisonment (*R v ICR Haulage Ltd* [1944] KB 551)).

Most criminal offences are created by statute and the statute in question will expressly state who can be convicted of the offence. As regards company law offences, it is common to provide that both the company and persons who caused the company to commit the offence can be convicted.

In most cases, determining who can be convicted of an offence poses no problems. However, some offences have proved problematic. Under the common law, it was extremely difficult to convict a company of manslaughter. As a result, the Corporate Manslaughter and Corporate Homicide Act 2007 was enacted, of which s. 1(1) provides that an organisation (which includes a company or partnership) will be guilty of corporate manslaughter if the way in which its activities are managed or organised causes a person's death, and amounts to a gross breach of a relevant duty of care owed by the organisation to the deceased. In practice, convictions for corporate manslaughter remain very rare.

6.2 Strict liability

Liability for certain civil wrongs and criminal offences can only be imposed if the defendant engaged in the unlawful act with a certain mental state (e.g. with malice or recklessly). As the company is not a natural person, it has no mind and so has no mental states. The law has remedied this problem via several means, one of which is the imposition of strict liability. Strict liability civil wrongs and criminal offences have no mental element and so all that need be established is that the prohibited act or omission was engaged in.

Strict liability arises most often in relation to criminal offences. Many offences established by the CA 2006 impose strict liability. For example, s. 248 of CA 2006 requires that minutes of all board meetings must be recorded. A failure to record such minutes results in an offence being committed by every person in default.

6.3 Vicarious liability

Vicarious liability involves a situation where one person is liable for the acts or omissions of another person. In the corporate context, it arises most commonly where a person acting on behalf of the company (a director or employee) commits some form of tortious act.

In such a case, the company may be found vicariously liable for the tortious act of the person acting on its behalf (although the claimant may also sue the person who committed the tortious act). In order to impose vicarious liability for civil wrongs, three requirements must be satisfied:

1. there must be an employer/employee relationship or a relationship of agency;
2. the employee or agent must have committed a tort; and
3. the tort must have been committed in the course of the employee's employment or the agent's agency.

As regards criminal liability, vicarious liability does not have a major role to play as most criminal offences impose personal or strict liability upon specified persons. However, vicarious liability can be imposed if a statute provides that a company can be liable for the criminal acts of others.

As vicarious liability is primarily a concept that arises under the law of torts, it will not be discussed further here. For a leading case involving a company being found vicariously liable for the tortious acts of others, see *Dubai Aluminium Co Ltd v Salaam* [2002] UKHL 48.

6.4 Attribution

It may be necessary to prove that the defendant had a certain state of mind (e.g. they acted maliciously) or they had certain knowledge to establish that certain civil wrongs and criminal offences have been committed.

A company, having no mind, will clearly lack the requisite state of mind or knowledge, but the law has been able to impose liability on companies via the use of 'identification theory' under which the state of mind or knowledge of certain persons (such as directors) can be attributed to the company. In other words, the state of mind/knowledge of such persons will be regarded as the state of mind/knowledge of the company.

The question that arises is whose state of mind/knowledge can be attributed to the company. In *Lennard's Carrying Co Ltd v Asiatic Petroleum Co Ltd* [1915] AC 705 (HL), Viscount Haldane LC stated that:

> 'a corporation is an abstraction. It has no mind of its own any more than it has a body of its own; its active and directing will must consequently be sought in the person of somebody who… is really the directing mind and will of the corporation, the very ego and centre of the personality of the corporation.'

Unfortunately, the House did not elaborate significantly upon whom exactly would constitute a company's 'directing mind and will'. This can usually be determined by looking at the company's constitution, especially if the articles contain the usual provision that vests managerial power in the directors (see article 3 of the model articles). In such a case, the directors will constitute a company's directing mind and will and their state of mind/knowledge can be attributed to the company. As to whether sub-board level employees can constitute the directing mind and will, Lord Reid in the case of *Tesco Supermarkets Ltd v Nattrass* [1972] AC 153 (HL) stated that:

> 'Normally the board of directors, the managing director and perhaps other superior officers of a company carry out the functions of management and speak and act as the company. Their subordinates do not. They carry out orders from above and it can make no difference that they are given some measure of discretion. But the board of directors may delegate some part of their functions of management giving to their delegate full discretion to act independently of instructions from them. I see no difficulty in holding that they have thereby put such a delegate in their place so that within the scope of the delegation he can act as the company. It may not always be easy to draw the line but there are cases in which the line must be drawn.'

However, in the following case, the House indicated that the 'directing mind and will' test will not be suitable in all cases and, in some cases, some other rule must be used.

Case law 3.13

***Meridian Global Funds Management Asia Ltd v Securities Commission* [1995] 2 AC 500 (PC)**

This case involved New Zealand company law, which provided that a person had to provide notice to specified persons if he became a 'substantial security holder' in a listed company. Meridian's chief investment officer and senior portfolio manager used Meridian's funds

to acquire 49% of the shares in another listed company, which they were authorised to do. However, they did not inform Meridian's board of this and so Meridian failed to notify anyone that it had become a 'substantial security holder' in the other company. Meridian argued that it had not breached the law as it did not know it had become a substantial security holder, and such knowledge could not be attributed to it as the chief investment officer did not constitute the company's directing mind and will.

Lord Hoffmann stated that the constitution, along with general legal principles of agency and vicarious liability, will usually be enough to determine who is liable. If not, the court may need to determine exactly how a particular rule applies to a company, which may involve the court having to 'fashion a special rule of attribution for the particular substantive rule'. In some cases, the 'directing mind and will' approach might be appropriate, but in other cases, it might not be. It will be a 'question of construction in each case as to whether the particular rule requires that the knowledge that an act has been done, or the state of mind with which it was done, should be attributed to the company'.

In *Meridian*, in terms of whose knowledge was to count as the knowledge of the company, Lord Hoffmann did not feel that this was a case where a special rule of attribution needed to be fashioned, as the case could be determined on agency principles. Accordingly, the person whose knowledge would be attributed to the company is 'the person who, with the authority of the company, acquired the relevant interest', namely the chief investment officer. To rule otherwise would allow the policy of the law to be defeated as it would encourage board members to pay little attention to what their investment managers were doing. On this basis, the chief investment officer's knowledge was attributed to Meridian and it was held liable.

As regards civil wrongs, the more contextual, if somewhat vague, approach in *Meridian* is the accepted approach. In criminal cases, *Meridian* has not gained the same foothold and the courts appear to first apply the directing mind and will test. If that does not result in guilt being established, the courts will decide whether to fashion a special rule of attribution.

Attribution as a defence

Most cases in this area attribute the wrongdoing of certain persons to the company in order to establish whether the company can be liable. In the following case, the issue was whether the actions of certain persons can be attributed to the company to establish a defence to a claim brought by the company itself. The defence in question is usually the illegality defence, which generally provides that a person cannot recover compensation for a loss which was caused by his own unlawful act.

Case law 3.14

***Bilta (UK) Ltd v Nazir (No 2)* [2015] UKSC 23**

It was alleged that the two directors of Bilta (UK) Ltd (one of whom was also the sole shareholder) had engaged in fraud which prevented the company from paying its tax liabilities. As a result, it was liquidated, owing £38 million to HMRC in unpaid tax. Bilta commenced proceedings against the two directors. The directors argued that their wrongdoing should be attributed to Bilta and therefore, as it was seeking to recover compensation for its own unlawful act, its claim should be struck out.

The strike out application was dismissed. Lords Toulson and Hodge stated that:

> **'where the company pursues a claim against a director or employee for breach of duty, it would defeat the company's claim and negate the director's or employee's duty to the company if the act or the state of mind of the latter were to be attributed to the company and the company were thereby to be estopped from founding on the wrong.'**

Accordingly, Lord Neuberger stated that:

> **'Where a company has been the victim of wrong-doing by its directors, or of which its directors had notice, then the wrong-doing, or knowledge, of the directors cannot be attributed to the company as a defence to a claim brought against the directors by the company's liquidator.'**

Not all the Justices employed the same reasoning and some questions remain unanswered (does the *ratio* of *Bilta* only apply to insolvent companies, for example). Lord Neuberger in *Bilta* recognised this and stated that the Supreme Court needed to address in a future case the proper approach to how the illegality defence applies to companies. While the Supreme Court did discuss the illegality defence in the subsequent case of *Patel v Mirza* [2016] UKSC 42, it did not focus on its application to companies. Clarification is still needed.

Chapter summary

- A promoter is a person involved in the formation of a company (except those involved through providing professional services).
- A promoter owes a duty to the unformed company and must not make a profit out of the company's promotion, unless they disclose the nature of the transaction and the profit made.
- Under s. 51 of the CA 2006, a pre-incorporation contract will be binding between the promoter and the third party.

- A company can be incorporated by registration submitting certain documentation to Companies House: the memorandum of association; the application for registration (Form IN01); and the statement of compliance.
- Upon successful incorporation, a company will be issued with a certificate of incorporation. Public companies will also need to obtain a trading certificate.
- The company is a body corporate and so is a legal person, and can therefore do many of the things that a natural person can (own property, enter into contracts, sue and be sued).
- The case of *Salomon* established that a company can be used to shield its members from liability, and that owning shares in a company is not enough to establish a relationship of agency or trusteeship.
- Statute may provide for a company's corporate personality to be disregarded.
- Following the case of *Prest*, the courts will only pierce the veil where 'a person is under an existing legal obligation or liability or subject to an existing legal restriction which he deliberately evades or whose enforcement he deliberately frustrates by interposing a company under his control'.
- The courts will only pierce the veil when other, more conventional remedies, have been of no assistance.
- The four methods used to impose liability on a company are
  - personal liability;
  - strict liability;
  - vicarious liability; and
  - liability imposed via attribution.

Chapter four
Legally binding the company

Contents

1. Introduction

As noted in the previous chapter, a company has contractual capacity and can enter into contracts. This chapter expands upon that by discussing how companies can be legally bound to others. It begins by looking at how companies enter into contracts, before discussing in detail the role of the company's constitution. Finally, the chapter looks at the capacity of a company and when persons have authority to contract on behalf of the company.

2. Company contracts

Contracts form an important day-to-day source of company law. It is vital to understand how companies enter into binding contracts. Sections 43 and 44 of the CA 2006 provide that a company can enter into a contract in three ways:

1. by affixing its common seal to a document (ss. 43(1)(a) and 44(1)(a));
2. by a person who has authority (express or implied) to contract on behalf of the company (s. 43(1)(b)); and
3. by complying with the rules in s. 44(2)–(8).

The first and third methods will be discussed here. The issue of who has authority to contract on behalf of the company is discussed later in this chapter.

2.1 Common seal

A company can enter into a contract by affixing its common seal to the contract, or it can execute a document by affixing its common seal to that document (ss.43(1)(a) and 44(1)(a)).

A common seal is effectively a stamp that can be used to 'sign' or execute a document by embossing the company's name onto the document in question. Companies are not legally required to have a common seal (CA 2006, s. 45(1)) and most do not. Companies that trade internationally may retain their common seal as some overseas countries still require that a seal be used.

Who may use the common seal and its use is a matter for the company's articles. The model articles provide that a common seal can only be used with the directors' authority. If the seal is affixed to a document, then the document should also be signed by an authorised person (namely a director, company secretary or any person authorised by the directors to sign documents to which the common seal is applied) (model articles for private companies, article 49; model articles for public companies, article 81).

2.2 Execution of documents

A document (such as a contract) may be validly executed if it is signed on behalf of the company by (i) two authorised signatories; or (ii) a director of the company in the presence of a witness who attests the signature (CA 2006, s. 44(2)). Every director of the company is an authorised signatory, as is the company secretary if the company has one (CA 2006, s. 44(3)).

Sections 43 and 44 set out the rules by which a company can enter into a contract, but they do not set out what contracts the company can enter into or who has authority to enter into certain contracts on behalf of the company. The remainder of this chapter looks at these issues.

Test yourself 4.1

1. **What are the three ways in which a company can enter into a contract?**
2. **What is a 'common seal' and is a company required to have one?**
3. **Who is an authorised signatory for the purpose of executing a document on behalf of the company?**

3. The constitution of a company

To a degree, the types of contract that a company can enter into and who has the ability to bind the company is dependent upon the statements in the company's constitution. The Companies Act 2006 empowers the company to engage in a wide range of acts, but it is not exhaustive. Companies need to be able to determine their own internal rules that set out what the company can and cannot do. Companies are afforded such flexibility by being able to create their own constitution. A company's constitution not only sets out the powers of a company, but also establishes certain powers, rights and obligations of the company's members and directors. It is a fundamental source of company law.

A company's constitution is not found in a single document. Instead, s. 17 of the CA 2006 provides that a company's constitution will include:

- the company's articles; and
- resolutions and agreements affecting the company's constitution, listed in s. 29(1).

The word 'include' in s. 17 indicates that other documents can also form part of the constitution. For example, s. 32(1) provides a member with the right to request a copy of certain 'constitutional documents' which includes the certificate of incorporation, the statement of capital and the statement of guarantee.

One document whose constitutional status is unclear is the memorandum of association. The CA 2006 does not refer to it as part of the constitution, but it did form a major part of the company's constitution prior to the CA 2006. Given the reduced importance of the memorandum under the CA 2006, the lack of clarity is not an issue in practice.

3.1 The memorandum of association

Under previous Companies Acts, the memorandum of association formed one of a company's two principal constitutional documents (the other being the articles). This is no longer the case under the CA 2006 and, while all companies are still required to have a memorandum (CA 2006, s. 7(1)(a)), the memorandum is no longer a key part of the company's constitution, nor is it a document of any real import.

This is because much of the information that used to be contained in the pre-2006 memorandum is now contained in the company's articles (CA 2006, s. 28(1)). Under s. 8(1) of the CA 2006, the memorandum merely states that the subscribers wish to form a company under the Act, agree to become members of the company and, in the case of a company with a share capital, to take at least one share each.

3.2 The articles of association

The articles of association form the company's principal constitutional document and set out the company's internal rules. All companies must have a set of articles (CA 2006, s. 18(1)). As companies can draft their own articles, this affords companies considerable flexibility in determining how the company is to be run. Further, the CA 2006 allows a company, via its articles, to exclude or modify certain statutory rules (for example, a private company can disapply pre-emption rights by including a provision in its articles to such effect).

Accordingly, knowing the content of a company's articles is vital to understanding how a company is to be run, with articles typically establishing rules and procedures relating to issues such as:

- the powers and responsibilities of the directors;
- the rules by which board meetings and general meetings will be run;
- the rules relating to the appointment and removal of directors;
- the rules relating to allotting shares and paying dividends; and
- the rules relating to capital and borrowing powers of the company.

Promoters, especially those setting up their first company, may find the task of drafting their own articles to be daunting and may be concerned that they will omit vital provisions. The law therefore provides several sets of model articles that can be used.

Model articles

Section 19(1) of the CA 2006 empowers the Secretary of State to make regulations setting out model articles, and these can be found in the Companies (Model Articles) Regulations 2008 (SI 2008/3229). As different types of company will have different internal rules, s. 19(2) of the CA 2006 provides that different model articles can be prescribed for different types of company. The 2008 Regulations provide three sets of model articles:

- model articles for private companies limited by shares (Schedule 1)
- model articles for private companies limited by guarantee (Schedule 2)
- model articles for public companies (Schedule 3).

If, when a company is first incorporated, the promoters do not register their own articles, then the applicable model articles will form the company's articles (CA 2006, s. 20(1)(a)). However, even if the promoters do register their own articles, the applicable model articles will still apply, insofar as they are not excluded or modified by the company's own articles (CA 2006, s. 20(1)(b)). This provides companies with a number of options.

Case study 4.1

Aya wishes to set up a private company limited by shares. In terms of the applicable articles, she has four choices:

1. **she can choose to not register a set of articles, in which case the model articles for private companies limited by shares will apply in full;**
2. **she can register her own articles and adopt all of the terms of the model articles;**
3. **she can register her own articles and adopt some of the terms of the model articles (this would be done by modifying or excluding the terms she did not wish to adopt); or**
4. **she can register her own articles which include a term stating that the terms of the model articles are excluded (which is what most larger companies do).**

Interpretation of the articles

Like any other source of law or legal document, there will be times when the meaning of an article provision is unclear. It may need to be interpreted by the courts, as occurred in the following case.

Case law 4.1

Rayfield v Hands **[1960] Ch 1 (Ch)**

Article 11 of the company's articles provided that '[e]very member who intends to transfer shares shall inform the directors who will take the said shares equally between them at a fair value'. A shareholder (Rayfield) wished to transfer his shares and so, in accordance with article 11, he informed the directors of this. However, the directors refused to take his shares on the ground the word 'shall' in article 11 did not require them to take the shares – it merely gave them the option to take them if they so wished. Rayfield sued.

The court stated that article 11 imposed an obligation upon the directors to take Rayfield's shares because article 11 stated that the directors 'will take the said shares' and this indicated a 'resultant prospective eventuality, in which the member has to sell his shares and the directors have to buy them'.

The courts' role when interpreting the articles was set out by Jenkins LJ in *Holmes v Keyes* [1959] Ch 199 (CA), who stated:

> 'the articles of association of the company should be regarded as a business document and should be construed so as to give them reasonable business efficacy, where a construction tending to that result is admissible on the language of the articles, in preference to a result which would or might prove unworkable.'

However, the courts' interpretative function is not boundless and limits are placed upon the courts' ability to interpret the articles. For example, the courts cannot add words to the articles to make them fairer or more reasonable (*Attorney General of Belize v Belize Telecom Ltd* [2009] UKPC 10). However, the courts can imply terms into the articles.

Implying terms into the articles

Implying terms into the articles does not constitute an addition to the articles because, as Lord Hoffmann stated in *Attorney General of Belize v Belize Telecom Ltd*, 'the implication of the term is not an addition to the instrument. It only spells out what the instrument means'. There are plenty of examples of cases where the courts have implied terms into the articles in order to give them efficacy or to protect a right provided for under the articles (see *Equitable Life Assurance Society v Hyman* [2002] 1 AC 408 (HL)).

Unfortunately, there is confusion regarding when it is appropriate for the courts to imply a term into the articles. In the leading case of *Attorney General of Belize v Belize Telecom Ltd* [2009] UKPC 10, Lord Hoffmann stated that:

> 'The court has no power to improve upon the instrument which it is called upon to construe, whether it be a contract, a statute or articles of association. It cannot introduce terms to make it fairer or more reasonable. It is concerned only to discover what the instrument means. However, that meaning is not necessarily or always what the authors or parties to the document would have intended. It is the meaning which the instrument would convey to a reasonable person having all the background knowledge which would reasonably be available to the audience to whom the instrument is addressed.'

In the subsequent Supreme Court case of *Marks & Spencer plc v BNP Paribas Securities Services Trust Co (Jersey) Ltd* [2015] UKSC 72, the Court appeared to be critical of Lord Hoffmann's test. In contract law, the courts will only usually imply a term into a contract where it is necessary to do so, but there was concern that Lord Hoffmann's formulation made it easier to imply terms into the articles by basing implication on reasonableness, rather than necessity. Lord Neuberger PSC stated:

> 'the notion that a term will be implied if a reasonable reader of the contract, knowing all its provisions and the surrounding circumstances, would understand it to be implied is quite acceptable, provided that (i) the reasonable reader is treated as reading the contract at the time it was made and (ii) he would consider the term to be so obvious as to go without saying or to be necessary for business efficacy… The second proviso is important because otherwise Lord Hoffmann's formulation may be interpreted as suggesting that reasonableness is a sufficient ground for implying a term… It is necessary to emphasise that there has been no dilution of the requirements which have to be satisfied before a term will be implied.'

Amending the articles

As companies and their lines of business change, the company may want to change the rules by which it is run. A company may amend its articles either by passing a special resolution (CA 2006, s. 21(1)) or if all of the members so agree (*Cane v Jones* [1980] 1 WLR 1451 (Ch)). In practice, the second method will only be relevant to smaller companies. In limited cases, the court can also order that a company amend its articles (see s. 98 of the CA 2006). Irrespective of how a company amends its articles, within 15 days of the amendment taking effect it must send a copy of the amended articles to Companies House (CA 2006, s. 26(1)). Failure to do so is a criminal offence (CA 2006, s. 26(3)).

A company's ability to amend its articles is subject to two notable limitations. First, the power to amend the articles may be restricted by statute. For example, while it is impossible for a company to make its articles unalterable, the CA 2006 does allow companies to make it more difficult to amend the articles by entrenching article provisions. An article provision that has been entrenched can only be amended or repealed 'if certain conditions are met, or procedures are complied with, that are more restrictive than those applicable in the case of a special resolution' (CA 2006, s. 22(1)). This could include requiring a higher majority or unanimity instead of the usual special resolution, or by requiring the alteration to be approved of by certain specified members or other persons. However, to prevent abuse, the Act does provide that an entrenched article provision can still be amended if all the members agree or if the court so orders (CA 2006, s. 22(3)).

Second, the courts have imposed several limitations on a company's ability to amend its articles, including the following.

- An amendment will not be valid if it deprives a member of a right that has already accrued, unless the member agrees to the amendment (*James v Buena Ventura Nitrate Grounds Syndicate Ltd* [1896] 1 Ch 456 (CA)).
- A company cannot contract out of the statutory ability to alter its articles (such as by placing a provision in its articles that seeks to render any part of the articles unalterable) (*Walker v London Tramways Co* (1879) 12 ChD 705 (Ch)).
- If the amendment of an article provision breaches a separate contract between the company and another person, the alteration will stand, but the company can be liable for breach of contract (*Southern Foundries (1926) Ltd v Shirlaw* [1940] AC 701 (HL)).

The most important common law limitation on a company's ability to amend its articles was established by Lindley MR in *Allen v Gold Reefs of West Africa Ltd* [1900] 1 Ch 656 (CA), who stated that the power to alter the articles must 'be exercised, not only in the manner required by law, but also bona fide for the benefit of the company as a whole'. The company here refers to the corporate entity, so if an amendment benefits the members, but not the company, then it will be invalid (*Brown v British Abrasive Wheel Co Ltd* [1919] 1 Ch 290 (Ch)). However, there will be cases where an amendment may not affect the company at all, but instead affects its members. In such cases, the courts will focus more on the effect that the amendment has on the members, as occurred in the following case.

Case law 4.2

***Greenhalgh v Arderne Cinemas Ltd* [1951] Ch 286 (CA)**

The articles of Arderne Cinemas Ltd (Arderne) provided that a shareholder would not sell his shares to an outsider if an existing shareholder was willing to purchase them. Mallard, who was Arderne's managing director and majority shareholder, wished to sell his shares to an outsider. He used his majority shareholding to amend the articles so that he did not have to offer them first to an existing shareholder. Greenhalgh, a minority shareholder, challenged the alteration on the ground that it did not benefit Arderne.

Evershed MR stated that 'the case may be taken of an individual hypothetical member and it may be asked whether what is proposed is, in the honest opinion of those who voted in its favour, for that person's benefit'. In determining this, the court would ask whether 'the effect of it were to discriminate between the majority shareholders and

the minority shareholders, so as to give to the former an advantage of which the latter were deprived'. Applying this, the court held that the amendment was valid because it might well be in a hypothetical member's benefit to sell his shares directly to an outsider. Further, the advantage obtained by Mallard was also obtained by all the other shareholders, so the amendment did not discriminate between majority and minority shareholders.

In *Citco Banking Corp NV v Pusser's Ltd* [2007] UKPC 13, Lord Hoffmann acknowledged that in cases where the amendment purely affects the shareholders or a group of them, the bona fide test will be of little aid and '[s]ome other test of validity is required'. Unfortunately, he did not set out what this other test was, leaving the law in a rather confused state. In practice, this may not be an issue due to the fact that minority shareholders can obtain better protection elsewhere, notably by bringing an unfair prejudice petition.

The use of the phrase 'bona fide' indicates that what matters is the subjective belief of the members who voted for the amendment. Accordingly, if those members honestly believed that the amendment was for the company's benefit as a whole, then the amendment would be valid, even if the court disagrees with the majority's assessment. The rationale behind this was set out by Scrutton LJ in *Shuttleworth v Cox Brothers & Co (Maidenhead) Ltd* [1927] 2 KB 9 (CA), who stated that '[i]t is not the business of the Court to manage the affairs of the company. That is for the shareholders and directors'.

However, other factors will also affect the court's decision. For example, if the amendment is motivated by fraud or malice, then it will not be bona fide (*Sidebottom v Kershaw Leese & Co Ltd* [1920] 1 Ch 154 (CA)). In the following case, the court held that the reasonableness of the amendment can be relevant.

Case law 4.3

***Shuttleworth v Cox Brothers & Co (Maidenhead) Ltd* [1927] 2 KB 9 (CA)**

The company's articles provided that its directors could hold office for as long as they wished, unless they engaged in one of six specified events. One of the directors, Shuttleworth, engaged in a financial irregularity that fell outside these six events. The other directors, who were also the majority shareholders, amended the articles to provide that a director would be required to resign if all the other directors so required. They then demanded that Shuttleworth resign. Shuttleworth stated that the amendment was not valid.

Bankes LJ confirmed that the test for altering the articles was subjective, but went on to discuss how the subjective belief of the shareholders should be ascertained, stating:

> **'The alteration may be so oppressive as to cast suspicion on the honesty of the persons responsible for it, or so extravagant that no reasonable men could really consider it for the benefit of the**

> **company. In such cases the Court is, I think, entitled to treat the conduct of shareholders as it does the verdict of a jury, and to say that the alteration of a company's articles shall not stand if it is such that no reasonable men could consider it for the benefit of the company.'**

Applying this, he stated that 'it seems to me impossible to say that the action of [Shuttleworth's co-directors] was either incapable of being for the benefit of the company or such that no reasonable men could consider it for the benefit of the company'. Accordingly, Shuttleworth's challenge failed and the amendment was deemed to be valid.

One particular type of article provision that has generated a notable amount of case law is so-called share expropriation or 'squeeze-out' provisions. These article provisions usually state that a shareholder can be forced to sell his shares to specified persons (usually the directors or other shareholders). As the following case demonstrates, such article provisions must be drafted carefully if they are to be valid.

Case law 4.4

***Dafen Tinplate Co Ltd v Llanelly Steel Co (1907) Ltd* [1920] 2 Ch 124 (Ch)**

Manufacturers of tinplates were invited to become shareholders in Llanelly Steel Co (1907) Ltd (Llanelly), on the understanding that the steel they used to manufacture the tinplates would be purchased from Llanelly. Dafen Tinplate Co Ltd (Dafen) became a shareholder of Llanelly, but soon thereafter started to source steel from another supplier. When Dafen refused to sell its shares to Llanelly, the majority shareholders of Llanelly amended the articles by inserting a new provision into them stating that the company could, by passing a resolution, force a shareholder to sell his shares to the board or to other persons as determined by the board at fair value. Dafen challenged the amendment.

Peterson J stated:

> **'It may be for the benefit of the majority of the shareholders to acquire the shares of the minority, but how can it be said to be for the benefit of the company that any shareholder, against whom no charge of acting to the detriment of the company can be urged, and who is in every respect a desirable member of the company, and for whose expropriation there is no reason except the will of the majority, should be forced to transfer his shares to the majority or to anyone else? Such a provision might in some circumstances be very prejudicial to the company's interest.'**

The court held that the amendment of the articles was not bona fide for the benefit of the company, and was therefore invalid.

It is important to note that Peterson J did not state that article provisions requiring a shareholder to sell his shares will always be invalid. The reason why the clause in *Dafen Tinplate* was invalidated was because it was too broad – as Peterson J stated '[t]o say that such an unrestricted and unlimited power of expropriation is for the benefit of the company appears to me to be confusing the interests of the majority with the benefit of the company as a whole'.

If the share expropriation clause is narrower and can benefit the company, it will be deemed valid. Thus, in *Sidebottom v Kershaw Leese & Co Ltd* [1920] 1 Ch 154 (CA), the articles were amended to provide that a shareholder who competed with the company could be required to sell his shares to the directors. The court held that such an article provision clearly benefitted the company and so it was deemed valid.

3.3 The constitution as a contract

Section 33(1) of the CA 2006 provides that '[t]he provisions of a company's constitution bind the company and its members to the same extent as if there were covenants on the part of the company and of each member to observe those provisions'. This means the constitution of a company forms a contract (often known as a 'statutory contract') between:

- the company and its members; and
- the members themselves.

A breach of a provision in the company's constitution can constitute breach of contract, allowing the company or a member to obtain a remedy. It should be noted that the contract created by s. 33 differs in several respects from a standard contract, with the principal differences being set out in Table 4.1.

	A standard contract	The s. 33 contract
Binding between	The parties to the contract at the time it was created	The company and its members (and the members themselves)
Alteration of terms	Alteration usually requires the consent of all parties to the contract	Can be altered by (i) passing a special resolution; (ii) with the consent of all the members; or (iii) by court order
Can be enforced by a third party	Only where s. 1(1) of the Contracts (Rights of Third Parties) Act 1999 applies	No, the s. 33 contract cannot be enforced by 'outsiders'
Enforcement of terms	Any term can be enforced	Only those terms that relate to membership rights can be enforced
Rectification of contract	Can be rectified	Cannot be rectified (*Scott v Frank F Scott (London) Ltd* [1940] Ch 749 (CA))
Defeasible on certain grounds	Can be defeated on the grounds of mistake, misrepresentation, duress or undue influence	Cannot be defeated on the grounds of mistake, misrepresentation, duress or undue influence (*Bratton Seymour Service Co Ltd v Oxborough* [1992] BCC 471 (CA))

Table 4.1 Differences between a standard contract and the s. 33 contract

Enforcing the s. 33 contract

The constitution forms a contract between the company and its members, and between the members themselves. Three consequences result from this. First, if a member breaches a term of the constitution, the company can sue the member for breach of contract.

Case law 4.5

***Hickman v Kent or Romney Marsh Sheepbreeders' Association* [1915] 1 Ch 881 (Ch)**

The company's articles stated that any dispute between it and a member should be referred to arbitration before any legal proceedings were issued. A dispute arose between the company and Hickman, one of its members. Hickman did not refer the dispute to arbitration and instead commenced legal proceedings against the company.

The constitution formed a contract between the company and Hickman, and Hickman had breached this contract. Accordingly, the court stayed the legal proceedings brought by Hickman and allowed the company to enforce the arbitration clause.

stayed
The suspension of proceedings.

Second, if the company breaches a term of the constitution, a member can sue the company for breach of contract.

Case law 4.6

***Wood v Odessa Waterworks Co* (1889) 42 ChD 636 (Ch)**

The articles provided that the directors could declare a dividend be paid to the members, providing that the dividend was sanctioned by the general meeting. The board proposed an ordinary resolution stating that debenture bonds would be issued to the members, instead of payment of a dividend. The resolution was passed by the general meeting, but one member (Wood) objected and sued the company on the ground that it had breached the articles.

Wood's action succeeded and an injunction was granted preventing the bonds from being issued. Stirling J stated that the articles provide that:

> **'the directors may, with the sanction of a general meeting, declare a dividend to be paid to the shareholders. *Prima facie* that means to be paid in cash. The debenture-bonds proposed to be issued are not payments in cash; they are merely agreements or promises to pay: and if the contention of the company prevails a shareholder will be compelled to accept in lieu of cash a debt of the company payable at some uncertain future period. In my opinion that contention ought not to prevail.'**

Third, if a member (or members) of the company breaches a term of the constitution, another member can sue for breach of contract.

Case law 4.7

***Rayfield v Hands* [1960] Ch 1 (Ch)**

The articles provided that any member who wished to sell his shares should first offer them to the directors and the directors would then purchase them. Rayfield, a member, informed the directors that he wished to sell his shares, but the directors refused to purchase them. As the directors were members of the company, Rayfield alleged that they had breached the s. 33 contract.

The directors had breached the articles and so Rayfield's action succeeded. The court ordered that the directors should purchase Rayfield's shares.

It is important to note that the ability of the company and its members to enforce the constitution is limited in two important ways in relation to (i) outsiders and outsider rights; and (ii) internal irregularities.

Outsiders and outsider rights

The privity of contract rule provides that only the parties to a contract can enforce it. An exception to this is where s. 1(1) of the Contracts (Rights of Third Parties) Act 1999 applies, but as noted in Table 4.1, s. 1(1) does not apply to the s. 33 contract. Accordingly, it follows that third parties (or 'outsiders') cannot enforce the constitution.

Case law 4.8

***Eley v Positive Government Security Life Assurance Co* (1876) LR 1 Ex D 88 (CA)**

A company's articles were drafted by its solicitor, Eley, and they provided that Eley could not be removed unless he engaged in some form of misconduct. Subsequently, Eley was removed as the company's solicitor as they engaged another firm of solicitors. Eley had not engaged in any misconduct, so he sued alleging that the company had breached its articles.

Although the company might have removed Eley in breach of the articles, Eley could not sue for breach because, as an outsider, he was not party to the s. 33 contract. Accordingly, his action failed.

While Eley was not a member of the company when he drafted the articles and when the company was incorporated, he was a member of the company at the time of the court case. This was not mentioned by the court at all, but it would likely have made no difference. This is because not only can outsiders not sue for breach of the s. 33 contract, but members cannot sue to enforce outsider rights (rights granted to them in their capacity other than members). As Astbury J stated in *Hickman v Kent or Romney Marsh Sheepbreeders' Association* [1915] 1 Ch 881 (Ch), '[a]n outsider to whom rights purport to be given by the articles in his capacity as such outsider, whether he is or subsequently becomes a member, cannot sue on those articles treating them as contracts between himself and the company to enforce those rights'.

The limitation was stated most clearly by Buckley LJ in *Bisgood v Henderson's Transvaal Estates* [1908] 1 Ch 743 (CA), who stated '[t]he purpose of the [constitution] is to define the position of the shareholder as shareholder, and not to bind him in his capacity as an individual'. It follows that members can usually only enforce the s. 33 contract if they bring a claim in their capacity as members, as the following case demonstrates.

Case law 4.9

***Beattie v E and F Beattie Ltd* [1938] Ch 708 (CA)**

Ernest Beattie (EB) was a member and director of the company. He was alleged to have improperly drawn a salary from the company and another member commenced a claim to recover this payment. The company's articles provided that, in the event of a dispute between the company and its members or between the members themselves, the member would not commence legal proceedings and would instead refer the matter to arbitration. EB argued that, as he was a member, this meant that the dispute should have been referred to arbitration and he sought a court order staying the legal proceedings.

Greene MR stated that 'the contractual force given to the articles of association... is limited to such provisions of the articles as apply to the relationship of the members in their capacity as members'. The dispute was between the company and EB in his capacity as a director, not in his capacity as a member. Accordingly, the arbitration article could not be enforced and the legal proceedings continued.

As the Law Commission has noted, the principle that a member must bring the claim in his capacity as a member has 'not been uniformly applied by the courts, particularly in cases involving shareholder directors' (Law Commission, *Shareholder Remedies* (Law Com CP No 142, 1996) para 2.17). It should be noted that, in relation to quasi-partnership companies (discussed in Chapter 10), the distinction between members and directors is blurred, so certain rights conferred upon directors may legitimately be regarded as membership rights.

An outsider right in the constitution can be enforced if a separate agreement outside of the constitution allows for such enforcement. This agreement can be express or implied.

Internal irregularities

A member whose constitutional membership rights have been breached will usually be prevented from enforcing such rights if the breach constitutes an 'internal irregularity', which occurs where the 'alleged wrong is a transaction which might be made binding on the corporation and on all its members by a simple majority of the members' (*Prudential Assurance Co Ltd v Newman Industries Ltd (No 2)* [1982] Ch 204 (CA)). Preventing the enforcement of such breaches is clearly a result of the principle of majority rule and seeks to prevent one individual from frustrating the wishes of the majority, as the following case demonstrates.

Case law 4.10

***MacDougall v Gardiner* (1875) 1 ChD 13 (CA)**

The articles provided that the chair could (i) adjourn a general meeting with the consent of the meeting; and (ii) provide for a vote to be taken by poll if five shareholders so demanded. At a general meeting, a majority of shareholders voted, by a show of hands, to adjourn the meeting. A group of shareholders demanded that the vote for an adjournment be put to a poll, but the chair refused. One of these shareholders commenced proceedings against the chair.

Mellish LJ stated:

> **'if the thing complained of is a thing which in substance the majority of the company are entitled to do, or if something has been done irregularly which the majority of the company are entitled to do regularly, or if something has been done illegally which the majority of the company are entitled to do legally, there can be no use in having a litigation about it, the ultimate end of which is only that a meeting has to be called, and then ultimately the majority gets its wishes.'**

Accordingly, the court held that, although the chair had breached the articles, the breach was an internal irregularity and so the shareholder's action failed.

As with the enforcement of outsider rights, the courts have not been consistent in their application of the internal irregularity rule. The courts have allowed the enforcement of breaches of internal irregularities in a number of cases, such as breaches of rules relating to notice (*Tiessen v Henderson* [1899] 1 Ch 861 (Ch)), wrongful exclusion of proxy votes (*Oliver v Dalgleish* [1963] 1 WLR 1274 (Ch)) and the wrongful exclusion of nominees' votes (*Pender v Lushington* (1877) 6 ChD 70 (Ch)). As a result, it cannot be predicted with certainty which constitutional rights can be enforced and which cannot.

Stop and think 4.1

The Law Commission considered expressly identifying in statute which constitutional rights would constitute an internal irregularity if breached, but ultimately rejected this idea. Do you think statute should define (i) which constitutional rights constitute membership rights; and (ii) which rights, if breached, would be unenforceable due to being an internal irregularity?

3.4 Shareholders' agreements

Shareholders' agreements do not typically form part of a company's constitution but they do supplement the constitution, so it is appropriate to discuss them here. A shareholders' agreement is an agreement (usually a contract) entered into by two or more members which usually sets out certain rules regarding the relationship of those members. If the company is also a party to the agreement, then it may also establish rules relating to the relationship between the company and the members. A shareholders' agreement can be entered into when the company is first incorporated or post-incorporation. They are typically only used by companies with a small number of members.

The following example demonstrates how a shareholders' agreement might work and why it may be preferable to place certain rights into a shareholders' agreement as opposed to placing them into the articles.

Case study 4.2

Louise is the promoter of a newly incorporated company, X-Corp Ltd. She is the only director of the company and owns 20% of the company's shares. The remaining shares are equally divided amongst three other shareholders. X-Corp and the four shareholders enter into a shareholders' agreement, which provides that (i) if a shareholder wishes to sell their shares, they must first offer those shares to the other shareholders; and (ii) Louise will be paid £30,000 per year for her services as a director.

The advantages of placing these rights in a shareholders' agreement, as opposed to the articles, are as follows.

1. **The agreement is confidential, whereas the articles are publicly available. However, in order to achieve this confidentiality, the agreement should not fall within s. 29 of the CA 2006.**
2. **All the terms of the agreement bind all the parties to it, whereas not all the terms contained in the constitution can be enforced. For example, if the term regarding Louise's pay was placed into the articles, she would probably be unable to enforce it as it is an outsider right.**

3. **The agreement can only be amended if all the parties to it so agree, whereas the terms of the constitution can be amended by the majority against the wishes of the minority. So, if the term regarding Louise's pay was placed in the articles, her pay could be reduced without her consent (assuming that her pay details were not also contained in her employment contract).**

Enforcement

The terms of a shareholders' agreement can be enforced by or against any person who is party to the agreement. This can provide the claimant access to several remedies, including damages, injunctions (to prevent the agreement being breached) or specific performance (to require the agreement to be complied with). Problems can arise where the company is party to the agreement and the agreement seeks to restrict the company's statutory rights. In such a case, the court may hold that the shareholders are bound by the agreement but the company is not.

Case law 4.11

***Russell v Northern Bank Development Corp Ltd* [1992] 1 WLR 588 (HL)**

A company entered into a shareholders' agreement with its five shareholders, with clause 3 of the agreement stating that the company would not issue any further share capital unless all the parties to the agreement so agreed in writing. The board tabled a resolution at a general meeting that provided for the company's share capital to be increased. One of the shareholders commenced proceedings, seeking an injunction to prevent the other members from voting for the resolution.

The House distinguished between the company and the five shareholders. The shareholders had simply agreed to exercise their votes in a particular way and so clause 3 was binding upon the shareholders. However, the effect of clause 3 upon the company was to unlawfully fetter the company's statutory powers (i.e. to increase its share capital) and so clause 3 was not binding upon the company. The House severed the part of clause 3 that sought to bind the company and declared binding the parts of clause 3 that affected the five shareholders.

severed
Where part of a transaction (e.g. a term of a contract) can be discarded while leaving the remainder of the transaction intact.

Test yourself 4.2

1. **What forms part of a company's constitution?**
2. **Is a company required to register a set of articles when it is incorporated?**
3. **How can the articles be amended?**

4. **What does s. 33(1) of the CA 2006 state?**
5. **Can all the terms of the constitution be enforced by the company or a member?**

4. Corporate capacity

As the company is a legal person it has the ability to enter into contracts. This is known as the company's 'contractual capacity'. This section discusses the extent to which the company can enter into contracts and the consequences of a company exceeding its contractual capacity.

4.1 The *ultra vires* doctrine

ultra vires
'Beyond one's powers.'

A company's contractual capacity can be limited or restricted by its constitution, and if a company exceeds its contractual capacity, then it is said to be acting ***ultra vires***. Historically, a company's capacity was restricted by including an objects clause in its memorandum with this clause stating the purpose for which the company was set up. The benefit of having an objects clause was that (i) it would clearly indicate to relevant persons (e.g. members, creditors) why the company was set up; and (ii) it helped ensure that the company engaged in activities in its area of expertise. If a company entered into a contract that was outside the scope of its objects clause, then that contract would be *ultra vires* and void (*Ashbury Railway Carriage and Iron Co Ltd v Riche* (1874-75) LR 7 HL 653 (HL)).

Unfortunately, the *ultra vires* doctrine gave rise to two notable problems. These two problems, and the extent to which they have been remedied by statutory reforms, are discussed next.

4.2 Unrestricted objects

At the time of *Ashbury*, the memorandum could not be altered and so neither could the objects clause. As a result, companies found it impossible to expand into areas of business that were outside their objects. This was a problem as, prior to the CA 2006, all companies had to include an objects clause in their memorandum. This is no longer the case: s. 31(1) of the CA 2006 states that '[u]nless a company's articles specifically restrict the objects of a company, its objects are unrestricted'.

A company incorporated under the CA 2006 does not need an objects clause and such a company will have unrestricted objects (although its capacity may be limited by the articles elsewhere). The objects clause is still of relevance for two reasons.

1. Companies incorporated under prior Companies Acts will still have an objects clause and this clause will still restrict their contractual capacity. However, the objects clause will now be regarded as forming part of the company's articles (CA 2006, s. 28(1)), so such companies can remove the objects clause by amending their articles.

2. Companies incorporated under the CA 2006 can choose to include an objects clause in their articles. This will restrict the company's contractual capacity.

If a company includes or decides to retain its objects clause, then acting outside of the objects will be *ultra vires*. However, a second major statutory reform has mitigated the effects of a company acting *ultra vires*.

4.3 Section 39 of the Companies Act 2006

A major problem of the *ultra vires* doctrine was that it meant that innocent third parties (such as Riche in *Ashbury*) might find contracts they entered into rendered void. This is no longer the case in most instances as s. 39(1) of the CA 2006 provides that '[t]he validity of an act done by a company shall not be called into question on the ground of lack of capacity by reason of anything in the company's constitution'. A contract entered into by a company cannot be invalidated on the ground that the contract is outside the scope of the company's contractual capacity. This provision is clearly designed to protect third parties – indeed, had s. 39 been in force at the time of *Ashbury*, then Riche could have enforced the contract and claimed damages.

As a result of s. 39, it has been stated that the *ultra vires* doctrine has been abolished, but this is not correct. From the point of view of third parties, the *ultra vires* doctrine is of little relevance as the contract will remain valid. However, from the point of view of the directors and members, the *ultra vires* doctrine is still relevant as an *ultra vires* act might result in the directors being in breach of duty (notably the duty to act in accordance with the constitution found in s. 171(a) of the CA 2006). This might result in the company suing the directors or the members suing the directors via a **derivative claim**.

derivative claim
An action brought by a member on behalf of the company to enforce a right belonging to the company.

Test yourself 4.3

1. **What is the objects clause and are companies required to have such a clause in their constitution?**
2. **What does s. 39(1) of the CA 2006 state?**

5. Agency

A company may have the capacity to enter into a contract but, as the company can only act through human actors (directors, employees etc.), it is also important to determine whether a person has the authority to enter into contracts on behalf of the company.

Case study 4.3

X-Corp is incorporated under the CA 2006 and has no objects clause. As a result, its contractual capacity is unrestricted. However, the articles provide that 'the directors may not, on behalf of the company, enter

into a loan agreement in excess of £50,000 without the approval of the members'. The board causes X-Corp to enter into a contract with Welsh Bank plc, under which X-Corp will borrow £100,000. Member approval was not obtained.

Here, X-Corp has the capacity to enter into loan agreements of any amount (as its capacity is unrestricted). However, the directors' authority to enter into loan agreements on behalf of X-Corp is limited and the directors do not have authority to enter into the agreement with Welsh Bank without member approval.

Section 43(1) of the CA 2006 provides that a company contract can be made on behalf of a company by a person acting under its authority. Typically, this refers to a person's authority as an agent of the company. A relationship of agency has been defined by Prof. Roy Goode as one 'arising where one person, the principal... appoints another, the agent... to bring about, modify, or terminate legal relations between the principal and one or more third parties'.

In the corporate context, the company is the principal and it will engage agents to act on its behalf (the directors are agents of the company). The question here is to what degree these agents have the ability to enter into contracts on behalf of the company. This will depend upon the authority that the agent has. There are two principal types of authority: actual authority and apparent authority. However, even if an agent lacks authority, the principal can ratify the agent's actions. For example, if a director acts without authority, the company can ratify the director's unauthorised acts, usually by passing an ordinary resolution (*Grant v United Kingdom Switchback Railway Co* (1888) 40 ChD 135 (CA)).

5.1 Actual authority

In *Freeman & Lockyer v Buckhurst Park Properties (Mangal) Ltd* [1964] 2 QB 480 (CA), Diplock LJ defined actual authority as:

> 'a legal relationship between the principal and agent created by a consensual agreement to which they alone are parties. Its scope is to be ascertained by applying ordinary principles of construction of contracts, including any proper implications from the express words used, the usages of the trade, or the course of business between the parties.'

This quote indicates that there are in fact two types of actual authority:

- express actual authority; and
- implied actual authority.

Express actual authority

Express actual authority is the most straightforward form of authority and refers to that authority that has been expressly bestowed upon an agent. Examples of express actual authority include the following.

- The articles may expressly confer authority upon an agent to engage in specified acts. For example, article 3 of the model articles expressly confers wide authority upon the directors by authorising them to exercise powers of management.

- The board of directors may expressly authorise an agent to engage in certain acts. For example, article 5 of the model articles authorises the directors to delegate to any person any powers conferred upon them by the articles. Accordingly, the directors can delegate their powers of management to others.

The articles, as well as conferring express actual authority upon a person, can also limit authority. For example, the articles could place limits upon the directors' powers of management (for example, requiring member approval for certain transactions).

Implied actual authority

Implied actual authority is more difficult to identify as it is based on the conduct of the parties, or the relationship between them. Implied actual authority tends to arise in several different ways.

- An agent who has express actual authority to engage in a certain act may need to undertake incidental activities in order to complete that act. Such an agent will usually have implied actual authority to engage in such incidental acts. For example, if a director has express actual authority to buy and sell goods, he will have implied actual authority to enter into negotiations for the price of those goods.
- An agent may be appointed to a particular role within the company, in which case the agent will usually have implied actual authority to do all such things as a person in that position usually has. The following case demonstrates this, along with demonstrating that a person need not be formally appointed to a role in order to obtain implied actual authority.

Case law 4.12

***Hely-Hutchinson v Brayhead Ltd* [1968] 1 QB 549 (CA)**

Richards had been formally appointed as chair of Brayhead Ltd. He had not been formally appointed as Brayhead's managing director, but he undertook this role with the board's acquiescence. This included the board acquiescing to Richards entering into contracts on Brayhead's behalf. Brayhead was planning to merge with Perdio Electronics Ltd. Richards, on behalf of Brayhead, entered into a contract with Hely-Hutchinson, under which Brayhead would indemnify Hely-Hutchinson for any losses he sustained in relation to Perdio. Perdio went into liquidation and Hely-Hutchinson sought to enforce the indemnity. Brayhead's board refused to indemnify Hely-Hutchinson on the ground that Richards had no authority to enter into the indemnity agreement on behalf of Brayhead. Hely-Hutchnson sued Brayhead.

Lord Denning MR stated:

> **'It is plain that... Richards had no express authority to enter into these... contracts on behalf of the company: nor had he any such authority implied from the nature of his office. He had been duly appointed chair of the company but that office in itself did not carry with it authority to enter into these contracts without the sanction of the board. But I think he had authority implied from the conduct of the parties and the circumstances of the case.'**

The conduct Lord Denning MR referred to was the fact that 'the board by their conduct over many months had acquiesced in [Richards] acting as their chief executive and committing Brayhead Ltd to contracts without the necessity of sanction from the board'. Accordingly, Richards had implied actual authority to enter into the indemnity on Brayhead's behalf and Hely-Hutchinson's claim succeeded.

Whether an agent has implied actual authority depends heavily on the facts. Placing an agent in a certain role (e.g. appointing a director as CEO) will bestow upon him a significant degree of implied actual authority, but the courts have placed some limits upon an agent's implied actual authority, including:

- implied actual authority will not be bestowed upon an agent where it would conflict with an express limitation or prohibition by the company; and
- implied actual authority (indeed, actual authority in general) will not be bestowed upon a director where he 'acts in a manner which is contrary to the interests of the company …' (*Re Capitol Films Ltd* [2010] EWHC 2240 (Ch)).

5.2 Apparent authority

To understand how apparent authority (or 'ostensible authority' as it is known in older cases) operates, consider the following example.

Case study 4.4

John is the managing director of X-Corp Ltd. X-Corp wishes to purchase a piece of machinery. The other directors of X-Corp authorise John to negotiate with potential sellers and to purchase the machinery, but only if the purchase price is less than £35,000. John enters into negotiations with Y-Corp and, on X-Corp's behalf, he enters into a contract with Y-Corp under which X-Corp will purchase the machinery for £40,000. John states that this was the best price possible, but the other directors refuse to accept this and X-Corp refuses to honour the contract on the ground that John had no authority to make it. Y-Corp sues X-Corp.

There is no doubt that John did not have actual authority to enter into the contract with Y-Corp on X-Corp's behalf. However, it is unlikely that Y-Corp could know this and, from its perspective, it would appear that John did indeed have authority to enter into the contract. It might be the case that John had apparent authority. Lord Denning has stated that 'apparent authority is the authority of an agent as it appears to others' (*Hely-Hutchinson v Brayhead Ltd* [1968] 1 QB 549 (CA)).

The authoritative definition of apparent authority, and the definition that sets out the requirements for apparent authority to exist, was provided by Diplock LJ in *Freeman & Lockyer v Buckhurst Park Properties (Mangal) Ltd* [1964] 2 QB 480 (CA), who stated that apparent authority is:

> 'a legal relationship between the principal and the contractor [i.e. a third party] created by a representation, made by the principal to the contractor, intended to be and in fact acted upon by the contractor, that the agent has authority to enter on behalf of the principal into a contract of a kind within the scope of the "apparent" authority, so as to render the principal liable to perform any obligations imposed upon him by such contract. It is irrelevant whether the agent had actual authority to enter into the contract.'

It is clear that there can be a considerable overlap between an agent's actual authority and his apparent authority. Lord Denning in *Hely-Hutchinson v Brayhead Ltd* [1968] 1 QB 549 (CA) acknowledged this and provided an example:

> 'when the board appoints one of their number to be managing director, they invest him not only with implied [actual] authority, but also with [apparent] authority to do all such things as fall within the usual scope of that office. Other people who see him acting as managing director are entitled to assume that he has the usual authority of a managing director.'

In many cases where both forms of authority exist, the effect of apparent authority will be to extend the agent's authority (as in the example given by Lord Denning above), but apparent authority can exist in cases where an agent has no actual authority at all. The key difference between actual authority and apparent authority is the relationship to which both forms of authority relate. Actual authority is about the authority that the principal has bestowed upon the agent. Conversely, in *Freeman & Lockyer v Buckhurst Park Properties (Mangal) Ltd* [1964] 2 QB 480 (CA), Diplock LJ stated that apparent authority is about the relationship between the principal and the third party: that the principal represents to the third party that the agent has authority to engage in the act in question and the third party then acts on that representation.

In order to establish that an agent has apparent authority, three requirements will need to be satisfied namely:

1. there must be a representation;
2. this representation must be relied upon; and
3. the person relying on the representation must alter their position.

Representation

As Diplock LJ stated, there must be representation that the agent has authority to enter into the contract in question on behalf of the principal. Diplock LJ was of the opinion that this representation must be made by someone who has actual authority (the company), but the case law suggests that the representation can be made by someone who has apparent authority (*ING Re (UK) Ltd v R&V Versicherung AG* [2006] EWHC 1544 (Comm)). What is accepted is that the agent himself cannot make this representation (*United Bank of Kuwait v Hammoud* [1988] 1 WLR 1051 (CA)).

The representation can be made orally or in writing, but in most cases it will be made by conduct. In *Armagas Ltd v Mundogas SA (The Ocean Frost)* [1986] AC 717 (HL), Lord Keith stated that this typically occurred where 'the principal has placed the agent in a position in which the outside world is generally regarded as carrying authority to enter into transactions of the kind in question'. The following case demonstrates this.

Case law 4.13

***Freeman & Lockyer v Buckhurst Park Properties (Mangal) Ltd* [1964] 2 QB 480 (CA)**

Kapoor was a director of Buckhurst Park (Mangal) Properties Ltd and, although he was never appointed as the company's managing director, he undertook this role with the other directors' acquiescence. Kapoor engaged a firm of architects to carry out work on Buckhurst's behalf, but when the architects sought payment, Buckhurst refused on the ground that Kapoor lacked authority to contract with the architects. The architects sued.

Diplock LJ stated:

> **'The representation which creates "apparent" authority may take a variety of forms of which the commonest is representation by conduct, that is, by permitting the agent to act in some way in the conduct of the principal's business with other persons. By so doing the principal represents to anyone who becomes aware that the agent is so acting that the agent has authority to enter on behalf of the principal into contracts with other persons of the kind which an agent so acting in the conduct of his principal's business has usually "actual" authority to enter into.'**

By acquiescing to Kapoor acting as managing director, Buckhurst had represented to the architects that Kapoor had the authority to engage in activities that a managing director would usually be authorised to undertake, including entering into contracts on behalf of the company. Accordingly, Kapoor had apparent authority to engage the architects and so Buckhurst was liable to pay them.

Reliance

The third party in question must rely on the representation.

- The third party must know of the existence of the representation. If it did not, it could not rely on it and apparent authority will not arise.
- The third party must know of the principal's existence (*AL Underwood Ltd v Bank of Liverpool* [1924] 1 KB 775 (CA)).
- The third party must not know, or ought not to have known, that the agent lacked authority (*Overbrooke Estates Ltd v Glencombe Properties Ltd* [1974] 1 WLR 1335 (Ch)). For example, if the third party knows that the contract is outside the scope of the company's articles, apparent authority will not arise (*Rolled Steel Products (Holdings) Ltd v British Steel Corp* [1986] Ch 246 (CA)).

Alteration of position

The third party must alter his position as a result of his reliance on the representation. In practice, this requirement is usually easy to satisfy as merely entering into the contract with the principal will indicate an alteration of position (*Polish Steamship Co v AJ Williams Fuels (Overseas Sales) (The Suwalki)* [1989] 1 Lloyd's Rep 511 (QB)). The third party need not show that the alteration of position caused him a detriment (*Rama Corporation Ltd v Proved Tin and General Investments Ltd* [1952] 2 QB 147 (QB)).

Test yourself 4.4

1. **What is a relationship of agency?**
2. **What is actual authority?**
3. **How does express actual authority differ from implied actual authority?**
4. **When will an agent have apparent authority?**

6. Board authority

As directors are agents of the company, the above agency rules apply to directors and determine what contracts they are authorised to enter into on behalf of the company. A company's articles typically vest general managerial power in the directors, which includes the ability to contract on behalf of the company. However, the articles may also limit the ability of the directors to contract on behalf of the company.

Case study 4.5

The articles of X-Corp Ltd vest managerial power in the directors, but the articles also provide that the directors' power to contract on behalf of X-Corp for the purchase of goods is limited to contracts worth a maximum of £20,000. If the price of the goods is higher, member approval is required. The directors enter into a contract on behalf of X-Corp under which X-Corp will purchase a piece of machinery from Y-Corp plc for £35,000. Member approval is not obtained.

The issue under discussion is whether there is a binding contract between X-Corp and Y-Corp, and what will the consequences be if the directors act beyond their authority under the articles. The answer is predominantly found in s. 40 of the CA 2006.

6.1 Section 40 of the Companies Act 2006

Section 40(1) provides that '[i]n favour of a person dealing with a company in good faith, the power of the directors to bind the company, or authorise others to do so, is deemed to be free of any limitation under the company's constitution'. If s. 40(1) applied to case study 4.5, then even though the directors have acted beyond their authority under the constitution, the contract would still be valid and could be enforced by either X-Corp or Y-Corp. Four points should be noted.

- Section 40 does not bestow authority upon the directors to enter into certain contracts – it merely provides that if they act outside their constitutional authority, the contract cannot be set aside due to this lack of authority.
- Section 40 protects the contract – it does not protect the directors, who may find themselves liable, potentially for breach of the s. 171(a) duty to act in accordance with the constitution (discussed in Chapter 7).
- Section 40 does not prevent the right of a member to bring proceedings to restrain an act that is beyond the power of the directors (CA 2006, s. 40(4)). A member is empowered to apply for an injunction preventing the directors from engaging in an act that is beyond their powers. However, in practice, this power is not especially useful as it can only be exercised if 'no such proceedings lie in respect of an act to be done in fulfilment of a legal obligation arising from a previous act of the company'. Given that the members (especially members of larger companies) will likely not know of a transaction until after a legal obligation has arisen, the power granted to the members under s. 40(4) is severely limited in practice.
- Section 40 cannot usually be used by a company that is a charity (s.42(1)).

Not all transactions fall within s. 40, and transactions not protected by s. 40 may be declared void (*Guinness plc v Saunders* [1990] BCLC 402 (HL)).

Persons dealing with the company
Section 40 can only be used by a 'person dealing with the company', and so it cannot be used by the company itself (such as to escape a contract entered into by directors who lacked the constitutional authority to do so). A person 'deals' with a company if 'he is a party to any transaction or other act to which the company is a party' (s. 40(2)(a)). The issue is slightly more complex in cases where the contract involves a director.

Where a director enters into a contract on behalf of the company with himself, then that director will usually be unable to rely on s. 40 (*Smith v Henniker-Major & Co* [2002] EWCA Civ 762). Section 41 provides that, where the validity of a transaction is dependent upon s. 40, then that transaction will be voidable at the company's instance if the transaction is between the company and (i) a director of the company; or (ii) any person connected with such a director (s. 41(2)). Any director who authorised such a transaction is liable to account for any gain he has made directly or indirectly by the transaction, and to indemnify the company for any loss or damage resulting from the transaction (s.41 (3)).

Dealing in good faith
A person can only rely on s. 40 if they deal with the company in good faith, but this requirement is very easily satisfied. Indeed, s. 40 itself helps establish good faith in three ways:

1. a person dealing with the company 'is not bound to enquire as to any limitation on the powers of the directors to bind the company or authorise others to do so' (s. 40(2)(b)(i));
2. a person dealing with the company 'is presumed to have acted in good faith unless the contrary is proved' (s. 40 (2)(b)(ii)); and
3. a person dealing with the company 'is not to be regarded as acting in bad faith by reason only of his knowing that an act is beyond the powers of the directors under the company's constitution' (s. 40 (2)(b)(iii)).

The power of the directors
One question that arises is whether s. 40 applies only to acts of the entire board. Section 40 refers to the power of 'the directors', whereas its predecessor (s. 35A of the Companies Act 1985) referred to the power of the 'board of directors'. This reformulation would indicate that s. 40 applies to acts of the entire board and acts of multiple directors. Pre-2006 case law held this to be the case (*Criterion Properties plc v Stratford UK Properties LLC* [2004] UKHL 28). The word 'directors' would appear to indicate that s. 40 cannot apply to the acts of a single director, but there is limited case law authority stating that it can apply to a single director (*International Sales & Agencies Ltd v Marcus* [1982] 2 CMLR 46 (QB)). The weight of opinion appears to be that s. 40 cannot apply to a single director, but clarification is desirable.

6.2 The 'indoor management' rule

In cases where s. 40 does not apply, then a common law principle known as the 'indoor management' rule (or the rule in *Turquand's* case) might be of use to a third party. The rule, which was established in the following case, provides that third parties that deal with the company can assume that the company's internal rules have been complied with.

Case law 4.14

***Royal British Bank v Turquand* (1856) 6 El & Bl 327**

The board of a company purported on behalf of the company to borrow £2,000 from a bank. The company's deed of settlement (essentially its articles) provided that the directors could only borrow sums on behalf of the company if authorisation was obtained from the general meeting. The directors did not obtain such authorisation. The company defaulted on the loan and the bank commenced legal proceedings against the company, which was in liquidation. The company's liquidator argued that (i) the directors had no authority to borrow the money on the company's behalf and so the company was not bound by the loan agreement; and (ii) the bank should bear the loss as it failed to inform itself of the directors' lack of authority.

Jervis CJ held that the company was bound to pay back the money to the bank. He stated that '[f]inding that the [directors'] authority might be made complete by a resolution, [the bank] would have a right to infer the fact of a resolution authorising that which on the face of the document appeared to be legitimately done'. In other words, the bank was entitled to assume that the directors had complied with the articles.

The passing of s. 40 has meant that, in many cases, recourse to the indoor management rule is no longer required (the bank could have easily enforced the loan agreement using s. 40). However, where s. 40 has no application, then the indoor management rule may still be of aid. It is important to remember the limitations of the indoor management rule:

- the rule does not apply in relation to transactions that are voidable under s. 41 (*Morris v Kanssen* [1946] AC 459 (HL)); and
- the rule will not apply where the third party has been put on notice that the company's internal rules have not been complied with (*Wrexham Association Football Club Ltd v CrucialMove Ltd* [2006] EWCA Civ 237).

Test yourself 4.5

1. **What does s. 40(1) of the CA 2006 state?**
2. **Who can rely on s. 40?**
3. **What does the 'indoor management' rule state?**

Chapter summary

- A company can enter into a contract (i) by affixing its common seal to a document; (ii) through a person who is authorised to contract on behalf of the company; or (iii) by complying with the rules in s. 44(2)–(8) of the CA 2006.
- The most important constitutional document is the company's articles of association. The memorandum of association used to be important but is much less so under the CA 2006.
- Statute provides a set of model articles that companies may use, or they may draft their own articles. Even if a company does draft its own articles, the model articles will still apply insofar as they are not excluded or modified by the company's own articles.
- The courts will interpret the articles in order to give them reasonable business efficacy.
- The courts can imply terms into the articles in certain circumstances.
- A company's articles can be amended by passing a special resolution, although both statute and case law impose limits on a company's ability to alter its articles, most notably the power to amend the articles must be exercised bona fide for the benefit of the company as a whole.
- The constitution forms a contract (i) between the company and its members; and (ii) between the members themselves. This contract differs from a standard contract in several ways.
- An outsider cannot generally enforce the constitution, nor can outsider rights generally be enforced.
- Shareholders are able to enter into agreements that set out certain rules regarding the relationship between those members. The parties to a shareholders' agreement (which can include the company) can enforce the terms of the agreement.
- Companies incorporated under the CA 2006 are not required to have an objects clause in their constitution.
- If the company acts outside of its constitution, it is said to be acting *ultra vires*. However, the validity of an act done by a company cannot generally be called into question on the ground that the company lacked capacity.
- A company may authorise an agent to engage in acts on the company's behalf. An agent's authority can be actual (express or implied) or apparent.
- Section 40 of the CA 2006 provides that, in favour of a person dealing with the company, the power of the directors to bind a company, or authorise others to do so, is deemed to be free of any limitation under the company's constitution. However, there are instances where s. 40 will not apply.

Part two

Chapter 5
The board of directors

Chapter 6
The role of the board

Chapter 7
Directors' duties

The board of directors

Overview

Part two focuses on the board of directors and the duties placed upon directors.

Chapter 5 begins by looking at what a director is and describes the various types of directors. It looks at how directors are appointed and paid, followed by an examination of the structure and composition of the board. The chapter ends by looking at how a director can vacate office.

Chapter 6 explores the role of the board. It discusses the division of power between the board and the members, followed by a discussion of the principal way in which directors exercise their powers, namely the rules relating to board meetings. The chapter ends by looking at the role of the company secretary.

Chapter 7 looks at the statutory duties placed upon directors. It discusses the scope and content of each of the seven general duties, followed by an examination of those transactions involving directors that require member approval.

At the end of this Part, students will be able to:

- explain what a director is and identify the various types of directors;
- discuss the process for appointing and remunerating directors;
- consider the various ways in which a director can cease to be a director;
- discuss the role of the board;
- understand the division of powers between the board and the members;
- demonstrate how board meetings should be conducted;
- appreciate the role of the company secretary;
- identify to whom directors owe their duties;
- understand the scope and operation of the general duties placed upon directors;
- consider how directors can avoid liability for breach of duty; and
- understand which transactions involving directors require member approval.

Chapter five
The board of directors

Contents

1. Introduction

This chapter outlines the basic information relating to the board of directors, beginning with the question of asking what a director is before moving on to look at the different types of director that exist. In recent years, the appointment, remuneration and composition of the board have become major governance issues, so these are all discussed. Finally, the chapter looks at the various ways in which a director may cease to be a director. The role, powers and duties of a director are discussed in subsequent chapters.

2. What is a director?

Many company law provisions apply only to directors, so it is important to know whether a person is a director or not. The CA 2006 does not seek to exhaustively define directors, simply stating that '[i]n the Companies Act "director" includes any person occupying the position of director, by whatever name called' (CA 2006, s. 250). Two points should be noted regarding s. 250.

- As s. 250 uses the word 'person', it follows that a legal person (such as a company or LLP) can currently be a director, although a company must have at least one director who is a natural person (s. 155(1)). However, concerns regarding the use of corporate directors have led to Parliament generally prohibiting the use of corporate directors, with s. 156A(1) stating that '[a] person may not be appointed as a director of a company unless the person is a natural person'. At the time of writing, s. 156A is not yet in force and the government is still determining what exceptions will exist to the s. 156A prohibition.

- Whether a director is called a director is irrelevant to the question of whether that person is a director: the key issue in determining the status of a person who may be a director under s. 250 is whether or not the person, 'by whatever name called', actually carries out the functions of a director.

2.1 Types of director

Several different types of director exist, although it is important to note that the CA 2006 does not generally distinguish between them (other than, in some cases, providing rules regarding shadow directors).

De facto *and* de jure directors

A *de jure* director is a person who has been validly appointed as a director (in accordance with the articles), whereas a *de facto* director is a person who acts as a director but has not been validly appointed. As s. 250 refers to 'any person occupying the position of director', it encompasses both *de jure* and *de facto* directors. The vast majority of provisions in the CA 2006 will apply to *de jure* and *de facto* directors but the courts may hold that, based on the construction of a provision, it may not apply to *de facto* directors.

Identifying whether a person is a *de facto* director is not always easy. Historically, *de facto* directors were directors who (i) were appointed as directors, but their appointment was defective; or (ii) their appointment came to an end, but they continued to act as director. The courts have now acknowledged that the term *de facto* director can also apply to a person who was never appointed as director (*Re Lo-Line Electric Motors Ltd* [1988] Ch 477 (Ch)). Over the years, the courts have stated that in order to be a *de facto* director, the person must:

- exercise real influence (otherwise than as a professional adviser) in the corporate governance of the company (*Re Kaytech International plc* [1999] BCC 390 (CA));
- undertake functions which could properly be discharged only by a director (*Re Hydrodam (Corby) Ltd* [1994] BCC 161 (Ch));
- participate in directing the affairs of the company and act on an equal footing with the *de jure* directors (*Secretary of State for Trade and Industry v Hollier* [2006] EWHC 1804 (Ch)).

An overview of the relevant authorities was provided by Lord Collins in *Revenue and Customs Commissioners v Holland* [2010] UKSC 51 [58]-[93] and Arden LJ in *Smithton Ltd v Naggar* [2014] EWCA Civ 939 [33]-[45].

Shadow directors

To understand why the law seeks to regulate shadow directors, consider the following example.

Case study 5.1

Sara and Cheryl are the only directors of X-Corp Ltd. Becky, who owns 95% of the shares in X-Corp, regularly tells the directors which transactions X-Corp should enter into and the directors usually follow her instructions.

Becky is not a director under s. 250 as she has not been appointed as a director, nor does she appear to occupy the position of director. Clearly, however, she controls the company and so should be subject to some form of regulation. As Lewison J stated in *Ultraframe (UK) Ltd v Fielding* [2005] EWHC 1638 (Ch), 'a person who effectively controls the activities of a company is to be subject to the same statutory liabilities and disabilities as a person who is a *de jure* director'. The law regulates the activities of such persons by designating them as 'shadow directors'. Certain statutory provisions expressly state that they apply to shadow directors. For example, the general duties can apply to shadow directors by virtue of s. 170(5).

Section 251(1) of the CA 2006 provides that a shadow director is 'a person in accordance with whose directions or instructions the directors of the company are accustomed to act'. It is important to know whether a person is a shadow director, so statute and the courts have issued guidance on some aspects of the s. 251 definition.

- Section 251(2) provides three instances where a person will not be a shadow director, namely where the person is:
  - giving advice in a professional capacity;
  - giving instructions, directions, guidance or advice in the exercise of a function conferred under an enactment; or
  - giving guidance or advice in a capacity as a Minister of the Crown.
- In *Ultraframe (UK) Ltd v Fielding* [2005] EWHC 1638 (Ch), the court stated that a person will not be a shadow director if the other directors do not act on their instructions. The court also stated that it must be shown that a 'governing majority of the board' was accustomed to acting on their instructions, and not merely a minority of the directors.
- In *Secretary of State for Trade and Industry v Deverell* [2001] Ch 340 (CA), Morritt LJ stated that the influence exerted by the purported shadow director need not cover the whole scope of the company's activities. He also stated that a person can openly be a shadow director and need not be shown to have 'lurked in the shadows'.
- As the directors must be 'accustomed' to acting on the shadow director's instructions, it follows that a person will not be a shadow director the first time such instructions are acted upon (*Re Unisoft Group Ltd (No 3)* [1994] BCC 766 (Ch)).

Executive and non-executive directors

Company law legislation does not distinguish between executive directors and non-executive directors (NEDs), although both fall within s. 250. An executive director is usually a full-time employee of the company and will be involved in the day-to-day management of the company. A NED is not usually an employee of the company, is part-time (usually around one to two days per month), and their managerial role is much more limited. The NEDs have an additional role, namely to 'scrutinise and hold to account the performance of management and individual directors against agreed performance objectives' (UK Corporate Governance Code, Provision 13).

Only the largest companies tend to have NEDs. In such companies, at least half the board, excluding the chair, should be made up of NEDs whom the board considers to be independent (UK Corporate Governance Code, Provision 11). The independence of NEDs is important in order to ensure that they provide effective scrutiny of the executive directors. Provision 10 of the UK Corporate Governance Code provides that the board should identify in the annual report each NED it considers to be independent. Provision 10 also provides a non-exhaustive list of circumstances which are likely to, or could appear to, impair a NED's independence:

- the NED is or has been an employee of the company or group within the last five years;
- the NED has, or has had within the last three years, a material business relationship with the company, either directly or as a partner, shareholder, director or senior employee of a body that has such a relationship with the company;
- the NED has received or receives additional remuneration from the company apart from a director's fee, participates in the company's share option or a performance-related pay scheme, or is a member of the company's pension scheme;
- the NED has close family ties with any of the company's advisers, directors or senior employees;
- the NED holds cross-directorships or has significant links with other directors through involvement in other companies or bodies;
- the NED represents a significant shareholder; or
- has served on the board for more than nine years from the date of their first appointment.

Where any of these or other relevant circumstances apply, and the board nonetheless considers that NED to be independent, the board should clearly explain why it considers that NED to be independent. In other words, whether a NED is independent is ultimately a matter for the board to determine.

Stop and think 5.1

When the FRC published its draft version of the 2018 Code, a NED would automatically be regarded as not independent if any of the above circumstances were present. The final version of the 2018 Code does not state this and merely provides that an explanation will be required (as was the case under prior versions of the Code). Do you think this is the right approach, or was the draft version of the 2018 Code preferable?

Alternate directors

A director may be temporarily unable to act as a director (due to illness, for example). In such a case, it may be desirable to appoint someone else to act on that director's behalf, with such a person being known as an 'alternate director'. The CA 2006 does not empower a director to appoint an alternate, so a director will only have such a power if it is provided for in the company's articles. The model articles for private companies do not contain such a power, but article 25(1) of the model articles for public companies does provide that a director (known as 'the appointer') may appoint another director, or any other person approved by a resolution of the directors, to exercise the appointer's powers and carry out the appointer's responsibilities. The articles will set out what the alternate director can and cannot do, and the circumstances under which his appointment will be terminated.

Nominee directors

Someone with an interest in the company (such as a major shareholder or creditor) might wish to safeguard that interest by having a say on the board. One way to do this is by negotiating with the company to obtain the ability to appoint a director. This power of appointment will usually be placed in the company's articles, but could also be set out in a shareholders' agreement. Such a director is known as a 'nominee director'. Two points should be noted regarding nominee directors.

- A nominee's duty is to the company, not the person who appointed him (*Scottish Co-Operative Wholesale Society Ltd v Meyer* [1959] AC 324 (HL)).
- A person who appoints a nominee could be regarded as a person with significant control (discussed in Chapter 3), and so will have to be identified on the PSC register.

2.2 Specific board roles

A director may be appointed to a specific board role. This appointment will affect the tasks undertaken by the director and his authority to act on behalf of the company. The model articles (article 19(1) for private companies; article 23(1) for public companies) provide that the director may 'undertake any services for the company that the directors decide'. It is common (especially in larger companies) for the board to appoint a chief executive officer (CEO) and/or chair.

A director can be appointed as CEO (or 'managing director') only if the articles so allow (the model articles contain no express provision for this, but the appointment of a CEO would fall under articles 19(1) and 23(1) above). The role and powers of a CEO are a matter for the company's articles (which may delegate certain powers to the CEO) and the CEO's service contract. Outside of this, a CEO does not acquire any additional powers simply by virtue of being appointed as CEO (*Mitchell & Hobbs (UK) Ltd v Mill* [1996] 2 BCLC 102 (QB)). The CEO is the head of the company with the FRC's Guidance on Board Effectiveness providing that '[a]s the most senior executive director, the chief executive is responsible for delivering the strategy as agreed by the board' (para 70).

A company may appoint a chair if the articles so provide, with article 12(2) of the model articles stating that the directors may appoint a director to chair their meetings. The role of the chair is not set out in statute, but Principle F of the UK Corporate Governance Code provides that '[t]he chair leads the board and is responsible for its overall effectiveness in directing the company'.

In practice, the CEO and the chair occupy positions of power within the company and, to avoid too much power being concentrated in one person, Provision 9 of the UK Corporate Governance Code recommends that the roles of CEO and chair should not be exercised by the same person.

Test yourself 5.1

1. **How does s. 250 of the CA 2006 define a director?**
2. **What is the difference between a *de jure* and a *de facto* director?**
3. **Define the following: (i) shadow director; (ii) alternate director; and (iii) nominee director.**

3. The appointment of directors

The CA 2006 says very little about the appointment of a director, preferring to leave the appointment process for companies to determine themselves via their articles. Before looking at this process, it is important to note that statute does state that certain persons are not eligible to act as a director:

- when s. 156A comes into force, a legal person will not be able to act as director, unless regulations provide for exceptions;
- a person under the age of 16 cannot act as director (CA 2006, s. 157);
- a company's statutory auditor cannot act as its director (CA 2006, s. 1214);
- a person subject to a disqualification order/undertaking commits a criminal offence if he acts as a director (CDDA 1986, ss. 1 and 13), unless he obtains leave to act; and

- an undischarged bankrupt cannot act as director, unless he obtains the leave of the court (CDDA 1986, s. 11(1)).

A company's articles may also contain provisions that prohibit or limit a person's ability to act as director.

3.1 The appointment process

A company's first directors will be appointed upon the company's incorporation (CA 2006, s. 16(6)). After that, the appointment of directors is a matter for the company's articles. If the company's articles say nothing about the appointment of directors, then the model articles will apply and provide that a director can be appointed by an ordinary resolution or by a decision of the directors (model articles for private companies, article 17(1); model articles for public companies, article 20). If such a company has excluded the model articles, then the power to appoint a director is exercised by the members passing an ordinary resolution (*Worcester Corsetry Ltd v Witting* [1936] Ch 640 (CA)).

The appointment of directors is a key governance topic. Concerns exist that the appointments process lacks independence, especially as in most companies the board can appoint a director. Principle J of the UK Corporate Governance Code provides that '[a]ppointments to the board should be subject to a formal, rigorous and transparent procedure'. Provision 17 recommends that the board should establish a nomination committee, whose role is 'to lead the process for appointments, ensure plans are in place for orderly succession to both the board and senior management positions, and oversee the development of a diverse pipeline for succession'.

To ensure the nomination committee is independent, Provision 17 goes on to state that the majority of the members of the nomination committee should be independent NEDs and the chair of the board should not chair the committee when it is dealing with the appointment of his successor.

3.2 The register of directors

Every company must keep a register of directors (CA 2006, s. 162(1)) which contains specified particulars regarding each director (ss. 162(2), 163, 164 and 166).

When a new director is appointed, the company must notify Companies House of the appointment within 14 days. This notice must contain (i) a statement of the particulars relating to the director that will be included in the register of directors; and (ii) a statement by the company that the director has consented to act as director (s.167(1)–(2)). The register can be inspected by any member without charge, and by any other person upon payment of a fee (s. 162(5)).

A private company may, instead of keeping its own register of directors, elect to keep the required information on the public register maintained by Companies House (ss. 167A–167E). Companies electing to do this will need to inform Companies House of relevant changes (s. 167D).

3.3 Defective appointments

It is possible that a director's appointment may not be conducted in accordance with the articles. The question is whether a defective appointment invalidates or affects in some other way the actions that director engaged in. If the answer is yes, this could have severe adverse consequences upon the company and any persons who dealt with that director. Fortunately, this is not normally the case. Section 161(1) of the CA 2006 provides that the acts of a person acting as a director are valid notwithstanding that it is afterwards discovered:

- that there was a defect in their appointment;
- that they were disqualified from holding office;
- that they had ceased to hold office; or
- that they were not entitled to vote on the matter in question.

However, s. 161 will not apply in three situations:

1. where the person seeking to rely on s. 161 has not acted in good faith (*Channel Collieries Trust Ltd v Dover, St Margaret's and Martin Mill Light Railway Co* [1914] 2 Ch 506 (CA));
2. where the person seeking to rely on s. 161 knew, at the time of the appointment, of the defect in the appointment and of the legal effect of the defect (*British Asbestos Co Ltd v Boyd* [1903] 2 Ch 439 (Ch)); or
3. where there was no purported appointment in the first place (*Morris v Kanssen and Others* [1946] AC 459 (HL)).

Test yourself 5.2

1. **Provide examples of persons who are ineligible to act as director.**
2. **Who has the power to appoint a director?**
3. **What does s. 161(1) of the CA 2006 state? Give three examples of when s. 161 will not apply.**

4. Directors' remuneration

Directors' remuneration in larger companies has become a major governance topic over the last few decades and the governance aspect will be discussed in the Corporate Governance module. Here, the relevant legal rules will be discussed alongside an overview of the relevant best practice principles.

The first issue to discuss is whether a director is entitled to be paid for acting as a director. In *Hutton v West Cork Railway Co* (1883) 23 ChD 654 (CA), Bowen LJ stated that '[a] director is not a servant; he is a person doing business for the company, but not upon ordinary terms. It is not implied from the mere fact that he is a director that he is to be paid for it.'

A director is *prima facie* an office holder and so is not entitled to be remunerated, unless authorised to do so. This authorisation can come from several sources, including:

- the company's members can approve the remuneration of a director (*Dunstan v Imperial Gas Light and Coke Co* (1832) 3 B & Ad 125);
- the company's articles can provide that a director is to be remunerated (as is provided for in article 19(2) of the model articles for private companies, and article 23(2) of the model articles for public companies); or
- a director's service contract can provide that a director is to be remunerated.

Absent such authorisation, any remuneration paid to a director will be deemed void (*Re George Newman & Co* [1895] 1 Ch 674 (CA)).

4.1 Who determines directors' pay?

Once it has been determined that a director is entitled to be paid, the next question to ask is how much is that director to be paid and what form the remuneration package will take. Who determines a director's pay is a matter for the company's articles, but if the articles say nothing on this, the directors' remuneration can be determined by the company in a general meeting (*Re George Newman & Co* [1895] 1 Ch 674 (CA)). The model articles provide that the directors themselves can determine their remuneration for their services to the company as directors, and for any other service which they undertake to the company (model articles for private companies, article 19(2); model articles for public companies, article 23(2)).

In larger companies, allowing directors to set their own pay is not regarded as good practice, with Principle Q of the UK Corporate Governance Code providing that '[n]o director should be involved in deciding their own remuneration outcome'. The Code therefore recommends that the board should establish a remuneration committee of at least three independent NEDs (Provision 32), which will then have delegated authority from the board to determine the company's remuneration policy and the remuneration of the chair, executive directors and senior management (Provision 33). Other roles of the remuneration committee as envisaged by the Code include:

- reviewing workforce remuneration, and taking workforce remuneration into account when setting executive remuneration (Provision 33);
- being responsible for appointing remuneration consultants (Provision 34); and
- ensuring that compensation commitments in directors' terms of appointment do not reward poor performance (Provision 39).

4.2 Disclosure

Companies are required to disclose specified information regarding directors' remuneration, with the disclosure requirements becoming more extensive depending upon the size of the company and whether it is quoted or unquoted. The CA 2006 provides that all companies must keep copies of the service contract of each director and shadow director (ss. 228(1) and 230), which can be inspected by any member free of charge (s. 229(1)). Failure to comply constitutes a criminal offence (s. 228(5) and (6)).

Schedule 5, para 1 of the Large and Medium-Sized Companies and Groups (Accounts and Reports) Regulations 2008 (SI 2008/410) provides that all large and medium-sized companies must disclose:

- the aggregate amount of remuneration paid to the directors;
- the aggregate amount of gains made by directors on the exercise of share options;
- the aggregate amount of money paid or assets received under a long-term incentive scheme; and
- the aggregate value of company contributions paid into directors' pension schemes.

Schedule 5, paras 2–5 of the Large and Medium-Sized Companies and Groups (Accounts and Reports) Regulations 2008 state that unquoted large and medium-sized companies must disclose additional information, namely:

- details regarding the pay of its highest paid director;
- details regarding retirement benefits paid to directors and past directors;
- details regarding payments made to directors for loss of office; and
- details regarding sums paid to third parties in respect of directors' services.

Quoted companies must prepare a remuneration report, which contains extensive details regarding the directors' remuneration. This report forms part of the company's annual report and so is discussed more in Chapter 14.

Finally, companies whose securities are listed must disclose additional remuneration-related information (e.g. details of any long-term incentive schemes) in order to comply with the Listing Rules (LR 9.8.4). Companies with a premium listing will also need to comply or explain against the disclosure-related Principles and Provisions in the UK Corporate Governance Code.

Test yourself 5.3

1. **Are directors entitled to be paid for their services?**
2. **Who determines how much a director will be paid?**

5. Board structure and composition

The CA 2006 has little to say regarding a board's structure and composition, meaning that the topic of board structure and composition is largely based on commercial and governance needs, as opposed to complying with legal obligations. As a result, the Corporate Governance module will discuss board structure and composition in more detail, but it is worth discussing some basic issues here.

5.1 Board structure and size

The vast majority of UK companies adopt a unitary board structure, under which all the directors are part of a single board that undertakes all board functions. In larger companies, certain tasks may be delegated to certain board committees, namely:

- the determination of directors' remuneration may be delegated to a remuneration committee;
- a nomination committee may be established to make recommendations to the board regarding directorial appointments; and
- an audit committee may be set up to recommend auditor appointments, monitor the internal audit function and monitor the company's internal financial controls.

In certain countries (such as Denmark and Germany), the dominant board structure is the two-tier board, under which executive directors form one board (a managerial board) with the NEDs forming another board (a supervisory board that supervises the managerial board).

Section 154 of the CA 2006 provides that a private company must have at least one director, and a public company must have at least two directors. The Act does not specify a maximum number of directors, but companies may specify a maximum in their articles (and a minimum, providing it does not fall below the minimum in s. 154). Unsurprisingly, small companies will likely have small boards and larger companies will have larger boards. The 2016 UK Corporate Governance Code stated that the board 'should be of sufficient size that the requirements of the business can be met and that changes to the board's composition and that of its committees can be managed without undue disruption, and should not be so large as to be unwieldy'. The 2018 Code makes no mention of board size.

5.2 Board composition

The topic of board composition is primarily a governance issue and so is discussed in more detail in the Corporate Governance module. It is worth briefly noting some composition-related principles that have been established.

Generally, it will be seen that these principles tend to apply only to the largest companies. For example, the UK Corporate Governance Code states that independent NEDs should comprise at least half of the boards of companies with a premium listing (Provision 11).

In recent years, the topic of board diversity has become a major governance issue, with Principle J of the UK Corporate Governance Code stating that board appointments should 'promote diversity of gender, social and ethnic backgrounds, cognitive and personal strengths'. The focus thus far has been on boardroom gender and ethnic diversity.

- A 2010 report entitled *Women on Boards* recommended that women should account for at least 25% of directors on FTSE 100 boards by the end of 2015. This figure was successfully reached and the Hampton-Alexander Review now recommends that FTSE 350 companies should aim for at least 33% female board representation by the end of 2020.
- The Parker Review recommends that each FTSE 100 board should have at least one director of colour by 2021, and each FTSE 250 board should have at least one director of colour by 2024.

6. Vacation of office

The final topic to discuss in this chapter are the various ways in which a director can cease to be a director. Four methods will be discussed: resignation, vacation in accordance with the articles, removal and disqualification.

6.1 Resignation

A director can vacate office at any time by resigning and the company must accept his resignation. The general rule is that a resigning director vacates office as soon as he notifies the company of his resignation (*OBC Caspian Ltd v Thorp* (1998) SLT 653), but it is common for a period of notice to be specified in the director's service contract. If the service contact provides for no notice period, a requirement to provide reasonable notice will be implied into the contract (*CMS Dolphin Ltd v Simonet* [2002] BCC 600 (Ch)).

6.2 Vacation in accordance with the articles

A company's articles may specify when a director is to vacate office. For example, the model articles (article 18 for private companies; article 22 for public companies) provide that a director will vacate office if:

- they cease to be a director by virtue of any provision of the CA 2006 or are prohibited from being a director by law;
- a bankruptcy order is made against them; or
- a registered medical practitioner who is treating that person gives a written opinion to the company stating that that person has become physically or mentally incapable of acting as a director and may remain so for more than three months.

Special mention should be made of article provisions requiring retirement by rotation, which occurs where a director is required to periodically vacate office and, if they so wish, seek re-election. The CA 2006 does not require retirement by rotation, but a company's articles may.

Unsurprisingly, small companies (especially family-run companies) do not require retirement by rotation, and so neither do the model articles for private companies. Larger companies do tend to require retirement by rotation. Article 21 of the model articles for public companies provides the following:

- the directors must retire at the company's first AGM and may seek re-election (article 21(1)); and
- at every subsequent AGM, any directors appointed by the directors since the last AGM or any directors who were not appointed or reappointed at one of the preceding two AGMs, must retire from office and may offer themselves for reappointment by the members (article 21(2)).

In practice, article 21(2) requires directors to retire every three years. Those directors may then seek re-election (which most do). Provision 18 of the UK Corporate Governance Code goes further and states that directors of companies with a premium listing be subject to annual re-election.

6.3 Removal

There are two principal ways in which a director can be removed, although in practice it is rare for a director to be removed.

Removal under the CA 2006
The first method of removing a director is found in s. 168(1) of the CA 2006, which provides that '[a] company may by ordinary resolution at a meeting remove a director before the expiration of his period of office, notwithstanding anything in any agreement between it and him'. The following rules must be complied with for the removal to be valid.

- As s. 168(1) specifies that the resolution take place at a meeting, the written resolution procedure cannot be used (CA 2006, s. 288(2)(a)).
- Special notice is required of a s. 168 resolution (s. 168(2)), namely 28 days (s. 312(1)).
- A copy of the resolution must be sent to the director(s) whose removal is sought (s. 169(1)).
- The director whose removal is sought has the right to protest against his removal and, to that end, may address the meeting (s. 169(2)) and circulate written representations to the meeting (s. 169(3)–(5)).

While s. 168 allows a company to remove a director, it will not deprive the director that has been removed of any compensation payable as a result of the removal (s. 168(5)(a)).

The s. 168 power to remove a director cannot be taken away from the members, but it is possible to make a removal more difficult by inserting a weighted voting rights clause in the articles. Such a clause provides that, in the event of a s. 168 resolution (or any other specified resolution), the voting power of specified persons (usually the director being removed) will be increased. The model articles do not provide for weighted voting rights and such clauses are prohibited under the Listing Rules (Listing Rules, LR 7.2.1A; Premium Listing Principle 3). The following case demonstrates how weighted voting rights can make a removal more difficult or even impossible.

Case law 5.1

***Bushell v Faith* [1970] AC 1099 (HL)**

Bushell, Faith and Bayne each held 100 shares in the company, and Bushell and Faith were the company's only directors. The articles provided that in relation to a resolution to remove a director, the shares of the director being removed would carry three votes per share. Bushell and Bayne tabled a resolution to remove Faith from office, but they could only muster 200 votes between them, whereas Faith was able to amass 300 votes (due to the weighted voting rights clause). Despite this, Bushell claimed that Faith had only amassed 100 votes and sought an injunction preventing Faith from acting as a director.

The Companies Act 1948 did not prohibit weighted voting rights clauses and so the clause was valid. Accordingly, the resolution was validly defeated by Faith and Bushell's claim failed.

The final point to note is that s. 168 does not derogate from any other power that may exist to remove a director (s. 168(5)(b)). Accordingly, the company can, via its articles, provide for other methods to remove a director.

Removal under the articles

The second method of removing a director is via a power of removal contained in the articles. The model articles do not contain any other methods of removal, but many companies (especially larger companies) insert a provision in the articles stating that a director will be required to vacate office if all the other directors so require. A consequence of removing a director via such an article provision is that it need not comply with the procedural rules found in s. 168 (*Browne v Panga Pty Ltd* (1995) 120 FLR 34 (Federal Court of Australia)).

6.4 Disqualification

Just as a driver can be disqualified from driving a car, so too can a director be disqualified from acting as a director. The relevant statute is the Company Directors Disqualification Act 1986 (CDDA 1986) which provides that a director can be disqualified on specified grounds.

- Where they are convicted of an indictable offence in connection with the promotion, formation, management, liquidation or striking off of a company, or with the receivership of a company's property, or with their being an administrative receiver of a company (s. 2).
- Where it appears that they have been persistently in default in relation to provisions of the companies legislation requiring any return, account or other document to be filed with, delivered or sent, or notice of any matter to be given, to the Registrar of Companies (s. 3).
- Where they have been found guilty of fraudulent trading under s. 993 of the CA 2006 or other fraud in relation to the company (s. 4).

- Where they have been convicted of a specified summary offence and they have, during the five-year period prior to the conviction, been convicted of similar offences at least three times (s. 5).
- Where they have been convicted of certain indictable offences overseas that involve (i) the promotion, formation, management, liquidation or striking off of a company; (ii) the receivership of a company's property; or (iii) a person being an administrative receiver of the company (s. 5A).
- Where they are or have been a director or shadow director of a company which has at any time become insolvent (whether while they were a director or subsequently), and their conduct as a director of that company (either taken alone or taken together with their conduct as a director/ shadow director of other companies) makes them unfit to be concerned in the management of a company (s. 6).
- Where, in the opinion of the Secretary of State, it is expedient in the public interest that a person who is, or has been, a director or shadow director should be disqualified (s. 8).
- Where they have exercised the requisite influence over a person disqualified under s. 6 (s. 8ZA) or s. 8 (s. 8ZD).
- Where they have breached competition law and their conduct makes them unfit to be concerned in the management of a company (s. 9A).
- Where they have been found liable for fraudulent trading or wrongful trading under IA 1986 (s. 10).
- Where a person is an undischarged bankrupt (s. 11).

Figure 5.1 summarises the grounds for disqualification, whether disqualification is mandatory and the relevant disqualification periods for each ground.

Disqualification orders and undertakings

Once it has been decided that a person should be disqualified, this can be put into effect in one of two methods. Both methods have the same effect – for a specified period, the disqualified person:

- shall not be a director of a company, act as receiver of a company's property or in any way, whether directly or indirectly, be concerned or take part in the promotion, formation or management of a company unless (in each case) he has the leave of the court; and
- shall not act as an insolvency practitioner (CDDA 1986, ss. 1(1) and 1A(1)).

Even though it is called the Company *Directors* Disqualification Act 1986 (italics added), the activities covered under ss. 1 and 1A can cover activities much wider than being a director. For example, a disqualified person could not act as a company secretary.

The first method of disqualification is that the court can issue a disqualification order, which is an order of the court providing that a person is to be disqualified (CDDA 1986, s. 1(1)). However, as a disqualification order is a court order, it can take a considerable amount of time for the case to reach court and for the order

Section	Ground	Disqualification period
2	Conviction of an indictable offence	15 years maximum
3	Persistent breaches of companies legislation	Five years maximum
4	Fraud or breach of duty during winding up	15 years maximum
5	Summary convictions relating to companies legislation	Five years maximum
5A	Conviction of certain offences abroad	15 years maximum
6	Unfitness in an insolvent company	2–15 years
8	Expedient in the public interest	15 years maximum
8ZA	Person instructing unfit director of insolvent company	2–15 years
8ZD	Person instructing unfit director	15 years maximum
9A	Breach of competition law	15 years maximum
10	Participation in fraudulent or wrongful trading under the Insolvency Act 1986	15 years maximum
11	Undischarged bankrupts	While order or undertaking remains in force

Figure 5.1 The grounds for disqualification

to be issued. As it is desirable for disqualification to occur quickly (to prevent the director in question from causing more damage), a second method of disqualification was introduced by the Insolvency Act 2000 – the disqualification undertaking. The Secretary of State can accept from the director in question an undertaking that he will not, for a specified period, engage in the activities set out in ss. 1(1) and 1A(1) above (s. 1A(1)).

Today, the majority of disqualifications occur via a disqualification undertaking, but they are subject to two notable limitations.

- They can only be used in relation to the grounds of disqualification found in ss. 5A, 7, 8, 8ZC, 8ZE or 9A, and if the Secretary of State is of the opinion that the person has engaged in the disqualifying conduct found in those sections.
- The Secretary of State can only accept the undertaking if it appears that an undertaking is 'expedient in the public interest'.

Disqualification orders and undertakings have the same legal force and, if either is breached, a criminal offence will be committed (s. 13). Further, the person in breach will, if he was involved in the management of the company, become personally liable for the debts of that company (s. 15(1)(a)). Personal liability can also be imposed on a person who is involved in the management of a company and acts upon instructions of a person who he knows is either (i) subject to a disqualification order or undertaking; or (ii) is an undischarged bankrupt (s. 15(1)(b)).

A person subject to a disqualification order or undertaking may apply to the court for 'leave to act' – to engage in any acts that are prohibited by the disqualification order or undertaking (s. 17). Such leave is rarely granted, with Arden LJ in *Re Tech Textiles Ltd* [1998] 1 BCLC 259 (Ch) stating that leave to act 'is not to be too freely given. Legislative policy requires the disqualification of unfit directors to minimise the risk of harm to the public, and the Courts must not by granting leave prevent the achievement of this policy.' When leave to act is granted, it is almost always subject to conditions.

Compensation orders and undertakings

Disqualifying a person under the CDDA 1986 may prevent that person from engaging in further wrongdoing, but it does not aid those who have already suffered loss due to such wrongdoing. To remedy this, the CDDA 1986 was amended in 2015 to allow for the courts to make compensation orders, and for the Secretary of State to accept compensation undertakings. A compensation order or undertaking can only be made if two conditions are met, namely:

- the person is subject to a disqualification order or undertaking; and
- the conduct to which the order or undertaking relates has caused loss to one or more creditors of an insolvent company of which the person has at any time been a director (s. 15A(3)).

A compensation order or undertaking will require the disqualified person to pay a specified amount to either (i) the Secretary of State for the benefit of the creditor(s) or class of creditor(s) specified; or (ii) as a contribution to the assets of the company (s. 15B(1) and (2)).

Test yourself 5.4

1. **What are four ways in which a director can vacate office?**
2. **How can a director be removed from office?**
3. **Identify five grounds for the disqualification of a director.**
4. **Explain the distinction between a disqualification order and a disqualification undertaking.**

Chapter summary

- Section 250 of the CA 2006 provides that the term 'director' includes 'any person occupying the position of director, by whatever name known'.
- A *de jure* director is a director who has been validly appointed to the role. A *de facto* director is a person who has not been formally appointed as a director, but who acts as a director.
- Section 251 provides that a shadow director is 'a person in accordance with whose directions or instructions the directors of the company are accustomed to act'.
- An executive director is usually a full-time employee of the company who is involved in the day-to-day management of the company. A non-executive director will be part-time and will not usually be an employee of the company. A non-executive director's role is to contribute to management and to monitor the executive directors. Only the largest companies will tend to have non-executive directors.
- An alternate director is a person who has been appointed to act on a director's behalf (for example, because that director is ill).
- A nominee director is a director appointed to safeguard the interests of another (such as a major creditor or shareholder).
- Companies may appoint directors to specific roles, such as chair or CEO, if their articles so allow.
- The appointment of directors is a matter for the company's articles. The model articles provide that a director can be appointed by an ordinary resolution or by a decision of the directors. Larger companies will conduct appointments through a nomination committee.
- Every company must keep a register of directors, although private companies may elect to keep the required information on the public register maintained by Companies House.
- Who determines directors' pay is a matter for the articles, with the model articles empowering the directors to determine their own pay. Executive pay in larger companies will be determined by a remuneration committee.
- A private company must have at least one director, and a public company must have at least two directors.
- In recent years, board composition has become a notable governance issue, with reports focusing on improving gender and ethnic diversity of FTSE 350 boards.
- A director can vacate office (i) by resigning; (ii) by being removed; (iii) by vacating office in accordance with the articles; and (iv) by being disqualified.

Chapter six
The role of the board

Contents

1. Introduction

This chapter outlines the role of the board. It begins by looking at the overall function of the board before examining the managerial powers of the board, especially how managerial power is divided between the board and the members. The procedures for board meetings are discussed in detail as board meetings are the principal way in which the board exercises its powers, and it is the company secretary's role to ensure that board meetings run smoothly. Although the company secretary is not usually a member of the board, the secretary's role can be of such importance that it is appropriate to discuss the secretary's role alongside the board.

2. The general functions of the board

The various pieces of company law legislation place a number of specific obligations upon directors but the law has very little to say regarding the general role of the board. The UK Corporate Governance Code's statement of the board's purpose is broad enough to apply to all types of company. Principle A states that '[a] successful company is led by an effective and entrepreneurial board, whose function is to promote the long-term sustainable success of the company, generating value for shareholders and contributing to wider society'.

The board's role will differ depending upon the company's size. In a small private company, the directors will likely play a part in all areas of the company's activities and will delegate few, if any, of their managerial powers. The directors will be unable to manage the full breadth of the company's activities in larger companies, and so will delegate significant managerial powers to others (the ability to delegate powers is discussed on page 118).

The result of this is that, in larger companies, much of the day-to-day management is not actually carried out by the board, but is instead carried out by sub-board level managers. The role of the board in such companies is to determine the strategic goals of the company, to put in place adequate governance arrangements and to monitor the activities of the managers to determine if the goals set are being attained.

3. The managerial powers of the board

The law does not set out the managerial powers of the board. These are instead a matter for the company's articles. The power to manage the company is initially vested in the members but it is impractical for the members to manage the company in all but the smallest companies (and the members will likely not wish to be involved in management). It is common for the members to delegate managerial power to the directors. Such delegation is usually extensive, as demonstrated by article 3 of the model articles which states that '[s]ubject to the articles, the directors are responsible for the management of the company's business, for which purpose they may exercise all the powers of the company'. This power is bestowed upon the directors collectively. A single director cannot exercise managerial power on his own (*Mitchell & Hobbs (UK) Ltd v Mill* [1996] 2 BCLC 102 (QB)) unless (i) he is the only director of the company; or (ii) the articles delegate such power to him personally.

Article 3 places a significant amount of power in the hands of directors, but the question is who has the ultimate right to manage the company: the directors or the members. To answer this, we need to look at the division of powers.

3.1 The division of powers

Questions regarding the division of power between the directors and the members rarely arise in small private companies as the directors and members are often the same persons.

The balance of power between the director and members is more relevant in companies where the directors do not control the majority of the company's shares. Most companies will have an article provision similar to article 3 delegating the power of management to the directors. Normally if *A* delegates a power to *B*, then *A* may still exercise that power. However, where the members have delegated managerial power to the directors, then the members lose the right to exercise that power, unless the articles provide otherwise. As Greer LJ stated in *John Shaw and Sons (Salford) Ltd v Shaw* [1935] 2 KB 113 (CA):

> 'If powers of management are vested in the directors, they and they alone can exercise these powers. The only way in which the general body of the shareholders can control the exercise of the powers vested by the articles in the directors is by altering their articles, or, if opportunity arises under the articles, by refusing to re-elect the directors of whose actions they disapprove. They cannot themselves usurp the powers which by the articles

are vested in the directors any more than the directors can usurp the powers vested by the articles in the general body of shareholders.'

The following case demonstrates this.

Case law 6.1

***Automatic Self-Cleansing Filter Syndicate Co Ltd v Cuninghame* [1906] 2 Ch 34 (CA)**

The articles delegated managerial power to the directors, which included the ability to sell the company's property on such terms as they deemed fit. The articles also stated that the shareholders could direct the directors to take action by passing an extraordinary resolution (which required a majority of at least 75%). The shareholders passed an ordinary resolution resolving to sell the company's assets. The director did not believe the sale was in the company's interests and refused to sell the assets in question.

The right to manage the company was vested in the directors and the shareholders could only interfere if the articles so provided. The shareholders had not passed an extraordinary resolution (they had merely passed an ordinary resolution), and so the directors were not compelled to comply with the shareholders' direction and could therefore refuse to sell the assets.

'Subject to the articles'

Article provisions that delegate managerial power to the director are often expressed as being 'subject to the articles'. Provisions can be inserted into the articles that affect the division of power between the directors and the members. In the following case, such a provision served to limit the directors' managerial power by giving specified persons a power of veto.

Case law 6.2

***Salmon v Quin & Axtens Ltd* [1909] 1 Ch 311 (CA)**

The articles provided that general powers of management were vested in the directors, subject to the articles. However, the articles also stated that board resolutions relating to the acquisition of certain properties could be vetoed by two named persons (who happened to be members of the company and its joint managing directors). The board passed a resolution resolving to acquire certain properties, but one of the managing directors exercised his veto. The other directors called an extraordinary general meeting and an ordinary resolution was passed by the members to acquire the properties. The managing director who vetoed the acquisition commenced proceedings to restrain the acquisition.

The power of management vested in the directors was subject to the articles, which gave the claimant a power of veto. The claimant had validly exercised this veto and so the court granted an injunction restraining the company from acquiring the properties.

It is common for a company's articles to provide the members with a power to direct the directors. For example, article 4(1) of the model articles provides that the members may 'by special resolution, direct the directors to take, or refrain from taking, specified action'. In practice, the use of a provision such as article 4(1) is rare. In small companies, it is not usually needed as the directors are often majority shareholders. In larger companies, it is difficult for shareholders to acquire the requisite number of votes. In any event, it is easier to simply remove the directors by passing an ordinary resolution under s. 168.

Reversion of powers

In certain cases, the power of management that the members delegate to the directors can revert back to the members. This usually arises where the directors are unwilling or unable to act, such as:

- where there is no board of directors (*Alexander Ward & Co Ltd v Samyang Navigation Co Ltd* [1975] 1 WLR 673 (HL));
- where the directors refuse to attend board meetings (*Barron v Potter* [1914] 1 Ch 895 (Ch)); or
- where the board cannot achieve quoracy and so cannot make any decisions (*Foster v Foster* [1916] 1 Ch 532 (Ch)).

3.2 Delegation of powers

In many companies, it is desirable (if not essential) for the directors to delegate some of their powers to others. In larger companies, much of the day-to-day managerial work is delegated to executive managers below board level. However, the board does not have the power to delegate its managerial powers to others by default – such delegation is only permissible if the articles allow for it. Given how useful delegation is, most companies will include a provision in their articles that allows the directors to delegate powers to others. Article 5(1) of the model articles provides the directors with wide powers of delegation, stating that:

> '[s]ubject to the articles, the directors may delegate any of the powers which are conferred on them under the articles–
>
> (a) to such person or committee;
> (b) by such means (including by power of attorney);
> (c) to such an extent;
> (d) in relation to such matters or territories; and
> (e) on such terms and conditions;
>
> as they think fit.'

Article 5(2) states that if the directors do delegate their powers to a person, the directors can authorise that person to delegate those powers to other persons (this is known as 'sub-delegation'). Under article 5(3), the directors are free to revoke any delegation of their powers, in whole or in part, or to modify the terms and conditions of the delegation. Delegation of a power does not deprive the board of the ability to continue exercising that power (*Huth v Clarke* (1890) 25 QBD 391 (QB)).

In many companies (especially larger companies), the delegation of powers is important from a governance perspective. For example, as discussed in Chapter 5, it is widely accepted that directors should not determine their own pay in larger companies. Provisions 32 and 33 of the UK Corporate Governance Code recommend that the board should establish a remuneration committee. The board should delegate to this committee responsibility for determining the company's remuneration policy and for setting the remuneration of the chair, executive directors and senior management.

Test yourself 6.1

1. **In whom is managerial power vested?**
2. **What does article 3 of the model articles state?**
3. **To what extent can the members interfere in management?**
4. **Can the directors delegate their managerial powers to others?**

4. Board meetings

The principal method by which directors exercise their managerial powers is by making decisions at board meetings. For obvious reasons, a company with only one director will not engage in board meetings. This is reflected in article 7(2) of the model articles for private companies, which provides that many of the rules relating to board meetings will not apply to a single-director company.

The CA 2006 has almost nothing to say about board meetings, with all the key rules being found in the company's articles. This affords the company a significant amount of flexibility in determining how its board meetings should be run.

4.1 Calling a meeting and notice

The power to call a board meeting is a matter for the company's articles, with the model articles providing that any director may call a board meeting, and such a meeting is called by providing notice of it to the other directors (model articles for private companies, article 9(1); model articles for public companies, article 8(1)–(3)).

The articles will specify the notice requirements. Generally, a failure to provide due notice will invalidate the board meeting (*Young v Ladies Imperial Cub Ltd* [1920] 2 KB 523 (CA)). The model articles (model articles for private companies, article 9(2)-(3); model articles for public companies, article 8(4)-(5)) set out the following notice requirements.

- Notice of a directors' meeting must be given to each director, but it need not be in writing. Companies are, of course, free to stipulate that notice must be provided in a specified way (in writing, for example).
- Notice of a meeting must state:
  - the date and time of the meeting;
  - where the meeting will take place; and
  - if it is expected that directors participating in the meeting will not be in the same place, how it is proposed that they should communicate with each other during the meeting.

The model articles (and most companies' articles) do not state how much notice must be provided. In the event of a dispute, this will depend upon the circumstances. The courts have held that notice periods can be very short – for example, in *Browne v La Trinidad* (1887) 37 ChD 1 (CA), the directors were provided with ten minutes notice and this was held to be sufficient and reasonable on the facts. Factors include how urgent the matter is and the usual practice of the board.

4.2 Quorum

quorum
A minimum number of qualifying persons required to be present in order to conduct business.

A board meeting can only transact business and make decisions if a **quorum** is present. What constitutes a quorum is a matter for the company's articles. If the articles are silent, a majority of directors will be required to attend (*York Tramways Co Ltd v Willow* (1882) 2 QBD 685 (CA)). The model articles provide that the quorum for a board meeting can be determined by a decision of the directors but it must not be less than two. If the directors have not decided what constitutes a quorum, it will be two (model articles for private companies, article 11(2); model articles for public companies, article 10(2)). This clearly will not apply to a single-director company (model articles for private companies, article 7(2)).

Not all directors present at a meeting will count towards the quorum – for example, if a director is not entitled to vote on a matter to be decided at a board meeting (e.g. because he has an interest that conflicts with that of the company), he will normally not count towards the quorum (*Re Greymouth Point Elizabeth Railway and Coal Co Ltd* [1904] 1 Ch 32 (Ch); model articles for private companies, article 14(1); model articles for public companies, article 16(1)).

An inquorate meeting cannot conduct any business (*Faure Electric Accumulator Co Ltd v Phillipart* (1888) 58 LT 525 (QB)) unless the articles provide otherwise (*Re Scottish Petroleum Co (No 2)* (1883) 23 ChD 413 (CA)).

4.3 Board decisions

How the board makes decisions at a meeting is a matter for the company's articles, with the model articles specifying different rules for private and public companies. Generally, if the votes for and against are equal, the decision is lost

(*Moodie v W&J Shepherd (Bookbinders) Ltd* [1949] 2 All ER 1044 (HL)). It is common for the articles to provide a director (usually the chair) with a casting vote (model articles for private companies, article 13(1); model articles for public companies, article 14(1)).

Private companies

Article 7(1) of the model articles for private companies provides that any decision of the directors must either be (i) a majority decision at a meeting; or (ii) a decision taken in accordance with article 8.

Articles 8(1) and (3) provide that a decision of the directors can be taken without a board meeting if all the directors eligible to vote on the matter indicate to each other, by any means, that they share a common view on the matter. This decision may take the form of a resolution in writing, copies of which have been signed by each director eligible to vote and in which each eligible director indicates his agreement (article 8(2)). Note that the article 8 procedure cannot be used if the eligible directors could not form a quorum had the decision been taken at a meeting (article 8(4)).

Public companies

Article 13 of the model articles for public companies provides that, subject to the articles:

- a decision is taken at a board meeting by a majority of the votes of participating directors; and
- each director participating in a board meeting has one vote.

Decisions may also be taken without a meeting via a directors' written resolution (not to be confused with written resolutions of the company). Any director may propose that a decision be taken by a directors' written resolution (article 17(1)) by giving notice of the proposed resolution to the other directors (article 17(3)). A proposed directors' written resolution will be adopted if all the directors entitled to vote on the matter sign a copy of the resolution (article 18(1)) and adoption of the resolution will be regarded as if the decision was taken at a directors' meeting (article 18(3)).

4.4 Minutes

One of the few areas regarding board meetings where the CA 2006 does establish rules is in relation to the keeping of **minutes**. The Act provides that every company must record all minutes of proceedings at directors' meetings (s. 248(1)) and must keep these records for at least 10 years from the date of the meeting (s. 248(2)). Failure to keep such minutes is a criminal offence (s. 248(3)), although decisions taken at the relevant meeting will be unaffected (*Re North Hallenbeagle Mining Co* (1866-67) LR 2 Ch App 321).

minutes
A written account providing records of a meeting.

The model articles also state that records must be kept, for a period of 10 years, of:

- every unanimous decision or majority decision taken by the directors (model articles for private companies, article 15); and

- every directors' written resolution (model articles for public companies, article 18(4)).

Test yourself 6.2

1. **Who has the power to call a board meeting?**
2. **In relation to board meetings, what constitutes a quorum?**
3. **How are board decisions taken in private companies and public companies?**
4. **For how long must a company keep minutes of its board meetings?**

5. The company secretary

A company secretary is not part of the board (unless the secretary is also a director), but they do attend board meetings. They are so vital to the effective operation of the board that it is appropriate to discuss the role of the company secretary alongside that of the board. A company secretary is an officer of the company (CA 2006, s. 1121(2)), so can face liability for breach of many company law statutory provisions.

5.1 Appointment and qualifications

A private company is not required to appoint a company secretary unless its articles state otherwise (CA 2006, s. 270(1)), but it may do so if it wishes. If a private company does not appoint a secretary, then:

- anything authorised or required to be sent to the secretary may be authorised or sent to the company itself (CA 2006, s. 270(3)(a)); and
- anything else required or authorised to be done by the secretary may be done by a director or a person authorised by the directors (s. 270(3)(b)).

A public company must appoint a company secretary (CA 2006, s. 271) and may have more than one secretary (who will be known as 'joint secretaries'). Under s. 273, the directors of a public company are under a duty to take all reasonable steps to ensure that the secretary (or each joint secretary) has the requisite knowledge and experience, and has one or more of the following qualifications:

- has acted as a secretary of a public company for at least three of the previous five years;
- is a member of a specific body set out in s. 273(3) (such as the Institute of Chartered Secretaries and Administrators or the Institute of Chartered Accountants of England and Wales);
- is a barrister, advocate or solicitor; or

- is a person who, by virtue of his holding or having held any other position or his being a member of any other body, appears to the directors to be capable of discharging the functions of company secretary.

If a public company does not appoint a secretary, the Secretary of State can direct the company to appoint a secretary. Failure to comply with this direction is a criminal offence (s. 272).

A company must keep a register of its secretaries (CA 2006, s. 275(1)), although a private company can elect to keep details of its secretaries on the public register at Companies House (ss. 274A, 279A–79E). Failure to keep a register when required to do so is a criminal offence (s. 275(6)).

5.2 Role and powers

The role of the secretary is not set out in the law, nor are there any activities that the secretary must carry out under the CA 2006 (although there are plenty that the secretary will carry out).

The company secretary is 'an officer of the company with extensive duties and responsibilities' (*Panorama Developments (Guildford) Ltd v Fidelis Furnishing Fabrics Ltd* [1971] 2 QB 711 (CA)). As s. 1173(1) of the CA 2006 expressly states that the secretary is an officer of the company, it follows that a secretary can be liable for any legal breach under which an officer can be held liable (for example, many provisions of the CA 2006 provide that liability for breach can be imposed on an officer of the company).

The precise role of the secretary will vary from company to company but, in many companies, the secretary will be 'the chief administrative officer of the company' (*Panorama Developments (Guildford) Ltd v Fidelis Furnishing Fabrics Ltd* [1971] 2 QB 711 (CA)). The secretary will engage in tasks such as:

- ensuring that the company's filing and disclosure requirements are fulfilled;
- preparing the agenda and minutes of board meetings and general meetings;
- ensuring that board meetings and general meetings are conducted in accordance with the law and the company's articles;
- maintaining the company's books and statutory registers;
- advising on the preparation and publication of annual reports and accounts, and other financial disclosures; and
- advising on compliance with legal requirements and best practice recommendations.

This focus on administrative matters is reflected in the authority that the secretary has as an agent of the company (agency is discussed in Chapter 4). An agent may be given express authority to engage in certain acts and, as the following case establishes, a secretary also has apparent authority to bind the company in relation to administrative matters.

Case law 6.3

***Panorama Developments (Guildford) Ltd v Fidelis Furnishing Fabrics Ltd* [1971] 2 QB 711 (CA)**

Using the company's notepaper, its company secretary hired a number of cars, stating that they would be used to transport the company's customers. This was not true and the secretary used the cars for personal use. The company refused to pay for the cars on the ground that the secretary did not have the authority to hire the cars.

Lord Denning MR stated that the company secretary:

> **'is an officer of the company with extensive duties and responsibilities.... He is no longer a mere clerk. He regularly makes representations on behalf of the company and enters into contracts on its behalf which come within the day-to-day running of the company's business. So much so that he may be regarded as held out as having authority to do such things on behalf of the company. He is certainly entitled to sign contracts connected with the administrative side of a company's affairs, such as employing staff, and ordering cars, and so forth. All such matters now come within the ostensible authority of a company's secretary.'**

Applying this, the court held that the hiring of cars was an administrative matter and so the secretary had apparent authority to enter into the contract on behalf of the company, which was therefore required to pay the hire charges.

Stop and think 6.1

In *Panorama*, Lord Denning MR noted that the historic perception of a secretary as a 'mere servant' was no longer correct, and that the secretary's role had increased in importance. However, Lord Denning MR still focused on the secretary's role as being primarily administrative. Do you think that this is still an accurate description of the secretary's role or do you think that the secretary's role is not purely administrative?

In larger companies, the role of the company secretary is often not merely administrative and will include governance matters. This is reflected in the UK Corporate Governance Code, with Provision 16 stating that '[a]ll directors should have access to the advice of the company secretary, who is responsible for advising the board on all governance matters'.

Test yourself 6.3

1. **Is a company required to appoint a company secretary?**
2. **What is the role of a company secretary?**
3. **What authority does a company secretary have as an agent?**

Chapter summary

- The power to manage the company is, by default, vested in the members, but in most companies, the members delegate managerial power to the directors via the articles.
- If the articles confer managerial power upon the directors, the members cannot usually interfere with such powers unless the articles state otherwise.
- In some cases (such as where the board is deadlocked or cannot achieve quoracy), the directors' powers of management can revert back to the members.
- The directors are able to delegate their powers only if the articles so provide.
- The rules by which board meetings are run is a matter for the company's articles.
- A board meeting can only conduct business and make decisions if a quorum is present. A quorum is the minimum number of directors required to be present, and this is a matter for the company's articles.
- Minutes of board meetings must be kept for at least 10 years.
- A public company must appoint a suitable, knowledgeable and qualified company secretary. A private company need not appoint a company secretary but may do so if it wishes.
- The company secretary is an agent of the company and has apparent authority to bind the company in relation to administrative matters.

Chapter seven
Directors' duties

Contents

1. Introduction

This chapter outlines the statutory duties that are placed upon directors under Part 10 of the CA 2006. A significant amount of power is concentrated in the directors, and there is a danger that the directors will use this power in a way that benefits themselves (often at the company's expense). One of the principal ways that such conduct is discouraged is by subjecting directors to a range of general duties, as well as requiring member approval for certain transactions involving directors.

2. The general duties

Until the CA 2006, the law relating to directors' duties was primarily found in case law spanning back over 150 years. To improve accessibility and to bring certain duties up to date, it was decided that the law relating to directors' duties would be partially **codified** and so the directors' duties are now found in ss. 170–187 of the CA 2006.

codification
The placing of law into statute.

The codified duties are referred to as 'the general duties', with s. 170(3) stating that these duties are 'based on certain common law rules and equitable principles as they apply in relation to directors and have effect in place of those rules and principles as regards the duties owed to a company by a director'.

Many of the general duties remain identical or similar to their common law predecessors. The case law that the common law duties were based upon continues to apply to the codified successors – as s. 170(4) states, 'regard shall be had to the corresponding common law rules and equitable principles in interpreting and applying the general duties'.

This lack of complete codification also applies to the remedies for breach of duty. The Companies Act 2006 does not state what the remedies are for breach of the general duties, with s. 178(1) merely stating that the consequences of breaching the general duties 'are the same as would apply if the corresponding common law rule or equitable principle applied'.

Stop and think 7.1

As the codification of directors' duties in only partial and pre-CA 2006 case law will continue to apply, do you think the codification of the general duties improves accessibility to a significant degree? Should the CA 2006 have sought to fully codify directors' duties?

Section 179 provides that '[e]xcept as otherwise provided, more than one of the general duties may apply in any given case'. The actions of a director may result in several general duties being breached, as the following example demonstrates.

Case study 7.1

The articles of X-Corp Ltd provide that a director of the company may enter into contracts on behalf of the company, providing that the value of the contract does not exceed £1,000. Contracts worth over £1,000 may only be approved by a resolution of the members.

Ellen, a director of X-Corp, enters into a £5,000 supply contract with Y-Corp plc. She does not disclose that she is the majority shareholder of Y-Corp and that she was paid £500 commission upon the contract being entered into.

In this situation, Ellen may have breached three duties:

- **in breaching the articles (by failing to obtain member approval), she would likely have breached the s. 171 duty to act within the company's constitution;**
- **as she is a shareholder of Y-Corp, she has a conflict of interest which could amount to a breach of the s. 175 duty to avoid conflicts of interest; and**
- **the receipt of the £500 commission payment could be in breach of the s. 176 duty not to accept third-party benefits.**

2.1 Scope

In determining the scope of the general duties, two questions must be answered.

1. To whom are the general duties owed?
2. To whom do the general duties apply?

Section 170(1) states that the general duties are owed by a director of a company to the company, meaning that:

- the directors do not owe their general duties to other persons (e.g. the members, employees, creditors etc.); and
- the only persons who can commence proceedings for breach of duty are the company itself and those persons who are empowered to bring claims on the company's behalf (e.g. the directors, the members via derivative claim).

The duties are owed by 'a director of the company', but this is subject to two caveats. First, the applicable general duty will also apply to a shadow director if it is capable of applying to a shadow director (s. 170(5)). Second, the duties in ss. 175 and 176 can also apply to former directors of a company (s. 170(2)).

2.2 Duty to act within powers

Section 171 effectively imposes two duties upon directors:

1. a duty to act in accordance with the company's constitution; and
2. a duty to only exercise powers for the purposes for which they are conferred.

Duty to act in accordance with the constitution
Section 171(a) provides that a director of a company must act in accordance with the company's constitution. The constitution (notably the articles) may place limits upon the directors' powers. If a director breaches the constitution, any contracts resulting from it will remain valid, but the director will be in breach of the s. 171(a) duty. A director in breach will be required to account for any gains made, or compensate the company for any losses it sustained, as a result of the breach.

Duty to exercise powers for the purposes for which they are conferred
Section 171(b) provides that a director must only exercise his powers for the purposes for which they are conferred (at common law, this was known as the 'proper purpose' duty). The test for determining whether a breach of s. 171(b) has occurred was set out by Lord Wilberforce in *Howard Smith Ltd v Ampol Petroleum Ltd* [1974] AC 821 (PC):

> 'it is necessary to start with a consideration of the power whose exercise is in question... Having ascertained, on a fair view, the nature of this power, and having defined as can best be done in the light of modern conditions the, or some, limits within which it may be exercised, it is then necessary for the court, if a particular exercise of it is challenged, to examine the substantial purpose for which it was exercised, and to reach a conclusion whether that purpose was proper or not.'

In *Extrasure Travel Insurances Ltd v Scattergood* [2003] 1 BCLC 598 (Ch), the court stated that this test involves four steps. First, the court will determine what power is being exercised. The s. 171(b) duty applies to any power granted to a director, but the bulk of the case law relates to the directors' power to allot shares on behalf of the company.

Second, the court will determine the proper purpose for which that power was delegated to the directors, which will involve the court determining 'the nature of the power [and] in light of modern conditions the, or some, limits within which it may be exercised'. (*Howard Smith Ltd v Ampol Petroleum Ltd* [1974] AC 821 (PC)).

Third, the court will determine the substantial purpose for which the power was exercised. Fourth, the court will determine if that purpose was proper. The reason why the courts focus on the substantial purpose is because the directors often exercise their powers for multiple purposes, with some being proper and others being improper. The courts will not seek to balance the proper and improper purposes. As the following case shows, it is the propriety of the substantial or dominant purpose that will determine if a breach of duty has occurred. If the substantial purpose is proper, no breach of s. 171(b) will occur, even if subservient improper purposes exist, or vice versa.

Case law 7.1

***Howard Smith Ltd v Ampol Petroleum Ltd* [1974] AC 821 (PC)**

A company (Miller) was subject to two rival takeover bids. Miller's board wanted the higher bid of Howard Smith Ltd (HS) to succeed, but this could not occur as the other bidder, Ampol, was Miller's majority shareholder and so could frustrate HS's bid. To prevent Ampol from frustrating HS's bid, the directors on Miller caused Miller to allot shares to HS. The purpose of the allotment was twofold:

1. **it would provide Miller with capital to build two oil tankers; and**
2. **it would convert Ampol's majority shareholding into a minority holding.**

Ampol commenced proceedings, on the ground that the allotment of shares to HS was for an improper purpose.

Lord Wilberforce stated that the substantial purpose of the allotment was to 'dilute the majority voting power held by Ampol... so as to enable a then minority of shareholders to sell their shares more advantageously'. As to whether this purpose was proper or improper, he stated that 'an issue of shares purely for the purpose of creating voting power has repeatedly been condemned'. Miller's directors were held to be in breach of duty and the share allotment was set aside.

However, the 'substantial purpose' approach was subject to criticism by Lord Sumption in *Eclairs Group Ltd v JKX Oil & Gas plc* [2015] UKSC 71, who stated that s. 171(b) provides that a director must only exercise his powers for the purposes for which they are conferred. Lord Sumption stated that the use of the word 'only' meant that the s. 171(b) duty would be breached if a director acted based on any improper purpose. Ultimately, Lord Sumption's criticism was *obiter*; although Lord Hodge did agree with Lord Sumption's view, Lord Mance did not and the other two Justices expressed no opinion on the matter. For now, the 'substantial purpose' approach of *Howard Smith* remains.

Any agreement entered into in breach of the s. 171(b) duty is voidable at the company's instance (*Howard Smith Ltd v Ampol Petroleum Ltd* [1974] AC 821 (PC)). It can be enforced against the company by a third party if the director had the authority to enter into it (*Criterion Properties plc v Stratford UK Properties LLC* [2004] UKHL 28). In addition, a director in breach may be required to account for any gains made, or compensate the company for any losses sustained, due to the breach (*Extrasure Travel Insurances Ltd v Scattergood* [2003] 1 BCLC 598 (Ch)).

2.3 Duty to promote the success of the company

Prior to the enactment of the CA 2006, directors were under a duty to act *bona fide* in the interests of the company (*Re Smith and Fawcett Ltd* [1942] Ch 304 (CA)). This duty has now been replaced by the duty in s. 172(1), which provides that '[a] director of a company must act in the way he considers, in good faith, would be most likely to promote the success of the company for the benefit of its members as a whole'.

The duty found in s. 172 is a broad one and can impact on the other general duties. One controversial way in which the s. 172 duty impacts upon the other general duties is demonstrated in the following example.

Case study 7.2

X-Corp Ltd has three directors: Karl, Katie and Allison. Karl has an interest in a proposed transaction involving X-Corp and a third party, but he has not disclosed this interest. He also knows that Katie also has the same interest and she has not disclosed it either. The company enters into the transaction meaning that both Karl and Katie have breached the duty in s. 177 and, if they do not declare their interest as soon as is reasonably practicable, they will be in breach of s. 182 too. Karl is aware that both he and Katie are in breach of duty.

The question is whether Karl's failure to disclose the breaches of duty is, in itself, a breach of the s. 172 duty. The answer appears to be yes. The courts have held that a director is under a duty to disclose his own breaches of duty (*Item Software (UK) Ltd v Fassihi* [2004] EWCA Civ 1244) and those of his fellow directors (*British Midland Tool Ltd v Midland International Tooling Ltd* [2003] EWHC 466 (Ch)) if he honestly believes that it is in the company's interests to know about the breaches.

Is the duty subjective or objective?

Section 172(1) provides that a director must act *in a way he considers, in good faith*, would be most likely to promote the success of the company. The italicised words here indicate that the duty is subjective, meaning that 'the question is whether the director honestly believed that his act or omission was in the interests of the company. The issue is as to the director's state of mind' (*Regentcrest plc v Cohen* [2001] BCC 494 (Ch)). This was confirmed in *Extrasure Travel Insurance Ltd v Scattergood* [2003] 1 BCLC 598 (Ch), where the court held that, as long as the decision of the directors was honest, no breach of duty will arise even if that decision was unreasonable.

A subjective approach is, however, only of use if the director actually considered whether his actions promoted the success of the company. If the director did not even consider this, then the approach to determining if s. 172 has been breached will cease to be subjective and an objective approach will be used.

Case law 7.2

***Charterbridge Corporation Ltd v Lloyds Bank Ltd* [1970] Ch 62 (Ch)**

This case concerned a group of companies. The board of one of the subsidiaries in the group entered into an agreement with a bank, under which the subsidiary would guarantee the indebtedness of all the other companies in the group. A dispute arose, and it was argued that the agreement between the subsidiary and the bank was invalid as the subsidiary's directors had breached the common law predecessor to s. 172.

Pennycuick J concluded that the directors of the subsidiary company did not consider how the agreement would affect the subsidiary – instead, they considered only how the agreement would affect the corporate group. A subjective test was therefore of no use: instead, the test to apply would be 'whether an intelligent and honest man in the position of a director of the company concerned, could, in the whole of the existing circumstances, have reasonably believed that the transactions were for the benefit of the company'. Based on this, the court held that no breach of duty had occurred.

Stop and think 7.2

Do you agree that an objective approach should be used in such cases? If a director does not consider at all whether their actions promote the success of the company, then could it be argued that this in itself is a breach of the s. 172 duty?

'The success of the company'

The directors must promote the success of the company. It is clear that the phrase 'the company' refers to the legal entity. What is not so clear is how the 'success' of the company is to be determined, as the Act provides no guidance. Although most companies will measure success in financial terms, the word 'success' can refer to non-financial gains too. It should not be assumed that the directors comply with the s. 172 duty simply by trying to maximise profits.

What amounts to success will depend on a wide array of factors, including what the company itself regards as success. To that end, companies are free to insert provisions into their articles specifying what the success model of the company will be (although very few companies do this).

'The benefit of its members as a whole'

The directors must promote the success of the company for the benefit of its members as a whole. Usually, the interests of the company and its members will align, but what happens if the interests of the company and its members conflict? The courts have held that where the interests of the company conflict with the interests of part of the company's membership, then the directors will not breach s. 172 if they favour the company's interests (*Mutual Life Insurance Co of New York v Rank Organisation Ltd* [1985] BCLC 11 (Ch)). No authority exists on whether the directors can prioritise the interests of the company over all of its members.

The s. 172(1) factors

When acting in a way that promotes the success of the company for the benefit of its members as a whole, the directors must have regard (amongst other matters) to a range of factors specified in s. 172(1):

1. the likely consequences of any decision in the long term;
2. the interests of the company's employees;
3. the need to foster the company's business relationships with suppliers, customers and others;
4. the impact of the company's operations on the community and the environment;
5. the desirability of the company maintaining a reputation for high standards of business conduct; and
6. the need to act fairly as between members of the company.

The inclusion of these factors in s. 172(1) was designed to give effect to the 'enlightened shareholder value' approach, which argues that long-term financial gain is best achieved if the company takes into account the interests of wider stakeholder groups in addition to the interests of its members. However, directors need only 'have regard' to these factors. Lord Goldsmith made three points regarding this phrase during the passage of the Companies Bill (HL Deb, 9 May 2006, vol 681, cols 845-846):

- the requirement to have regard to the s. 172(1) factors is subordinate to the principal duty to promote the success of the company for the benefit of its members as a whole;
- a director must give 'such consideration to the factors identified as is necessary for the decision that he has to take, and no more than that'; and
- where there are conflicting courses of action, or where the s. 172(1) factors compete, the course of action to be taken is a matter for the director's 'good faith business judgment'.

It will be noted that the company's creditors are not expressly mentioned in the s. 172(1) list of stakeholders (although certain persons in the list can be creditors, such as suppliers and customers). Instead, s. 172(3) provides that the s. 172 duty has effect subject to any enactment or rule of law requiring directors to consider or act in the interests of the company's creditors in certain circumstances. In a number of pre-CA 2006 cases, the courts had held that, as the company nears insolvency, the interests of the company's creditors become more pressing and can even eclipse those of the members. As Nourse J stated in *Brady v Brady* [1987] 3 BCC 535 (CA), where the company is 'both going and solvent, first and foremost come the shareholders... Conversely, where the company is insolvent, or even doubtfully solvent, the interests of the company are in reality the interests of the existing creditors alone.'

It is clear that the directors are under a duty to consider the creditors' interests, but it is not clear when this duty arises. In some cases (e.g. *BTI 2014 LLC v Sequana SA* [2016] EWHC 1686 (Ch)), the test adopted by the court is based on how close the company is to insolvency, whereas in other cases (e.g. *Re HLC Environmental Projects Ltd* [2013] EWHC 2876 (Ch)), the court adopted a test based on whether the company could pay its debts. Judicial clarification is required.

A large company must include, within its strategic report, a 'section 172(1) statement' that sets out how the company has had regard to the s. 172(1) factors (discussed on p. 278).

Remedies
An agreement in breach of the s. 172 duty is voidable at the company's instance. If a breach of the s. 172 duty causes the company loss, the director in breach may be required to compensate the company (*Extrasure Travel Insurances Ltd v Scattergood* [2003] 1 BCLC 598 (Ch)).

Test yourself 7.1

1. **Is the s. 172 duty subjective or objective?**
2. **Can the directors prioritise the interests of the company over the interests of its members?**
3. **Identify the six factors listed in s. 172(1) that the directors must have regard to.**
4. **What are the remedies for a breach of the s. 172 duty?**

2.4 Duty to exercise independent judgment

The common law has long provided that directors should not fetter their discretion when exercising their powers. This duty has now been replaced by the duty in s. 173, which provides that a director of a company must exercise independent judgment (s. 173(1)).

Exceptions
Section 173(2) establishes two instances where the s. 173 duty will not be breached. First, no breach will occur where a director acts in accordance with an agreement duly entered into by the company that restricts the future exercise of discretion by its directors (s. 173(2)(a)). This is largely a codification of a common law principle that provided that the directors could fetter their discretion if they believed it was in the company's interests. The following case provides an example of this.

Case law 7.3

***Fulham Football Club Ltd v Cabra Estates plc* [1992] BCC 863 (CA)**

A company (Vincenza) owned the freehold to a stadium that it wished to redevelop. The stadium was home to Fulham Football Club (the Club) and the redevelopment work would require the Club to relocate. The local council did not want this to happen and so it refused planning permission for the redevelopment. In order to convince the council, Vincenza entered into an agreement with the directors of Fulham Football Club Ltd (Fulham), under which the Club would receive payments in return for Fulham's directors agreeing to support the redevelopment. The Club later changed its mind and wished to remain at the stadium, and so it argued that the agreement was invalid as it involved the directors of Fulham fettering their discretion by agreeing to support the redevelopment scheme.

Neill LJ stated that:

> **'it does not follow from that proposition that directors can never make a contract by which they bind themselves to the future exercise of their powers in a particular manner, even though the contract taken as a whole is manifestly for the benefit of the company. Such a rule could well prevent companies from entering into contracts which were commercially beneficial to them.'**

Here, the directors of Fulham honestly believed that the agreement was in Fulham's interests and it did indeed confer significant benefits upon Fulham. The court held that the duty had not been breached and the agreement between Vincenza and Fulham was valid.

Second, no breach of duty will occur where the director acts in a way that is authorised by the company's constitution (s. 173(2)(b)). So, for example, if the articles provide that a nominee director must follow the instructions of the person who nominated him, then no breach of the s. 173 duty will occur if the nominee director follows those instructions (*Scottish Cooperative Wholesale Society Ltd v Meyer* [1959] AC 324 (HL)). However, following such instructions will not absolve a director from a breach of the other general duties, notably the duties in ss. 172 and 174.

Remedies
Any agreement entered into in breach of s. 173 is voidable at the company's instance. Those directors in breach may be required to account for any gains made or compensate the company for any losses sustained.

2.5 Duty to exercise reasonable care, skill and diligence

Section 174(1) of the CA 2006 provides that '[a] director of a company must exercise reasonable care, skill and diligence'. In determining whether a director has breached the s. 174 duty, the principal question is what standard of care directors are required to meet.

The standard of care
Section 174(2) states that the care, skill and diligence expected of a director is that which would be exercised by a reasonably diligent person with:

(a) the general knowledge, skill, and experience that may reasonably be expected of a person carrying out the functions carried out by the director in relation to the company (the objective test); and

(b) the general knowledge, skill, and experience that the director has (the subjective test).

The standard established by s. 174(2) differs from the prior common law standard. The prior common law duty provided that '[a] director need not exhibit in the performance of his duties a greater degree of skill than may reasonably be expected from a person of his knowledge and experience' (*Re City Equitable Fire Insurance Co Ltd* [1925] Ch 407 (CA) (Romer J)). This standard was clearly subjective as it was based on the skill and knowledge that the director actually had. A director with little skill or knowledge was subject to a low standard of care (see e.g. *Re Brazilian Rubber Plantations and Estates Ltd* [1911] 1 Ch 425 (Ch)). The s. 174(2) standard contains an objective and a subjective standard.

- Section 174(2)(a) above imposes an objective standard based on the skill, care and diligence that may reasonably be expected of a director. It does take into account the functions of the director, so the director of a one-person small private company would likely be subject to a different standard to the CEO of a FTSE 100 company. This objective standard essentially lays down a minimum standard that all directors must meet.
- Section 174(2)(b) imposes a subjective standard based on the knowledge, skill and experience that the director actually has. It will only apply where the director has some skill, qualification or experience that merits raising the standard expected of him, for example, a finance director will be expected to have a higher degree of skill and knowledge in relation to financial matters (*Re Brian D Pierson (Contractors) Ltd* [2001] 1 BCLC 275 (Ch)). The subjective standard cannot be used to lower the standard of care expected of the director below the objective minimum in s. 174(2)(a).

Section 174(2) sets out the standard of care but s. 174 provides no guidance on how that standard should be applied. Fortunately, the courts have sought to lay down guidance, with the leading case being *Re Barings plc (No 5)* [1999] 1 BCLC 433 (Ch), one of many arising out of the collapse of Barings Bank following the unlawful activities of the rogue trader Nick Leeson. In this case, Jonathan Parker J laid down several principles, which were affirmed when the case reached the Court of Appeal (*Re Barings Bank plc (No 5)* [2001] BCC 273 (CA)). Before looking at these principles, Jonathan Parker J noted that such principles may not apply to all cases as '[t]he extent of the duty, and the question whether it has been discharged, must depend on the facts of each particular case'.

The first principle set out by Jonathan Parker J was that:

> '[d]irectors have, both collectively and individually, a continuing duty to acquire and maintain a sufficient knowledge and understanding of the company's business to enable them properly to discharge their duties as directors.'

This is backed up by the FRC's 2018 Guidance on Board Effectiveness, which states that the chairman should ensure that 'all directors continually update their skills, knowledge and familiarity with the company to fulfil their role both on the board and committees' (para 61). In order to acquire such knowledge, the directors may need to rely on others (such as professional advisers, employees within the company and so on). Where the directors are provided with inaccurate information, this may result in a director not being in breach of the s. 174 duty. However, a breach will not be avoided if the director knew or ought to have known that the information was inaccurate (*Re Queens Moat Houses plc* [2004] EWHC 1730 (Ch)).

The second principle is that:

> '[w]hilst directors are entitled (subject to the articles of association of the company) to delegate particular functions to those below them in the management chain, and to trust their competence and integrity to a reasonable extent, the exercise of the power of delegation does not absolve a director from the duty to supervise the discharge of the delegated functions.'

Generally, a director will not breach s. 174 if he delegates a function to another person and that person performs that function unlawfully or with a lack of skill and care (*Dovey v Corey* [1901] AC 477 (HL)). However, this is subject to several exceptions.

- The directors must exercise reasonable skill and care when deciding to whom their functions are delegated. If they fail to do so, and the delegated functions are performed unlawfully or without due skill and care, the directors could be in breach of the s. 174 duty.
- As Jonathan Parker J stated above, the directors are required to supervise those persons to whom they have delegated their powers. A failure to supervise such persons can result in a breach of the s. 174 duty.
- Although a director can delegate functions, he cannot delegate so many of them that he ends up taking little or no part in the running of the

company. A director who is inactive will almost certainly be in breach of the s. 174 duty (*Dorchester Finance Co Ltd v Stebbing* [1989] BCLC 498 (Ch)).

Remedies
A director will be required to compensate the company for any loss it sustains due to his breach of the s. 174 duty.

Test yourself 7.2

1. **How does the standard of care in s. 174 differ from its common law predecessor?**
2. **When will the subjective element of the s. 174 duty apply?**
3. **If a director delegates one of his functions to another person, and that person does not perform with the requisite skill and care, will the director be in breach of the s. 174 duty?**
4. **What is the remedy for a breach of the s. 174 duty?**

2.6 Duty to avoid conflicts of interest

Section 175(1) provides that a director 'must avoid a situation in which he has, or can have, a direct or indirect interest that conflicts, or possibly may conflict, with the interests of the company'.

When will a conflict arise?
The key question is what sort of interest will constitute a conflict. Section 175 provides limited guidance on what does and does not amount to a conflict.

- The s. 175 duty does not apply to a conflict that arises in relation to a transaction or arrangement with the company itself (s. 175(3)). Such conflicts are covered by ss. 177 and 182. Accordingly, s. 175 applies to conflicts that arise from a transaction or arrangement with a third party.
- The s. 175 duty will not be infringed where the situation cannot reasonably be regarded as likely to give rise to a conflict of interest (s. 175(4)(a)).
- References to a conflict of interest in s. 175 include a conflict of interest and duty and a conflict of duties (s. 175(7)).

Perhaps the key piece of statutory guidance is found in s. 175(2), which states that the s. 175 duty 'applies in particular to the exploitation of any property, information or opportunity (and it is immaterial whether the company could take advantage of the property, information or opportunity)'. Many cases involving the s. 175 duty and its common law predecessor involve a director who has personally exploited information or an opportunity that could rightfully be regarded as belonging to the company. A range of case law principles have been developed that are often referred to as 'the corporate opportunity doctrine'.

Section 175(2) expressly states that the s. 175 duty applies even where the company cannot take advantage of the property, information or opportunity in question (for an example of this, see *Regal (Hastings) Ltd v Gulliver* [1967] 2 AC 134 (HL)). As the following case demonstrates, this is also the case where the company could take advantage of the property, information or opportunity, but chose not to.

Case law 7.4

***Bhullar v Bhullar* [2003] EWCA Civ 424**

A company that let commercial properties was run by the families of two brothers (M and S). Relations broke down between the two families and it was decided that the families would go their separate ways. In order to more easily divide the company's assets among the two families, the directors from M's family proposed that the company should not acquire any more properties, and the directors from S's family agreed.

A short time later, by chance and not while acting in the course of the company's business, a director from S's family discovered a piece of property close to a piece of property owned by the company. Through another company he controlled, S acquired this property. M was not informed of this acquisition, but later found out about it and commenced proceedings against S.

Jonathan Parker LJ stated that:

> **'the relevant question ... is not whether the party to whom the duty is owed ... had some kind of beneficial interest in the opportunity: in my judgment that would be too formalistic and restrictive an approach. Rather, the question is simply whether the fiduciary's exploitation of the opportunity is such as to attract the application of the rule.'**

Applying this, the court held that even though S had not acquired the property while acting for the company, he did have a duty to inform the company of the opportunity so that it could decide whether to acquire the property or not. By failing to do so, the s. 175 duty had been breached. The fact that the company had agreed not to acquire any more properties was irrelevant.

Stop and think 7.3

Do you agree with the strict approach evidenced in *Bhullar*? Do you think that, once it had been agreed that the company would not acquire any properties, the directors of the company should have been free to acquire the property themselves?

An obvious example of a situation where a director could exploit information or an opportunity belonging to a company is where that director is also a director of a rival company. Directors are free to sit on the boards of multiple companies (providing it is not prohibited by the articles, or the director's service contract or letter of appointment), but one would imagine that a director of one company could not also sit on the board of a rival company due to the conflict this would present. Surprisingly, there is no such rule and a director is generally free to sit on the board of a rival company (*London and Mashonaland Exploration Co Ltd v New Mashonaland Exploration Co Ltd* [1891] WN 165). However, in the following case, the court appeared to argue that this was not a general rule, and whether such a director is acting in breach of duty will depend upon the facts.

Case law 7.5

In Plus Group Ltd v Pyke **[2002] EWCA Civ 370**

Pyke suffered a stroke and so could not continue as director (although he did not vacate office). The company (IPG) was therefore managed solely by another director, Plank. Pyke recovered, but Plank would not allow him to be involved in IPG's management. Pyke set up a rival company and obtained contracts from IPG's main customer. Some ten months later, Plank removed Pyke as a director of IPG and IPG commenced proceedings against Pyke.

Brooke LJ stated that '[t]here is no completely rigid rule that a director may not be involved in the business of a company which is in competition with another company of which he was a director' and Sedley LJ stated that cases involving directors taking up rival directorships were 'fact-specific'. However, Sedley LJ did go on to state that the situations where a director can take up a rival directorship were 'very narrow indeed'.

The court agreed that this was one such situation (although the reasoning of the judges did differ in parts) and that Pyke had not acted in breach of duty as he had been excluded from management, he was not permitted to withdraw his money from IPG, and he had not used any confidential information he acquired while at IPG.

Former directors

Unlike many other general duties, the s. 175 duty can also apply to a former director (s. 170(2)(a)). This is to prevent a director from vacating office as a director and then competing with the company using information and opportunities he acquired while he was a director of that company. It should be noted that the mere act of resigning and setting up a rival business is not a breach of s. 175 (*Balston Ltd v Headline Filters Ltd* [1990] FSR 385 (Ch)). A breach will only arise where the former director exploits any property, information or opportunity of which he became aware at a time when he was a director of the company (s. 170(2)(a)).

Case law 7.6

***Industrial Development Consultants Ltd v Cooley* [1972] 1 WLR 443**

Cooley, the managing director of a company, entered into negotiations with the Eastern Gas Board to construct a series of depots. The Gas Board decided not to award the contract to the company. A year later, a director of the Gas Board told Cooley that it had still not found someone to build the depots. Cooley did not inform the company of this and instead resigned as a director (and did so without the required notice by falsely claiming that he was ill). Cooley then entered into negotiations with the Gas Board on his own behalf and secured the contract to build the depots. The company commenced proceedings against Cooley.

Cooley was held in breach of duty and had to account for the profits he made. Cooley should have told the company that the Gas Board was once again looking for someone to build the depots. By not doing so and obtaining the contract himself, he 'embarked upon a deliberate policy and course of conduct which put his personal interest as a potential contracting party with the Eastern Gas Board in direct conflict with his pre-existing and continuing duty as managing director of the plaintiffs'. He had exploited an opportunity he became aware of while he was a managing director and resigned so that he could take advantage of it himself.

It should be stressed that the facts of the case will affect whether the former director is in breach of the s. 175 duty. For example, the court may be less likely to hold that a breach of s. 175 has occurred where the director's reason for resigning is not to compete with his former company (*Island Export Finance Ltd v Umunna* [1986] BCLC 460 (QB)) or where the director resigned because he was excluded from management by his fellow directors (*Foster Bryant Surveying Ltd v Bryant* [2007] EWCA Civ 200).

Authorisation

The s. 175 duty will not be infringed where the conflict has been authorised by the company (s. 180(4)(a)) or by the directors (s. 175(4)(b)). The directors' ability to provide such authorisation is as follows.

- The directors cannot authorise a conflict where statute requires member approval to be provided (e.g. a third-party benefit under s. 176, or certain transactions requiring member approval).
- In the case of a private company, the directors may authorise the conflict providing that the company's constitution does not invalidate such authorisation (s. 175(5)(a)). The model articles for private companies do not invalidate the directors' ability to authorise a conflict.
- In the case of a public company, the directors may only authorise a conflict if there is a provision in the articles enabling them to do so (s. 175(5)(b)). The model articles for public companies do not contain such a provision.

Where the directors are so empowered to authorise a conflict, several rules need to be complied with, including:

- authorisation must be obtained prior to the director entering into the agreement that results in a conflict;
- the directors' authorisation will only be valid if, when they vote on the matter, the director with the conflict does not count towards the quorum and his vote is not counted (s. 175(6));
- when deciding whether to authorise the conflict, the directors must act in accordance with their general duties; and
- authorisation may avoid the conflicted director being in breach of the s. 175 duty, but it may not avoid the director being in breach of other general duties.

Remedies

A contract entered into in breach of the s. 175 duty is voidable at the company's instance, as long as the other party to the contract knew of the breach (*Hely-Hutchinson & Co Ltd v Brayhead Ltd* [1968] 1 QB 549 (CA)). The director in breach can be required by the company to account for any gains made (*Aberdeen Rly Co v Blaikie Bros* (1854) 1 Macq 461 (HL)).

Test yourself 7.3

1. **What types of situation do not amount to a conflict under s. 175?**
2. **Are directors able to sit on the boards of competing companies?**
3. **Does the s. 175 duty apply to former directors of a company?**
4. **When will a director in a position of conflict not be in breach of the s. 175 duty?**
5. **Can directors authorise a s. 175 conflict?**

2.7 Duty not to accept benefits from third parties

The common law has long provided that a person in a fiduciary position cannot accept a bribe or a secret commission (*Attorney General of Hong Kong v Reid* [1994] 1 AC 324 (PC)). The duty in s. 176 is wider as it does not only apply to bribes or secret commissions. Section 176(1) provides that a director of a company must not accept a benefit from a third party conferred by reason of:

- his being a director; or
- his doing (or not doing) anything as a director.

Key to the scope of the s. 176 duty is what constitutes a 'benefit'. The CA 2006 does not define what a benefit is, so the issue will be left to the courts who have not sought to apply any technical interpretation of the word. The Act does, however, state that certain benefits will not fall within s. 176, including:

- a benefit received from the company or a person acting on behalf of the company (s. 176(2));
- a benefit received by a director from a person by whom his services (as a director or otherwise) are provided to the company (s. 176(3)); and
- a benefit that cannot reasonably be regarded as likely to give rise to a conflict of interest (s. 176(4)).

Stop and think 7.4

Given that the s. 176 duty only applies to third-party benefits that can reasonably be regarded to give rise to a conflict of interest, it follows that every benefit that falls within s. 176 could also amount to a conflict under s. 175. Why does the s. 176 duty exist? Why do you think a separate duty is required for third-party benefits?

A director who has received a third-party benefit will not be in breach of the s. 176 duty if:

- the benefit has been approved by the members (s. 180(4)(a)); or
- the articles contain provisions for dealing with conflicts of interest, and the director acts in accordance with those provisions (s. 180(4)(b)).

Remedies and offences

A breach of the s. 176 duty can result in a number of consequences, including:

- the contract that provides for the benefit can be rescinded by the company (*Shipway v Broadwood* [1899] 1 QB 369 (CA));
- the company can recover the benefit from the director, or claim damages from the director or third party (*Mahesan v Malaysia Government Officers' Co-operative Housing Society Ltd* [1979] AC 374 (PC));
- the company can summarily dismiss the director (*Boston Deep Sea Fishing Co v Ansell* (1888) 39 ChD 39 (CA)); and
- an offence will be committed if the benefit amounts to a bribe (Bribery Act 2010, s. 2).

2.8 Duty to declare interest in transactions or arrangements

Sections 177 and 182 establish rules regarding directors having to disclose their interest in certain transactions or arrangements.

Proposed transactions or arrangements

Section 177(1) provides that if a director of a company is in any way, directly or indirectly, interested in a proposed transaction or arrangement with the company, he must declare the nature and extent of that interest to the other directors. A few points should be noted.

- Section 177 only applies where the transaction or arrangement is with the company. If the transaction or arrangement is not with the company (for example, it is with a third party), then s. 177 will not apply and s. 175 will be the relevant duty.
- Section 177 applies where a director is 'interested' in a proposed transaction. This will obviously include a situation where a director proposes to contract with the company (*Movitex Ltd v Bulfield* [1988] BCLC 104 (Ch)), but it will also include situations where a director is not party to the contract, but has some form of interest in it (e.g. where company A contracts with company B, and a director of company A is a shareholder in company B (*Gwembe Valley Development Co Ltd v Koshy* [2003] EWCA Civ 1048)).

In order to avoid a breach of s. 177, a director will need to declare the nature and extent of his interest to the other directors before the transaction or arrangement is entered into (s. 177(4)). Obviously, this will not apply where the company only has one director. Section 177 goes on to specify a number of other instances where a declaration will not be required:

- where the director is not aware of the interest, or is not aware of the transaction or arrangement (s. 177(5));
- where the interest cannot reasonably be regarded as likely to give rise to a conflict of interest (s. 177(6)(a));
- where the other directors are already aware of the interest (s. 177(6)(b)); or
- where the interest concerns the terms of the director's service contract that have been or are to be considered by the directors (s. 177(6)(c)).

Once the director has declared his interest, the board can then decide if it wishes to proceed with the transaction or arrangement. The articles will usually provide that the director who has the interest cannot vote on the matter and will not count towards the quorum (the model articles do contain such a provision).

A breach of the s. 177 duty will result in the transaction or arrangement being voidable at the company's instance (*Hely-Hutchinson v Brayhead Ltd* [1968] 1 QB 549 (CA)). It would appear that the director in breach faces no liability, which has attracted considerable criticism.

Existing transactions or arrangements

Section 182 is not a general duty in its own right, but nevertheless imposes a notable obligation upon directors. Section 182(1) provides that where a director of a company is in any way, directly or indirectly, interested in a transaction or arrangement that has been entered into by the company, he must declare the nature and extent of the interest to the other directors. There are several notable differences between the s. 182 duty and the s. 177 duty.

- The s. 177 duty applies to proposed transactions or arrangements, whereas s. 182 applies to transactions or arrangements that the company has entered into.

- Under s. 177, the declaration must be made before the transaction/arrangement is entered into. Under s. 182, the declaration must be made as soon as is reasonably practicable (s. 182(4)).
- A breach of s. 177 results in civil consequences only. Conversely, a breach of s. 182 is a criminal offence (s. 183).

A declaration will not be required in the same instances as those found under s. 177(6) noted above (s. 182(6)). A director who makes the requisite declaration under s. 177 will not be required to make another declaration under s. 182 (s. 182(1)). If, however, the director does not make a s. 177 declaration, and then does not make a declaration when the transaction is entered into, he can be in breach of both ss. 177 and 182.

Test yourself 7.4

1. **Explain the various differences between the duties in ss. 177 and 182.**
2. **How can a director with an interest in a proposed transaction with the company avoid a breach of the s. 177 duty?**
3. **Does a breach of ss. 177 or 182 result in criminal liability?**

3. Avoiding liability

A director who is found liable for breach of duty (or certain other legal wrongs) can attempt to avoid liability in certain ways:

- through a provision excluding or limiting his liability;
- through a provision indemnifying the director for any liability he may face; or
- by seeking to be relieved from liability.

As discussed below, each of these forms of liability avoidance is regulated by the CA 2006.

3.1 Exclusion and indemnity provisions

A director who is liable for breach of duty may seek to obtain protection from liability via a provision in the articles or in his employment contract. A director's ability to do this is greatly limited by s. 232 of the CA 2006, which provides that:

- any provision that purports to exempt a director of a company (to any extent) from any liability that would otherwise attach to him in connection with any negligence, default, breach of duty or breach of trust in relation to the company is void (s. 232(1)); and
- any provision by which a company directly or indirectly provides an indemnity (to any extent) for a director of the company, or of an associated

company, against any liability attaching to him in connection with any negligence, default, breach of duty or breach of trust in relation to the company of which he is a director is void (s. 232(2)).

However, a provision indemnifying the director will not be void in three situations:

1. where the company purchases and maintains insurance for a director against such liability (ss. 232(2)(a) and 233);
2. where the company indemnifies a director against liability to a person other than the company (i.e. a third party) (ss. 232(2)(b) and 234); or
3. where the company indemnifies a director who is a trustee of an occupational pension scheme against liability incurred in connection with the company's activities as trustee of the scheme (ss. 232(2)(c) and 235).

3.2 Relief from liability

A director who could be found liable for engaging in certain conduct can, in specified circumstances, be relieved of liability by the members or the courts.

Ratification

Section 239 of the CA 2006 allows the members to ratify the conduct of a director, which includes a former director or shadow director (s. 239(5)), that amounts to negligence, default, breach of duty or breach of trust in relation to the company (s. 239(1)). Section 239(2) provides that the decision to ratify such conduct must be made by a resolution of the members of the company, but s. 239(6)(a) also provides that the decision can be taken by unanimous consent (so the unanimous assent rule, discussed on page 169, will apply).

If the director whose conduct is being voted on is also a member, then his vote will be disregarded, as will those of persons connected to him (s. 239(3) and (4)). However, if the vote takes place via a resolution at a meeting, then such persons can still count towards the quorum (s. 239(4)).

Even if the director's acts or omissions are ratified in accordance with the above rules, ratification may still be ineffective for two reasons. First, s. 239(7) provides that s. 239 does not affect any other enactment or rule of law imposing additional requirements for valid ratification, and if these additional requirements are not met, the ratification will be invalid. The courts have created several additional requirements, including:

- the ratification of the members must be informed (*Knight v Frost* [1999] 1 BCLC 364 (Ch)); and
- the decision to ratify must be 'honest, bona fide and in the best interest of the company' (*Madoff Securities International Ltd v Raven* [2011] EWHC 3102 (Comm) (Flaux J)).

Second, s. 239(7) also provides that s. 239 does not affect any rule of law as to acts that are incapable of being ratified by the company. The courts have held that certain acts cannot be ratified, including:

- illegal acts (*Re Exchange Banking Co (Flitcroft's Case)* (1882) 21 ChD 519 (CA)); or
- acts which are not bona fide and honest (*Bowthorpe Holdings Ltd v Hills* [2002] EWHC 2331 (Ch)).

Relief from the court

Section 1157(1) of the CA 2006 provides that where an officer or auditor of the company has been held liable for negligence, default, breach of duty or breach of trust, then the court may relieve him of liability (in whole or in part) if it appears to the court that he acted honestly and reasonably, and that having regard to all the circumstances of the case, he ought fairly to be excused. The following case demonstrates the courts' power to grant relief.

Case law 7.7

***Re Duomatic Ltd* [1969] 2 Ch 365 (Ch)**

The company's three directors (E, H and T) held all of its ordinary shares. E and T wanted to remove H from office but, in order to avoid a legal dispute, they caused the company to pay him £4,000 so that he would leave (this payment was not disclosed to all the members). H resigned as a director and transferred his shares to E.

The company's articles provided that the directors' remuneration had to be authorised by the members. Such authorisation was never formally obtained, but all the members who were entitled to vote knew and approved of the remuneration payments. The company encountered financial difficulties and entered liquidation. The liquidator sought to recover three sums from the directors:

(a) the salaries drawn by E and T;

(b) a £9,000 payment made to E a month before the company entered liquidation; and

(c) the £4,000 payment made to H.

The court held that all three payments were made in breach of duty, so the question was whether to grant relief to the directors concerned. The court held:

- **as regards payment (a), relief was granted on the ground that all the members knew and approved of the remuneration payments;**
- **as regards payment (b), relief was granted as E had merely followed a practice that had been followed in previous years; and**
- **as regards payment (c), relief was not granted as such a loss of office payment should have been disclosed to, and authorised by, the members of the company and this had not occurred.**

The courts have stated that relief from liability cannot be granted where the director was completely inactive (*Lexi Holdings plc v Luqman* [2007] EWHC 2652 (Ch)) or where the director is liable for wrongful trading (*Re Produce Marketing Consortium Ltd* [1989] 1 WLR 745 (Ch)).

Test yourself 7.5

1. **Can a director avoid liability for breach of duty by including a provision in the articles excluding such liability?**
2. **Explain the two ways by which a director can obtain relief from liability.**
3. **When will a court grant relief under s. 1157?**

4. Transactions requiring member approval

Part 10, Ch 4 of the CA 2006 regards certain transactions involving directors as potentially giving rise to significant conflicts of interest, namely:

- long-term service contracts;
- substantial property transactions;
- loans, quasi-loans and other credit transactions; and
- remuneration and payments for loss of office.

Compliance with the general duties alone will be insufficient in relation to such transactions and the transaction in question will need to be approved by the members (CA 2006, s. 180(3)). Approval takes the form of a resolution of the members, which will be an ordinary resolution, unless the articles require a higher majority or unanimity (s. 281(3)). The unanimous assent rule (discussed on page 169) can also apply.

4.1 Service contracts

Section 188 applies to a provision (such as in an employment contract) under which the guaranteed term of a director's employment with the company is, or may be, longer than two years (s. 188(1)). In such a case, the company cannot agree to such a provision unless it has been approved by a resolution of the members (s. 188(2)). To ensure that the members are fully informed on the matter, the resolution must not be passed until a copy of the proposed contract incorporating the provision is made available to the members (s. 188(5)).

Stop and think 7.5

Why do you think member approval is required for director service contracts over two years in length? What problems would arise if a director had an extremely lengthy service contract?

Note that s. 188(2) only requires the provision in question to be approved – it does not require the entire contract to be approved. If the required approval is not obtained, then the provision in question is void, to the extent of the contravention (s. 189(a)). The remainder of the contract will remain valid, but it will be deemed to contain a term entitling the company to terminate it at any time by giving reasonable notice (s. 189(b)).

Where the company has a premium listing, then Provision 39 of the UK Corporate Governance Code states that contract periods should be one year or less. Such contracts are now standard in listed companies.

4.2 Substantial property transactions

Section 190 applies to an arrangement under which:

- a director of a company or its holding company, or a person connected with such a director, acquires or is to acquire from the company (directly or indirectly) a substantial non-cash asset; or
- the company acquires or is to acquire a substantial non-cash asset (directly or indirectly) from such a director or a person so connected (s. 190(1)).

In either case, the company must not enter into the arrangement unless it has been approved by a resolution of the members or is conditional upon such approval being obtained (s. 190(1)).

Substantial non-cash asset

The requirement for member approval only applies to 'substantial non-cash assets'. A 'non-cash asset' is defined broadly as 'any property or interest in property, other than cash' (s. 1163(1)). A non-cash asset will be 'substantial' if it is:

- over £100,000; or
- exceeds 10% of the company's asset value and is more than £5,000 (s. 191(2)).

Connected persons

The requirement of member approval also applies where the arrangement is entered into with a person who is 'connected' to a director. The concept of a 'connected person' also applies to other transaction requiring member approval. Section 252(2) provides that the following persons are connected with a director:

(1) members of the director's family (as defined in s. 253);

(2) a body corporate with whom the director is connected (as defined in s. 254);

(3) trustees of a trust, the beneficiaries of which include the director or members of his family or a connected body corporate, or the terms of which confer a power on the trustees that may be exercised for the benefit of any such person;

(4) any partner of the director or the partner of a person connected to the director by virtue of (1), (2) or (3) above; or

(5) a firm that is a legal person under the law and (i) in which the director is a partner; or (ii) one of the partners is connected to a director by virtue of (1), (2) or (3) above.

Exceptions

Certain arrangements are excluded from the requirement for member approval, including:

- where the transaction relates to anything to which a director is entitled under his service contract (s. 190(6)(a));
- where the transaction relates to a director's payment for loss of office (s. 190(6)(b));
- where the transaction is between a company and a person in his capacity as a member of that company (s. 192(a));
- where the transaction is between a holding company and its wholly-owned subsidiary, or between two wholly-owned subsidiaries of the same holding company (s. 192(b));
- where the company is being wound up (unless it is a members' voluntary winding up) (s. 193); and
- where the company is in administration (s. 193).

Consequences of contravention

If member approval under s. 190 is required and not obtained, then s. 190(3) specifically states that the company is not liable. Instead, the consequences can include the following.

- The transaction is voidable at the company's instance, unless:
  - restitution of any money or other asset that was the subject matter of the arrangement or transaction is no longer possible;
  - the company has been indemnified in pursuance of this section by any other persons for the loss or damage suffered by it; or
  - rights acquired in good faith, for value and without actual notice of the contravention by a person who is not a party to the arrangement or transaction would be affected by the avoidance (s. 195(2)).
- The transaction will also cease to be voidable if it is approved by a resolution of the members within a reasonable period of the company entering into it (s. 196).
- Whether or not the transaction is avoided, a director (including any director who authorised the transaction) or connected person is liable:
  - to account to the company for any gain that he has made directly or indirectly by the arrangement or transaction; and

- is jointly and severally with any other person so liable to indemnify the company for any loss or damage resulting from the arrangement or transaction (s. 195(3) and (4)).

- A director who authorised the transaction or a connected person can avoid liability if they can show that, at the time the transaction was entered into, they did not know of the relevant circumstances that constituted the contravention (s. 195(7)).

4.3 Loans, quasi-loans and credit transactions

Sections 197–214 provide that three types of transactions require member approval. The first transaction occurs where a company makes a loan to a director of the company or its holding company, or gives a guarantee or provides security in connection with a loan made by any person to such a director (s. 197(1)). A company must not enter into such a transaction unless it is approved by a resolution of the members (s. 197(1)).

The second transaction occurs where a public company (or a company associated with a public company) makes a quasi-loan to a director of the company or of its holding company, or gives a guarantee or provides security in connection with a quasi-loan made by any person to such a director (s. 198(1) and (2)). A public company must not enter into such a transaction, unless the transaction has been approved by a resolution of the members of the company (s. 198(2)). Two terms here require defining:

- A company is 'associated' with a public company if one is the subsidiary of the other, or if they are both subsidiaries of the same company (s. 256).
- A 'quasi-loan' is a transaction under which one party (the creditor) agrees to pay a sum for another person (the borrower) or agrees to reimburse expenditure incurred by another party for another (the borrower):
  - on terms that the borrower (or a person on his behalf) will reimburse the creditor; or
  - in circumstances giving rise to a liability on the borrower to reimburse the creditor (s. 199(1)).

The third transaction occurs where a public company (or a company associated with a public company) enters into:

- a credit transaction as creditor for the benefit of a director of the company or of its holding company, or a person connected with such a director; or
- it gives a guarantee or provides security in connection with a credit transaction entered into by any person for the benefit of such a director, or a person connected with such a director (s. 201(1) and (2)).

A public company must not ether into such a transaction unless it has been approved by a resolution of the members (s. 201(2)). A 'credit transaction' is a transaction under which one party:

- supplies any goods or sells any land under a hire-purchase agreement or a conditional sale agreement;

- leases or hires any land or goods in return for periodical payments; or
- otherwise disposes of land or supplies goods or services on the understanding that payment is to be deferred (s. 202(1)).

Exceptions
The requirement for member approval will not apply in several situations, including:

- where the transaction provides a director with funds to meet expenditure incurred by him:
  - for the purposes of the company or for the purpose of enabling him to perform his duties as an officer of the company; or
  - to enable any such person to avoid incurring such expenditure (s. 204(1));
- where the value of the transaction in question does not exceed £50,000 (s. 204(2));
- where the transaction provides the director with funds to meet expenditure incurred by him in defending specified legal proceedings (s. 205(1));
- where a loan or quasi-loan does not exceed £10,000 (s. 207(1);
- where a credit transaction does not exceed £15,000 (s. 207(1)); and
- where a loan, quasi-loan or credit transaction is made to an associated body corporate (s. 208).

Consequences of contravention
The following consequences apply if member approval is required and not obtained.

- The transaction is voidable at the company's instance, unless:
  - restitution of any money or other asset that was the subject matter of the arrangement or transaction is no longer possible;
  - the company has been indemnified in pursuance of this section by any other persons for the loss or damage suffered by it; or
  - rights acquired in good faith, for value and without actual notice of the contravention by a person who is not a party to the arrangement or transaction would be affected by the avoidance (s. 213(2)).
- The transaction will also cease to be voidable if it is approved by a resolution of the members within a reasonable period of the company entering into it (s. 214).
- Whether or not the transaction is avoided, a director (including any director who authorised the transaction) or connected person is liable:
  - to account to the company for any gain that he has made directly or indirectly by the arrangement or transaction; and
  - is jointly and severally with any other person so liable to indemnify the company for any loss or damage resulting from the arrangement or transaction (s. 213(3) and (4)).

- A director who authorised the transaction or a connected person can avoid liability if they can show that, at the time the transaction was entered into, they did not know of the relevant circumstances that constituted the contravention (s. 213(7)).

4.4 Remuneration and payments for loss of office

Sections 215–222 and 226A–226F provide that member approval is required for certain remuneration and loss of office payments. The rules differ depending on whether the company is unquoted or quoted.

Stop and think 7.6

In recent years, payments made to directors for loss of office have become extremely controversial. Why do you think this is?

Unquoted companies

An unquoted company must not make a payment for loss of office to a director unless the payment has been approved by a resolution of the company (s. 217(1)). A payment for loss of office means a payment made to a director or past director:

- by way of compensation for loss of office as director of the company;
- by way of compensation for loss, while director of the company, of any other office or employment in connection with the management of the affairs of the company or any subsidiary undertaking of the company;
- as consideration for or in connection with his retirement from his office as director of the company; or
- as consideration for or in connection with his retirement, while director of the company, from any other office or employment in connection with the management of the affairs of the company, or any subsidiary undertaking of the company (s. 215(1)).

In several situations, member approval is not required for a loss of office payment, including:

- a payment made in good faith to discharge an existing legal obligation (s. 220(1)(a), which is defined as an obligation of the company, or any body corporate associated with it, that was not entered into in connection with, or in consequence of, the event giving rise to the payment for loss of office (s. 220(2));
- a payment made in good faith by way of damages for breach of an existing legal obligation (s. 220(1)(b));
- a payment made in good faith by way of settlement or compromise of any claim arising in connection with the termination of a person's office or employment (s. 220(1)(c));

- a payment made in good faith by way of pension in respect of past services (s. 220(1)(d)); and
- a payment made by the company or any of its subsidiaries that does not exceed £200 (s. 221(1)).

If member approval is required and not obtained, then the recipient of the payment holds it on trust for the company that made the payment, and any director who authorised the payment is jointly and severally liable to indemnify the company that made the payment and for any loss resulting from it (s. 222(1)).

Quoted companies

Sections 226B(1) and 226C(1) provide that a quoted company may not make a remuneration payment or a loss of office payment to a person who is, or is to be or has been, a director of the company unless:

- the payment is consistent with the approved directors' remuneration policy; or
- the payment is approved by a resolution of the members.

A payment made in breach of ss. 226B or 226C will be held by the recipient on trust for the company or other person making the payment, and any director who authorised the payment is jointly and severally liable to indemnify the company that made the payment and for any loss resulting from it (s. 226E(1)).

Test yourself 7.6

1. **What four transactions require member approval?**
2. **What are the consequences of a director not obtaining member approval for a long-term service contract?**
3. **What is a substantial property transaction?**
4. **What is a quasi-loan?**
5. **Does a loss of office payment made to a director of a quoted company require member approval?**

Chapter summary

- In the CA 2006, directors' duties are referred to as 'the general duties' of which there are seven in ss. 171–177.
- The general duties of a director are owed to the company.
- Section 171 (the duty to act within powers) provides that directors are (i) under a duty to act in accordance with the company's constitution; and (ii) to only exercise powers for the purposes for which they are conferred.

- Section 172 provides that directors must act in a way they consider would be most likely to promote the success of the company for the benefit of its members as a whole.
- Section 173 provides that a director of a company must exercise independent judgment.
- Section 174 provides that a director of a company must exercise reasonable care, skill and diligence.
- Section 175 provides that a director must avoid a situation in which they have, or can have, a direct or indirect interest that conflicts, or possibly may conflict, with the interests of the company.
- Section 176 provides that directors of a company must not accept a benefit from a third party conferred by reason of (i) their being a director; or (ii) their doing (or not doing) anything as a director.
- Section 177 provides that if a director of a company is in any way, directly or indirectly, interested in a proposed transaction or arrangement with the company, they must declare the nature and extent of that interest to the other directors.
- Section 182 provides that where a director of a company is in any way, directly or indirectly, interested in a transaction or arrangement that has been entered into by the company, they must declare the nature and extent of the interest to the other directors.
- A provision will be void if it:
  - purports to exempt a director of a company from any liability that would otherwise attach to them in connection with any negligence, default, breach of duty or breach of trust in relation to the company; or
  - provides that a company provides an indemnity (to any extent) for a director of the company, or of an associated company, against any liability attaching to them in connection with any negligence, default, breach of duty or breach of trust in relation to the company of which he is a director.
- A director can be relieved from liability if the members ratify his breach of duty, or if the court grants relief from liability.
- Four transactions involving directors require member approval:
  - long-term service contracts (i.e. those over two years in length);
  - substantial property transactions;
  - loans, quasi-loans and other credit transactions; and
  - remuneration and payments for loss of office.

Part three

Chapter 8
Membership

Chapter 9
Company meetings and decision making

Chapter 10
Members' remedies

Membership of a company

Overview

Part three looks at company membership, the role of the company's members, company meetings and members' remedies.

Chapter 8 looks at the membership of the company. The chapter begins by looking at what membership is, how a person becomes and ceases to be a member and how the law seeks to make company membership transparent.

Chapter 9 discusses company meetings and decision making. This involves a discussion of how companies make decisions, the rules relating to the running of company meetings and the extent to which members engage with such meetings.

Chapter 10 discusses the three principal remedies designed to protect members, especially minority shareholders, namely the derivative claim, the unfair prejudice petition and the petition for winding up.

At the end of this Part, students will be able to:

- understand how a person becomes, and ceases to be, a member;
- discuss how the law has sought to improve the transparency of company membership;
- identify the various ways that companies make decisions;
- understand the rules by which company meetings are run;
- appreciate the differences between general meetings and class meetings;
- discuss the extent to which members engage with company meetings;
- appreciate the difference between personal actions and corporate actions, and when a representative action or group litigation order can be brought;
- discuss the operation of the statutory member remedies, namely the derivative claim, the unfair prejudice petition and the petition to wind up the company; and
- understand the relationship between the various statutory member remedies.

Chapter eight
Membership

Contents

1. Introduction

This chapter discusses the concept of membership, beginning with how the law defines a member. In some cases, a person will only be a member if their name is entered into the register of members, so this register is discussed. In recent years, there has been a significant focus on how to make company ownership more transparent and so the chapter examines the register of interests disclosed and the PSC register. The chapter concludes by looking at how a person's membership can be brought to an end.

2. What is membership?

Company law bestows numerous rights upon members and also imposes a range of obligations upon them. It is important to be able to determine whether a person is a member. Before looking at how the CA 2006 defines membership, it is important to note that being a member and being a shareholder are not synonymous (although, in many cases, a shareholder will be a member and vice versa). For example, a company without a share capital will have members, but will not have shareholders. Even a company with a share capital may have persons who:

- are shareholders, but not members (because there are good reasons not to enter their name onto the register of members, as discussed on p. 158); or
- are members, but not shareholders (see e.g. *Re Nuneaton Borough Association Football Club Ltd* [1989] 5 BCC 377 (CA)).

Section 112 of the CA 2006 provides for two ways by which a person can become a member.

1. The subscribers of a company's memorandum are deemed to have agreed to become members of the company. Upon the company's registration, they become members and their names must be entered as such in the register of members (s. 112(1)).
2. Every other person who agrees to become a member of the company and whose name is entered in its register of members is a member of the company (s. 112(2)).

Both methods require that that the person has agreed to become a member, but how agreement occurs differs based on the method used.

- When the company is first incorporated, the subscribers to the memorandum are deemed to have agreed to become members.
- In all other cases, the person must agree to become a member. There are no specific requirements regarding acceptance. For example, acceptance need not be in writing or take the form of a contract. All that is required is that the prospective member assents to becoming a member (*Re Nuneaton Borough Association Football Club Ltd* [1989] 5 BCC 377 (CA)).

Both methods also talk about the prospective member's name being entered onto the register of members (this register is discussed on p. 159). This is not a requirement of membership under the first method: subscribers will become members even if their names are not entered onto the register of members (CA 2006, Explanatory Notes, para 239), although the company is required to enter their names into the register of members. Under the second method, a person will not become a member unless their name is entered into the register of members.

2.1 Restrictions on membership

The directors decide whether a person's name should be entered into the register of members. There are several instances where the directors may validly decide to refuse to enter a prospective member's name into the register.

- Unincorporated associations (such as partnerships) have no legal personality and so they should not be accepted as members. In the case of a sole proprietorship, the name of the sole proprietor should be entered into the register. In the case of an ordinary partnership, the names of the partners should instead be entered into the register.
- Companies are able to become members of other companies, but there are limits to this. For example, a company cannot generally be a member of itself (*Trevor v Whitworth* (1887) 12 App Cas 409 (HL)), and so its name should not be entered into its own register of members (although an exception for this is provided for in relation to treasury shares (CA 2006, s. 124(2)).

Test yourself 8.1

1. **Are all shareholders in a company also members of that company?**
2. **What are the two ways by which a person can become a member under s. 112 of the CA 2006?**
3. **Does a person need to have their name entered into the register of members in order to become a member?**
4. **Provide an example of a situation where the directors should refuse to enter someone's name into the register of members.**

3. The register of members

Section 113(1) of the CA 2006 provides that every company must keep a register of its members, although private companies may instead elect to keep their membership data on the central register at Companies House (ss. 128A–128B). Failure to keep a register of members is a criminal offence (s. 113(7)). If a company elects to keep its own register, then s. 114(1) provides that this register must be kept at either the company's registered office or its **single alternative inspection location** (SAIL). A company's SAIL is a location other than the company's registered office, where documents may be kept available for inspection (CA 2006, s. 1136; Companies (Company Records) Regulations 2008 (SI 2008/3006), reg 3).

single alternative inspection location
The location other than the company's registered office, where documents may be kept available for inspection.

3.1 Legal status and content

Despite the importance of the register, it does not actually provide conclusive proof regarding issues of membership – instead, it merely provides *prima facie* evidence of any matters that the CA 2006 requires to be included in the register (ss. 127 and 128H(1)). Sections 113(2) and (3) provide that the information that must be included in the register consists of:

- the names and addresses of each member;
- the date on which each person was registered as a member;
- the date on which any person ceased to be a member;
- if the company has a share capital, the register must contain a statement of the shares of each member, setting out:
  - the number of shares the member holds and, if applicable, the class of shares; and
  - the amount paid or agreed to be considered as paid on the shares; and
- if the company does not have a share capital, but it does have more than one class of member, then the register must identify to which class each member belongs.

If the register contains an error, the company cannot rectify the error (*Gardiner v Victoria Estates Co Ltd* (1885) 12 R 1356). Instead, the company must apply to the court for a rectification order which, under s. 125(1) of the CA 2006, can be sought if:

1. the name of any person is, without sufficient cause, entered in or omitted from a company's register of members; or
2. default is made or unnecessary delay takes place in entering on the register the fact of any person having ceased to be a member.

3.2 Inspection of the register

Any member of the company has a right to inspect the register of members free of charge. Anyone else may inspect the register upon paying a fee (s. 116(1)). To exercise this right of inspection, a person must make a request to the company to that effect. This request must provide specified information, such as the person's name and address, the purpose for which the information will be used, and whether the information will be disclosed to others (s. 116(3)–(4)).

The company must either comply with the request or apply to the court for an order (known as a 'no-access order') that the request was not made for a proper purpose (s. 117(1) and (3)) within five working days of the receipt of the request. If such an order is made, the court will direct that the company not comply with the request and can also direct that it need not comply with requests for a similar purpose (s. 117(3)–(4)). The exercise of the courts' ability to issue a no-access order under the CA 2006 was first examined in the following case.

Case law 8.1

***Re Burry & Knight Ltd* [2014] EWCA Civ 604**

In the 1990s, Knight asked for a company to be investigated due to concerns he had regarding its management, but this request was refused. Several decades later, he once again made allegations regarding the company and so sought to inspect the register, stating that the purpose of the inspection was to (i) study B&K's shareholding; (ii) tell the other members his concerns regarding B&K's directors; and (iii) advise the other members to obtain professional advice regarding share valuation in the future. A no-access order was sought on the ground that Knight's request was for an improper purpose.

Arden LJ stated that the information Knight sought would not provide any benefit to the members. Further, she agreed with the contention that Knight wished to inspect the register in order conduct a vendetta against the controllers of the company. This was held to be an improper purpose and so the no-access order was granted.

Test yourself 8.2

1. **What information must be included in the register of members?**
2. **Can the company rectify an error in the register of members?**
3. **Who has the right to inspect the register of members, and what procedure must they follow?**

4. Transparency and membership

It is important to be able to identify who controls a company, in order to hold companies and those who control them to account. A company is controlled by a combination of its directors and members and, although it is straightforward to identify a company's directors, identifying a company's members can be more difficult. One might think that all that need be done is to look at the register of members, but the register of members might not reveal the true identity of the person who controls the shares. This is because when a person buys shares in a company, he can have those shares registered in the register of members in the name of someone else (known as the 'nominee'). In such a case, the nominee's name must be entered into the register of members and so the nominee will be the member and **legal owner** of the shares.

legal owner
The legal owner of shares is the person whose name is entered into the register of members in respect of those shares.

Case study 8.1

X-Corp plc's register of members states that its share capital (which consists of 10,000 £1 shares) is equally divided amongst two shareholders, namely A-Corp plc and B-Corp plc. However, B-Corp plc is a nominee of A-Corp.

In the above example, A-Corp and B-Corp are the legal owners of 5,000 shares each. It would appear, based on the register of members, that A-Corp and B-Corp each have equal control over X-Corp. This is not the case as A-Corp actually controls all 10,000 shares (the person who ultimately controls the shares is said to be their **beneficial owner**). Due to this distinction between legal ownership and beneficial ownership of shares, X-Corp plc's register of members does not provide an accurate account of who actually controls the shares in X-Corp.

beneficial owner
The beneficial owner of shares is the person who ultimately controls those shares.

The use of nominees can be completely legitimate but concerns have existed that nominees could use a company to engage in unlawful activity (such as tax evasion or money laundering) while concealing their identity from regulators. To combat this, there are two methods by which company law seeks to make corporate control more transparent, namely:

- the register of interests disclosed; and
- the PSC register.

4.1 Register of interests disclosed

In the example above, A-Corp has an interest in B-Corp's shares, but this interest is not evident from the register of members. Under s. 793 of the CA 2006, X-Corp could issue a notice to A-Corp requiring A-Corp to confirm whether it has an interest in X-Corp's shares and, if it does have such an interest, to provide further information regarding that interest.

An 'interest in shares' is defined extremely widely and includes 'an interest of any kind whatsoever in the shares' (s. 820(2)(a)). If X-Corp refused to issue a s. 793 notice, then the members holding at least 10% of the company's paid-up capital can require X-Corp to issue a s. 793 notice (s. 803). Note the following restrictions on the use of s. 793.

- It can only be used by a public company (s. 791). In practice, private companies would not need to use s. 793 as they can ask for further information regarding a shareholder prior to registering the shares.
- A public company can only issue a s. 793 notice if it knows or has reasonable cause to believe that a person is interested in its shares, or if a person has been so interested in the previous three years (s. 793(1)).

A person who fails to comply with a s. 793 notice, or who provides false information when complying with a s. 793 notice, commits a criminal offence (s. 795).

The company must keep a register of any information disclosed to it under s. 793 (s. 808(1)) and this register is known as the register of interests disclosed. Failure to keep this register is a criminal offence (s. 808(5)). Any information received under s. 793 must be entered into this register within three days (s. 808(2)) and must be kept on the register for at least six years (ss. 815(1) and 816). Any person can inspect this register free of charge (s. 811(1)).

4.2 The PSC register

The major weakness of a s. 793 notice is that it can only be used by a company if it knows or has reasonable cause to believe that a person is interested in its shares. Many companies will lack such knowledge, and so the register of interests disclosed may not provide full information on all persons who have an interest in the company's shares, especially the beneficial owners. To provide more transparency in terms of who the beneficial owners of a company's shares are, the Small Business, Enterprise and Employment Act 2015 (SBEEA 2015) introduced a new Part 21A into the CA 2006, which requires companies to maintain a register of persons with significant control (a PSC register).

Any company to which Part 21A applies must keep a PSC register (s. 790M(1)), although private companies may instead elect to keep their PSC information on the central register of Companies House (ss. 790W–790ZD). Part 21A applies to all companies, except (i) companies subject to chapter 5 of the DTRs; and (ii) companies excluded from Part 21A by regulations (s. 790B(1)). Companies subject to Part 21A must take reasonable steps to find out if there is a registrable person/entity in the company and, if so, to identify them (s. 790D(1)). Registrable persons are also under a duty to notify the company if they are registrable (s. 790G).

The company must keep a register of any registrable persons who have significant control over the company, and failure to keep such a register is a criminal offence (s. 790M(12)). Schedule 1A, Part 1 of the CA 2006 provides that a person will have significant control if any one of the following conditions are satisfied:

(a) a person holds, directly or indirectly, more than 25% of the company's shares;

(b) a person holds, directly or indirectly, more than 25% of the company's voting rights;

(c) a person holds the right, directly or indirectly, to appoint or remove a majority of the company's directors;

(d) a person has the right to exercise, or actually exercises, significant influence or control over the company; or

(e) the trustees of a trust or the members of the firm that is not a legal person (i) meet any of the conditions in (a) to (d) above in relation to the company or would do so if they were individuals; and (ii) have the right to exercise, or actually exercise significant influence or control over the activities of that trust or firm.

Case study 8.2

John is the majority shareholder of Y-Corp Ltd and holds 51 of the company's 100 shares. The remaining 49 shares are held by Sarah (who holds 25 shares) and Natalie (who holds 24 shares). Y-Corp has been experiencing financial difficulties and so it enters into negotiations with BigBank plc. BigBank agrees to lend Y-Corp £50,000, but only if Y-Corp changes its articles to provide that Y-Corp cannot borrow any money nor grant any security without BigBank's consent.

In this example, John is a PSC under (a) and (b). Neither Sarah nor Natalie are PSCs. BigBank is a PSC under (d) as, by having a veto over Y-Corp's borrowing, it exercises significant control over Y-Corp.

Section 790K specifies what information the register must contain regarding registrable persons, including the person's name, address, country of residence, nationality, the date the person became a registrable PSC and the nature of his control over the company. Any person can inspect the PSC register free of charge (ss. 790N(1) and 790O(1)).

Test yourself 8.3

1. **What is a 'nominee'?**
2. **What information is found in the register of interests disclosed?**
3. **What is a person with significant control?**

5. Termination of membership

A person's membership of a company is terminated if their name is removed from the register of members. This can happen for a number of reasons, including:

- the member dies;
- the member transfers, transmits or gifts his shares in a company to another person, and that person's name is entered into the register of members in respect of those shares;
- the member's shares are **forfeited** (*Re China Steam Ship Co* (1868) LR 6 Eq 232) or **surrendered** (*Trevor v Whitworth* (1887) 12 App Cas 409 (HL));
- where the contract to sell shares to the member is subsequently rescinded (for example, due to misrepresentation) or declared void (for example, due to mistake);
- where an event occurs that, under the articles, will cause the member to cease being a member (*Sidebottom v Kershaw Leese & Co Ltd* [1920] 1 Ch 154 (CA)); or
- where the member is declared bankrupt and his shares are registered in the name of his trustee in bankruptcy.

forfeiture
Where the company or directors exercise a power (e.g. in the articles) to take away a person's shares.

surrendered
Where shares are given up by a member.

Chapter summary

- Section 112 of the CA 2006 provides two ways by which a person can become a member:
  - the subscribers of a company's memorandum are deemed to have agreed to become members of the company and, upon the company's registration, they become members and their names must be entered as such in the register of members; or
  - every other person who agrees to become a member of the company and whose name is entered in its register of members is a member of the company.
- Every company must keep a register of members, although private companies can choose to keep their membership data on the central register at Companies House.

- Anyone can inspect the register of members (although non-members must pay a fee).
- Public companies must keep a register of interests disclosed that provides information on persons who have an interest in the company's shares.
- Companies must keep a PSC register that provides details of persons with significant control over the company.
- A member's membership of the company is terminated once their name is removed from the register of members.

Chapter nine

Company meetings and decision making

Contents

1. Introduction

This chapter outlines the various ways in which companies make decisions, of which the principal mechanism is the general meeting. Significant decision-making power is placed in the hands of the company's members and this chapter looks at how the members exercise that power. Company meetings are subject to numerous procedural rules. It is the responsibility of the company secretary to ensure that meetings are run smoothly and in compliance with the relevant rules.

2. How companies make decisions

Companies can make decisions via two different methods: (i) by passing resolutions; or (ii) by unanimous assent. Both methods are available to public and private companies, but the method that is most appropriate and practical will depend on the type of company and its size.

- Decisions of a public company must be made via resolutions at a meeting, unless the unanimous assent rule is used (s. 281(2) and (4)). In larger public companies, the unanimous assent rule is not practical, and so company decisions are taken via resolutions at the annual general meeting.
- Decisions of a private company can be made by a resolution at a meeting, by a written resolution, or by unanimous assent (s. 281(1) and (4)). Most private companies have a very small number of members and so holding

meetings is usually pointless (especially those where the directors and members are the same persons). Accordingly, most private companies will make decisions by written resolution or unanimous assent.

3. Resolutions and the unanimous assent rule

As noted above, companies make decisions either by passing resolutions or by unanimous assent. Both decision-making methods will now be discussed.

3.1 Resolutions

A resolution is simply a vote under which the company resolves itself (or those who act on its behalf, notably the directors) to a particular course of action if a certain majority of those voting vote in favour of the resolution. Public companies must pass resolutions at a meeting (s. 281(2)), whereas private companies can pass resolutions at a meeting or using the written resolution procedure (s. 281(1)). Votes are calculated differently based on whether a resolution is at a meeting or if the written resolution procedure is used.

- Where the resolution is tabled at a meeting, the requisite majority is calculated based on the votes cast by those eligible to vote (ss. 282(3) and (4) and 283(4) and (5)). In other words, the votes are calculated based only on those who actually vote.
- Where a written resolution is used, the requisite majority is calculated based on the voting rights of the total number of members eligible to vote (ss. 282(2) and 283(2)), not just those who actually do vote.

Case study 9.1

X-Corp Ltd's share capital consists of 100 shares that are equally divided amongst 10 members. It is proposed that the company change its name, which requires the passing of a special resolution (which requires a majority of not less than 75%). Only four of the members vote, with three voting in favour and one voting against.

- **If the resolution took place at a meeting, it would pass as 75% of those who did vote voted in favour.**
- **If the resolution was a written resolution, it would not pass as only 40% of those eligible to vote voted for it.**

Both methods of voting are based on those who are eligible to vote, albeit in differing ways. Although the general rule is that anyone on the register of members is eligible to vote (*Pender v Lushington* (1877) 6 ChD 70 (Ch)), this is a general rule. Certain members may not be eligible to vote (such as those who have non-voting shares or those who are excluded from voting by the articles).

Ordinary resolutions, special resolutions and resolutions

The Companies Act 2006 provides for three types of resolutions. The type of resolution will determine the majority required in order to pass it, and legislation will specify when each type of resolution applies.

1. An ordinary resolution is a resolution that is passed by a simple majority (s. 282(1) (i.e. over 50%). If there is an exact 50:50 split between those voting in favour and against, the resolution fails.
2. A special resolution is a resolution that is passed by a majority of not less than 75% (s. 283(1)).
3. A resolution (one that is not specified as ordinary or special) will be classed as an ordinary resolution (and so will require a simple majority), unless the company's articles specify a higher majority or unanimity (s. 281(3)).

Written resolutions

The rules relating to company meetings are procedurally burdensome, especially for smaller companies. The Companies Act 2006 provides an easier method of making decisions by resolution by allowing private companies to make a decision via a written resolution (s. 288). Any resolution that can take place at a meeting can also take place as a written resolution, except a resolution to remove a director or auditor before their period of office has expired (s. 288(2)).

Figure 9.1 sets out the written resolution procedure.

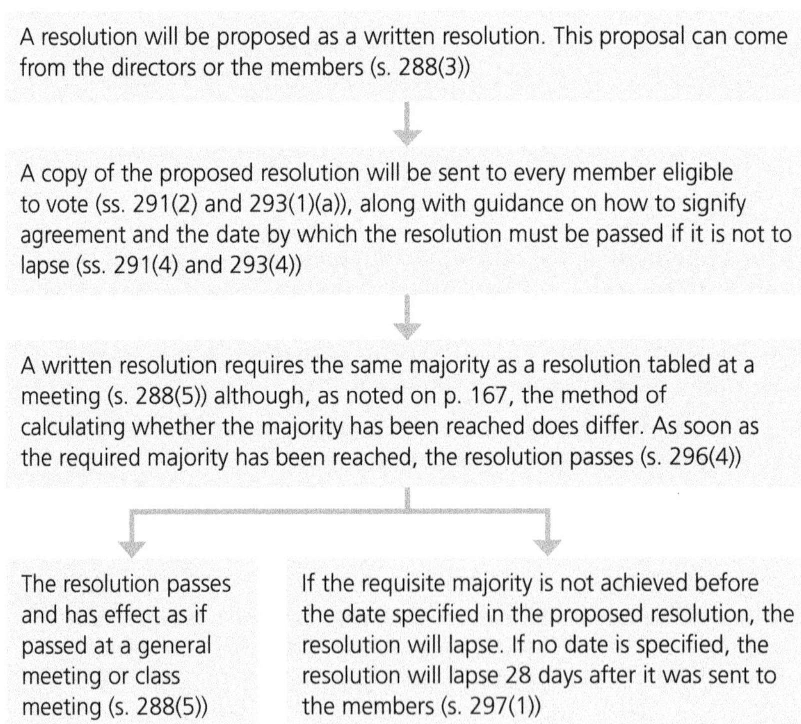

Figure 9.1 The written resolution process

3.2 Unanimous assent

Where all the members of a company know that they agree on a matter, making the decision via a resolution seems like a redundant and administratively burdensome exercise (especially in smaller companies). Common law has long allowed companies to make decisions by unanimous assent: if all of the members agree on a matter, the decision will be validly made even if no meeting takes place and no resolution is passed. The rule originated in the case of *Baroness Wenlock v The River Dee Co* (1883) 36 ChD 675 (CA) but the unanimous assent rule is often known as the '*Duomatic* principle', named after the following case.

Case law 9.1

***Re Duomatic Ltd* [1969] 2 Ch 365 (Ch)**

The two directors of Duomatic Ltd held all the company's voting shares between them and drew a salary from the company. Duomatic's articles provided that its directors' pay would be determined by a resolution at a general meeting, but no resolution was ever passed. Duomatic went into liquidation and the liquidator sought to recover from the directors the salaries paid to them on the ground that their remuneration had not been approved by the company.

Buckley J stated 'where it can be shown that all shareholders who have a right to attend and vote at a... meeting of the company assent to some matter which a general meeting of the company could carry into effect, that assent is as binding as a resolution in general meeting would be'. The directors held all the voting shares and their unanimous assent was regarded as a decision of the company. Accordingly, the liquidator's claim failed.

It must be emphasised that what is required is unanimity, and not merely an overwhelming majority. Thus, in *Re D'Jan of London* [1994] 1 BCLC 561 (Ch), a member who held 99% of the company's voting rights could not, by himself, take a decision by unanimous assent.

Scope

A wide range of decisions can be taken by unanimous assent and it can take the place of almost any resolution (subject to some limitations). It can be used to replace ordinary and special resolutions (*Cane v Jones* [1980] 1 WLR 1451 (Ch)), and decisions taken at general meetings and class meetings (*Re Torvale Group Ltd* [2000] BCC 626 (Ch)). Where statute states that a resolution is required, then whether the unanimous assent rule can be used will depend on whether the provision expressly or impliedly excludes the operation of the rule (such as by requiring a decision be taken at a meeting).

However, the rule is not universal and is subject to a number of conditions and restrictions, including:

- the unanimous assent rule will not apply where statute requires that a decision be taken at a meeting (*Re Oceanrose Investments Ltd* [2008] EWHC 3475 (Ch));
- in *EIC Services Ltd v Phipps* [2003] EWHC 1507 (Ch), the court stated that the unanimous assent rule can only be used in cases where:
  - the members who assented had appropriate or full knowledge of the matter in question;
  - all the members gave their actual assent (if a member's assent is not sought, the rule will not apply even if the member would likely have assented); and
- the rule cannot be used to make a decision that could not have been made by a resolution (e.g. to declare an unlawful dividend (*Secretary of State for Business, Innovation and Skills v Doffman* [2010] EWHC 3175 (Ch)).

Test yourself 9.1

1. **Explain the difference in the ways that votes are calculated at a meeting and by using the written resolution procedure.**
2. **Explain the difference between an ordinary resolution, a special resolution and a resolution.**
3. **What does the unanimous assent rule state?**
4. **What types of decisions cannot be taken by unanimous assent?**

4. General meetings

General meetings are so-called because all the members are usually entitled to attend. Prior to the CA 2006, there were two types of general meeting, namely (i) annual general meetings (AGMs); and (ii) extraordinary general meetings (EGMs), which was any general meeting that was not an AGM. The Companies Act 2006 no longer refers to EGMs and the AGM is simply regarded as a special form of general meeting that has its own additional rules.

A private company may never need to hold a general meeting as there are more straightforward ways for such companies to make decisions (the written resolution procedure or via unanimous assent). As a result, general meetings are only important in relation to larger private companies and public companies.

4.1 Calling a meeting

The power to call a general meeting is vested in several persons.

- The directors can call a general meeting (s. 302). This power is usually exercised by the board passing a resolution at a board meeting. In practice, almost all meetings are called by the directors.

- Members representing 5% of the company's paid-up share capital (or 5% of the voting rights if the company does not have a share capital) can require the directors to call a general meeting (s. 303(1) and (2)). Upon receipt of a valid request, the directors must call a meeting within 21 days and it must be held within 28 days following the date that notice of the meeting was provided (s. 304(1)). If the directors fail to comply with a valid request, the members who requested the meeting can call a meeting themselves at the company's expense (s. 305(1) and (6)).
- The court can call a general meeting if, for any reason, it is impracticable to call a meeting or conduct a meeting in the manner prescribed by the company's articles or the CA 2006 (s. 306(1)) (for example, where the meeting became disorderly and was closed down by the police (*Re British Union for the Abolition of Vivisection* [1995] BCLC 1 (Ch)). There are some situations where the court will not call a meeting, such as where it would affect the class rights of members, *Harman v BML Group Ltd* [1994] 1 WLR 893 (CA).

4.2 Notice

Each person entitled to attend a general meeting must be given sufficient notice of that meeting. A failure to provide sufficient notice will usually render the meeting invalid (*Smythe v Darley* (1849) HL Cas 789 (HL)), except where the failure to provide notice is accidental (CA 2006, s. 313(1)).

Notice of a general meeting must be provided to every member and director (s. 310(1)), as well as the company's auditor (s. 502(2)(a)), although the articles may provide that certain members and directors are not entitled to notice (s. 310(4)(b)). Notice may be provided in hard copy form, in electronic form, or by means of a website (s. 308). Notice of a meeting must provide the following:

- the time, date and place of the meeting (s. 311(1));
- the general nature of the business to be dealt with at the meeting (s. 311(2));
- if a special resolution is tabled at a meeting, the text of the resolution should be included and the intention to propose the resolution as a special resolution should be stated (s. 283(6)(a));
- the notice must contain, with reasonable prominence, a statement informing the member of his rights in relation to appointing a proxy (s. 325(1));
- the notice of an AGM of a public company must state that the meeting is an AGM (s. 337(1));
- certain resolutions will require additional information to be included (where a resolution is tabled to remove a director, the notice must contain any representations made by the director in question (s. 169(3)); and
- in the case of a traded company, the notice must provide the details of a website that contains specified information that must be provided prior to the meeting (s. 311(3)(a)), including specified details regarding the company's shares and voting rights (s. 311A(1)).

The notice will usually be accompanied by a circular which provides additional information on the meeting's agenda and the resolutions tabled. It has been suggested that the directors are under a duty to provide the members with sufficient information to enable them to decide whether to vote for or against the resolutions tabled at the meeting (*Tiessen v Henderson* [1899] 1 Ch 861 (Ch)) and a failure to include certain information could invalidate a resolution (for example, a director's failure to disclose an interest in a resolution (*Kaye v Croydon Tramways Co* [1898] 1 Ch 358 (CA)).

Length of notice

The amount of notice that must be provided is as follows.

- The general rule is that at least 14 clear days' notice must be given (s. 307(1) and (2)(b)). The reference to 'clear days' means that the day on which the notice is given and the day on which the meeting takes place are excluded (s. 360).
- In the case of the AGM of a public company, at least 21 clear days' notice must be provided (s. 307(2)(a)).
- If the company is a **traded company**, then at least 21 clear days' notice must be provided (s. 307A(1)(b)) but this can be reduced to 14 clear days if:
  - the meeting is not an AGM;
  - the company offers the members the ability to vote by electronic means; and
  - a special resolution is passed reducing the notice period to not less than 14 clear days (s. 307A(1)(a) and (2)–(4)).

traded company
A company with any shares that (i) carry rights to vote at general meetings; and (ii) are admitted to trading on a regulated market in an EEA state by or with the consent of the company.

The above notice periods are minimum periods, so the company is free to specify longer notice periods in its articles (ss. 307(3) and 307A(6)). The articles cannot specify a shorter notice period than those noted above but a company can provide shorter notice than that required by statute if the members agree as follows:

- in a private company, at least 90% of the members must agree to the shorter notice period (s. 307(6)(a));
- in a public company, at least 95% of the members must agree to the shorter notice period (s. 307(6)(b)); and
- as regards the AGM of a public company, all the members must agree to the shorter notice period (ss. 307(7) and 337(2)).

Certain resolutions require special notice (namely at least 28 clear days) to be provided (s. 312(1)). The resolutions are:

- a resolution to remove a director (s. 168);
- a resolution at a meeting to appoint someone in place of a director that was removed at that meeting;
- a resolution to remove an auditor (s. 511); and
- a resolution to appoint a new auditor (s. 515).

4.3 Quorum

In order for a general meeting to validly make decisions, a minimum number of 'qualifying persons' needs to be present (this is known as a 'quorum'). For the purposes of a general meeting, s. 318(3) provides that a qualifying person is:

- an individual who is a member of the company;
- a representative of a corporate member (corporate representatives are discussed on p. 175); or
- a proxy of the member (proxies are discussed on p. 175).

The number of qualifying persons that constitutes a quorum is as follows.

- In the case of a limited company that only has one member, one qualifying person present at the meeting will constitute a quorum (s. 318(1)).
- In all other cases, the general rule is that two qualifying persons present at the meeting will constitute a quorum, unless the only two persons present are two corporate representative or two proxies of the same person (s. 318(2)). This is subject to the articles, so companies can specify a different number in their articles.

A meeting that lacks a quorum when it starts cannot proceed (*Re Cambrian Peat, Fuel and Charcoal Co Ltd* (1875) 31 LT 773). A meeting that starts with a quorum, but then becomes inquorate, must stop unless the articles provide otherwise (*Re Hartley Baird Ltd* [1955] Ch 143 (Ch)).

4.4 Voting

A member's ability to vote is one of the most important membership rights and so a range of rules exist to ensure that the voting process is fair. The law does not seek to tell members how to vote – as Lord Maugham stated in *Carruth v Imperial Chemical Industries Ltd* [1937] AC 707 (HL) 'the shareholder's vote is a right of property, and prima facie may be exercised by a shareholder as he thinks fit in his own interest'. Despite this, a member's ability to vote can be taken away or restricted in several ways, including:

- a member will be unable to vote if his shares have no voting rights;
- a company's articles may place restrictions upon a member's ability to vote; and
- statute may limit a member's ability to vote (for example, a director who is also a member cannot vote on a resolution to ratify his negligence or breach of duty (s. 239(3) and (4)).

How members exercise their vote

There are two different ways to pass resolutions at a meeting. The first method is a show of hands, under which the members attending raise their hands to signify support for, or opposition to, a resolution. Each member will have one vote, unless the articles state otherwise (s. 284(2) and (4)). Resolutions are to be taken on a show of hands unless the articles provide otherwise. The model articles state that a vote will be taken on a show of hands unless a poll is demanded in accordance with the articles (model articles for private companies limited by shares, article 42; model articles for public companies, article 34). The chair will count the votes and declare if the resolution is passed or not. The following example indicates how this works in practice.

Case study 9.2

Ten members attend a general meeting of X-Corp Ltd. Two ordinary resolutions have been tabled.

- **As regards the first resolution, six members raise their hands in support and so the chair declares that the resolution is passed.**
- **As regards the second resolution, three members raise their hands in support. This does not mean that the resolution has failed as some members may abstain. Accordingly, the chair asks those members who oppose the resolution to raise their hands. Only two members raise their hands, and so the resolution is passed.**

The second method is a poll vote, under which each member has one vote per share, unless the company has no share capital, in which case, each member has one vote (s. 284(3) and (4)). In larger companies, votes are conducted by a poll because the shareholders want voting power commensurate with their shareholding. Members have a statutory right to demand that a vote be taken by poll. This right cannot be taken away by the articles, but it can be restricted (s. 321). The model articles (model articles for private companies, article 44(2); model articles for public companies, article 36(2)) state that a poll may be demanded by:

- the chair;
- the directors;
- two or more persons having the right to vote on the resolution; or
- a person or persons representing not less than one tenth of the total voting rights of all the shareholders having the right to vote on the resolution.

The following example shows a poll vote in action, and how it compares to a vote on a show of hands.

Case study 9.3

Ten members attend a general meeting of Y-Corp Ltd. Nine of the members hold 10 shares each, while the tenth member (*X*) holds 910 shares. Two ordinary resolutions have been tabled and *X* demands that the first one is taken by poll:

- **As regards the first resolution (taken by poll), nine of the members vote for it and *X* votes against, and so the resolution is defeated.**

- **As regards the second resolution (taken on a show of hands), three members support the resolution and two (including *X*) vote against it. The resolution is passed.**

Where a vote is taken by a poll at a meeting of a quoted or traded company, then s. 341 provides that the company must ensure that certain information is placed on its website, including:

- the date of the meeting;
- the text of the resolution;
- the number of votes cast in favour; and
- the number of votes against.

Voting by proxy

A member is entitled to appoint another person (known as a 'proxy') to exercise all or any of his rights to attend, speak and vote at a meeting of the company (s. 324(1)). Most members of larger companies do not attend the AGM and so the ability to appoint a proxy is especially useful. When the company sends out notice of the meeting, that notice must include, with reasonable prominence, a statement informing members of their right to appoint a proxy (s. 325(1)). Members are free to choose who acts as their proxy, but in larger companies, the company will usually nominate a proxy (usually the chair). The member can then accept this nomination or ignore it and choose his own proxy.

A proxy attending the meeting of a traded company must be appointed in writing (s. 327(A1)). No such formality is required in other companies unless the articles so provide, and it is common for companies to require that some form of document be filed with the company in order to validly appoint a proxy (the model articles require that a proxy notice be filed with the company). A proxy's appointment can be terminated by the member who appointed him.

Section 324A provides that a proxy must vote in accordance with any instructions given by the member who appointed them. If no such instructions have been provided, then the proxy may vote as they wish.

Corporate representatives

A corporate representative is a person who has been authorised by a resolution of the directors of a company (*A*) to represent *A* at a meeting of another company (*B*) in which *A* is a member (s. 323(1)). That representative can then exercise on behalf of *A* the same powers as *A* could exercise as if he were an individual member of *B* (s. 323(2)). In other words, from *B*'s perspective, the representative is a member of *B* and has all the rights of *A*.

Instead of appointing a corporate representative, *A* could simply appoint a proxy. The advantage of *A* appointing a corporate representative is that it does not need to comply with any procedural rules relating to proxies – the representative can simply turn up to the meeting.

Test yourself 9.2

1. **Identify three possible limitations on a member's ability to vote.**
2. **What are the two methods of voting on a resolution and how do they differ?**
3. **What is a proxy?**
4. **What is a corporate representative?**

4.5 Annual general meetings

The requirements placed upon companies to hold an AGM are as follows.

- A private company does not need to hold an AGM, but it can do if it so wishes. A private company will be required to hold an AGM if it is a traded company (s. 336(1A)) or if its articles require that an AGM be held (Companies Act 2006 (Commencement No. 3, Consequential Amendments, Transitional Provisions and Savings) Order, Schedule 3, para 32).
- A public company must hold an AGM every year within a six-month period beginning with the day following its accounting reference date (s. 336(1)). This period is increased to nine months in the case of a traded company (s. 336(1A)).

The business that is typically dealt with at an AGM includes:

- laying the accounts and the various reports before the meeting (discussed more in Chapter 14);
- a resolution providing that the members agree to receive and adopt the accounts and reports;
- approving the remuneration report (if the company is quoted);
- approving the appointment/re-appointment of directors and the auditor;
- declaration of a final dividend; and
- providing directors of the company with authorisation to engage in certain acts (such as allot shares, disapply pre-emption rights or authorise the company to purchase its own shares).

4.6 Adjourning a meeting

The common law provides the chair with a power to adjourn a meeting in limited circumstances, such as where a poll has been demanded, but it cannot be taken forthwith (*Jackson v Hamlyn* [1953] Ch 577 (Ch)). In practice, a company's articles will increase the chair's powers of adjournment, with the model articles (model articles for private companies, articles 41(2) and (3); model articles for public companies, articles 33(2) and (3)) stating that:

- if a meeting is not quorate within half an hour of the time it was due to start, or if it starts quorate but then becomes inquorate, then the chair must adjourn the meeting;
- the chair may adjourn the meeting if the meeting consents to an adjournment;
- the chair may adjourn the meeting if it appears to him that an adjournment is necessary to protect the safety of any person attending the meeting or ensure that the business of the meeting is conducted in an orderly manner; and
- the chair must adjourn a general meeting if directed to do so by the general meeting.

The articles will normally provide that, when the chair adjourns a meeting, he will set the time and date of the adjourned meeting, and this adjourned meeting will be regarded as a continuation of the original meeting.

4.7 Records of meetings and resolutions

It is vital that records of meetings and resolutions are kept so that the records can be referred to if a dispute arises. Specified records must be kept by a company for at least 10 years (s. 355(2)) and any member can inspect these records free of charge (s. 358(3)). The records that must be kept are:

- copies of all resolutions of members passed otherwise than at general meetings (e.g. written resolutions);
- minutes of all proceedings of general meetings; and
- details of decisions taken by a sole member (ss. 355(1) and 357).

Test yourself 9.3

1. **What types of company must hold an AGM?**
2. **Identify five items of business that typically arise at an AGM.**
3. **Under the model articles, when can a chair adjourn a meeting of the company?**
4. **What records of meetings and resolutions must the company keep, and for how long must they be kept?**

5 Class meetings

Class meetings are meetings where only one class of member is entitled to attend, not all the members of the company (although other members can attend if no objection is raised). They are held when a decision is taken that affects only a particular class of member (such as a decision to vary class rights).

The rules relating to class meetings are largely the same as those for general meetings but the following differences should be noted.

- As discussed on page 171, both the members and the courts have the power to call a general meeting, but they do not have the power to call a class meeting (CA 2006, ss. 334(2)(a) and (b) and 335(2)(a) (and (b)).
- The quorum for a class meeting can differ to that of a general meeting, notably where the class meeting is to decide on a variation of class rights (ss. 334(3) and 335(3)).
- The rules relating to the right to demand a poll found in s. 321 only apply to general meetings. As regards a class meeting to approve a variation of class rights, any holder of shares of the class in question can demand a poll (s. 334(6)).

6. Member engagement

Providing the members with a forum in which to make decisions and engage with the company does not mean they will actually do so. Concerns have long existed that members of larger companies do not engage sufficiently and that, as a result, the general meeting is not an effective forum for shareholder democracy.

In the Cadbury Report, Sir Adrian Cadbury stated that '[i]f too many Annual General Meetings are at present an opportunity missed, this is because shareholders do not make the most of them and, in some cases, boards do not encourage them to do so'. Principle D of the UK Corporate Governance Code provides that the board should ensure effective engagement with, and encourage participation from, the shareholders, but other than that it has little to say regarding general meetings – although paras 34–44 of the FRC's accompanying Guidance on Board Effectiveness (2018) does contain further guidance on how companies should engage with stakeholders.

A detailed discussion of the effectiveness of general meetings is outside the scope of this text, but a brief discussion of several ways in which engagement could be improved will be of use.

6.1 Electronic meetings

One possible method of improving member engagement at company meetings is through the use of electronic meetings (including by telephone). The courts have long recognised that the members do not need to physically be in each other's presence in order for a company meeting to take place (see e.g. *Byng v London Life Association Ltd* [1970] Ch 170 (CA)), and s. 360A(1) of the CA 2006 provides that nothing in Part 13 is to be taken to preclude the holding and conducting of a meeting in such a way that persons who are not present together at the same place may attend, speak and vote at it by electronic means.

Accordingly, companies can, through their articles, choose between physical meetings, electronic meetings or a combination of the two. To date, very few companies have chosen to hold electronic meetings. Only one UK-listed company (Jimmy Choo plc) has held a fully electronic meeting.

6.2 Institutional investors

Institutional investors (such as insurance companies, pension funds and banks) control a significant portion of shares in UK quoted companies. It was hoped that these powerful shareholders could use their concentrated shareholdings to better hold companies to account, but institutional investors have been criticised for not being as active as they could be (both the Walker Review and the Kay Report criticised institutional investors for a lack of engagement).

To encourage institutional investors to engage more with companies, the FRC published the UK Stewardship Code in 2010. This was updated in 2012, with a new Code due to be published in 2019 (see the FRC website for updates on this). The structure of the 2019 Code has been amended to make it more similar to the 2018 UK Corporate Governance Code. Accordingly, the 2019 Stewardship Code consists of a series of Principles and Provisions. It is proposed that signatories to the Code are required to apply the Code's Principles and state how they have done so (this is known as 'apply and explain'). The Code's Provisions adopt a comply or explain approach, meaning that signatories are expected to comply with the Provisions and explain how they have done so. Signatories that choose not to comply with a Provision should explain why and disclose what alternative approach they have taken.

The FRC monitors compliance and assigns signatories to the Stewardship Code to one of two tiers (although the FRC is consulting on whether this is the best approach to monitor compliance).

1. Tier 1 signatories provide a good quality and transparent description of their approach to stewardship and explanations of an alternative approach where necessary.
2. Tier 2 signatories meet many of the reporting expectations but report less transparently on their approach to stewardship or do not provide explanations where they depart from provisions of the Code.

Institutional investors and the UK Stewardship Code are discussed in more detail as part of the Corporate Governance unit.

Chapter summary

- Companies can make decisions via two different methods: by passing resolutions or by unanimous assent.
- Decisions of a public company must be made via resolutions at a meeting, unless the unanimous assent rule is used (in practice, public companies will rarely use this rule).
- Decisions of a private company can be made by a resolution at a meeting, by a written resolution or by unanimous assent.
- A resolution is a vote under which the company resolves itself to a particular course of action if a certain majority of those voting vote in favour of the resolution.
- An ordinary resolution is passed if a simple majority vote in favour (i.e. over 50%), whereas a special resolution requires a majority of not less than 75%.
- If all of the members agree on a matter, the decision will be validly made even if no meeting takes place and no resolution is passed. However, there are some decisions that cannot be taken by unanimous assent and must be made via a formal resolution.
- A general meeting is a meeting where all the members are entitled to attend. A class meeting is a meeting where only one class of member is entitled to attend.
- A general meeting can be called by:
  - the directors;
  - members representing 5% of the company's paid-up share capital or, if the company does not have a share capital, 5% of the voting rights can require the directors to call a general meeting; or
  - the court.
- Fourteen days' clear notice must be provided of a company meeting, but this is increased to 21 clear days in the case of the AGM of a public company or the general meeting of a traded company.
- In order for a general meeting to validly make decisions, a minimum number of 'qualifying persons' needs to be present, which is:
  - one qualifying person in the case of a limited company that has only one member; or
  - two qualifying persons in all other cases.
- There are two methods of voting on a resolution, namely:
  - on a show of hands, under which each member has one vote; or
  - by a poll, under which each member has one vote per share, unless the company has no share capital, in which case, each member has one vote.
- A member is entitled to appoint another person (a proxy) to exercise all or any of his rights to attend, speak and vote at a meeting of the company.

- Private companies do not generally need to hold an AGM, but can do if they so wish. A public company must hold an AGM every year within a six-month period beginning with the day following its accounting reference date.
- Records of meetings and resolutions must be kept for at least 10 years.
- In order to encourage institutional investors to engage more with their companies, the FRC published the UK Stewardship Code. An updated Code will be published in 2019.

Chapter ten
Members' remedies

Contents

1. Introduction

This chapter outlines a range of remedies available to members who feel they have been wronged in some way. Although the remedies discussed in this chapter apply to members in general, they are primarily aimed at minority shareholders who have suffered loss due to the actions of those who control the company. Without the remedies in this chapter, such minority shareholders would be largely powerless to obtain redress.

The chapter largely focuses on the three principal statutory member remedies:

- the derivative claim under Part 11 of the CA 2006;
- the unfair prejudice petition under Part 30 of the CA 2006; and
- the winding up petition under s. 122 of the IA 1986.

Before looking at these statutory member remedies, it is first important to understand the differences between personal, representative and corporate actions.

2. Personal, representative and corporate actions

If a member sustains loss due to the actions of another person, they may have a personal right to bring proceedings against that person. For example, if a member sustains loss due to the company or another member breaching the constitution then, as the constitution forms a contract (CA 2006, s. 33, discussed in Chapter 4), the member may be able to sue for breach of contract. Examples of personal actions are discussed throughout this text. Two issues will be discussed here:

- what happens if a third party's act or omission causes loss to both the company and a member; and
- in what circumstances can a member (*X*) bring a claim on behalf of other members who have suffered a loss arising out of the same circumstances that caused loss to *X*.

2.1 The relationship between personal and corporate actions

A person may cause loss to both the company and its members. The issue is whether both the company and its members can sue, or only one party. The general rule is that both the company and its members have a personal right to sue the wrongdoer (*Pender v Lushington* (1877) 6 ChD 70 (Ch)). An exception to this is where the 'no reflective loss' principle applies.

The 'no reflective loss' principle

A person may engage in an act or omission that causes loss to both the company and its members. Normally, both the company and its members can sue the wrongdoer, but the members will be prevented from suing where the no reflective loss principle applies. This principle states that where the members' losses are reflective of the loss sustained by the company, then it is the company that should recover the loss and company's claim will 'trump that of the shareholder' (*Day v Cook* [2001] EWCA Civ 592 (Arden LJ)). An obvious example of such a situation is where a person causes loss to the company, which in turn causes the company's share price to drop. Both the company and its shareholders have suffered a loss, but the loss suffered by the shareholders is merely reflective of that suffered by the company. The rationale behind preventing the members from claiming was set out by Lord Millett in *Johnson v Gore Wood & Co (No 1)* [2002] AC 1 (HL) 62, who stated:

> 'If the shareholder is allowed to recover in respect of such loss, then either there will be double recovery at the expense of the defendant or the shareholder will recover at the expense of the company and its creditors and other shareholders. Neither course can be permitted ... Justice to the defendant requires the exclusion of one claim or the other; protection of the interests of the company's creditors requires that it is the company which is allowed to recover to the exclusion of the shareholders.'

Over time, the no reflective loss principle has been refined, with *Johnson v Gore Wood & Co (No 1)* itself now providing the key facets of the no reflective loss principle.

- Lord Millett stated that '[n]o action lies at the suit of a shareholder suing in that capacity and no other to make good a diminution in the value of the shareholder's shareholding where that merely reflects the loss suffered by the company'.

- Members can sue for a reduction in the value of their shareholding if:
  - they have a cause of action to do so; and
  - the company has suffered loss, but has no cause of action to recover that loss.
- Lord Bingham stated '[w]here a company suffers loss caused by a breach of duty to it, and a shareholder suffers a loss separate and distinct from that suffered by the company caused by breach of a duty independently owed to the shareholder, each may sue to recover the loss caused to it by breach of the duty owed to it but neither may recover loss caused to the other by breach of the duty owed to that other'.

In the following case, the courts have created an exception to the no reflective loss principle. A member can bring a claim against a person for losses that are reflective of those sustained by the company if the company is unable to claim due to that person's conduct.

Case law 10.1

***Giles v Rhind* [2002] EWCA Civ 1428**

Giles and Rhind were directors and shareholders of Surrey Hill Foods Ltd (SHF). Rhind resigned and the terms of his resignation provided that he would not set up a new company that competed with SHF. Rhind did set up a rival company and diverted clients from SHF to this new company. SHF commenced proceedings against Rhind, but Rhind's actions had driven SHF to insolvency and so it did not have sufficient funds to continue the claim. Therefore, Giles commenced a personal claim against Rhind for the reduction in value of the shares he held in SHF.

The court noted that, in *Johnson*, it was held that a member could sue for a reduction in the value of his shareholding if the company did not have a cause of action. Here, Waller LJ stated that 'the same should be true of a situation in which the wrongdoer has disabled the company from pursuing that cause of action'. Giles' personal action against Rhind was therefore allowed to continue.

2.2 Representative actions and GLOs

It may be the case that the interests of multiple members, or even all the members, will be adversely affected by a person's act or omission. The issue being discussed here is whether all the members affected have to sue individually in order to obtain a remedy or whether one action can be brought on behalf of all the members affected.

The UK has no American-style 'class action' system but Part 19 of the Civil Procedure Rules (CPR) establishes two mechanisms that allow for collective action, namely:

- the representative action; and
- the group litigation order.

Representative actions
Where more than one person has the same interest in a claim, then a representative action may be commenced by one or more of the persons who have the same interest as representatives of any other persons who have that interest (CPR, r 19.6(1)). A member who has suffered loss can, on his own or with other affected members, bring a claim along with (or on behalf of) the affected members. If the case succeeds, any judgment or order made by the court binds all the parties represented in the claim. It can also be enforced on persons not party to the claim with the permission of the court (CPR, r 19.6(4)(a)).

Group Litigation Orders
In a representative action, all the affected members will obtain the same remedy. If some members wish to obtain different remedies, then a group litigation order (GLO) will be preferable. Rule 19.10 of the CPR provides that a GLO is effectively a mechanism to manage multiple cases that arise from common or related issues of fact or law. Affected persons who opt in to the GLO will be placed on a 'group register' and their cases will be heard by the court. Each claimant who opts in brings their claim in an individual capacity but the case will be heard in a single court, avoiding multiple proceedings. If the case succeeds, any judgment or order made by the court binds all the parties on the group register, unless the court orders otherwise (CPR, r 19.12(1)(a)).

Test yourself 10.1

1. **If a third party causes loss to both the company and its members, can both sue to recover their loss?**
2. **What is the no reflective loss principle?**
3. **In what situation will the no reflective loss principle not apply?**
4. **What is the difference between a representative action and a group litigation order?**

3. The derivative claim

Part 11 of the CA 2006 establishes the rules relating to the derivative claim. The derivative claim (the successor to the derivative action) provides a mechanism under which a member can sue to obtain redress for a wrong done to the company. Before looking at how the derivative claim operates, it is first important to understand why it was created and why, as a general rule, members cannot usually sue on behalf of the company. To do this, the rule in *Foss v Harbottle* must be examined.

3.1 The rule in *Foss v Harbottle*

As a general rule, if a person sustains loss due to the act or omission of another person, then only the person who suffered the loss can sue to obtain redress. As the Court of Appeal stated '*A* cannot, as a general rule, bring an action against *B* to recover damages or secure other relief on behalf of *C* for an injury done by *B* to *C*. *C* is the proper plaintiff because *C* is the party injured, and, therefore, the person in whom the cause of action is vested' (*Prudential Assurance Co Ltd v Newman Industries Ltd (No 2)* [1982] Ch 204 (CA)). In the corporate context, this means that if a wrong is committed against a company, then only the company can sue for redress and its members cannot sue on the company's behalf. This is known as the 'proper claimant' principle as the company is the proper claimant. The proper claimant principle forms one half of the rule in *Foss v Harbottle* and *Foss* itself demonstrates the proper claimant principle in action.

Case law 10.2

***Foss v Harbottle* (1843) 2 Hare 461**

Foss and Turton were shareholders of a company. They alleged that the company's directors and certain other shareholders defrauded the company by entering into a series of fraudulent transactions. They therefore commenced proceedings against the wrongdoers 'on behalf of themselves and all the other members of the corporation, except those who committed the injuries complained of'.

The court held that the conduct engaged in by the defendants had not just caused loss to Foss and Turton – it was 'an injury to the whole corporation'. Wigram V-C stated that '[i]t was not, nor could it successfully be, argued that it was a matter of course for any individual members of a corporation thus to assume to themselves the right of suing in the name of the corporation'. There was nothing preventing the company from commencing proceedings to obtain redress and, as it was the proper claimant, Foss and Turton's claim failed.

The principal rationale behind the proper claimant principle is a desire to prevent excessive claims being brought. As Mellish LJ stated in *Macdougall v Gardiner* (1875) 1 ChD 13 (CA):

> 'Looking to the nature of these companies, looking at the way in which their articles are formed, and that they are not all lawyers who attend these meetings, nothing can be more likely than that there should be something more or less irregular done at them – some directors may have been irregularly appointed, some directors as irregularly turned out, or something or other may have been done which ought not to have been done according to the proper construction of the articles. Now, if that gives a right to every member of the company to file a bill to have the question decided, then if there happens to be one cantankerous member, or one member who loves litigation, everything of this kind will be litigated; whereas, if the bill must be filed in the name of the company, then, unless

> there is a majority who really wish for litigation, the litigation will not go on. Therefore, holding that such suits must be brought in the name of the company does certainly greatly tend to stop litigation.'

In *Prudential Assurance Co Ltd v Newman Industries Ltd (No 2)* [1982] Ch 204 (CA), the court held that the proper claimant principle is but one half of the rule in *Foss v Harbottle*. The other half of the rule consists of the 'irregularity principle', which basically provides that a member cannot bring a claim in relation to an irregularity that could be remedied or ratified by a simple majority of the members. Mellish LJ also set out the rationale behind this principle:

> 'if the thing complained of is a thing which in substance the majority of the company are entitled to do, or if something has been done irregularly which the majority of the company are entitled to do regularly, or if something has been done illegally which the majority of the company are entitled to do legally, there can be no use in having a litigation about it, the ultimate end of which is only that a meeting has to be called, and then ultimately the majority gets its wishes.'

However, the rule in *Foss v Harbottle* contained a notable exception, namely the derivative action.

The derivative action

The rule in *Foss v Harbottle* is eminently sensible but it did give rise to a notable problem. Lord Denning MR in *Wallersteiner v Moir (No 2)* [1975] 2 WLR 389 (CA) noted that if a company is:

> 'defrauded by a wrongdoer, the company itself is the one person to sue for the damage... But suppose it is defrauded by insiders who control its affairs – by directors who hold a majority of the shares – who then can sue for damages? Those directors are themselves the wrongdoers. If a board meeting is held, they will not authorise the proceedings to be taken by the company against themselves. If a general meeting is called, they will vote down any suggestion that the company should sue them themselves. Yet the company is the one person who is damnified. It is the one person who should sue.'

As a result, Denning MR stated that 'some means must be found for the company to sue. Otherwise the law would fail in its purpose. Injustice would be done without redress.' The law's answer was to allow members to commence proceedings on behalf of the company in certain cases. This was known as a derivative action, as the member was bringing an action based on a right derived from the company.

In *Edwards v Halliwell* [1950] 2 All ER 1064 (CA), Jenkins LJ stated that there were four instances where a derivative action could be brought, namely:

1. where the act complained of was illegal or *ultra vires*;
2. where the act complained of infringed the personal rights of a member;
3. where the act complained of could only be done or sanctioned by the passing of a special resolution; and
4. where the act complained of constituted a 'fraud on the minority'.

In reality, the first three are examples of personal rights and so are not true derivative actions. It is only the fourth instance that constitutes a true derivative action. The 'fraud on the minority' instance was created to deal with the exact type of situation as noted by Denning MR in *Wallersteiner*, namely where those who controlled the company commit some form of fraud against the company.

The operation of the rule in *Foss* and the development of the derivative claim was deemed complex and unwieldy by the Law Commission and so it was proposed to simplify the procedure and codify it in statute. The result is Part 11 of the CA 2006 which establishes the statutory derivative claim.

3.2 The statutory derivative claim

Before looking at the derivative claim itself, it should be noted that Part 11 does not significantly affect the rule in *Foss v Harbottle* itself. Instead, Part 11 largely replaces the derivative action with a statutory derivative claim.

A derivative claim is a claim brought by a member of a company in respect of a cause of action vested in the company, which seeks relief on behalf of the company (CA 2006, s. 260(1)). This simple definition results in several important consequences:

- The claim must be brought by a member. A person who was a member and had a cause of action cannot commence a derivative claim once he ceases to be a member. However, if the person is a current member, it does not matter whether the cause of action arose before or after they became a member (CA 2006, s. 260(4)). The claimant need not be a minority member, but the courts will usually only grant permission for a majority shareholder to bring a claim in exceptional circumstances (*Cinematic Finance Ltd v Ryder* [2010] EWHC 3387 (Ch)).
- As the cause of action must be vested in the company, a derivative claim cannot be brought for a cause of action that is personally vested in the member (unless that cause of action also gives rise to a claim on behalf of the company, in which case the member's claim will likely be prevented from continuing due to the no reflective loss principle).
- Any benefits of the derivative claim go to the company and not the member bringing the claim. To this end, r 19.9(3) of the CPR provides that the company will be made a party to a derivative claim, so that it is able to enforce the court's judgment.

The statutory derivative claim largely replaces the common law derivative action, but there are two instances where the provisions relating to the statutory derivative claim do not apply and so, in these instances, the common law derivative action will continue to be relevant:

- The first instance is where a 'multiple derivative action' is involved. A multiple derivative action occurs where a member is seeking relief not on behalf of the company in which he is a member, but on behalf of another company (normally a subsidiary of the company of which he is a member). Such an action is permitted in very limited cases, but it will fall outside the scope of the statutory derivative claim (*Re Fort Gilkicker Ltd* [2013] EWHC 348 (Ch)).

- The second instance is where the claimant is a member of a company that is not registered under a Companies Act. The principal example of this is where the claim relates to a foreign company (*Novatrust Ltd v Kea Investments Ltd* [2014] EWHC 4061 (Ch)).

3.3 Causes of action

Not all causes of action vested in the company are grounds for a derivative claim – instead, s. 260(3) provides that a derivative claim can only derive from an actual or proposed act or omission involving negligence, **default**, breach of duty or breach of trust by a director of the company. Although s. 260(3) states that the act or omission must be engaged in by a director, this does not mean that a derivative claim can only be made against a director. A claim can be made against a director or another person (or both) (s. 260(3)). A claim can only be made against a person who is not a director 'where the damage suffered by the company arose from an act involving a breach of duty etc on the part of the director (such as for knowing receipt of money or property transferred in breach of trust or for knowing assistance in a breach of trust)' (Explanatory Notes to the CA 2006, para 494).

default
A failure to perform a legally obligated act.

3.4 The derivative claim procedure

The Companies Act 2006 and the Civil Procedure Rules (CPRs) set out the procedure that must be followed in order to bring a derivative claim. The first step is for the derivative claimant to issue a claim form (CPR, r 19.9(2)) which must be accompanied by an application for permission to continue the claim (CPR, r 19.9A(2)). This application is necessary because s. 261(1) of the CA 2006 provides that a member who brings a derivative claim must apply to the court for permission to continue it. The claimant must provide evidence supporting his claim and why permission should be granted, and the defendant may also submit evidence in answer to the claim.

The process for determining whether permission is granted involves a two-stage process.

Stage 1: Establishing a prima facie *case*

The first stage involves the court determining if, based on the evidence provided by the claimant, there is a *prima facie* case for granting permission to continue the claim (s. 261(2)). The purpose of this stage is to weed out frivolous or unmeritorious claims, and so the company is not involved at this stage. In practice, stage 1 is not especially difficult to overcome and most claimants are able to establish a *prima facie* case.

At the end of stage 1, there are three possible outcomes (s. 261(4)):

- The court may adjourn the proceedings and give such directions as it thinks fit.
- If the court decides that a *prima facie* case has not been established, it must dismiss the claimant's application, and the court may make any consequential order that it considers appropriate (s. 261(2)).

- If the court decides that a *prima facie* case has been established, then the court may give directions to the company as to the evidence that it must produce and may adjourn the proceedings to allow such evidence to be obtained (s. 261(3)). The case will then proceed onto the second stage.

Stage 2: Determining whether to grant permission

The second stage involves a hearing to determine if permission to continue the claim should be granted. The starting point is s. 263(2), which sets out three circumstances in which permission to continue the claim must be refused. The first is where the court is satisfied that a person acting in accordance with s. 172 (duty to promote the success of the company) would not seek to continue the claim (s. 263(2)(a)). The courts have set out guidance on what factors may be relevant in determining this. In *Iesini v Westrip Holdings Ltd* [2009] EWHC 2526 (Ch), Lewison J stated that relevant factors include:

> 'the size of the claim; the strength of the claim; the cost of the proceedings; the company's ability to fund the proceedings; the ability of the potential defendants to satisfy a judgment; the impact on the company if it lost the claim and had to pay not only its own costs but the defendant's as well; any disruption to the company's activities while the claim is pursued; whether the prosecution of the claim would damage the company in other ways (e.g. by losing the services of a valuable employee or alienating a key supplier or customer) and so on.'

The second circumstance is where the court is satisfied that the cause of action arises from an act or omission that is yet to occur, and the act or omission has been authorised by the company (s. 263(2)(b)). Whether authorisation has occurred will depend on whether statute specifies the process for obtaining authorisation. If such a process exists, it must be followed. If no such process exists, the common law rules will apply (s. 180(4)) and typically involve the members providing authorisation by passing a resolution.

The third circumstance is where the court is satisfied that the cause of action arises from an act or omission that has already occurred, and the act or omission was authorised by the company before it occurred or has been ratified by the company since it occurred (s. 263(2)(c)). Again, what constitutes authorisation or ratification will depend upon whether a specific statutory process exists or not, but it should be noted that a process for ratification does exist under s. 239 (discussed in Chapter 9).

If none of these three circumstances apply, then the court will have discretion as to whether to grant permission for the claim to continue. In determining this, s. 263(3) provides that the court must take into account six factors.

- The first factor is whether the member is acting in good faith in seeking to continue the claim. Examples of situations where a lack of good faith has been established include where the claimant was a party to the conduct complained of (*Iesini v Westrip Holdings Ltd* [2009] EWHC 2526 (Ch)), and where the claimant was pursuing the claim for an ulterior motive (e.g. to further the claimant's interest as a creditor of the company, *Abouraya v Sigmund* [2014] EWHC 277 (Ch)).

- The second factor is the importance that a person acting in accordance with s. 172 (duty to promote the success of the company) would attach to the claim.
- The third factor is where the cause of action results from an act or omission that is yet to occur, whether the act or omission could be, and in the circumstances would be likely to be, authorised or ratified.
- The fourth factor is where the cause of action arises from an act or omission that has already occurred, whether the act or omission could be, and in the circumstances would be likely to be, ratified by the company.
- The fifth factor is whether the company has decided not to pursue the claim. If a company decides not to pursue the claim for valid reasons, then the court will likely refuse permission to continue the claim (*Kleanthous v Paphitis* [2011] EWHC 2287 (Ch)). Note, however, that where the claim is being brought against directors who constitute the majority of the board, then the fact that the company decides not to pursue the claim will carry 'very little weight' (*Cullen Investments Ltd v Brown* [2015] EWHC 473 (Ch)) as those directors will use their power to prevent the company from pursuing the claim.
- The sixth factor is whether the act or omission in respect of which the claim is brought gives rise to a cause of action that the member could pursue in his own right rather than on behalf of the company. The mere existence of another remedy will not, in itself, cause permission to be refused. The key issue is whether it is more appropriate for the member to pursue this alternative remedy, rather than the derivative claim (*Franbar Holdings Ltd v Patel* [2008] EWHC 1534 (Ch)). If the claimant has a good reason not to pursue that alternative remedy, then this factor will not result in permission being refused.

These factors must be taken into account, but s. 263(3) does not provide an exhaustive list of relevant factors, so other factors can also be taken into account (*Franbar Holdings Ltd v Patel* [2008] EWHC 1534 (Ch)). A further factor is stated in s. 263(4) which provides that 'the court shall have particular regard to any evidence before it as to the views of members of the company who have no personal interest, direct or indirect, in the matter'.

If permission to continue the case is refused, then the claimant's application will be dismissed. If permission to continue the claim is granted, then the claim will continue like any other claim brought by the company and the court will determine what remedies (if any) are appropriate. As noted, because the claim is brought on behalf of the company, any remedy awarded will be awarded to the company, and not the derivative claimant.

Stop and think 10.1

To date, the majority of derivative claims brought have failed on the ground that the court refused to grant permission to continue. Do you think that the claimant should be required to obtain the court's permission? Do you think that the courts, in refusing to grant permission more often, are being overly strict?

3.5 Costs

The usual rule in UK litigation is that the losing party pays their costs and those of the successful party (CPR, r 44.2(2)(a)), but this rule does not necessarily apply in relation to derivative claims. Instead, the court can order that the company pays the costs, with the rationale for this being set out by Buckley LJ in *Wallersteiner v Moir (No 2)* [1975] 2 WLR 389 (CA):

> 'where a shareholder has in good faith and on reasonable grounds sued as plaintiff in a minority shareholder's action, the benefit of which, if successful, will accrue to the company and only indirectly to the plaintiff as a member of the company, and which it would have been reasonable for an independent board of directors to bring in the company's name, it would... clearly be a proper exercise of judicial discretion to order the company to pay the plaintiff's costs.'

Rule 19.9E of the CPR provides that '[t]he court may order the company, body corporate or trade union for the benefit of which a derivative claim is brought to indemnify the claimant against liability for costs incurred in the permission application or in the derivative claim or both'. Note that the court is not obliged to order that the company will pay the costs, but it has a discretion to do so.

Test yourself 10.2

1. **What two principles form the rule in *Foss v Harbottle*?**
2. **In what situations could a common law derivative action be brought?**
3. **What is a derivative claim and what causes of action can form the basis of a derivative claim?**
4. **Briefly explain the process used by the court to determine whether a derivative claim should be permitted to continue.**

4. The unfair prejudice remedy

Prior to 1948, the only statutory remedy available to a member was to petition the court for a winding up order. A less severe remedy was desirable and so the Companies Act 1948 allowed a member to obtain a remedy where he was subject to oppressive conduct. However, only a few cases succeeded and so the 1962 Jenkins Committee recommended that the oppressive conduct remedy be replaced by the unfair prejudice remedy. Today, this remedy is found in Part 30 of the CA 2006, notably s. 994(1), which allows a member to petition the court for a remedy where:

- the company's affairs are being or have been conducted in a manner that is unfairly prejudicial to the interests of members generally, or of some part of its members (including at least himself); or
- an actual or proposed act or omission of the company (including an act or omission on its behalf) is or would be so prejudicial.

The unfair prejudice petition is now the most popular statutory member remedy and can apply to a wide range of situations.

4.1 Petitioners and respondents

Before looking at the type of conduct that can form the basis of a s. 994 petition, it is important to understand who can petition the court and whose conduct can form the basis of a s. 994 petition.

Who may petition the court?
Section 994(1) provides that a petition may be made by 'a member of a company'. Any person who is a member within s. 112 may petition the court. Note that former members are not able to petition the court (*Re a Company (No 00330 of 1991)* [1991] BCLC 597 (Ch)). Non-members may also petition the court in two situations.

- A person who is not a member may petition the court if shares have been transferred or transmitted to him by the operation of law (s. 994(2)).
- The Secretary of State may bring a petition in certain circumstances (s. 995), although such petitions are extremely rare (see e.g. *Re Scitec Group Ltd* [2012] EWHC 661 (Ch)).

Who may a petition be brought against?
The persons against whom a petition can be brought depends upon whether the claim is based on s. 994(1)(a) or 994(1)(b). Section 994(1)(a) applies where the company's affairs are being or have been conducted in a manner that is unfairly prejudicial to the interests of members generally, or of some part of its members (including the petitioner). Paragraph (a) does not identify whose conduct must be unfairly prejudicial, and so a claim under (a) can be based on the actions of a wide variety of persons, including the company, the directors, other members or third parties (notably those who have 'improperly assisted' the alleged unfairly prejudicial conduct, *Re Fahey Developments Ltd* [1996] BCC 320 (Ch)).

Section 994(1)(b) applies where an actual or proposed act or omission of the company is or would be unfairly prejudicial to the interests of members generally, or of some part of its members (including the petitioner). As this refers to an actual or proposed omission *of the company*, the courts have held that 'the petitioner must identify something which the company does or fails to do' (*Graham v Every* [2014] EWCA Civ 191 (Arden LJ)).

4.2 Unfairly prejudicial conduct

It is important to understand what types of conduct can amount to unfairly prejudicial conduct. To a significant degree, this depends upon how the courts have interpreted certain words and phrases within s. 994(1).

'The company's affairs'

Section 994(1)(a) applies where the company's affairs are being or have been conducted in a manner that is unfairly prejudicial to the interests of members generally, or of some part of its members (including at least himself). Section 994(1)(a) therefore only applies to conduct that relates to 'the company's affairs'. As a result, a petition based on s. 994(1)(a) will not succeed if it is based on the conduct of a person acting in relation to his own affairs, and not those of the company. The following case demonstrates this.

Case law 10.3

***Re Legal Costs Negotiators Ltd* [1999] BCC 547 (CA)**

The share capital of a company was divided equally amongst its four directors. One of these directors, Hateley, was dismissed as an employee due to alleged mismanagement, and he later resigned as a director. The remaining three directors offered to purchase Hateley's shares, but he refused. The directors alleged that, in keeping his shares, Hateley had engaged in unfairly prejudicial conduct. This was because the company was a quasi-partnership and there was a legitimate expectation that each member would contribute to the company and be engaged full-time on its business. As Hateley could no longer do this, he had breached this legitimate expectation and so had engaged in unfairly prejudicial conduct.

Peter Gibson LJ stated that Hateley's decision to keep the shares did not constitute conduct relating to the company's affairs – the conduct complained of related to Hateley's own affairs as a member. The directors' petition was struck out.

In practice, the courts have not placed too strict an interpretation on what amounts to the company's affairs, as the following case demonstrates.

Case law 10.4

***Re Home & Office Fire Extinguishers Ltd* [2012] EWHC 917 (Ch)**

A company's shares were owned by two brothers (Simon and Guy), and they were its only directors. Guy refused to provide Simon with an advance on his salary, which resulted in Simon attacking Guy with a

hammer (although Simon stated that Guy attacked him). Guy purported to terminate Simon's employment. Each brother petitioned the court, alleging that the other brother had acted in an unfairly prejudicial manner.

The court was satisfied that, based on the available evidence, it was Simon that attacked Guy. One might assume that Simon attacking Guy would not constitute conduct relating to the company's affairs, but the court held that it did. This was because Simon's conduct 'was a breach of the implied understanding that he and Guy, would act properly and in good faith towards each other, and it was also a single event which made it impossible for them to continue their association as directors of, and shareholders in, the Company'. Guy's petition succeeded and Simon was ordered to sell his shares to Guy.

A final point to note is that the company's affairs do not have to be the affairs of the company in which the petitioner is a member – the court has held that a member of a parent company can bring a s. 994 petition is relation to its subsidiary (*Re Citybranch Group Ltd* [2004] EWCA Civ 815) or vice versa (*Scottish Co-operative Wholesale Society Ltd v Meyer* [1959] AC 324 (HL)).

'Actual or proposed act or omission'

Section 994(1)(b) relates to 'an actual or proposed act or omission' that is unfairly prejudicial. In the case of an actual act or omission, the petitioner need not have been a member when the unfairly prejudicial conduct occurred, so a member can bring a claim based on conduct that occurred before he became a member (*Lloyd v Casey* [2002] 1 BCLC 454 (Ch)).

It used to be the case that a petition could not be brought based on proposed unfairly prejudicial conduct, and so a member had to wait until the conduct was actual before petitioning the court. This is no longer the case as s. 994 expressly covers a proposed act or omission.

'Unfairly prejudicial'

The conduct complained of must be unfairly prejudicial, but the Act provides no guidance as to how to determine this, and so the matter has been left to the courts. The courts have not sought to place a technical or restrictive interpretation on the words 'unfairly prejudicial'. As Neill LJ stated in *Re Saul D Harrison and Sons plc* [1995] 1 BCLC 14 (CA), '[t]he words "unfairly prejudicial" are general words and they should be applied flexibly to meet the circumstances of the particular case...'

Note that in order for a s. 994 petition to succeed, the petitioner must show that the conduct complained of is both unfair and prejudicial. As Neill LJ stated in *Re Saul D Harrison and Sons plc* [1995] 1 BCLC 14 (CA), the conduct complained of 'must be both prejudicial (in the sense of causing prejudice or harm to the relevant interest) and also unfairly so: conduct may be unfair without being prejudicial or prejudicial without being unfair, and it is not sufficient if the conduct only satisfies one of these tests'. In the following case, the conduct in question was deemed to be prejudicial, but not unfair.

Case law 10.5

***Grace v Biagioli* [2005] EWCA Civ 1222**

The three directors of Telpro Ltd each held one quarter of its shares. One of Telpro's directors, Grace, was unhappy about the board's decision regarding a dividend payment and, unbeknownst to the other directors, he entered into negotiations to purchase a company that competed with Telpro. The other directors discovered this and exercised a power in the articles to remove Grace as a director. Grace brought a claim against the other directors, alleging that his removal amounted to unfairly prejudicial conduct.

The court held that, in removing Grace from office, the other directors had indeed treated him in a prejudicial manner. However, his removal was not unfair because, by entering into negotiations to purchase a rival company, Grace had placed himself in a position of actual or potential conflict with his duties as a director. The other directors were justified in removing Grace from office.

Note that Grace also claimed that the company's decision regarding the payment of dividends was unfairly prejudicial, and this petition did succeed.

When determining whether the conduct is unfair, the court adopts an objective approach. As Slade J stated in *Re Bovey Hotel Ventures Ltd* (Ch, 31 July 1981):

> 'The test of unfairness must, I think, be an objective, not a subjective, one. In other words, it is not necessary for the petitioner to show that the persons who have de facto control of the company have acted as they did in the conscious knowledge that this was unfair to the petitioner or that they were acting in bad faith; the test, I think, is whether a reasonable bystander observing the consequences of their conduct, would regard it as having unfairly prejudiced the petitioner's interests.'

When determining whether conduct is prejudicial, Harman J in *Re Unisoft Group Ltd (No 3)* [1994] BCC 766 (Ch) stated that '[t]he requirement of prejudice means that the conduct must be shown to have done the members harm and I believe harm in a commercial sense, not in a merely emotional sense'. This does not mean that only financial harm is covered and prejudice can occur even where the petitioner's financial interests have not been adversely affected. However, as David Richards J stated in *Re Coroin Ltd* [2012] EWHC 2343 (Ch) '[w]here the acts complained of have no adverse financial consequence, it may be more difficult to establish relevant prejudice'.

Whether conduct is unfairly prejudicial will depend strongly on the facts of the case, but examples of conduct that have been held to amount to unfairly prejudicial conduct include the following.

- Abuse of a controlling position can amount to unfair prejudice, with examples including the directors:

- selling company assets at an undervalue to another company they control (*Re Little Olympian Each Ways Ltd (No 3)* [1995] 1 BCLC 636 (Ch));
- transferring business to another company they control (*Re London School of Electronics Ltd* [1986] Ch 211 (Ch)); or
- paying themselves excessive remuneration (*Re Cumana Ltd* [1986] BCLC 430 (CA)).

- Mismanagement of the company will not normally constitute unfair prejudice (*Re Elgindata Ltd* [1991] BCLC 959 (Ch), but serious mismanagement can do (*Re Macro (Ipswich) Ltd* [1994] 2 BCLC 354 (Ch)).
- A breach of directors' duties (see e.g. *Re Cumana Ltd* [1986] BCLC 430 (CA)).
- A breach of the company's constitution or statutory rights (see e.g. *Re a Company (No 00789 of 1987)* [1990] BCLC 384 (Ch)).
- Criminal conduct (*Bermuda Cablevision Ltd v Colica Trust Co Ltd* [1998] AC 198 (PC)).
- Exclusion from management of a quasi-partnership company (*Re Ghyll Beck Driving Range Ltd* [1993] BCLC 1126 (Ch)).
- A failure to consider paying dividends (*Re McCarthy Surfacing Ltd* [2008] EWHC 2279 (Ch)), the payment of derisory dividends (*Re Sam Weller & Sons Ltd* [1990] Ch 682 (Ch)), or refusing to pay a declared dividend (*Grace v Biagioli* [2005] EWCA Civ 1222).

4.3 The 'interests of members'

The conduct complained of must be unfairly prejudicial to the interests of members generally, or of some part of its members (including the petitioner). This leads us to ask what the interests of the members are. An important point to note is that a breach of a member's rights can form the basis of a s. 994 petition, but a member's interests are wider than his rights. In the following case, the petitioner's rights were not unfairly prejudiced, but his interests were.

Case law 10.6

***Re Sam Weller & Sons Ltd* [1990] Ch 682 (Ch)**

A company had undistributed profits of £464,000 but had paid the same derisory dividend for the previous 37 years. A group of members commenced a s. 994 petition alleging, *inter alia*, that the payment of low dividends constituted unfairly prejudicial conduct. The company and its director (who received a salary) sought to strike out the petition on the ground that the dividend payment was not prejudicial as it affected all the members equally.

The court held that the payment of low dividends did not breach the petitioners' rights as members. However, Peter Gibson J went on to state that '[t]he word "interests" is wider than a term such as "rights"

... Parliament recognised that members may have different interests, even if their rights as members are the same'. The director was also a member, and his interests differed to those of the other members. The director might wish to retain profits in order to bolster the value of his own shareholding. As regards the other members, however, Peter Gibson J stated:

> **'It may well be in the interests of the other shareholders, including the petitioners, that a more immediate benefit should accrue to them in the form of larger dividends. As their only income from the company is by way of dividend, their interests may be not only prejudiced by the policy of low dividend payments, but unfairly prejudiced.'**

The director's strike out application was dismissed.

qua
'In the capacity of.'

Member qua *member*

A s. 994 petition will only succeed if it is the petitioner's interests as a member that have been unfairly prejudiced. From this, the courts have held that the member must bring his claim in his capacity as a member, and not in any other capacity (case law refers to this as a member acting member ***qua*** member). So, for example, if a petitioner who is a member and employee of the company brings his claim in his capacity as an employee (i.e. the petition relates to his interests as an employee), then the petition will likely fail (*Re John Reid & Sons (Strucsteel) Ltd* [2003] EWHC 2329 (Ch)).

However, in determining whether the member is acting in his capacity as a member, the courts have adopted a broad and flexible approach that will depend upon the facts of the case. For example, in a quasi-partnership company (quasi-partnerships are discussed on p. 204), the roles of member and director are blurred and so holding the office of director might amount to a member interest (*Re a Company (No 00477 of 1986)* (1986) 2 BCC 99171 (Ch)). In the case of *Gamlestaden Fastigheter AB v Baltic Partners Ltd* [2007] UKPC 26, the court went even further and allowed a petitioner to bring a claim to protect his rights as a creditor. Lord Scott stated:

> 'in a case where an investor in a joint venture company has, in pursuance of the joint venture agreement, invested not only in subscribing for shares but also in advancing loan capital, the investor ought not ... to be precluded from the grant of relief ... on the ground that the relief would benefit the investor only as loan creditor and not as member.'

'Equitable considerations'

The courts have stated that, in certain companies, regard must be had to 'equitable considerations' when determining if the petitioner's interests as a member have been unfairly prejudiced. Such equitable considerations often involve 'a fundamental understanding between the shareholders which formed the basis of their association but was not put into contractual form' (*Re Saul D Harrison and Sons plc* [1995] 1 BCLC 14 (CA) (Hoffmann LJ)). In other words, the breach of such an understanding can amount to unfairly prejudicial conduct. The following case is the leading case in this area.

Case law 10.7

***O'Neill v Phillips* [1999] 1 WLR 1092 (HL)**

Phillips was the sole director and shareholder of a company. He transferred 25% of his shares to O'Neill and appointed him as a director. Phillips retired as director, leaving O'Neill as the *de facto* managing director. Phillips was entitled to 75% of the company's profits with O'Neill entitled to the remaining 25%, but Phillips waived this entitlement and the profits were split equally between them. Phillips indicated in principle that he would be willing to increase O'Neill's shareholding to 50% if certain targets were met, but no formal agreement was reached on this.

Following a downturn in the company's financial performance, Phillips became concerned about O'Neill's management of the company, and so Phillips resumed personal command of the company while O'Neill became a manager of the company's German branch. Given O'Neill's reduced status, Phillips once again asserted his right to claim 75% of the company's profits.

O'Neill left the company and brought a s. 994 petition, alleging that Phillips, in reducing O'Neill's share of the profit and in failing to give him an equal shareholding, had engaged in unfairly prejudicial conduct.

Lord Hoffmann stated that:

> **'a member of a company will not ordinarily be entitled to complain of unfairness unless there has been some breach of the terms on which he agreed that the affairs of the company should be conducted. But... there will be cases in which equitable considerations make it unfair for those conducting the affairs of the company to rely upon their strict legal powers. Thus unfairness may consist in a breach of the rules or in using the rules in a manner which equity would regard as contrary to good faith.'**

The House held that Phillips had not promised to transfer any shares to O'Neill, nor had he promised that O'Neill would always receive an equal share of the company's profits. There had been no breach of the company's constitution (so O'Neill's rights had not been breached) and there were no facts indicating that 'equitable considerations' were relevant here.

Whether such equitable considerations arise will largely depend upon the company involved. Jonathan Parker J in *Re Astec (BSR) plc* [1999] BCC 59 (Ch) stated that equitable considerations:

> 'can have no place in the context of public listed companies... If the market in a company's shares is to have any credibility, members of the public dealing in that market must it seems to me be entitled to proceed on the footing that the constitution of the company is as it appears in the company's public documents, unaffected by any extraneous equitable considerations and constraints.'

It would appear that equitable considerations will only likely arise in quasi-partnership companies (discussed on p. 204). Cases involving such companies have largely involved a petitioner who has been excluded from managing the company and has alleged that this exclusion constitutes unfairly prejudicial conduct. As one of the defining characteristics of a quasi-partnership is an expectation that the members will be involved in management, the courts have held that exclusion from the management of such a company can amount to unfairly prejudicial conduct (*Re Ghyll Beck Driving Range Ltd* [1993] BCLC 1126 (Ch)). However, this will only be the case if the expectation to manage is legitimate and was actually agreed upon. The court may still, depending on the facts of the case, hold that an exclusion was not unfairly prejudicial (e.g. where the petitioner was excluded from management due to his own adverse conduct, *Woolwich v Milne* [2003] EWHC 414 (Ch)).

4.4 Remedies

Section 996(1) provides that if the court is satisfied that the s. 994 petition is well founded, it may make such order as it thinks fit for giving relief. It is clear that s. 996 provides the court with a great deal of discretion in determining what type of remedy to make, as it can make 'any order that it thinks fit'. This discretion is further enhanced in three ways. First, the use of the word 'may' in s. 996(1) indicates that even if the petitioner's interests as a member have been unfairly prejudiced, the court is not obliged to provide the petitioner with a remedy and reasons may exist to deny the petitioner a remedy. For example, the court may decline the petitioner a remedy under s. 996 if other remedies exist, especially if the petitioner could end the prejudicial state of affairs himself (for example, by passing a resolution, as in *Re Legal Costs Negotiators Ltd* [1999] BCC 547 (CA)).

Second, although the petitioner must specify the remedy that he seeks (Companies (Unfair Prejudice Applications) Proceedings Rules 2009 (SI 2009/2469), article 3(2)), the court is not bound to provide this remedy (*Hawkes v Cuddy* [2009] EWCA Civ 291).

Third, although an unfair prejudice petition is not subject to a limitation period, the court may deny the petitioner a remedy where a substantial period has elapsed between the unfairly prejudicial conduct and the petition being brought. Thus, in *Re Grandactual Ltd* [2005] EWHC 1415 (Ch), a nine-year delay between the conduct in question and the petition being brought resulted in the court holding that the petitioner should not be awarded a remedy.

Although the court can make any order that it thinks fit, s. 996(2) provides a non-exhaustive list of remedies that the court can award, including:

- an order regulating the conduct of the company's affairs in the future (for example, where the defendant is a director, the court may strip that director of certain powers, as occurred in *Re HR Harmer Ltd* [1959] 1 WLR 62 (CA));
- an order requiring the company to refrain from doing an act complained of, or to perform an act that it has failed to perform;
- an order authorising civil proceedings to be brought in the name and on behalf of the company by such persons and on such terms as the court may direct;
- an order requiring the company not to make any, or any specified, alterations in its articles without the leave of the court;
- an order providing for the purchase of the shares of any members of the company by other members or by the company itself and, in the case of a purchase by the company itself, a reduction of the company's capital. This is by far the most common remedy sought and ordered under s. 996 and so is discussed in more detail next.

Share purchase orders

In *Grace v Biagioli* [2005] EWCA Civ 1222, Patten J stated:

> 'In most cases, the usual order to make will be the one requiring the Respondents to buy out the petitioning shareholder at a price to be fixed by the court… The reasons for making such an order are in most cases obvious. It will free the petitioner from the company and enable him to extract his share of the value of its business and assets in return for foregoing any future right to dividends. The company and its business will be preserved for the benefit of the Respondent shareholders, free from his claims and the possibility of future difficulties between shareholders will be removed. In cases of serious prejudice and conflict between shareholders, it is unlikely that any regime or safeguards which the court can impose, will be as effective to preserve the peace and to safeguard the rights of the minority.'

A share purchase order, under which the court orders that the respondent buys the shares of the petitioner, is the usual remedy. The court may also order that the company buys the petitioner's shares, or even that the respondent must sell his shares to the petitioner (see e.g. *Re Hedgehog Golf Co Ltd* [2010] EWHC 390 (Ch)).

Where a share purchase order is made, the key issue to determine is at what price the shares must be purchased. When determining how the shares should be valued, Nourse J in *Re Bird Precision Bellows Ltd* [1984] Ch 149 (Ch) stated that the dominant concern is that 'the price fixed by the court must be fair'. The court will take into account a wide array of factors in valuing the shares, but given that most s. 994 petitioners are minority shareholders, one key issue is whether the share price should be discounted to reflect the minority shareholder's lack of control. Where the petitioner is a minority shareholder, a discount normally will be applied (*Re Elgindata Ltd (No 1)* [1991] BCLC 959), but this depends on the facts. For example, where the petitioner is a member of a quasi-partnership, then the usual approach adopted is that the shares will be valued on a *pro-rata* basis and no discount will be applied (*Re Bird Precision Bellows Ltd* [1984] Ch 149 (Ch)).

Another key issue is at what date should the shares be valued. Several possibilities exist.

- A date before the unfairly prejudicial conduct took place.
- The date of the petition.
- The date of the trial.
- The date that the remedial order is made under s. 996.

The starting point will be that '*[p]rima facie*, an interest in a going concern ought to be valued at the date on which it is ordered to be purchased' (*Re London School of Electronics Ltd* [1986] Ch 211 (Ch) (Nourse J)). However, this is a starting point only and it may be the case that, in order to achieve a fair valuation, a different date may need to be chosen. For example, where the respondent's conduct causes the value of the shares to decrease, then the court is more likely to value the shares at a date before the unfairly prejudicial conduct took place (*Re OC Transport Services Ltd* (1984) 1 BCC 99068 (Ch)).

Winding up

One issue that has not been clarified is whether the court can wind up a company under s. 996. Conflicting views exist. In *Apex Global Management Ltd v FI Call Ltd* [2015] EWHC 3269 (Ch), Hildyard J implied that winding up was available by stating that 'the court should not ordinarily make a winding-up order pursuant to section 996, given the specific provisions for such a remedy...' However, the Law Commission has argued that winding up is not available based on the judgment of Ferris J in *Re Full Cup International Trading Ltd* [1995] BCC 682 (Ch). In practice, it will be very rare for a s. 994 petitioner to seek a winding up order, but clarification is still desirable.

Test yourself 10.3

1. **A s. 994 petition can be made by which parties?**
2. **A s. 994 petition can be brought against which parties?**
3. **Provide eight examples of conduct that has been held to amount to unfairly prejudicial conduct.**
4. **Give five examples of the types of remedy that the court can order under s. 996.**
5. **When determining the value of shares, when will the court discount the price of the shares?**
6. **Can the court wind up a company under s. 996?**

5. The petition for winding up

A company can be wound up by the court on specified grounds. For our purposes, the key ground is that found in s. 122(1)(g) of the IA 1986, which allows a member (and other specified persons) to petition the court for an order winding up the company. The court may grant such an order if it is 'of the opinion that it is just and equitable that the company should be wound up'.

5.1 Who can apply?

Section 124(1) sets out who can apply to the court for a winding up order. The full list is discussed in Chapter 18 – here, the focus is on whether a member can apply. Members and shareholders are not expressly listed in s. 124(1), but s. 124(1) does provide that a winding up petition can be made by a contributory or contributories. A 'contributory' is a 'person liable to contribute to the assets of a company in the event of its being wound up' (IA 1986, s. 79(1)). An obvious example of a contributory would be a shareholder who had not fully paid for his shares. One would imagine that a shareholder whose shares were fully paid up would not be a contributory, but such a shareholder will be able to petition the court for a winding up order if he can show that he has a 'tangible interest' that entitles him to ask for a winding up petition (*Re Rica Gold Washing Co* (1879) 11 ChD 36 (CA)). Usually, this will require the shareholder to show '*prima facie* probability that there will be assets available for distribution amongst the shareholders' (*Re Othery Construction Ltd* [1966] 1 WLR 69 (Ch)), or that the winding up would 'achieve some advantage, or avoid or minimise some disadvantage, which would accrue to him by virtue of his membership of the company' (*Re Chesterfield Catering Co Ltd* [1977] Ch 373 (Ch)).

5.2 'Just and equitable'

Once a petition has been made, the question for the court to determine is whether it is just and equitable to wind up the company based on the disputed conduct. When deciding this, Neville J in *Re Blériot Manufacturing Aircraft Co Ltd* (1916) 32 TLR 253 stated that '[t]he words "just and equitable" are words of the widest significance, and do not limit the jurisdiction of the court to any case. It is a question of fact, and each case must depend upon its own circumstances'. It cannot be said that certain conduct will definitely merit the making of a winding up order, but below are examples of conduct that have resulted in a company being wound up on just and equitable grounds:

- If a company is formed for a particular purpose (its 'substratum') and this purpose is stated in its objects clause, then a company may be wound up if it becomes impossible to fulfil this purpose. For example, in *Re German Date Coffee Co* (1882) 20 ChD 169 (CA), the company's objects stated that it was formed in order to take advantage of a patent for making coffee out of dates. However, the patent was never granted, and so the court ordered that the company be wound up.
- A company may be wound up where it becomes deadlocked. In *Re Yenidje Tobacco Co Ltd* [1916] 2 Ch 426 (CA), the company's only two

directors fell out, refused to talk to one another and the company became deadlocked. The court ordered that the company be wound up.

- A company may be wound up if it was set up for an unlawful purpose. In *Re International Securities Corp* (1908) 99 LT 581, a company that was set up to deal in unlawful lottery bonds was wound up by the court.
- A company may be wound up if it was set up for a fraudulent purpose. In *Re Thomas Edward Brinsmead & Sons* [1897] 1 Ch 406 (CA), a company was set up to manufacture pianos that would be passed off as being made by a much more well-established piano-maker. The company was wound up by the court.
- In *Loch v John Blackwood Ltd* [1924] AC 783 (PC), Lord Shaw stated that a company may be wound up where there is a 'justifiable lack of confidence in the management of the company's affairs'. This covers a wide range of conduct, and examples of where companies have been wound up for this reason are (i) where the controller of the company acts in an oppressive manner (*Re HR Harmer Ltd* [1959] 1 WLR 62 (CA)); (ii) where the company fails to publish accounts or hold meetings when required (*Loch v John Blackwood Ltd* [1924] AC 783 (PC)); or (iii) where a director sold company assets to a rival company he controlled (*Re Concrete Column Clamps Ltd* [1953] 4 DLR 60). Note that a company will not be wound up for this reason merely because it is being run negligently or carelessly (*Re Five Minute Car Wash Service Ltd* [1966] 1 WLR 745 (Ch)).

Quasi-partnerships and equitable considerations

Where the company in question is a quasi-partnership, the scope of the winding up remedy (and also the unfair prejudice remedy) broadens as the court will take into account 'equitable considerations' when deciding whether to order the winding up of a company. The following leading case discusses what 'equitable considerations' are and when a company will be a quasi-partnership.

Case law 10.8

***Ebrahimi v Westbourne Galleries Ltd* [1973] AC 360 (HL)**

Two people, E and N, formed a partnership on the understanding that they would both manage the firm. Some years later, they incorporated their business with E and N becoming the company's directors. Subsequently, N's son, G, also became a director. A dispute arose and N and G removed E under what is now s. 168 of the CA 2006. As the company distributed its profits via directors' fees (as opposed to a dividend), E was no longer able to share in the company's profits. E petitioned the court for a winding up order.

There was no doubt that the removal of E was conducted in accordance with statute and the company's articles, but this did not mean that the just and equitable remedy would not apply. Lord Shaw stated that the words 'just and equitable' are:

> 'a recognition of the fact that a limited company is more than a mere legal entity, with a personality in law of its own: that there is room in company law for recognition of the fact that behind it, or amongst it, there are individuals, with rights, expectations and obligations *inter se* which are not necessarily submerged in the company structure. That structure is defined by the Companies Act and by the articles of association by which shareholders agree to be bound. In most companies and in most contexts, this definition is sufficient and exhaustive, equally so whether the company is large or small. The "just and equitable" provision does not... entitle one party to disregard the obligation he assumes by entering a company, nor the court to dispense him from it. It does, as equity always does, enable the court to subject the exercise of legal rights to equitable considerations; considerations, that is, of a personal character arising between one individual and another, which may make it unjust, or inequitable, to insist on legal rights, or to exercise them in a particular way.'

Lord Wilberforce stated that these equitable considerations could arise if the company in question was a quasi-partnership, stating:

> 'It would be impossible, and wholly undesirable, to define the circumstances in which these considerations may arise. Certainly the fact that a company is a small one, or a private company, is not enough. There are very many of these where the association is a purely commercial one, of which it can safely be said that the basis of association is adequately and exhaustively laid down in the articles. The superimposition of equitable considerations requires something more, which typically may include one, or probably more, of the following elements: (i) an association formed or continued on the basis of a personal relationship, involving mutual confidence – this element will often be found where a pre-existing partnership has been converted into a limited company; (ii) an agreement, or understanding, that all, or some... of the shareholders shall participate in the conduct of the business; (iii) restriction upon the transfer of the members' interest in the company – so that if confidence is lost, or one member is removed from management, he cannot take out his stake and go elsewhere.'

Here, the company was a quasi-partnership and so equitable considerations would apply. The relevant consideration here was the understanding that E and N would be involved in management of the business, and there was an indisputable inference that 'the character of the association would, as a matter of personal relation and good faith, remain the same'. The House therefore held that, by removing E from office, N and G had breached this understanding and so the court ordered that the company be wound up.

It is now well accepted that, if a company is a quasi-partnership, the exclusion of a member from management will likely justify a winding up on just and equitable grounds (*Re Davis and Collett Ltd* [1935] Ch 693 (Ch); *Tay Bok Choon v Tahansan Sdn Bhd* [1987] 1 WLR 413 (PC)).

5.3 Relationship with other remedies

Winding up a company is a drastic remedy and the courts are understandably reluctant to wind up a company if some alternative solution exists. Section 125(2) of the IA 1986 provides that, where a contributory or contributories present a winding up petition on just and equitable grounds, the court must not make a winding up order if (i) some other remedy is available to the petitioner; and (ii) the petitioner is acting unreasonably in seeking to have the company wound up and not pursuing that other remedy.

This 'other remedy' can be any remedy (and not simply the member remedies discussed in this chapter). The most notable alternative remedy is the unfair prejudice remedy, and so it is important to understand the relationship between the two remedies.

Winding up and the unfair prejudice remedy

Prior to 1948, the only statutory member remedy was to petition the court for a winding up order. In 1948, the unfair prejudice remedy was introduced and the number of winding up petitions on just and equitable grounds decreased. However, a new problem presented itself. Claimants would often bring an unfair prejudice petition and a winding up petition, with the following example demonstrating the rationale behind this.

Case study 10.1

Anja is a member of X-Corp Ltd. She is unhappy at how the company has treated her and she brings a claim against the company alleging that her interests as a member have been unfairly prejudiced. She also petitions the court for an order winding up X-Corp. Bringing the winding up petition alongside the unfair prejudice petition places considerable pressure on X-Corp because the winding up starts as soon as the petition is presented to the court (IA 1986, s. 129(2)). By commencing the winding up, Anja has prevented X-Corp from engaging in certain acts (e.g. disposing of property, transferring shares (IA 1986, s. 127(1)). This may pressure the directors into agreeing a settlement, even if they feel that Anja's claims have no merit.

To prevent claimants from placing this sort of pressure on defendants, the court issued a Practice Direction stating that a winding up petition should only accompany an unfair prejudice petition if winding up 'is the relief which the petitioner prefers or if it is considered that it may be the only relief to which he is entitled' (*Practice Direction (Companies Court: Contributory's Petition)* [1990] 1 WLR 490 (Ch)).

Test yourself 10.4

1. **What is a contributory?**
2. **Provide five examples of the type of conduct that may result in the company being wound up.**
3. **What are three characteristics of a quasi-partnership?**
4. **Can a claimant bring a winding up petition and an unfair prejudice petition in relation to the same conduct?**

Chapter summary

- If a member sustains loss due to the actions of another person, he may have a personal right to bring proceedings against that person.
- Where a person has caused loss to both the company and its members, the general rule is that both the company and its members have a personal right to sue the wrongdoer.
- The no reflective loss principle provides that where the members' losses are reflective of the loss sustained by the company, then it is the company that should recover the loss and the member will usually not be able to do so.
- The no reflective loss principle will not apply where the member's losses are reflective of those sustained by the company, but the company is unable to claim due to that person's conduct.
- The rule in *Foss v Harbottle* provides that:
  - where a wrong is done to the company, it is the proper claimant to seek redress; and
  - a member cannot bring a claim in relation to an irregularity that could be remedied or ratified by a simple majority of the members.
- A derivative claim is a claim brought by a member of a company in respect of a cause of action vested in the company, which seeks relief on behalf of the company.
- A derivative claim can only derive from an actual or proposed act or omission involving negligence, default, breach of duty or breach of trust by a director of the company.
- A member who brings a derivative claim must apply to the court for permission to continue the claim. The court will first determine if there is a *prima facie* case for granting permission to continue and, if so, it will then decide whether to grant permission or not.
- Section 994 of the CA 2006 allows a member to petition the court for a remedy where:
  - the company's affairs are being or have been conducted in a manner that is unfairly prejudicial to the interests of members generally, or of some part of its members (including at least himself); or

  - an actual or proposed act or omission of the company (including an act or omission on its behalf) is or would be so prejudicial.
- In order for an unfair prejudice petition to succeed, the conduct complained of must be both unfair and prejudicial.
- A s. 994 petition will only succeed if it is the petitioner's interests as a member that have been unfairly prejudiced.
- In certain cases, notably where the company is a quasi-partnership, the court will take into account 'equitable considerations' when determining whether unfairly prejudicial conduct has occurred.
- Where the court decides that an unfair prejudice petition is well founded, the court may make such order as it thinks fit for giving relief in respect of the matters complained of. The usual remedy is a share purchase order, under which the respondents are ordered to purchase the petitioner's shares.
- Section 122(1)(g) of the IA 1986 provides that the court may wind up a company if it is of the opinion that it is just and equitable that the company should be wound up.
- Reasons for winding up a company on just and equitable grounds include:
  - loss of substratum;
  - the company becoming deadlocked;
  - the company was set up for an unlawful or fraudulent purpose; or
  - there is a justifiable lack of confidence in the management of the company's affairs.
- A quasi-partnership will normally have one or more of the following characteristics:
  - it was formed on the basis of a personal relationship involving mutual confidence;
  - there was an agreement that all or some of the members will be involved in management; and
  - there will be a restriction upon the transfer of the members' interest in the company.
- A winding up petition should only accompany an unfair prejudice petition if winding up is the relief which the petitioner prefers or if it is considered that it may be the only relief to which he is entitled.

Part four

Capital and corporate transparency

Overview

Part four focuses on capital and corporate transparency. It looks at the two main sources of capital, namely share capital and debt capital, and the capital rules designed to protect creditors.

Chapter 11 examines shares and share capital. It begins by looking at what a share is and the different types of share capital. It discusses the rules relating to the allotment of shares, including allotting shares of different classes and the special rules relating to offering shares to the public. The chapter ends by looking at how shares can be transferred or transmitted.

Chapter 12 discusses the capital maintenance rules – a series of rules that are designed to protect creditors by preventing capital from being returned to shareholders.

Chapter 13 considers the role of loan capital by looking at the various sources of loan capital and the steps that providers of such capital can take to ensure repayment.

Chapter 14 looks at those measures designed to make companies more transparent. It discusses the range of disclosure obligations placed upon companies.

Chapter 15 looks at market abuse by discussing the offence of insider dealing, offences relating to financial services and the market abuse regime.

At the end of this Part, students will be able to:

- understand what a share is and the different types of share capital;
- discuss the processes by which shares can be allotted, transferred and transmitted;
- discuss the operation of the capital maintenance rules;
- identify the various sources of loan capital;
- discuss the various forms of security available to creditors, notably charges;
- identify the key disclosure obligations placed upon companies;
- appreciate the importance of the role undertaken by the company's auditor;
- demonstrate awareness of the operation of the rules relating to the offence of insider dealing and those offences that relate to financial services; and
- understand the operation of the market abuse regime.

Chapter eleven
Shares and share capital

CONTENTS

1. Introduction

This chapter outlines the rules relating to shares and share capital. The vast majority of UK companies have a share capital and being able to allot shares is one of the most important advantages of incorporation. The rules relating to shares and share capital are complex, especially if the company wishes to offer its shares to the public. Before looking at the various rules relating to shares and share capital, it is important to cover some basic information, beginning with what a share is and the different terms used to describe share capital.

2. What is a share?

The CA 2006 provides limited guidance on the definition and nature of a share. Section 540(1) provides that a 'share' means a share in the company's share capital. Section 541 provides slightly more help by stating that a share constitutes personal property, so once a share is allotted and issued, it belongs to the shareholder and not the company (*Pilmer v Duke Group Ltd* [2001] 2 BCLC 773). As a share is an item of personal property, the shareholder may also transfer or transmit the share to others. In *Colonial Bank v Whinney* (1886) 11 App Cas 426, the court confirmed that the type of personal property that a share constitutes is a **thing in action**, meaning a share is simply an intangible asset other than land.

thing in action
A 'thing' is an asset other than land, with a 'thing in action' being an intangible thing.

The classic judicial definition of a share was laid down by Farwell J in *Borland's Trustee v Steel Bros & Co Ltd* [1901] 1 Ch 279 (Ch), who stated that:

> '[a] share is the interest of a shareholder in the company measured by a sum of money, for the purpose of liability in the first place, and of interest in the second, but also consisting of a series of mutual covenants entered into by all the shareholders.... A share is ... an interest measured by a sum of money and made up of various rights contained in the contract.'

3. Terms used to describe share capital

Before examining the various rules relating to shares and share capital, it is important to explain some important terms that will commonly arise in relation to a company's share capital.

3.1 Nominal value and the share premium

nominal value
A fixed value that must be attached to all the shares in a limited company.

Section 542(1) of the CA 2006 provides that shares in a limited company must each have a fixed **nominal value** with s. 542(2) providing that a failure to fix a nominal value to an allotment of shares will render that allotment void. The nominal value of a share may not bear any resemblance to what the share is actually worth, leading some to question why shares must be given a nominal value. The answer is twofold:

- the nominal value represents the minimum value that a share can be allotted for; and
- the nominal value helps determine how much a shareholder will be required to contribute upon the company's liquidation – if the shareholder has paid the nominal value, he will not be required to contribute any more.

share premium
The amount paid for a share that is over the nominal value.

Shares are often allotted for more than their nominal value, and the excess is known as the **share premium**, with the following example demonstrating how this works in practice.

Case study 11.1

X-Corp plc allots 1,000 shares with a nominal value of £1 each. The shares are allotted for £1.50, so the share premium is 50 pence per share. All 1,000 shares are sold and, as the company is a public company, all the shareholders must fully pay the premium at the time of allotment (s. 586(1)). The share premium received (£500 in total) does not form part of X-Corp's share capital, and instead must be transferred to an account called the 'share premium account' (s. 610(1)).

authorised share capital
The maximum total nominal value of shares that a company may issue.

3.2 Authorised and allotted share capital

A company's **authorised share capital** represents the maximum nominal value of shares that a company can issue. Prior to the CA 2006, all companies had to state their authorised minimum capital in their memorandum, but this requirement has now been abolished. Companies incorporated under prior Companies Acts are now free to remove their authorised share capital if they so wish, and companies incorporated under the CA 2006 will not have an authorised minimum capital, unless they choose to include one in their articles.

Stop and think 11.1

Why do you think the CA 2006 abolished the requirement for a company to state its authorised share capital? Did the requirement serve any useful purpose?

The total nominal value of shares that have actually been allotted is known as the **allotted share capital** (s. 546(1)(b)). The following example demonstrates authorised and allotted share capital in practice.

allotted share capital
The total nominal value of shares that a company has allotted.

Case study 11.2

The authorised share capital of X-Corp plc is £50,000. To date, it has allotted 10,000 shares with a nominal value of £4 each. Its allotted share capital is £40,000. The company can only allot shares with a total nominal value of £10,000 before it is prevented from allotting any more due to its authorised share capital. If the company wishes to allot shares beyond this, it will either need to amend its articles to either (i) increase its authorised share capital; or (ii) remove the authorised share capital entirely.

3.3 Issued and unissued share capital

Once shares have been allotted to a person and that person's name has been entered into the register of members in respect of those shares, those shares have been issued (*National Westminster Bank plc v Inland Revenue Commissioners* [1995] 1 AC 119 (HL)). The total nominal value of shares that have been issued is called the **issued share capital** (s. 546(1)(a)). If a company has an authorised share capital, then the difference between its issued capital and its authorised capital is known as its 'unissued share capital' (the total nominal value of shares that can be issued before the authorised share capital is reached).

issued share capital
The total nominal value of shares that a company has issued.

3.4 Paid-up share capital

A company can allot shares without requiring full payment for them upon allotment – shares may instead be nil-paid (nothing paid on allotment, with full payment due later) or part-paid (part-payment is made at allotment, with the remainder due later). A company's **paid-up share capital** represents the combined total of the nominal value of shares that has actually been paid, although in some cases, the share premium account can be regarded as forming

paid-up share capital
The combined total of the nominal value of shares that has actually been paid.

part of the company's paid-up share capital (such as in relation to a reduction of capital (CA 2006, s. 610(4)).

3.5 Called-up and uncalled share capital

called-up share capital The paid-up share capital plus any payment called for or any instalment due.

uncalled share capital The amount that a company can call on before the shares are fully paid for.

Where shares are nil-paid or part-paid on allotment, the company can call for the remainder to be paid or require that payment is made in instalments on set dates (depending on the terms of the allotment). A company's **called-up share capital** represents the paid-up share capital plus the amount called for/ instalment amount due (irrespective of whether this payment is actually made). The amount that the company can call on before the shares are fully paid for is known as the **uncalled share capital**.

Case study 11.3

X-Corp Ltd has allotted and issued 100 shares with a nominal value of £1 each (so the allotted/issued capital is £100). The terms of the allotment provide that the allottees will pay 50 pence on allotment, with the remainder due at a later date. X-Corp's paid-up capital is therefore £50.

A month later, the company calls on all shareholders to pay 20 pence of the outstanding amount. X-Corp's called-up share capital will be £70. All of the shareholders pay the required amount, and so the company's paid-up capital increases to £70. The uncalled share capital is £30.

Test yourself 11.1

1. **Explain the distinction between a share's nominal value and the share premium.**
2. **Explain the distinction between a company's allotted share capital and its issued share capital.**
3. **Explain the distinction between a company's paid-up share capital and its called-up share capital.**

4. Allotment and issuing of shares

A person can become a shareholder by (i) having new shares allotted to them; or (ii) by acquiring existing shares from an existing shareholder. In this section, the rules relating to the allotment of shares are discussed. As discussed, there is a difference between a company's allotted share capital and its issued share capital, and this difference exists because there is a distinction between when shares are allotted and when they are issued.

- Shares are allotted 'when a person acquires the unconditional right to be included in the company's register of members in respect of the shares' (CA 2006, s. 558).

- Shares are issued when the person's name is actually entered into the register of members (*National Westminster Bank v Inland Revenue Commissioners* [1995] 1 AC 119 (HL)).

As a result, shares will first be allotted to a person with the issuing of shares occurring subsequently. A person only acquires legal title to the shares once they have been issued.

4.1 Authority to allot shares

As a company has no mind of its own, a decision to allot shares must be taken on its behalf by the directors. The question is whether the directors have the authority to allot shares on the company's behalf. The answer depends upon the type of company, the contents of the company's articles and the type of share that the proposed allotment relates to.

Where a private company has only one class of shares, then the directors are authorised to allot more shares of that same class on behalf of the company (s. 550). This power is, however, subject to the articles. The articles may exclude or limit the directors' ability to allot shares (the model articles contain no such exclusions or limitations).

In all other cases, the directors will only have the authority to allot shares on behalf of the company if they are authorised to do so by the company's articles or by a resolution of the company (s. 551(1)). The model articles contain no such authorisation, and instead state that 'the company may issue shares with such rights or restrictions as may be determined by ordinary resolution' (model articles for private companies, article 22; model articles for public companies, article 43). In practice, many companies will include in their articles a provision granting authority to the directors to allot shares. Irrespective of how authority is granted upon the directors, it is subject to the following:

- authorisation can be given for a specific allotment only or it can be granted to the directors generally (s. 551(2));
- authorisation can be unconditional or subject to conditions (s. 551(2));
- the authorisation must:
  - state the maximum amount of shares that may be allotted under it; and
  - specify the date on which it will expire, which cannot be more than five years from the date the authorisation is granted (s. 551(3));
- authorisation can be renewed for a further period of up to five years by a resolution of the company (s. 551(4)(a));
- authorisation can be revoked or varied at any time by a resolution of the company (s. 551(4)(b)); and
- a resolution to give, vary, revoke or renew authorisation may be an ordinary resolution, even though the effect of the resolution is to alter the company's articles (s. 551(8)).

Within one month of making an allotment of shares, the company must deliver to Companies House a return on the allotment (Form SH01) that provides specified information on the allotment (s. 555).

Share warrants

Mention should be briefly made of share warrants. A share warrant (also known as 'bearer shares') is a document that states that the person who holds the warrant is the holder of the shares specified in the warrant. The person is not a member of the company as their name is not entered in the register of members. The shares held under the warrant can be transferred simply by handing the warrant to someone else (and, as a result, no one's name is stated on the warrant). As a result of this, it was very difficult for a company to know who held such shares and this opacity could be used to facilitate unlawful activities such as tax evasion and money laundering.

To prevent this, the ability to allot share warrants has been abolished (CA 2006, s. 779(4)). Schedule 4 of the SBEEA 2015 provides that existing share warrant holders had until the 26 February 2016 to surrender their warrants to the company. The company would then convert the warrants into registered shares and enter their holders' names into the register of members. Any warrants not surrendered by 26 February were cancelled, but the nominal value of the shares held under the warrant can be claimed by the warrant holder.

4.2 Minimum share capital

Public companies are subject to a minimum allotted share capital requirement. As noted in Chapter 3, a public company must not conduct any business until it has been issued with a trading certificate (CA 2006, s. 761(1)), and the registrar should not issue a public company with a trading certificate unless the nominal value of the company's allotted share capital is not less than the authorised minimum (s. 761(2)). This authorised minimum is £50,000 or the prescribed euro equivalent (s. 763(1)).

Private companies are not subject to the minimum capital requirement, and so a private company with a share capital can be incorporated with a single one pence share.

4.3 Pre-emption rights

If shares are allotted to a person who is not already an existing shareholder, the effect of the allotment will be to dilute the voting rights (and future dividend payments) of the existing shareholders. To prevent this from happening without the consent of the existing shareholders, s. 561(1) of the CA 2006 provides that a company must not allot equity securities to a person unless:

- it has made an offer to each person who holds ordinary shares in the company to allot to them, on the same or more favourable terms, a proportion of those securities equal to the proportion in nominal value held by them (as near as practicable) of the ordinary share capital of the company; and

- the period during which any such offer may be accepted has expired or the company has received notice of the acceptance or refusal of every offer so made.

Pre-emption rights only apply to the allotment of 'equity securities'. These are defined as ordinary shares in the company, rights to subscribe for, or to convert securities into, ordinary shares in the company (s. 560(1)). The following example demonstrates pre-emption rights in practice.

Case study 11.4

X-Corp Ltd has allotted 100 £1 ordinary shares divided up amongst four shareholders, namely Kathryn, Rhoda, Walter and Amelia. John has expressed an interest in purchasing shares in X-Corp and so the directors of X-Corp decide to allot a further 300 £1 shares. As the existing shareholders have pre-emption rights, they must first be offered enough of the new shares to allow them to maintain their existing holding, as follows.

Shareholder	Shareholding before allotment	Pre-emption offer of new shares
Kathryn	40 shares (40%)	120 shares (160 shares (40%))
Rhoda	30 shares (30%)	90 shares (120 shares (30%))
Walter	20 shares (20%)	60 shares (80 shares (20%))
Amelia	10 shares (10%)	30 shares (40 shares (10%))

Kathryn, Walter and Amelia accept the offer and subscribe for the shares. Rhoda turns down the offer and decides not to purchase any more shares. John purchases the remaining shares. The table below shows each shareholder's holding post-allotment.

Shareholder	Shareholding post-allotment
Kathryn	160 shares (40%)
Rhoda	30 shares (7.5%)
Walter	80 shares (20%)
Amelia	40 shares (10%)
John	90 shares (22.5%)

By accepting the pre-emption right offer, Kathryn, Walter and Amelia's voting rights have not been diluted.

bonus shares
Shares that are issued fully paid up to existing shareholders in proportion to their existing holdings.

Three types of share allotment will not be subject to pre-emption rights:

- **bonus shares** (s. 564);
- shares that are, or are to be, wholly or partly paid up otherwise than in cash (s. 565); and
- shares that are allotted as part of an employee share scheme (s. 566).

In addition to the above exceptions, pre-emption rights can be excluded by the company in a number of situations, including:

- the articles of a private company can exclude pre-emption rights (s. 567);
- the s. 561 pre-emption right will not apply where the company's articles already contain such a corresponding right and that article provision has been complied with (s. 568);
- the directors of a company with only one class of share may ignore pre-emption rights if they are empowered to do so by the articles or by a special resolution of the company (s. 569);
- where the directors are authorised to allot shares under s. 551, then they may be given the power, either through the articles or via a special resolution of the company, to allot shares without pre-emption rights applying (s. 570); and
- where the directors are authorised to allot shares under s. 551, then the company may, by passing a special resolution, exclude or modify pre-emption rights in relation to a specified allotment, providing that the directors make a statement setting out specified information (e.g. their reasons for excluding pre-emption rights) (s. 571).

4.4 Payment for shares

When shares are allotted, the terms of the allotment will specify whether the shares allotted will be:

- fully paid (i.e. the full purchase price is payable on allotment);
- partly paid (i.e. part of the purchase price is due on allotment, with the remainder at a later date); or
- nil paid (nothing is due on allotment, with the full price to be paid at some point in the future).

Where shares are not fully paid on allotment, the company can either require the allottee to pay the remainder via a series of fixed instalments or the company can issue a 'call notice', which requires the allottee to pay a specified amount (which may be the full remaining payment or part of it).

The risk with allotting partly-paid or nil-paid shares is that the allottee may not pay the remaining amount (if they have insufficient funds, for example). In such a case, the articles will usually provide the company with some form of remedy. For example, the model articles for public companies provide that if an allottee fails to pay an instalment or comply with a call notice, then:

- the company will have a lien over any partly-paid shares and, if the required payment is not received within 14 days, the company can sell those shares (articles 52 and 53); or
- the company can send the allottee a notice of intended forfeiture and, if payment is not then received within 14 days, the directors may decide that the shares are forfeited (articles 58 and 59).

The allottee will cease to be a member, but remains liable for the sums payable (article 60(3)). Forfeited shares are deemed to be the company's property and so can be sold, re-allotted or otherwise disposed of as the directors see fit (article 60(2)).

Note that the model articles for private companies do not contain such remedies. This is because private companies almost always require shares to be paid in full on allotment.

Means of payment

Section 582(1) provides that shares allotted by a company, and any premium on them, many be paid up in money or money's worth (including goodwill and know-how). It is therefore possible to pay for shares with non-cash consideration such as goods and services, but this is limited in the case of shares in a public company in several ways.

- A public company must not accept, in payment for its shares or any premium on them, an undertaking from a person that he or someone else will do work or perform services for the company (s. 585(1)). If a public company does accept such an undertaking, the undertaking remains enforceable (s. 591(1)). The person who gave the undertaking is liable to pay the nominal value and any premium in relation to the shares received (s. 585(2)), and they will commit an offence (s. 590).
- A public company cannot accept as payment an undertaking which is to be performed more than five years after the date of the allotment (s. 587(2)). If the company does accept such an undertaking, the undertaking remains enforceable (s. 591(1)). The person who gave the undertaking is liable to pay the nominal value and any premium in relation to the shares received (s. 587(2)), and they will commit an offence (s. 590).
- A public company cannot accept non-cash consideration as payment for shares, unless the non-cash consideration has been independently valued and a copy of the valuation report made available to the company and the proposed allottee (s. 593(1)). A breach of these rules can result in the allottee being liable to repay to the company an amount equal to the nominal value of the shares received and any premium on them (s. 593(3)). An offence will also be committed (s. 607).

Allotment of shares at a discount

Section 580(1) of the CA 2006 provides that a company's shares must not be allotted at a discount (namely, for less than their nominal value). If shares are allotted at a discount, then the allottee is liable to pay the company an amount equal to the discount plus interest (s. 580(2)). However, there is an exception to this in relation to commission payments. Consider the following example to understand this exception.

Case study 11.5

X-Corp Ltd enters into an agreement with John, under which it agrees to pay him 10% commission if he purchases shares in the company. A week later, X-Corp allots 20 shares to John, with each share having a nominal value of £1. John pays £18 for the shares (£20 minus the £2 commission payment). The commission payment made to John means that he has acquired the shares at a discount.

Section 552 aims to combat this by prohibiting a company from paying commission to a person who agrees to subscribe for shares or who procures or agrees to procure subscriptions for shares in the company. However, such commission can be paid if:

- the payment of commission is authorised in the company's articles (article 44 of the model articles for public companies provides such authorisation); and
- the commission paid, or agreed to be paid, does not exceed 10% of the price at which the shares are issued or the amount or rate authorised by the articles, whichever is the lesser (s. 553).

Stop and think 11.2

The restrictions on paying for shares with non-cash consideration only apply to public companies. Is it therefore straightforward for private companies to evade the prohibition on allotting shares at a discount by overvaluing the non-cash consideration received?

4.5 Share certificates

A company must, within two months of the allotment of shares, have ready share certificates for delivery to the relevant holders in relation to the allotment (s. 769(1)). A failure to do so is a criminal offence (s. 769(3)). However, a company need not complete and deliver share certificates if:

- the conditions of the share allotment provide that share certificates will not be delivered (s. 769(2)(a));
- the shares are allotted to a financial institution (s. 769(2)(b)); or
- the shares that are allotted are uncertificated (Uncertificated Securities Regulations 2001 (SI 2001/3755), reg 38(2)).

A share certificate fulfils two functions. First, it provides basic information about the shares to which it relates (the information contained in a share certificate is a matter for the company's articles).

Second, the share certificate provides evidence that the person named on it holds legal title to the shares the certificate relates to. In *Re Bahia and San Francisco Railway Co Ltd* (1867-68) LR 3 QB 584, Cockburn CJ stated that a share certificate is:

> 'a declaration by the company to all the world that the person in whose name the certificate is made out, and to whom it is given, is a shareholder in the company, and it is given by the company with the intention that it shall be so used by the person to whom it is given and acted upon in the sale and transfer of shares.'

However, the share certificate only provides *prima facie* evidence of the holder's title to the shares (s. 768(1)), meaning that the holder's claim to hold legal title to the shares can be rebutted. Conclusive evidence as to who holds shares is found in the register of members.

Test yourself 11.2

1. **What is the difference between allotting and issuing shares?**
2. **A private company that has allotted ordinary shares wishes to allot preference shares. Do the directors have the authority to allot these shares?**
3. **Explain the concept of a minimum share capital.**
4. **What are pre-emption rights?**
5. **Explain the distinction between fully paid, partly-paid and nil-paid shares.**
6. **What limitations are placed upon a public company's ability to accept non-cash consideration as payment for shares?**
7. **What two functions does a share certificate fulfil?**

5. Offering shares to the public

One decision that a public company will make is whether to offer to sell its shares to the public at large. Private companies must not offer, allot or agree to allot any securities to the public (CA 2006, s. 755(1)). If a private company breaches the s. 755(1) prohibition, then the allotment of shares remains valid (s. 760), but the court can (i) order the company to stop contravening s. 755; (ii) order the company to re-register as public; or (iii) make a remedial order and/or order that the company be wound up (ss. 757–759).

There is no doubt that offering shares to the public brings some significant advantages, notably the ability to raise significant amounts of money through issuing new shares (especially if the shares are admitted to trading on a stock exchange). However, there are also significant disadvantages – companies that offer their shares to the public are subject to a significant amount of additional regulation, especially if they wish to admit their shares to trading on a stock exchange.

5.1 The regulatory framework

Before looking at the process by which public companies can offer their shares to the public, it is first important to set out the legal framework under which public offers of shares are regulated.

EU Law

The free movement of capital is a pillar of the EU. It has long been the EU's goal to create an integrated European financial market that allows capital and financial services to flow throughout the EU. To that end, a significant body of UK capital regulation derives from EU law, notably a series of EU directives including:

- the Consolidated Admission and Reporting Directive (Directive 2001/34/EU) (CARD) which seeks to harmonise the rules relating to the listing of securities;
- the Prospectus Directive (Directive 2003/71/EC), which sets out rules regarding prospectuses, but will eventually be replaced by the Prospectus Regulation (Regulation 2017/1129/EU); and
- the Transparency Obligations Directive (Directive 2004/109/EU), which sets out disclosure rules for companies who trade on a regulated market.

Financial Services and Markets Act 2000

The Financial Services and Markets Act 2000 (FSMA 2000) regulates financial services by requiring that certain 'regulated activities' (which are set out in Schedule 2 and include dealing in investments or providing investment advice) are only undertaken by authorised persons (e.g. those persons authorised by the Financial Conduct Authority (FCA) to undertake regulated activities).

In addition, Part IA of the FSMA 2000 establishes the bodies who regulate financial services, with the principal regulator being the FCA.

The FCA and the FCA Handbook

EU Member States are required to appoint one of more 'competent authorities' who are responsible for enforcing CARD (CARD, Article 105). In the UK, this body is the FCA which acts as the UK Listing Authority (UKLA), although it should be noted that the FCA has stated that it intends to stop using the term UKLA as it has proven confusing. As regards securities regulation, the FCA has two key functions. First, it determines which securities are admitted to the official list, and maintains the official list (FSMA 2000, s. 74).

Second, the FCA is empowered to make rules in order to achieve its objectives (s. 137A(1)). These rules are found in the FCA Handbook. The Handbook is divided into a series of blocks, with block 7 being relevant for our purposes as it contains the following rules:

- the Listing Rules, which set out the rules for listing shares and the rules that listed companies must comply with;
- the Prospectus Rules, which set out rules regarding the preparation and publication of prospectuses; and
- the Disclosure Guidance and Transparency Rules (DTRs), which impose a range of disclosure obligations on listed companies.

If a company breaches these rules or a provision in Part VI of FSMA 2000, then the FCA can impose on that company a financial penalty of such amount as it considers appropriate (FSMA 2000, s. 91). Instead of imposing a financial penalty, the FCA may publish a statement censuring the person in breach (FSMA 2000, s. 91(3)). The most severe sanction available to the FCA is to suspend (s. 77(2)) or discontinue (s. 77(1)) a listing of securities.

5.2 Types of public offer and stock exchanges

Two questions will need to be answered when a public company decides to offer its shares to the public.

- What type of offer will the company make?
- Will the company trade its shares on a stock exchange?

Types of offer

The first time that a company offers it shares to the public is called an initial public offering (IPO), and the company may follow this up over time with subsequent offerings to the public. There are several ways that a company can offer its shares to the public.

- An offer for subscription involves the company offering to the public a certain amount of shares. Note that the company cannot allot the shares unless all the shares offered are subscribed for or the terms of the offer provide that shares may be allotted even if all the shares are not subscribed for (CA 2006, s. 578(1)).
- An offer for sale involves an investment bank subscribing for all the shares being offered by the company, and the bank then offering those shares to the public.
- A placing usually involves an investment bank 'placing' its shares with selected purchasers (normally institutional investors selected by the bank), rather than the public at large. The bank is essentially identifying which persons may wish to purchase the shares. Once the placing is made, those persons can then decide whether to purchase the shares or not. Often the investment bank that placed the shares will agree to purchase any shares that are not placed.
- A rights issue is an offer made to existing shareholders of the company, under which each shareholder is offered shares in proportion to their existing shareholding. It is often the case that shareholders who choose

not to take up the rights offer can sell the right to purchase the shares to another person (if the shareholder does not have this right, it is known as an 'open offer').

Stock exchanges

The company will need to decide if it wishes to trade its shares on a stock exchange and, if so, what stock market. In the UK, the principal stock exchange is the London Stock Exchange (LSE). If a company wishes for its shares to be traded on the LSE, it will need to decide which of the LSE's markets the shares will be traded on. There are two principal markets.

- The Main Market, which is the LSE's flagship market. The shares traded on the Main Market are those of larger, well-established companies and only listed securities can be traded on the Main Market. In addition to complying with the legal rules discussed on p 226, companies whose shares are listed on the Main Market will also have to comply with the Rules of the London Stock Exchange.
- AIM (formerly known as the Alternative Investment Market) is aimed at smaller and medium-sized companies. Securities traded on AIM are not listed and are subject to less regulation than shares on the Main Market. It is common for companies to first trade their shares on AIM and then to progress to the Main Market at a later date. Companies with shares on AIM must comply with the AIM Rules for Companies.

A UK company need not trade on a UK stock exchange – it may trade on a stock exchange elsewhere, or it may trade its shares on several exchanges. For example, a number of FTSE 100 companies will have a primary listing on the LSE's Main Market and a secondary listing on a market overseas (e.g. the New York Stock Exchange).

5.3 Listing

An additional decision for a company is whether to list its shares or not. Listed securities are those securities that are admitted onto the official list that is maintained by the FCA. There are good reasons why a company would seek to list its shares, as certain share markets (such as the LSE's Main Market) will only accept listed securities. However, this must be balanced with the fact that listed companies are subject to additional rules that unlisted companies are not.

If a company does decide to apply to the FCA to have its shares listed, it will need to first decide which of the two types of listing it wants – a standard listing or a premium listing. The difference is that companies with a premium listing are subject to greater regulation and the UK Corporate Governance Code applies to companies with a premium listing.

Stop and think 11.3

Given the additional regulatory burdens of a premium listing, why do you think a company would seek a premium listing? What do you think are the advantages and disadvantages of a premium listing over a standard listing?

Not all public companies are eligible for listing. In order to apply for a listing, a company must meet a range of eligibility criteria, including:

- the company must be duly incorporated and operating in accordance with its constitution (Listing Rules, LR 2.2.1);
- the shares to be listed must comply with the law of the company's place of incorporation, be authorised under the company's constitution and have any statutory and other necessary consents (LR 2.2.2);
- the shares to be listed must be freely transferable, fully paid and free from all liens and restrictions on the right to transfer (LR 2.24);
- the expected aggregate of the shares to be listed must be at least £700,000 (LR 2.2.7(1)); and
- an FCA-approved prospectus must be published (LR 2.2.10).

The above eligibility requirements are for a standard listing. A company that seeks a premium listing will need to comply with additional eligibility requirements found in LR6.

The listing process

The listing process is set out in LR3 of the Listing Rules. The company will book a date on which its listing application will be heard. Two days before this date, the company must submit to the FCA:

- a completed Application for Admission of Securities to the Official List;
- an approved prospectus or listing particulars;
- any circular that was published in connection with the application; and
- written confirmation of the number of shares to be allotted (LR 3.3.2).

The FCA will notify the company of its decision within six months of the application being received (FSMA 2000, s. 76(1)). If the application is successful and the FCA decides to admit the shares to the official list, it will notify the company in writing (FSMA 2000, s. 76(3)). The listing will become effective once it is announced by a regulatory information service (Listing Rules, LR 3.2.7). If the application is not successful and the FCA decides to not admit the shares to the official list, then it must notify the company of this (FSMA 2000, s. 76(5)). The company may appeal the FCA's decision to the Upper Tribunal (FSMA 2000, ss. 76(6) and 417(1)).

Continuing obligations

In order to maintain its listing, the company will need to comply with a range of continuing obligations found in the DTRs and the Listing Rules. All listed companies must comply with the two Listing Principles (LR 7.2.1):

1. a listed company must take reasonable steps to establish and maintain adequate procedures, systems and controls to enable it to comply with its obligations (Listing Principle 1); and
2. a listed company must deal with the FCA in an open and co-operative manner (Listing Principle 2).

In addition, companies with a premium listing must comply with the six Premium Listing Principles, which state:

1. a listed company must take reasonable steps to enable its directors to understand their responsibilities and obligations as directors (Premium Listing Principle 1);
2. a listed company must act with integrity towards the holders and potential holders of its premium listed shares (Premium Listing Principle 2);
3. all equity shares in a class that has been admitted to premium listing must carry an equal number of votes on any shareholder vote (Premium Listing Principle 3);
4. where a listed company has more than one class of equity shares admitted to premium listing, the aggregate voting rights of the shares in each class should be broadly proportionate to the relative interests of those classes in the equity of the listed company (Premium Listing Principle 4);
5. a listed company must ensure that it treats all holders of the same class of its listed equity shares that are in the same position equally in respect of the rights attaching to those listed equity shares (Premium Listing Principle 5); and
6. a listed company must communicate information to holders and potential holders of its listed equity shares in such a way as to avoid the creation of a false market in those listed equity shares (Premium Listing Principle 6).

5.4 The prospectus

Recital 18 of the Prospectus Directive sets out why, in certain cases, companies are required to prepare and publish an approved prospectus before they offer their shares to the public:

> 'The provision of full information concerning securities and issuers of those securities promotes, together with rules on the conduct of business, the protection of investors. Moreover, such information provides an effective means of increasing confidence in securities and thus of contributing to the proper functioning and development of securities markets. The appropriate way to make this information available is to publish a prospectus.'

The relevant rules relating to prospectuses are found in the FSMA 2000 (notably ss. 84–87I) and the Prospectus Rules in the FCA Handbook. In 2017, the EU Prospectus Regulation was passed which will amend some of these rules when it comes into force by July 2019.

When is a prospectus required?

Sections 85(1) and (2) of the FSMA 2000 provide that it is unlawful for transferable securities to be offered to the public, or request that shares be admitted to trading on a UK regulated market, unless an approved prospectus has been made available before the offer/request is made. Breach of these requirements is an offence (s. 85(3)).

However, a number of exceptions exist to the s. 85 requirement. In certain cases, a prospectus will not be required:

- where the shares are only offered to qualified investors (s. 86(1)(a));
- where the offer is made or directed at fewer than 150 persons, other than qualified investors, per EEA state (s. 86(1)(b));
- where the minimum consideration payable by each person under the offer is at least €100,000 (or equivalent amount) (s. 86(1)(c));
- where the total consideration for the transferable securities being offered in EEA states cannot exceed €8 million (or equivalent amount) (s. 86(1)(e));
- where the transferable securities are being sold or placed through a financial intermediary (s. 86(1A)); or
- where the transaction is one that falls within Schedule 11A (s. 85(5) and (6)), with an example being where the total consideration for the securities being offered is less than €1 million (Schedule 11A, para 9).

Some of these exceptions apply simply to an offer of shares to the public, whereas others apply to requests to admit shares to a regulated market. An offer of shares may be exempt from the requirement to draw up a prospectus but may nevertheless still need to draw up a prospectus if the company wants to admit the shares to a regulated market.

Content of the prospectus

PR2 of the Prospectus Rules sets out the format and content of the prospectus. In terms of the format, PR 2.2.1 provides that the prospectus can be drawn up as a single document, or it can be divided up into separate documents. If it is drawn up as separate documents, then three separate documents are required (PR 2.2.2(1)).

1. The registration document, which contains information about the company issuing the shares in question.
2. The securities note, which contains information about the shares to which the prospectus relates.
3. The summary, which must convey concisely, in non-technical language and in an appropriate structure, the key information relevant to the securities which are the subject of the prospectus. When read with the rest of the

prospectus, this must be an aid to investors considering whether to invest in the securities (FSMA 2000, s. 87A(6)). The 'key information' that must be provided is set out in s. 87A(10).

Exactly what information is required in these documents will depend upon the nature of the shares and the company that is issuing them (FSMA 2000, s. 87A(4)). The rules are complex, but basically every company must provide a 'base prospectus' that contains certain mandatory information (as set out in PR 2.3.1). Depending on the company and the shares being issued, the prospectus may need to provide additional information that the Prospectus Rules refer to as 'building blocks'.

Approval and publication of the prospectus

A prospectus cannot be published until it has been approved by the FCA (FSMA 2000, s. 85(1) and (7)). Three criteria will need to be satisfied to gain approval:

1. the UK is the company's home state;
2. the prospectus contains the necessary information; and
3. all the other relevant requirements found in Part VI of the FSMA 2000 or the Prospectus Directive have been complied with (FSMA 2000, s. 87A(1)).

If the FCA is not satisfied that these criteria have been satisfied, it will refuse to grant approval and must state why approval has not been granted (s. 87D(4)–(5)). If the FCA does approve the prospectus, then it must be made available to the public as soon as practicable, at a reasonable time in advance of, and at the latest at the beginning of the offer or the admission of the shares to trading (Prospectus Rules, PR 3.2.2). A prospectus will be deemed to be made available to the public if it is:

- published in one or more newspapers that are circulated throughout, or widely circulated in, the EEA states in which the offer for shares has been made;
- available in printed form, free of charge, to the public at the LSE or the company's registered office; or
- made available in electronic form on the company's website or the website of the LSE (PR 3.2.4).

A significant benefit of acquiring approval is that, if a competent authority of an EEA state approves a prospectus, then that prospectus will be approved in all other EEA states (Prospectus Directive, Article 17). This 'passporting' of prospectuses facilitates the cross-border offering of shares. However, it is likely that UK companies will lose their passporting rights upon the UK's exit from the EU (unless an agreed trade deal preserves passporting rights).

Liability for untrue or misleading statements etc.

Section 90(1) of the FSMA 2000 provides that any person responsible for the prospectus is liable to pay compensation to a person who has:

- acquired securities to which the prospectus applies; and
- suffered loss in respect to those securities as a result of:
  - any untrue statement in the prospectus;
  - any misleading statement in the prospectus; or
  - the omission from the prospectus of any required information.

Liability can be imposed on 'any person responsible' for the prospectus, with PR 5.5 setting out who such persons are. The rules are complex and based on the type of security in question, but as an example, where the prospectus relates to equity shares, the persons responsible include:

- the company;
- the directors of the company;
- persons who accept responsibility for the prospectus and are so named in the prospectus; and
- persons not stated above who authorised the content of the prospectus (PR 5.5.3).

When determining how much compensation is payable, the House of Lords stated that, in relation to a predecessor of s. 90, damages should be determined in the same way as damages for the tort of deceit (*Clark v Urquharticle* [1930] AC 28 (HL)) and it is likely that this will also apply to s. 90. The significance of this is that unforeseeable losses can be claimed for.

Section 90(6) of FSMA 2000 provides that nothing in s. 90 affects any other form of liability. So, for example, if a person makes an untrue or misleading statement in the prospectus, he could be liable under s. 90 and also liable for misrepresentation.

A number of situations (set out in Schedule 10) are excluded from s. 90(1) and so liability cannot be imposed, including:

- where the person responsible for the prospectus reasonably believed that the statement was true and not misleading, or that the information that was omitted was properly omitted (Schedule 10, para 1); and
- where the person who suffered the loss acquired the securities knowing that the information in the prospectus was false or misleading, or knew that it contained omitted material (Schedule 10, para 6).

5.5 Underwriting

When a company makes a public offer of its shares, it is common for that offer to be underwritten. An underwriting agreement typically involves the company entering into an agreement with an underwriter (usually an investment bank), under which the underwriter agrees to subscribe or purchase any shares that are not taken up by the public. The advantage of this, from the company's perspective, is that the company knows that all of the shares offered will be subscribed for or purchased. The downside of this is that the underwriter does not provide the underwriting service for free, and it will charge the company commission (which is usually calculated based on a percentage of the nominal value of the shares being offered).

Test yourself 11.3

1. **What three sets of rules within the FCA Handbook are relevant to the public offering of shares?**
2. **Identify the four main types of public offering of shares.**
3. **Explain the distinction between a standard listing and a premium listing.**
4. **When will a company be required to prepare and publish a prospectus?**
5. **If a company decides to divide a prospectus up into separate documents, what are these documents? Briefly explain what they cover.**
6. **What is underwriting?**

6. Classes of share

Most companies with a share capital will have only one class of share, and most companies without a share capital will only have one class of member. However, companies may have multiple classes of share with each class having different rights, providing that the articles authorise the directors to allot shares of a different class or the articles are so altered to provide such authorisation (*Andrews v Gas Meter Co* [1897] 1 Ch 361 (CA)).

Where a company does have multiple classes of share, the rights of the various classes are usually expressly and clearly stated in the company's articles. In such a case, determining what amounts to a class right is simple. Where the class rights are not so expressly provided, it can be more difficult to determine a class right. Section 629(1) of the CA 2006 provides limited guidance by stating that 'shares are of one class if the rights attached to them are in all respects uniform'.

As noted, most companies will have only one class of share, which will be known as 'ordinary shares' and will carry the usual rights (such as the right to vote at general meetings). Companies may create as many classes of share as they wish with whatever rights they wish. A common form of share class is the preference share, which will usually provide that the holder is entitled to a fixed dividend that is payable before a dividend is paid to the ordinary shareholders. Unless otherwise stated, this entitlement to a fixed dividend is cumulative (*Webb v Earle* (1875) LR 20 Eq 556). If a dividend is not paid one year, it is carried over to the next and the shareholder will receive double (if the company has sufficient distributable profits).

6.1 Variation of class rights

A company may seek to vary the rights of a particular class of shareholder. Before looking at the statutory procedure to vary class rights, it is important to note that this procedure only applies to a 'variation' of class rights, so we must first discuss what constitutes a variation of class rights.

The Companies Act 2006 does not define what a 'variation' of class rights is, merely providing limited guidance:

- any amendment of a provision contained in a company's articles for the variation of the rights attached to a class of shares, or the insertion of any such provision into the articles, is itself to be treated as a variation of those rights (ss. 630(5) and 631(5)); and
- abrogation (repealing or abolishing) of a class right will constitute a variation (ss. 630(6) and 631(6)).

The task of determining what amounts to a variation has been left to the courts. The approach adopted by the courts was set out in *White v Bristol Aeroplane Co Ltd* [1953] Ch 65 (CA), where Evershed MR stated that 'there is to my mind a distinction, and a sensible distinction, between an affecting of the rights and an affecting of the enjoyment of the rights, or of the stockholders' capacity to turn them to account'. In other words, a distinction is drawn between an alteration that affects a class right and an alteration that affects the enjoyment of a class right, with only the former being capable of amounting to a variation. The following case provides a stark example of this distinction in action.

Case law 11.1

***Re Mackenzie and Co Ltd* [1916] 2 Ch 450 (Ch)**

The company's preference shareholders were entitled to a 4% dividend on the amount paid up on their shares. As the preference shares had a nominal value of £20 and were all fully paid up, this meant that each preference shareholder was entitled to a dividend of 80 pence per share. It was proposed that the nominal value of the preference shares would be reduced to £12, which would have the knock-on effect of reducing the dividend payment to 48 pence per share. The question was whether this amounted to a variation of the preference shareholders' class rights.

The reduction of the nominal value of the preference shares did not constitute a variation of the preference shareholders' class rights. The reason for this was that the class right itself had not changed – the preference shareholders were still entitled to a 4% dividend on the amount paid up on their shares. All that had changed is their enjoyment of the class right (i.e. the right was less valuable).

As long as the right itself remains the same, the fact that the right is rendered less valuable, or even worthless, will not be enough to classify the alteration of the class right as a variation (*Dimbula Valley (Ceylon) Tea Co Ltd v Laurie* [1961] Ch 353 (Ch)).

How to vary class rights?

Sections 630 and 631 provide that there are only two ways to vary class rights. First, where the company's articles contain a provision stating how class rights are to be varied, class rights can be varied by complying with that provision (ss. 630(2)(a) and 631(2)(a)). The model articles contain no such provision, but companies (especially companies with multiple classes of share) will frequently add one.

Second, where the articles contain no provision for the variation of class rights, then class rights can be varied as follows.

- In order to vary rights attached to a class of shares, the consent of the holders of shares of that class will need to be obtained (s. 630(2)(b)). The consent required is either:
  - consent in writing from the holders of at least three-quarters in nominal value of the shares of that class; or
  - a special resolution passed at a class meeting of holders of the class of shares in question (s. 630(4)).
- In order to vary the rights of a class of members in a company without a share capital, the consent of members of that class will need to be obtained (s. 631(2)(b)). The consent required is either:
  - consent in writing from at least three-quarters of the members of that class; or
  - a special resolution passed at a class meeting of the members of the class in question (s. 631(4)).

When deciding whether to consent to a variation, the shareholders/members must decide this based on whether the dominant purpose of the variation is to benefit the class as a whole. If they do not do so, the variation may be invalidated, as occurred in the following case.

Case law 11.2

***British America Nickel Corp Ltd v MJ O'Brien Ltd* [1927] AC 369 (PC)**

A company issued bonds, the terms of which provided that the bondholders' rights could be modified if three-quarters of the bondholders in value consented to the variation. A modification was proposed and was passed due to the support of a bondholder called Booth. However, unknown to the other bondholders, Booth had been promised $2 million worth of shares in the company if he supported the variation. Upon discovering this, a bondholder who opposed the variation commenced proceedings against the company.

Viscount Haldane stated that the power to vote on the variation of a class right 'must be exercised for the purpose of benefitting the class

as a whole, and not merely individual members only'. Here, Booth had supported the variation to benefit himself, and not the bondholders as a whole. The court therefore held that the resolution approving the variation was invalid.

Had Booth disclosed the existence of the incentive, then the decision may very well have been different. In *Azevedo v Imcopa Importação* [2013] EWCA Civ 364, Lloyd LJ stated that a payment made to a shareholder/member to support a variation in class rights was not objectionable providing that it was 'open and above board'.

Right of objection

Shareholders/members of the class in question who did not consent to the variation have the right to apply to the court to object to the variation, provided that they represent:

- not less than 15% of the issued shares of the class of shares in question (in the case of a company with a share capital); or
- not less than 15% of the class of members in question (in the case of a company without a share capital) (ss. 633(2) and 634(2)).

If such an application is made, the variation will have no effect until it is confirmed by the court (ss. 633(3) and 634(3)). If the court is of the opinion that the variation would unfairly prejudice the class represented by the applicant(s), then it may disallow the variation (ss. 633(5) and 634(5)).

Test yourself 11.4

1. **What are class rights?**
2. **What approach have the courts adopted in order to determine if an alteration of class rights amounts to a variation?**
3. **What are the two methods of varying class rights?**

7. Transfer and transmission of shares

This section discusses the two ways by which existing shares can be passed from one person to another: (i) by transfer; or (ii) by transmission. Transmission occurs where a person acquires shares by the operation of law. Shares are transferred where they pass from one person to another via a method such as sale.

7.1 Transfer of shares

Shares are items of personal property and so can be transferred from one person to another (CA 2006, s. 544(1)). This most commonly occurs where a shareholder sells some or all of their shares to another person. However, a shareholder's ability to transfer their shares is not completely free, as s. 544(1) of the CA 2006 provides that a company's shares are transferable in accordance with its articles. From this, it follows that a company's articles can place limits upon the ability to transfer its shares. In practice, it only tends to be private companies that do this, with article 26(5) of the model articles for private companies stating that the directors may refuse to register a transfer of shares. Another form of limitation may be to provide that a shareholder who wishes to transfer his shares must first offer them to specified persons (such as other shareholders of the company).

The process for transferring shares depends on whether the shares being transferred are certificated (a share certificate has been issued in relation to them) or uncertificated (no share certificate has been issued).

Transfer of certificated shares

A company will not register a transfer of certificated shares unless it has received a proper instrument of transfer (CA 2006, s. 770(1)). A company's articles may specify what amounts to a 'proper instrument of transfer' but this usually refers to the 'stock transfer form' found in Schedule 1 of the Stock Transfer Act 1963 (indeed, this form will still be a proper instrument of transfer, even if the articles specify a different instrument). In such a case, the process for transferring shares is as follows.

- The transferor and transferee will agree the terms of the transfer (how many shares will be transferred, and for what price etc).
- The transferor will complete the stock transfer form and sign it.
- The transferee will pay the agreed price.
- If the transferor is transferring all their shares to a single transferee, they will send the stock transfer form and the share certificate to the transferee. In all other cases, the transferor will send the stock transfer form and the share certificate to the company, and the company will send the stock transfer form to the relevant transferee(s).
- If applicable, the transferee will pay stamp duty and the stock transfer form will be stamped to confirm payment.
- The transferee will send the stamped stock transfer form and, if applicable, the share certificate to the company.
- The company registers the transfer of shares (CA 2006, s. 771(1)) and provides a new share certificate to the transferee. If the transferor only sold some shares, they will be provided with a new share certificate that reflects their updated shareholding. Alternatively, the company may refuse to register the transfer of shares, in which case it must provide the transferee with its reasons for refusing the transfer within two months (s. 771(1)).

Transfer of uncertificated shares

The transfer of uncertificated shares occurs most commonly in relation to the shares of listed companies, under rules set out in the Uncertificated Securities Regulations 2001 (USR 2001). Under these regulations, a transfer occurs via a 'registered system', which is 'a computer-based system, and procedures, which enable title to units of a security to be evidenced and transferred without a written instrument, and which facilitate supplementary and incidental matters' (USR 2001, reg 2(1)). A registered system is run by an Operator, and the only approved Operator to date is Euroclear UK and Ireland Ltd. The system that Euroclear operates is called CREST. The process for transferring shares under CREST is as follows.

- The transferor and transferee will agree the terms of the transfer (e.g. how many shares will be transferred, for what price and on what date).
- The transferor and transferee will instruct CREST to transfer the shares. CREST will then check whether the instructions of both parties match, and whether the transferor has the shares in question.
- On the specified date, CREST will remove the requisite shares from the transferor's account and deposit them in the account of the transferee. At the same time, it will transfer the agreed price from the transferee's bank to the transferor's bank. Euroclear's register of members will be updated to reflect the transfer, and the company whose shares were being transferred will be sent a message to inform it that it needs to update its register of members.

7.2 Transmission of shares

Shares are transmitted where a person acquires them by the operation of law. In such a case, the shares are not transferred and so the above procedures need not be followed (no instrument of transfer is required, CA 2006, s. 770(1)). The transmission of shares occurs in three situations.

1. The death of a shareholder will cause his shares to be transmitted to their personal representative. The personal representative will then deal with the shares, usually by transferring them to others in accordance with the deceased's will.
2. The shares of a shareholder who has been declared bankrupt will be transmitted to their trustee in bankruptcy (IA 1986, ss. 283(1) and 306), who will then usually sell them to pay off the bankrupt's debts.
3. The shares of a shareholder who becomes a patient under the Mental Health Act 1983 will be transmitted to a receiver appointed by the Court of Protection.

Test yourself 11.5

1. **Explain the difference between the transfer and transmission of shares.**
2. **What document is required to transfer certificated shares?**
3. **In what three situations will the transmission of shares occur?**

Chapter summary

- A share is an item of personal property called a thing in action.
- All shares in a limited company must have a fixed nominal value and this represents the minimum price that a share can be allotted for. If a share is allotted for more than the nominal value, the excess is known as the share premium.
- Where a private company has only one class of shares, then the directors are authorised to allot more shares of that same class on behalf of the company. In all other cases, the directors will only have the authority to allot shares on behalf of the company if they are authorised to do so by the company's articles or by a resolution of the company to allot further shares.
- The registrar should not issue a public company with a trading certificate unless it has an allotted share capital of not less than £50,000.
- Where an allotment of shares is made, the shares should first be offered to the existing shareholders to allow them to maintain their holdings (known as 'pre-emption rights'). In specified cases, pre-emption rights will not apply or can be excluded.
- Shares can be fully paid (the full price is payable on allotment), partly paid (part of the price is due on allotment, with the remainder at a later date), or nil paid (nothing is due on allotment, with the full price to be paid at some point in the future).
- A company is prohibited from allotting shares at a discount (for below the nominal value).
- A share certificate provides *prima facie* evidence of title to the shares the certificate relates to.
- The key domestic law relating to the public offering of shares is found in the Financial Services and Markets Act 2000 and the FCA Handbook (notably the Listing Rules, the Prospectus Rules and the Disclosure Guidance and Transparency Rules).
- The main types of public offer are:
  - an offer for subscription;
  - an offer for sale;
  - a placing; and
  - a rights issue.
- The principal stock exchange in the UK is the London Stock Exchange and its principal market is the Main Market.
- A company lists its securities by applying to the FCA to have those securities admitted to the official list.
- It is unlawful for transferable securities to be offered to the public, or request that shares be admitted to trading on a UK regulated market, unless an approved prospectus has been made available before the offer/request is made.

- A prospectus can be drawn up as a single document, or it can be divided up into separate documents, namely the (i) registration document; (ii) the securities note; and (iii) the summary.
- A prospectus cannot be published until it has been approved by the FCA.
- A person responsible for a prospectus can be liable to pay compensation to a person who has suffered loss as a result of:
  - any untrue statement in the prospectus
  - any misleading statement in the prospectus; or
  - the omission from the prospectus of any required information.
- It is possible for a company to have different classes of member or share with different rights and these are known as class rights.
- The Companies Act 2006 provides that a variation of class rights can only be made:
  - by complying with the process in the articles for varying class rights (if the articles provide such a process); or
  - by obtaining the consent of the holders of the class right in question.
- Shares are transmitted where shares pass from one person to another due to the operation of law. Shares are transferred when they pass from one person to another in a manner that is not due to the operation of law.
- Transferring certificated shares requires a proper instrument of transfer to be delivered to the company. The transfer of uncertificated shares is usually carried out via a registered computer system, such as CREST.
- The transmission of shares occurs where:
  - a shareholder dies;
  - a shareholder is declared bankrupt; and
  - a shareholder becomes a patient under the Mental Health Act 1983.

Chapter twelve
The capital maintenance rules

Contents

1. Introduction

This chapter outlines those rules designed to protect creditors by ensuring that share capital is not unduly reduced. These rules are collectively referred to as the 'capital maintenance rules' (or the 'capital maintenance doctrine'). The principal purpose behind these rules was set out by Lord Wilson in *Trevor v Whitworth* (1887) 12 App Cas 409 (HL), who stated that the effect of these rules:

> 'is to prohibit every transaction between a company and a shareholder, by means of which the money already paid to the company in respect of his shares is returned to him, unless the Court has sanctioned the transaction. Paid-up capital may be diminished or lost in the course of the company's trading... but persons who deal with, and give credit to a limited company, naturally rely upon the fact that the company is trading with a certain amount of capital already paid, as well as upon the responsibility of its members for the capital remaining at call; and they are entitled to assume that no part of the capital which has been paid into the coffers of the company has been subsequently paid out, except in the legitimate course of its business.'

The legal rules discussed in this chapter are:

- the rules relating to alterations of share capital (particularly reductions in share capital);
- the rules relating to a company acquiring its own shares;
- the rules relating to a company providing financial assistance to others to acquire its shares; and
- the rules relating to distributions (notably dividend payments).

2. Alteration of share capital

A company is able to alter its share capital. Section 617 of the CA 2006 sets out the ways in which this can be done, including:

- increasing capital by allotting new shares;
- sub-dividing shares (e.g. converting 100 £2 shares into 200 £1 shares); or
- consolidating shares (e.g. converting 100 £10 shares into 10 £100 shares).

None of the above reduces the amount of share capital – allotting new shares increases share capital, and sub-division and consolidation maintains the level of share capital. These alterations do not adversely affect the creditors and concerns regarding capital maintenance do not arise. Sub-division or consolidation of shares may increase the company's level of capital by making it easier for the company to raise capital. However, a reduction of the company's share capital can adversely affect the creditors' position and so specific rules exist regarding such reductions that aim to protect the company's creditors.

2.1 Reduction of share capital

The courts have long held that a company may only reduce its share capital in a manner permitted by the Companies Act (*Trevor v Whitworth* (1887) 12 App Cas 409 (HL)). The CA 2006 provides for two methods to reduce capital:

- special resolution followed by court confirmation
- special resolution followed by solvency statement.

The methods above set out the processes that must be followed in order to reduce capital but, as long as these processes are followed, a company may reduce its share capital in any way it chooses (CA 2006, s. 641(3)). This is subject to two limitations:

- a company that seeks to reduce its capital by special resolution supported by solvency statement cannot do so if the result of the reduction is that there would be no members of the company holding shares other than redeemable shares (s. 641(2)); and
- a company may not reduce its share capital by either method if the reduction is part of a scheme under which a person is to acquire all the shares in the company or all the shares in one or more classes, other than those they already hold (s. 641(2A)).

A company does not require authorisation from its articles in order to reduce its share capital, but the articles may exclude or restrict the company's ability to reduce its share capital (s. 641(6)). If a reduction amounts to a variation of class rights, then the process for varying class rights must be followed.

Special resolution and court confirmation

The first method of reducing share capital is available to both public and private companies (although it is unlikely that private companies would use this method, given that the second method is much less cumbersome). It involves a special resolution and court confirmation (s. 641(1)(b)). The company must first pass a special resolution resolving to reduce its share capital. If this resolution passes, the company can then apply to the court for an order confirming the reduction (s. 645(1)).

When deciding whether to confirm the reduction, the primary concern of the courts is the interests of the company's creditors. A reduction will only be confirmed if the 'creditors of the company are safeguarded so that money cannot be applied in any way that would be detrimental to creditors' (*Re Ratners Group plc* (1988) 4 BCC 293 (Ch) 295 (Harman J)). However, the creditors are not the only relevant group, and the court will consider the interests of others.

- In *Re Jupiter House Investments (Cambridge) Ltd* [1985] 1 WLR 975 (Ch), Harman J stated that the court will only confirm the reduction if 'the cause of the reduction … was properly put to shareholders so that they could exercise an informed choice, and that the cause is proved by the evidence before the court' and 'the proposed reduction affects all shareholders of equal standing in a similar manner, or that those treated in a different manner from their equals have consented to that different treatment'.
- In *Poole v National Bank of China Ltd* [1907] AC 229 (HL), Lord Macnaghten stated that the court can take into account 'the interest of those members of the public who may be induced to take shares in the company'.

As a reduction can adversely affect the position of the company's creditors, s. 646 of the CA 2006 provides every creditor with the right to object to a reduction if the following conditions are met:

1. the proposed reduction involves a diminution of liability in respect of unpaid share capital or the payment to a shareholder of any paid-up share capital (s. 645(2)); and
2. the creditor can show that there is a real likelihood that the reduction would result in the company being unable to discharge his debt or claim when it fell due (s. 646(1)).

The court will draw up a list of such creditors (s. 646(2)) and will not confirm the reduction unless it is satisfied that every creditor on that list has either (i) consented to the reduction; or (ii) their debt or claim has been discharged, has determined or has been secured (s. 648(2)). In practice, it is rare for creditors to object as the company will usually seek to obtain the creditors' consent prior to the reduction commencing or will pay the creditors off.

If the court confirms the reduction, then the company must deliver to Companies House a copy of the court order and a statement of capital, and the registrar will then register it (s. 649(1)). The reduction will take effect once these documents have been registered (s. 649(3)).

Special resolution and solvency statement

The second method of reducing share capital is only available to private companies. It involves the company passing a special resolution supported by a solvency statement (s. 641(1)(a)). The solvency statement, which must be made not more than 15 days before the date of the resolution (s. 642(1)(a)), is a statement that each of the directors has formed the opinion that:

- as regards the company's situation at the date of the statement, there are no grounds on which the company could then be found to be unable to pay (or otherwise discharge) its debts; and
- the company will be able to pay (or otherwise discharge) its debts as they fall due during the year immediately following the date of the statement.

Alternatively, if it is intended to commence the winding up of the company within twelve months of the date of the statement, each director must be of the opinion that the company will be able to pay (or otherwise discharge) its debts in full within twelve months of the commencement of the winding up (s. 643(1)).

The statement is only valid if made by all the directors. If the directors make a solvency statement without having reasonable grounds for the opinions expressed in it, and the statement is delivered to the registrar, then an offence is committed by each director in default (s. 643(4)) and the reduction will be void (*Macpherson v European Strategic Bureau Ltd* [2002] BCC 39 (CA)).

Within 15 days of the resolution being passed, the company must deliver to Companies House a statement of capital and copies of the resolution and the solvency statement (s. 644(1)). The reduction will not take effect until the registrar registers these documents (s. 644(4)).

Test yourself 12.1

1. **What are the two methods by which a company can reduce its share capital?**
2. **What two limitations are placed on a company's ability to reduce its share capital?**
3. **When deciding whether to confirm a reduction, what is the court's principal concern?**
4. **What does a solvency statement state?**

3. Acquisition of own shares

Section 658(1) of the CA 2006 establishes a general rule that a company cannot acquire its own shares, with contravention of s. 658 being a criminal offence. There are several justifications for this prohibition, including:

- such an acquisition would return capital to the shareholders which is generally prohibited under the capital maintenance rules;
- a company could purchase its own shares in an attempt to manipulate its own share price; and
- such an acquisition would reduce the company's share capital and could therefore allow a company to avoid the procedures for reducing share capital discussed in the previous section.

However, recognising that such an acquisition may be justifiable in some cases, the CA 2006 does provide for a number of exceptions to this general prohibition. Several are listed in s. 659:

- a limited company may acquire any of its own fully-paid shares otherwise than for valuable consideration;
- a company may acquire its own shares as part of a valid reduction of capital; and
- the court may order that a company purchase its own shares from a member if the member's interests have been unfairly prejudiced under s. 994 of the CA 2006.

Two notable exceptions to the general prohibition relate to redeemable shares and a company purchasing its own shares.

3.1 Redeemable shares

Redeemable shares are shares issued by the company on the condition that they will be redeemed (bought back) by the company if the company or the shareholder so requires (s. 684(1)). A public company may only issue redeemable shares if authorised to do so by its articles (s. 684(3)). A private company does not require authorisation from its articles, but its articles may exclude or restrict the company's ability to issue redeemable shares (s. 684(2)).

Only fully paid up shares can be redeemed (s. 686(1)) and the company must pay for the shares upon redemption (s. 686(3)), unless the company and the shareholder agree to payment being made on a later date (s. 686(2)). In order to prevent capital being returned to the shareholders, the payment for the shares must come from the company's distributable profits or from the proceeds of a fresh issue of shares made for the purpose of the redemption (s. 687(2)). As discussed on page 245, a process exists whereby a private company can pay for redeemable shares using capital.

When redeemable shares are redeemed, they are cancelled and the company's share capital must be reduced by the nominal value of the shares redeemed (s. 688). If the shares were redeemed wholly out of the company's profits, the amount by which the company's issued share capital was diminished must be transferred to an account called the 'capital redemption reserve' (s. 733(1) and (2)(a)). Within one month of the redemption, the company must notify Companies House of the redemption, specify the shares redeemed, and provide a statement of capital (s. 689).

3.2 Purchase of own shares

Section 690(1) provides the company with a more wide-ranging ability to purchase its shares, as it applies to all the company's shares (including redeemable shares). However, this power is subject to several limitations, including:

- the company's articles may exclude or restrict the company's ability to purchase its own shares (s. 690(1)(b));
- a company cannot purchase its own shares if, as a result of the purchase, there would no longer be any shares other than redeemable shares or shares held as treasury shares (s. 690(2)); and
- only fully paid shares can be purchased (s. 691(1)).

Authorisation
The purchase of the shares must be authorised, with the process for authorisation differing depending on whether the purchase is a market purchase or an off-market purchase.

A market purchase is one that takes place on a recognised investment exchange and is subject to a marketing arrangement on the exchange (s. 693(4)). A company that purchased its own listed shares would constitute a market purchase (s. 693(3)(a)). A company can only make a market purchase of its own shares if it is first authorised to do so by a resolution of the company (s. 701(1)).

An off-market purchase is one that: (i) does not take place on a recognised investment exchange; or (ii) does take place on a recognised investment exchange but is not subject to a marketing arrangement on the exchange (s. 693(2)). Before making an off-market purchase of its own shares, the company must first obtain one of the following forms of approval:

- the terms of the contract for the share purchase must be authorised by a resolution of the company before the contract is entered into; or
- the contract must provide that no shares may be purchased until its terms have been authorised by a resolution of the company (s. 694(2)).

Payment and cancellation
The shares must be paid for on purchase (s. 691(2)) unless a private limited company is purchasing shares for the purposes of or pursuant to an employee share scheme (s. 691(3)). The purchase of shares must generally be paid for out of the company's distributable profits or out of the proceeds of a fresh issue of shares made for the purpose of financing the purchase (s. 692(2)(a)). A process exists whereby a private company can purchase its own shares out of capital, but this process is complex. A simpler process for purchasing shares out of capital is available to a private company if:

- the purchase is authorised by the company's articles; and
- the total price paid for the shares in the financial year does not exceed £15,000 or the nominal value of 5% of its fully paid-up share capital at the beginning of the financial year, whichever is the lower (s. 692(1ZA)).

Directors' statement

The directors must make a statement specifying how much capital will be required to pay for the shares (known as the 'permissible capital payment') and including a statement of solvency (s. 714(1)–(5)). The directors' statement must be available for inspection (s. 720) and a copy must be made available to the members (s. 718).

↓

Auditor's report

The directors' statement must be accompanied by a report by the company's auditor which states (i) the amount specified as the permissible capital payment is properly determined; and (ii) he is not aware of anything to indicate that the opinion expressed by the directors in their solvency statement is unreasonable in all the circumstances (s. 714(6)). The auditor's report must be available for inspection (s. 720) and a copy must be made available to the members (s. 718).

↓

Special resolution

Within one week of the directors' statement, the payment out of capital must be approved by a special resolution of the company (s. 716).

↓

Public notice

Within one week following the special resolution being passed, the company must publish a notice in *The Gazette* stating that the company has approved a payment out of capital for the purpose of acquiring its own shares by redemption or purchase (or both) (s. 719).

↓

Payment

The payment out of capital must be made no earlier than five weeks after the resolution, and no later than seven weeks after the resolution (although the seven-week period can be extended by the court if an application is made to the court for an order cancelling the resolution) (s. 723).

Figure 12.1 Redeeming or purchasing shares out of capital

Once purchased by the company, the shares are then cancelled and the company's share capital must be reduced by the nominal value of the shares cancelled (s. 706(b)). If the shares were purchased wholly out of the company's profits, the amount by which the company's issued share capital was diminished must be transferred to the capital redemption reserve (s. 733(1) and (2)(b)). Within 28 days of the purchase, the company must deliver a return to Companies House (Form SH03), which must state the number and nominal value of the shares purchased and the date on which they were delivered to the company (s. 707(1) and (3)).

3.3 Acquisition of shares out of capital

As noted above, a company can only generally redeem or purchase its own shares out of distributable profits or the proceeds of a fresh issue of shares. However, this may not be possible for private companies (who may lack such profits or cannot sell sufficient shares). The CA 2006 allows private companies to redeem or purchase their own shares out of capital, providing that the company has first used any available profits and the proceeds of any fresh issue of shares made for the purpose of redemption or purchase (s. 710(1)).

The Act sets out a strict procedure that must be followed. This procedure, which is rather cumbersome, is summarised in Fig. 12.1.

Any member (other than one who voted for the resolution) or creditor of the company may, within five weeks of the special resolution, apply to the court for an order cancelling the resolution (s. 721(1)–(2)). The court will then make an order either cancelling or confirming the resolution, and it may do so on such terms and conditions and it thinks fit (s. 721(4)).

Test yourself 12.2

1. **Why are companies generally prohibited from acquiring their own shares?**
2. **What are redeemable shares?**
3. **Does a company require authorisation in its articles in order to issue redeemable shares?**
4. **If a company wishes to redeem or purchase its own shares, where must the payment come from?**
5. **What happens to a company's shares when it redeems or purchases them?**

4. Financial assistance to acquire shares

The Greene Committee of 1926 stated that a company providing financial assistance to others to acquire their shares was open to the 'gravest abuses', noting that it could:

- allow a company to manipulate its share prices; and
- allow a company (*A*) to provide financial assistance to another company (*B*), and *B* could then use that money to purchase shares in *A* and take it over.

To prevent such abuses, the Companies Act 1929 prohibited companies from providing financial assistance to others to acquire their shares. The problem with the prohibition was that it also caught certain innocent transactions, especially those involving private companies. A 'whitewash' procedure was introduced by the Companies Act 1981 which allowed private companies to provide financial assistance if certain conditions were met. Unfortunately, this procedure was complex and private companies could not rely on it with certainty, and so the CA 2006 abolished the prohibition in relation to private companies. The provisions relating to financial assistance (found in ss. 677–683 of the CA 2006) only apply to public companies.

4.1 Financial assistance

Section 677(1) of the CA 2006 provides that, as regards the rules in ss. 677–83, 'financial assistance' means financial assistance given by way of gift, guarantee, security, indemnity, release or waiver, or loan, and any other financial assistance given by a company where the net assets of the company are reduced to a material extent by the giving of the assistance or the company has no assets. This broad definition covers a wide range of financial assistance, including:

- where a company lends money to a person and that person uses that money to buy shares in the company;
- where a company guarantees a loan made by a bank to another person and that person uses that money to buy shares in the company; and
- where a person (*X*) borrows money from a bank and uses it to buy enough shares to control a company. *X* then uses the resources of the company to repay the money loaned by the bank.

When determining whether a company has financial assistance, the court will:

> 'examine the commercial realities of the transaction and decide whether it can properly be described as the giving of financial assistance by the company, bearing in mind that the section is a penal one and should not be strained to cover transactions which are not fairly within it' (*Charterhouse Investment Trust v Tempest Diesels Ltd* [1986] BCLC 1 (Ch) (Hoffmann J)).

4.2 Prohibited financial assistance

The CA 2006 provides that four types of financial assistance are prohibited.

1. Where a person is acquiring, or proposing to acquire, shares in a public company, then that company or a subsidiary of that company is prohibited from giving financial assistance directly or indirectly for the purpose of the acquisition before or at the same time as the acquisition takes place (s. 678(1)).
2. Where a person is acquiring or proposing to acquire shares in a private company, it is not lawful for a public company that is a subsidiary of that company to give financial assistance directly or indirectly for the purpose of the acquisition before or at the same time as the acquisition takes place (s. 679(1)).

3. Where a person has acquired shares in a company and a liability has been incurred (by that person or another) for the purpose of the acquisition, then that company, or a subsidiary of that company, may not give financial assistance directly or indirectly for the purpose of reducing or discharging the liability if, at the time the assistance is given, the company in which the shares were acquired is a public company (s. 678(3)).
4. Where a person has acquired shares in a private company and a liability has been incurred (by that person or another) for the purpose of the acquisition, then a public company that is a subsidiary of that company may not give financial assistance directly or indirectly for the purpose of reducing or discharging the liability (s. 679(3)).

The 'principal purpose' and 'incidental part' exceptions

Each of the above forms of prohibited financial assistance is subject to an exception, namely where:

- the assistance is given in good faith in the interests of the company; and
- the company's principal purpose in giving the assistance is not for the purpose of acquiring the shares, or the giving of assistance is for the purpose of acquiring shares, but only an incidental part of some larger purpose of the company (ss. 678(2) and (4) and 679(2) and (4)).

An example of a 'larger purpose' would be where the financial assistance was part of a scheme designed to restructure a corporate group in order to rescue a company (*Re Uniq plc* [2011] EWHC 749 (Ch)). However, as the following case indicates, the courts have adopted a narrow approach in the application of this exception.

Case law 12.1

***Brady v Brady* [1989] AC 755 (HL)**

Two brothers were the directors and majority shareholders of a group of companies. They had an argument and the companies became deadlocked. It was decided that the business would be divided between the two brothers. This process was complex and involved one company providing another company in the group with financial assistance to acquire its shares. It was argued that this financial assistance was not prohibited because it was part of a larger purpose (the division of the business) and it was incidental to that purpose.

The financial assistance did not fall within the exception and so was prohibited. As regards whether the assistance was given for the purpose of acquiring the shares, Lord Oliver stated that 'it is important to distinguish between a purpose and the reason why a purpose is formed'. The reason for the assistance was to divide the business between the brothers, but the purpose of the assistance was indeed to provide financial assistance to acquire shares.

As regards the assistance being for an incidental purpose, Lord Oliver went on to state that a 'larger' purpose is not the same as a 'more important' purpose. The assistance was 'not a mere incident of the scheme devised to break the deadlock. It was the essence of the scheme itself and the object which the scheme set out to achieve.' The financial assistance was not an incidental part of a larger purpose.

4.3 Exceptions to the general prohibition

Section 681 sets out a number of transactions that will not constitute prohibited financial assistance, including:

- a distribution of a company's assets by way of dividend lawfully made;
- a distribution of a company's assets made in the course of its winding up;
- an allotment of bonus shares;
- a reduction of capital made in accordance with statute;
- a redemption or purchase of shares made in accordance with statute; and
- anything done in pursuance of a court order under a scheme of reconstruction or scheme of arrangement.

Section 682 provides a further list of transactions that will not constitute prohibited financial assistance if the company giving the assistance is a private company, or the company giving the assistance is a public company, and (i) the company has net assets that are not reduced by the giving of the assistance; or (ii) to the extent that the assets are so reduced, the assistance is provided out of distributable profits. The list includes:

- where the lending of money is part of the ordinary business of the company;
- the provision by the company, in good faith and in the interests of the company or its holding company, of financial assistance for the purposes of an employee share scheme; and
- the making of loans to persons (other than directors) employed in good faith by the company with a view to enabling those persons to acquire fully paid shares in the company or its holding company to be held by them by way of beneficial ownership.

4.4 Consequences of providing prohibited financial assistance

The CA 2006 only states one consequence of a company engaging in prohibited financial assistance, namely that the company and every officer in default commits a criminal offence (s. 680(1)). However, a number of civil consequences have been established by the courts.

- An agreement to provide unlawful financial assistance is unenforceable in its entirety (*Heald v O'Connor* [1971] 1 WLR 497 (QB)). However, if the agreement to provide assistance can be severed from the agreement to purchase shares, then the agreement to purchase shares can be enforced (*Carney v Herbert* [1985] AC 301 (PC)).

- A director who is party to a transaction that amounts to prohibited financial assistance may be held in breach of duty (see e.g. *Re In a Flap Envelope Co Ltd* [2003] EWHC 3047 (Ch)), or disqualified (*Re Continental Assurance Co of London plc (No 1)* [1996] BCC 888 (Ch)).
- The court in *Belmont Finance Corp v Williams Furniture Ltd (No 2)* [1980] 1 All ER 393 (CA) held that (i) a recipient of prohibited financial assistance will be liable to account for the sum received if he knew or ought to have known of the impropriety of the transaction; and (ii) a person who knowingly assists the directors to cause the company to provide prohibited financial assistance can be personally liable to the company.

Test yourself 12.3

1. **Why was the prohibition on providing financial assistance introduced?**
2. **What types of company are prohibited from providing financial assistance to acquire their shares?**
3. **What is 'financial assistance'? Provide three examples of such assistance.**
4. **Explain the 'principal purpose' and 'incidental part' exceptions.**
5. **What are the consequences of a company providing prohibited financial assistance?**

5. Distributions

Many persons who purchase shares in a company (especially larger companies) will expect a return on that investment, usually through receiving a share in the company's profits via a dividend payment. However, it should be noted that the members do not have a right to share in the company's profits, unless the company has sufficient profits to distribute and the articles provide that a distribution must be made to the members.

Companies have an implied power to distribute their profits to members (*Burland v Earle* [1902] AC 83 (PC)), but such a power must be closely regulated to ensure that capital is not returned to the members. The relevant rules can now be found in Part 23 of the CA 2006, which also preserves the relevant common law rules (s. 851(1)).

5.1 What is a 'distribution'?

The definition of 'distribution' in the CA 2006 is extremely wide. It means 'every description of distribution of a company's assets to its members, whether in cash or otherwise' (s. 829(1)). It is important that the definition is wide and flexible because companies may try to disguise a contribution to a member in order to avoid the rules relating to distributions, with examples of disguised distributions including:

- selling company property at an undervalue to a person who is a member (*Aveling Barford Ltd v Perion Ltd* (1989) 5 BCC 677 (Ch));
- the company purchasing property at an inflated price from a person who is a member;
- paying excessive director's fees to a director who is also a member (*Re Halt Garage* (1964) Ltd [1982] 3 All ER 1016 (Ch)); and
- paying excessive remuneration to an employee who is also a member.

Disguised distributions may, depending on the facts, be distributions under s. 829. However, s. 829 does provide that the following will not amount to a distribution:

- an issue of shares as fully or partly-paid bonus shares;
- the reduction of share capital (i) by extinguishing or reducing the liability of any of the members on any of the company's shares in respect of capital not paid up; or (ii) by repaying paid-up share capital;
- the redemption or purchase of the company's own shares; and
- a distribution of assets to members of the company on its winding up.

Dividends

The s. 829 definition covers a wide range of distributions, but the most common distribution is a dividend. A dividend is simply a distribution of part or all of the company's profits to its members, with each member usually getting *X* pence for each share they own. The more shares a member holds, the greater the dividend they will receive.

There are two types of dividend payment:

- A final dividend, which is a dividend paid out once the company's final accounts have been prepared (it is paid following the end of the relevant financial year). The articles usually provide that the members 'declare' a final dividend by passing an ordinary resolution.
- An interim dividend, which is a dividend normally paid out before the company's final accounts have been prepared (it is paid during the relevant financial year). A company's articles usually provide that the directors can pay out an interim dividend without obtaining member approval.

The type of company will often determine how dividends are paid. In small private companies, the directors and members are often the same people and so a combination of dividends and remuneration will be used in order to provide the most tax efficient way of distributing the company's profits. In larger public companies, the members will expect profits to be distributed by way of a dividend payment, with larger companies paying a quarterly or half-yearly interim dividend followed by a final dividend.

From a capital maintenance perspective, the key issue is the source of the dividend payment.

5.2 Profits available for distribution

The common law has long held that a company cannot pay a dividend out of capital (*Re Exchange Banking Co, Flitcroft's Case* (1882) 21 ChD 519 (CA)). This rule has been codified by s. 830(1) of the CA 2006, which states that '[a] company may only make a distribution out of profits available for the purpose', which are defined by s. 830(2) as the company's:

> 'accumulated, realised profits, so far as not previously utilised by distribution or capitalisation, less its accumulated, realised losses, so far as not previously written off in a reduction or reorganisation of capital duly made.'

Key to understanding this definition is understanding what are (i) accumulated profits and losses; and (ii) realised profits and losses.

Accumulated profits and losses

The inclusion of the word 'accumulated' means that companies need to take into account previous years' performance when determining whether they have profits available to distribute. A company cannot issue a dividend based on a profit it makes in one year if that profit has not offset any losses sustained in previous years. The following example demonstrates how accumulated profits and losses can affect the amount of profit that is available for distribution.

Case study 12.1

X-Corp Ltd was incorporated in January 2014. The following table sets out its realised profits and losses for a five-year period. During this time, it makes no distributions, but the table shows how much profit X-Corp could have distributed each year.

	2015	2016	2017	2018	2019
Realised profits (RP)	**£10,000**	**£15,000**	**£10,000**	**£5,000**	**£0**
Realised losses (RL)	**£5,000**	**£10,000**	**£5,000**	**£10,000**	**£5,000**
RP – RL	**£5,000**	**£5,000**	**£5,000**	**–£5,000**	**–£5,000**
Profits available for distribution	**£5,000**	**£10,000**	**£15,000**	**£10,000**	**£5,000**

This table shows how the amount that the company has to distribute is affected by the performance in the current year and previous years. If a dividend is paid, then this will also need to be taken into account. The following table gives an example of this.

	2015	2016	2017	2018	2019
Cumulative RP – RL	**£5,000**	**£10,000**	**£15,000**	**£10,000**	**£5,000**
Dividends paid	**£0**	**£5,000**	**£0**	**£5,000**	**£0**
Cumulative dividends	**£0**	**£5,000**	**£5,000**	**£10,000**	**£10,000**
Profits available for distribution	**£5,000**	**£5,000**	**£10,000**	**£0**	**£0**

Realised profits and losses

It used to be the case that a company could make a distribution based on estimated profits. The problem that arose was that, if the actual profit ended up being lower than the estimated profit, then profit made by the company might be less than the distribution made. In such a case, the shortfall would have to come out of capital. To prevent this, the company's distributable profits must be calculated based on realised profits and losses.

The CA 2006 does not define what 'realised' means. Instead, it states realised profits and losses are 'such profits or losses of the company as fall to be treated as realised in accordance with principles generally accepted at the time when the accounts are prepared, with respect to the determination for accounting purposes of realised profits or losses' (s. 853(4)). In other words, the CA 2006 states that realised profits and losses will be determined based on generally accepted accounting practices at the time.

- Paragraph 28 of Financial Reporting Standard 18 provides that profits are realised 'only when realised in the form either of cash or of other assets, the ultimate cash realisation of which can be assessed with reasonable certainty'.
- Realised losses are defined as (i) any amount written off by way of providing for depreciation or diminution in the value of assets; or (ii) any amount retained as reasonably necessary for the purpose of providing for any liability, the nature of which is clearly defined and which is either likely to be incurred, or certain to be incurred but uncertain as to amount or as to the date on which it will arise (CA 2006, s. 841(2); Small Companies and Groups (Accounts and Directors' Report) Regulations 2008, Schedule 7, paras 1, 2 and 6; Large and Medium-Sized Companies and Groups (Accounts and Reports) Regulations 2008, Schedule 9, paras 1, 2 and 8).

More detailed guidance on realised profits and losses is provided by the Institute of Chartered Accountants in England and Wales (ICAEW) and the Institute of Chartered Accountants in Scotland (ICAS) in Technical Release Tech 02/17BL.

Net asset rules

In addition to distributions having to be paid from distributable profits, a public company can only make a distribution if the amount of its net assets is not less than the aggregate of its called-up share capital and undistributable reserves (s. 831(1)).

A company's net assets are defined as 'the aggregate of the company's assets less the aggregate of its liabilities' (s. 831(2)). A company's undistributable reserves are:

- its share premium account;
- its capital redemption reserve;
- the amount by which its accumulated, realised profits (not previously utilised by capitalisation) exceed its accumulated, realised losses (not previously written off in a reduction or reorganisation of capital duly made); and
- any other reserve which the company is forbidden from distributing by any enactment or by its articles (s. 831(4)).

5.3 Reference to relevant accounts

It is important that a company, when determining whether it has distributable profits, does so based on accurate and reliable data. This allows a company to justify the distribution should a query arise. Section 836(1) therefore states that whether a distribution may be made by the company is determined by reference to 'relevant accounts', with such accounts usually being the company's last annual accounts (s. 836(2)) that were circulated to the members in accordance with the CA 2006's requirements (s. 837(1)). These accounts can only be relied on if:

- the accounts were properly prepared in accordance with the CA 2006 (s. 837(2)); and
- the auditor has reported on the accounts, unless the company is exempt from audit and the directors took advantage of this exemption (s. 837(3)).

If these requirements are not met, then the accounts cannot be relied upon and the distribution will be treated as unlawful (s. 836(4)).

5.4 The payment of a dividend

If a company has distributable profits and it is decided that a distribution by dividend will be made, the company must then follow the relevant process for payment of the dividend. On this, the CA 2006 has nothing to say – the process for paying a dividend is a matter for the company's articles, with many companies adopting the following three-stage process (this is also the process found in the model articles).

1. The directors will recommend an amount of distributable profit to be distributed by way of a dividend.
2. In the case of a final dividend, the company will 'declare' that a dividend be paid by the members passing an ordinary resolution. The company

cannot declare a dividend if the directors have not made the above recommendation, and the company cannot declare a dividend that exceeds the amount recommended by the directors (although it can declare a lower amount). As noted, an interim dividend does not usually require member approval and so this stage will not apply.

3. The dividend is paid based on the rights of the members.

There are a number of different ways of paying a dividend, with the standard method being to send each member a dividend warrant. This is essentially a cheque authorising the company's bank to pay the member's bank the dividend amount. However, the articles may provide for another method of payment – the model articles allow members to write to the company requesting their dividend be paid directly into their bank account (model articles for private companies, article 31(1)(a); model articles for public companies, article 72(1)(a)). Companies with a large number of members tend to send their members a dividend mandate form to complete, which instructs the company to pay the dividend into a bank account of the member's choosing.

Dividends must generally be paid in cash (*Wood v Odessa Waterworks Co* (1889) 42 ChD 636 (Ch)) unless the company's articles provide for some other form of payment. The model articles provide that a company may pay all or part of a dividend by transferring non-cash assets of equivalent value to its members (model articles for private companies, article 34(1); model articles for public companies, article 76(1)). This could allow a company to pay a scrip dividend, under which the member can choose whether to receive the dividend in the form of cash or in the form of newly issued, fully paid-up shares.

Stop and think 12.1

From the point of view of the company and its members, what are the advantages of paying out a dividend in shares as opposed to cash? How can a company encourage members to take dividends in the form of shares as opposed to cash?

5.5 Consequences of payment of an unlawful distribution

The payment of an unlawful distribution is not, in itself, a criminal offence. Instead, s. 847 and the common law (the rules of which are preserved by s. 847(3)) provide for a number of civil remedies against (i) members who receive an unlawful distribution; and (ii) directors who recommend or authorise an unlawful distribution. The company's auditor may also face liability if an unlawful distribution was paid out based on audited accounts and the audit was not conducted with reasonable skill and care (*Re Thomas Gerrard & Son Ltd* [1968] Ch 455 (Ch)).

Liability of the directors

The CA 2006 says nothing about the liability faced by a director who authorises an unlawful distribution, but the common law does state that the directors who authorised the payment of an unlawful distribution are liable to repay the amount of the distribution to the company (*Re Exchange Banking Co, Flitcroft's Case* (1882) 21 ChD 519 (CA)).

Case law 12.2

***Bairstow v Queens Moat Houses plc* [2001] EWCA Civ 712**

The company declared a dividend but, due to the accounts being misleading, the dividend paid out was unlawful as the company had no distributable profits. The directors were dismissed and they sued for wrongful dismissal. The company counterclaimed and sought to recover from the directors involved the amount of the unlawful dividend that was paid out.

The directors' claim for wrongful dismissal failed and they were ordered to repay the company over £78.5 million. Robert Walker LJ provided guidance regarding director liability.

- **The directors are liable to repay an unlawful dividend payment irrespective of whether the company is solvent or insolvent.**
- **Where an unlawful dividend is paid based on improperly prepared accounts, then the directors will be liable to repay the full amount of the unlawful dividend. This is the case even if the company could pay out a dividend had the accounts been prepared properly.**
- **Relief under s. 1157 of the CA 2006 (discussed in Chapter 7) would only be granted where the directors had acted honestly and reasonably in paying out the unlawful dividend.**

In *Bairstow*, the company's accounts were improperly prepared and so the directors were liable to repay the whole of the dividend payment. In *Re Marini Ltd* [2003] EWHC 334 (Ch), the court held that where a company has distributed profits based on properly prepared accounts, then the directors will only be liable for the amount that is unlawful (i.e. that amount in excess of the company's distributable profits).

A director that is ordered to repay dividends to the company can seek recovery of that amount from those members who were aware of the illegality. The amount that the director can recover from such a member is limited to the amount that the member received (*Moxham v Grant* [1900] 1 QB 88 (CA)).

Liability of the members

Section 847 applies where a distribution, or part of one, made by a company to its members is unlawful (s. 847(1)). If, at the time of the distribution, a member knows or has reasonable grounds for believing that it was made unlawfully, the member is liable:

- to repay the distribution (or part of it, as the case may be) to the company; or

- in the case of a distribution not made in cash, to repay the company a sum equal to the value of the distribution (or part) at the time (s. 847(2)).

In determining whether a member knew or had reasonable grounds to believe that the distribution was unlawful, Chadwick LJ in *It's a Wrap (UK) Ltd v Gula* [2006] EWCA Civ 544 stated that:

> 'it is enough that the member has the relevant knowledge of facts which, if they exist, lead to the conclusion that the distribution does contravene the statutory provisions; it is not necessary that the member has the relevant knowledge of the legal rules and the consequences of those rules when properly applied to the facts.'

Test yourself 12.4

1. **How does the CA 2006 define a 'distribution'?**
2. **What is a dividend? Explain the differences between a final dividend and an interim dividend.**
3. **A distribution must be paid out of what assets of the company?**
4. **What is the usual three-stage process for paying a final dividend?**
5. **Do dividends have to be paid in cash?**
6. **If an unlawful dividend is paid, to what extent will the company's directors and members be liable?**

Chapter summary

- The principal purpose of the capital maintenance rules is to prevent share capital being returned to the company's members, as this can adversely affect the creditors' interests.
- Any company can reduce its share capital by passing a special resolution followed by court confirmation. A private company can reduce its share capital by passing a special resolution supported by a solvency statement.
- A company is generally prohibited from acquiring its own shares.
- A company can acquire its own shares if (i) those shares are redeemable; or (ii) the company follows the procedure in ss. 690–708 of the CA 2006. Payment must generally come from the company's profits or via a fresh issue of shares.
- A process exists that allows a private company to redeem or purchase its own shares out of capital.
- A public company is generally prohibited from providing financial assistance to others to acquire its shares, but there are exceptions. This prohibition no longer applies to private companies.

- A company may only make a distribution out of profits available for the purpose. The principal type of distribution is a dividend which is a distribution of part or all of the company's profits to its members, with each member usually getting *X* pence for each share they own.
- The usual process for paying a final dividend (as found in the articles) is that (i) the directors will recommend an amount of profit to be distributed by way of dividend; (ii) the company will declare the dividend by passing an ordinary resolution; and (iii) the dividend will be paid to the members based on their rights.
- If an unlawful distribution is made, the directors who authorised the distribution, the members who received the distribution and the auditor who prepared the accounts on which the distribution was based can incur civil liability.

Chapter thirteen
Loan capital

Contents

1. Introduction

This chapter outlines the role, sources of and rules relating to loan capital. For many companies, loan capital can be a very useful source of capital. Having access to loan capital can be vital for several reasons.

- Most companies have very few members and so their share capital may be minimal. Such companies may therefore have to borrow in order to fund the company's start-up costs or expansion plans (although less well-established companies may find it difficult to obtain loan capital).
- For companies that are financially struggling or unable to pay their debts, raising capital through selling shares may be impossible. The only way for a company to try and fend off liquidation and pay off its debts might be to borrow more from others (although creditors may be reluctant to lend to such a company).
- A company that is making a profit may not wish to use that profit to pay off its debts. It may instead wish to use its profits to pay out a dividend or expand its business. The company may therefore borrow to pay off its immediate debts.

A person who borrows money is known as the 'borrower' or 'debtor', whereas the persons lending the money is known as the 'creditor' or 'lender'. In this text, the terms borrower and creditor will be used.

2. Sources of loan capital

If the company does decide to borrow, it then has to determine what form of borrowing to undertake. There are three principal sources of loan capital.

- A term loan involves the borrower borrowing a sum from the creditor, with repayment of this sum plus interest due by a certain date. Repayment can be made at once or via a series of instalments.
- An overdraft involves the borrower withdrawing from its bank account more money than it has deposited in it. An overdraft limit will be agreed upon and the borrower can draw on the overdraft until the limit is reached (if the limit is reached regularly, the borrower and bank can negotiate an increased overdraft limit).
- A debt security (which is principally used by larger companies) is a financial instrument issued by the company which will typically provide that the company will pay the holder of the security a specified sum plus interest on a certain date. Debt securities are similar to shares in that they are issued by the company, they can be transferred and they can be traded on a stock exchange. As a form of security, they are also subject to the statutory rules relating to securities (notably those in the CA 2006, the FSMA 2000 and the FCA Handbook).

2.1 Debentures

In *Levy v Abercorris Slate and Slab Co* (1888) LR 37 ChD 260, Chitty J stated that a debenture refers to 'a document which either creates a debt or acknowledges it'. He went on to correctly note that there is no precise legal definition of a debenture, with the CA 2006 merely stating that the term debenture 'includes debenture stock, bonds and any other securities of the company, whether or not constituting a charge on the company' (s. 738).

Companies can issue corporate bonds or debenture stock, which can then be sold to others in a manner similar to shares. Debenture holders, as holders of debt securities, are creditors of the company. The bonds or stock issued to them are evidence of a loan made to the company. Debenture holders are not, therefore, shareholders, but it is possible for the company to issue convertible debentures that grant the holder the right to convert their debentures into shares.

3. The power to borrow

A company is free to borrow from others subject to two limitations. First, a public company must not exercise any borrowing powers unless it has first been issued with a trading certificate (CA 2006, s. 761(1)). Second, a company's articles can restrict its ability to borrow (for example, by requiring that loans of a certain amount be subject to member approval). Borrowing in breach of such restrictions will not usually invalidate the loan (CA 2006, s. 39).

The ability of other persons (notably directors) to borrow on behalf of the company will depend on the articles and the authority that has been conveyed upon them as agents. The articles typically confer wide managerial powers upon the directors: they will usually have actual authority to enter into loan agreements on behalf of the company and, by implication, to grant security over the company's assets (unless the articles state otherwise). The articles can limit the directors' ability to borrow on behalf of the company but breaching such limitations will not usually invalidate the loan agreement (CA 2006, s. 40).

4. Security

When a creditor lends money to the company, there is no guarantee that the creditor will be repaid. For example, the company might be liquidated with insufficient assets to repay the loan. It is common for creditors to take steps to ensure or to increase the chances of repayment being made. One way to do this is to obtain a right or interest over an asset or the business of the company. For example, the agreement under which the security is created might provide that if the company defaults on the loan, the creditor can appropriate a specified company asset, sell it, and use the proceeds of the sale to repay the loan. Where such a right or interest is obtained, the loan is said to have been 'secured' as the creditor has sought to secure his chances of being repaid. In *Bristol Airport plc v Powdrill* [1990] Ch 744 (CA), Browne-Wilkinson V-C defined 'security' as follows:

> 'Security is created where a person (the creditor) to whom an obligation is owed by another (the debtor) by statute or contract, in addition to the personal promise of the debtor to discharge the obligation, obtains rights exercisable against some property in which the debtor has an interest in order to enforce the discharge of the debtor's obligation to the creditor.'

A creditor who obtains some form of security is known as a 'secured creditor', whereas a creditor who does not obtain security is known as an 'unsecured creditor'. Secured creditors are in a stronger position than unsecured creditors for several reasons:

- if the company breaches the loan agreement, the creditor will have rights over the company's assets that have been secured (for example, selling the asset and recovering the proceeds);
- if the company is liquidated, secured debts are paid ahead of unsecured debts, meaning that secured creditors have a better chance of being repaid; and
- a secured creditor may be able to negotiate other benefits that unsecured creditors do not have (such as the right to consult with the board in certain cases).

4.1 Types of security

If a creditor does decide to secure the loan, the creditor will need to decide what form of security to use. There are two broad categories of security:

- possessory security, under which the creditor will have physical possession of the secured asset and will return this asset once the loan is paid off; and
- non-possessory security, under which the borrower retains possession of the asset and can continue to use it (although the usage may be restricted).

Stop and think 13.1

Depending on the company's circumstances and the nature of the asset to be secured, possessory and non-possessory forms of security each have their own advantages and disadvantages. What are the advantages and disadvantages of each type of security from the point of view of the company and the creditor?

There are two main types of possessory security.

1. A pledge, under which the creditor takes possession of the secured asset and keeps possession of it until the debt is repaid. If the borrower breaches the loan agreement, the creditor usually has an implied right to sell the secured asset.
2. A lien, under which the borrower will deliver the secured asset to the creditor, and the creditor can retain possession of this asset until the loan is repaid. Note that the creditor has no implied power to sell the asset if the borrower defaults – such a power will only arise if provided for in the loan agreement.

There are two main types of non-possessory security.

1. A mortgage under which the creditor obtains title to the secured assets from the borrower. If the borrower defaults, the creditor can possess the secured asset and, if the loan agreement so provides, sell it. If the borrower does not default and pays off the loan, title in the assets will be returned.
2. An equitable charge, under which the creditor has the right to appropriate the charged asset if the borrower defaults on the loan. If the charge so provides, the creditor can then sell the charged asset. Note that, unlike a charge, title in the goods does not pass to the creditor.

The Companies Act 2006 does not really distinguish between mortgages and equitable charges. It simply provides that the word 'charge' includes a mortgage (CA 2006, s. 859A(7)).

Test yourself 13.1

1. **Explain the difference between secured and unsecured borrowing.**
2. **What are the advantages of taking security over a company's assets?**
3. **Explain the differences between, and types of, possessory and non-possessory security.**

5. Charges

The most common form of security taken over a company's assets is a charge. Where a company borrows money, it is common for the company to grant the creditor a charge over an asset or assets (or even over the entire business of the company). The person who granted the charge (the company) is known as the 'chargor'. The person to whom the charge is granted (the creditor) is known as the 'chargee' or 'chargeholder'.

There are two types of charge, namely fixed and floating charges. Both are discussed in more detail below, but Table 13.1 sets out the principal differences between them.

	Fixed charge	Floating charge
Suitable to be taken over which types of assets	A specific, identifiable asset or assets	A class of assets, or the entire undertaking
Chargeholder's ability to deal with the charged asset	The ability of the chargeholder to deal with the charged asset will usually be limited or prohibited	The chargeholder will usually be free to deal with the charged assets, until the charge crystallises
Charged assets availability to the liquidator	No	Yes
Prescribed part must be set aside	No	Yes
Ranking upon liquidation	Effectively ranks ahead of all other debts	Ranks behind debts secured by fixed charge, liquidation expenses and preferential debts
Charge can be set aside by liquidator or administrator	No	Yes

Table 13.1 Fixed and floating charges

A creditor may wish to secure the loans via both types of charge – this is done by obtaining a fixed charge over specific assets, along with a floating charge taken over all the assets and the business itself. This gives the creditor maximum protection in the event of the company defaulting or being wound up.

5.1 Fixed charges

A fixed charge is a charge taken over a specific asset of the company (such as a building or piece of equipment). Depending upon the terms of the charge, it will provide the chargeholder with certain rights and impose upon the chargor certain limits. The exact rights contained within a fixed charge will depend upon its terms, but typically fixed charges will provide the following.

- Should the company default on the loan or if it enters liquidation, then the chargeholder will typically be able to appropriate the charged asset and sell it to recover the money owed. The charge may also empower the chargeholder to appoint a receiver to take possession of the charged asset on its behalf.
- The company will usually be unable to sell or deal with the charged asset, unless it first repays the chargeholder or obtains the chargeholder's consent to sell or deal with the charged assets (*Agnew v Inland Revenue Commissioner* [2001] UKPC 28). The advantage of this is that it ensures that the chargeholder remains in control of the charged assets and that the charged assets are available to the chargeholder if the company defaults or enters liquidation. If the company does sell or deal with the charged asset, the chargeholder can sue for breach of contract. As the charge document prohibits the company from disposing of the charged assets, it is not suitable to take a fixed charge over an asset that the company needs to dispose of or use (e.g. raw materials used in the production of goods).
- The charge instrument usually provides that no subsequent fixed charges can be granted over the charged assets, unless the chargeholder so agrees. If the instrument does not state this and a subsequent fixed charge is granted over the same asset, then they will rank in order of time when they were first created (the first takes priority over the second, and so on). Where a fixed charge and a floating charge are taken over the same assets, then the fixed charge takes priority even if it was created after the floating charge (*Re Castell & Brown Ltd* [1898] 1 Ch 315 (Ch)).

A major advantage of a fixed charge is that assets secured by the fixed charge are not available to the liquidator if the company enters liquidation. This effectively means that debts secured by fixed charge rank ahead of all other debts.

5.2 Floating charges

A fixed charge is inflexible as it prevents the company from dealing with the charged asset. A more flexible form of security was desirable and this led to the creation of the floating charge. In *Agnew v Inland Revenue Commissioner* [2001] UKPC 28, Lord Millett described a floating charge as follows:

> 'The floating charge is capable of affording the creditor, by a single instrument, an effective and comprehensive security upon the entire undertaking of the debtor company and its assets from time to time, while at the same time leaving the company free to deal with its assets and pay its trade creditors in the ordinary course of business without reference to the holder of the charge.'

In *Re Yorkshire Woolcombers Association Ltd* [1903] 2 Ch 284 (CA), Romer LJ identified the three key characteristics of a floating charge:

- the charge is taken over a class of assets present or future (in practice, it is common for a floating charge to be taken over all the assets and business of the company);
- that class of assets is one which, in the ordinary course of the company's business, would be changing from time to time (e.g. stock in trade); and
- until some future step is taken by the chargeholder, the company is free to use the charged assets

In *Agnew v Inland Revenue Commissioner* [2001] UKPC 28, Lord Millett noted that a fixed charge may have the first two characteristics, but it is the third characteristic that really distinguishes a floating charge from a fixed charge. A floating charge is so called because it effectively floats over the charged assets where it remains dormant until the occurrence of some specified event or the chargeholder intervenes. While the charge remains floating, the chargor has considerable flexibility in that it can sell the charged assets or deal with them in the course of its business.

A floating charge can be taken over assets covered by an existing floating charge (*Wheatley v Silkstone and Haigh Moor Coal Co* (1885) 29 ChD 715 (Ch)), subject to some limitations.

- In *Re Benjamin Cope & Sons Ltd* [1914] 1 Ch 800 (Ch), the court stated that a company cannot grant a floating charge over all the same assets as a prior floating charge and have the subsequent floating charge rank ahead of the original charge, unless the terms of the original charge allow this. The court also stated that where a floating charge is taken over all the assets and business of the company, a subsequent floating charge may also be taken over all the company's assets and business, but the prior charge will retain priority.
- A subsequent floating charge can be created over part of the assets subject to a prior floating charge (*Re Automatic Bottle Makers Ltd* [1926] Ch 412 (CA)). It is common for the prior charge to contain a 'negative pledge clause' that provides that the company will not create any subsequent floating charges over the assets of the prior floating charge that will rank in priority to the first floating charge.

Crystallisation

A floating charge 'floats' over the charged assets until some event occurs, at which point it becomes a fixed charge over the charged assets (although it will not rank as a fixed charge for the purposes of liquidation). The process by which a floating charge becomes fixed is known as 'crystallisation'. Upon crystallisation, the chargor will be unable to dispose or deal with the charged assets unless the chargeholder consents (*Evans v Rival Granite Quarries Ltd* [1910] 2 KB 979 (CA)). As Lord Macnaghten stated in *Illingworth v Illingworth* [1904] AC 355 (HL)), a floating charge is 'ambulatory and shifting in its nature, hovering over and so to speak floating with the property which it is intended to affect until some event occurs or some act is done which causes it to settle and fasten on the subject of the charge within its reach and grasp'.

The question is what events will cause a floating charge to crystallise. The charge instrument may specify which events will cause crystallisation. It is common for the instrument to specify that the charge will crystallise if the company defaults on the loan or if the chargeholder gives notice of crystallisation. It is generally implied that crystallisation will occur upon the following events (although the charge instrument can provide that they will not cause the charge to crystallise):

- the company goes into liquidation (*Re Panama New Zealand and Australian Royal Mail Co* (1870) LR 5 Ch App 318 (CA));
- the company's business ceases (*Re Woodroffes (Musical Instruments) Ltd* [1986] Ch 366 (Ch)); or
- a receiver is appointed (*Re Carshalton Park Estate Ltd* [1908] 2 Ch 62 (Ch)).

It used to be the case that crystallisation required the chargeholder to intervene in some way, but this is no longer the case. The instrument can include an 'automatic crystallisation clause' which provides that crystallisation can occur automatically upon some specified event (*Re Brightlife Ltd* [1987] Ch 200 (Ch)).

It appears to be possible to include within a charge a term providing that, if the charge crystallises, it can be 'de-crystallised' by the chargeholder (*Covacich v Riordan* [1994] 2 NZLR 502 (New Zealand High Court)).

Test yourself 13.2

1. **What is a fixed charge and why do they provide such a powerful form of security?**
2. **What are the three key characteristics of a floating charge?**
3. **What does 'crystallisation' mean and when will a floating charge crystallise?**

5.3 Determining the type of charge

It is vital to be able to distinguish between fixed and floating charges for several reasons.

- In the event of a company being liquidated, the liquidator will distribute the company's assets among its creditors in the relevant order, meaning that some creditors may not be paid if there are insufficient assets. However, assets secured by fixed charge are not available to the liquidator, meaning that fixed chargeholders effectively rank ahead of other creditors.
- In the event of a liquidation, a portion of the debt owed to floating chargeholders is set aside to pay off the company's unsecured creditors. This amount is not set aside in relation to a debt owed to a fixed chargeholder.
- Certain floating charges are vulnerable to being set aside by the liquidator, whereas fixed charges cannot be set aside by a liquidator.

In *Agnew v Inland Revenue Commissioner* [2001] UKPC 28, Lord Millett stated that the court should adopt a two-stage approach to determine the type of charge:

> 'At the first stage [the court] must construe the instrument of charge and seek to gather the intentions of the parties from the language they have used. But the object at this stage of the process is not to discover whether the parties intended to create a fixed or a floating charge. It is to ascertain the nature of the rights and obligations which the parties intended to grant each other in respect of the charged assets. Once these have been ascertained, the Court can then embark on the second stage of the process, which is one of categorisation. This is a matter of law. It does not depend on the intention of the parties. If their intention, properly gathered from the language of the instrument, is to grant the company rights in respect of the charged assets which are inconsistent with the nature of a fixed charge, then the charge cannot be a fixed charge however they may have chosen to describe it.'

From this, it follows that the instrument's classification of the charge is relevant, but not conclusive (*Street v Mountford* [1985] AC 809 (HL)). The key factor in determining the type of charge is, based on the charge instrument, what rights and obligations the parties intended to grant each other in respect of the charged assets. The court may conclude that a charge that is described as floating is actually a fixed charge (*Russell Cooke Trust Co Ltd v Elliot* [2007] EWHC 1443 (Ch)) or, as occurred in the following case, a charge described as fixed was a floating charge.

Case law 13.1

***Agnew v Inland Revenue Commissioner* [2001] UKPC 28**

A company had granted its bank security in the form of a fixed and floating charge. The purported fixed charge was taken over the company's book debts (discussed below) and any proceeds that the bank required to be paid into a specified bank account. Any proceeds that the bank had not required to be paid into the account could be collected by the company, and proceeds were subject to the floating charge. The bank never did require that the proceeds be paid into the account, so the company was free to collect these proceeds. In doing so, it took them out of the scope of the fixed charge. The company went into receivership and a dispute arose regarding the status of the purported fixed charge.

Lord Millett stated that the key issue in determining the status of the charge was whether 'the company should be free to deal with the charged assets and withdraw them from the security without the consent of the holder of the charge; or, to put the question another way, whether the charged assets were intended to be under the control of the company or of the charge holder'. The company controlled the charged assets as it was able to collect the proceeds and place them

outside the scope of the fixed charge. This was held to be 'inconsistent with the nature of a fixed charge' and so the purported fixed charge was held to be a floating charge.

Charges over changing assets

A company is restricted in how it uses assets that are subject to a fixed charge. Park J in *Re ASRS Establishment Ltd* [2000] 1 BCLC 727 (Ch) 732 stated that a fixed charge 'does not fit so comfortably in the case of assets which come and go in the normal routine of business operations. It was for assets of that sort that the idea of a floating charge evolved.' However, he went on to say:

> 'a fixed charge confers the best type of security on a creditor. A floating charge is considerably better than no charge at all, but it is not as good as a fixed charge. Any creditor will want to have a fixed charge if it can. There is therefore every incentive for a creditor to whom a debenture is being issued to express it as creating fixed charges rather than floating charges over as many of the debtor's assets as possible. Further, the creditor tends to have the whip hand in this respect. It puts forward the terms of the debenture, and the debtor is likely to accept them... As long as the creditor takes care so to word the debenture that, if it fails to create a fixed charge over an asset of the debtor, it succeeds in creating a floating charge... there is nothing to be lost by stating that a charge is to be a fixed charge.'

A creditor may seek to take a fixed charge over assets that are changing in the course of the company's business, most notably the company's book debts. The Insolvency Service defines book debts as 'sums of money owed to a bankrupt, partnership or company ... usually for goods or service supplied or work carried out'.

Case study 13.1

X-Corp Ltd manufactures electrical components that it sells to the manufacturers of electrical goods. On 1 January, X-Corp sells a batch of components to three customers: (i) TVBuild Ltd (£10,000); (ii) Motherboard plc (£20,000); and (iii) TechCorp Ltd (£15,000). The terms of the sale provide that payment is due within 60 days of the invoice being received by the customer. The sums owed are book debts and are an asset of the company. The following events occur:

- **On 20 January, TVBuild Ltd pays the sum owed. Its book debt is extinguished and the money paid is transferred into X-Corp's bank account.**
- **On 1 February, X-Corp sells a batch of components to BioTech Ltd for £5,000.**
- **A book debt, being an asset of the company, can be sold. On 5 February, X-Corp sells the book debt of Motherboard plc to Y-Corp plc. This book debt is removed from X-Corp's books.**

- **TechCorp Ltd has still not paid the sum owed by 10 March. X-Corp can sue TechCorp to recover the debt owed.**

It can therefore be seen that a company's book debts are constantly fluctuating, as the following table shows

Book debts of X-Corp Ltd		
1 January	**1 February**	**1 March**
◆ TVBuild Ltd (£10,000)	◆ Motherboard plc (£20,000)	◆ TechCorp Ltd (£15,000)
◆ Motherboard plc (£20,000)	◆ TechCorp Ltd (£15,000)	◆ BioTech Ltd (£5,000)
◆ TechCorp Ltd (£15,000)	◆ BioTech Ltd (£5,000)	
Total: £45,000	**Total: £40,000**	**Total: £20,000**

As a company's book debts fluctuate, one might imagine that they would not be a suitable asset over which to take a fixed charge. However, for the reasons noted above by Park J, there have been several cases where creditors have purported to take a fixed charge over a company's book debts. The question is whether this is possible. In the following case, the Supreme Court stated that it was possible, but only if the chargeholder has the requisite control over the charged assets.

Case law 13.2

***Re Spectrum Plus Ltd* [2005] UKHL 41**

A company's bank overdraft was secured by what was expressed to be a specific charge (a fixed charge) over the company's book debts. The charge restricted the company's ability to deal with its book debts and stated that the proceeds of the book debts had to be paid into a specified account that the company held with the bank. As long as the company did not exceed its overdraft limit, it was free to draw from the bank account into which the proceeds of the book debts were paid.

The company was wound up owing the bank a considerable sum. A number of the company's preferential creditors questioned the status of the fixed charge. The bank sought a declaration from the court as to the charge's status.

Lord Scott stated that:

> **'the essential characteristic of a floating charge, the characteristic that distinguishes it from a fixed charge, is that the asset subject to the charge is not finally appropriated as a security for the payment**

> **of the debt until the occurrence of some future event. In the meantime, the chargor is left free to use the charged asset and to remove it from the security.'**

As the company was free to draw from the bank account into which the proceeds of the book debts were paid, it was able to remove such sums from the scope of the fixed charge. The bank did not have sufficient control over the charged assets for the charge to be categorised as fixed, and it was held to be a floating charge.

The House stated that in order to create a fixed charge over a company's book debts, the chargeholder should have sufficient control over the charged assets so that the assets are preserved for the benefit of the chargeholder. Lord Hope stated how this could occur:

- **the charge could prevent the company from dealing with the book debts in any way, so they are preserved for the benefit of the chargeholder's security; or**
- **the charge could prevent all dealings with the book debts other than their collection, and to require the proceeds when collected to be paid (i) to the chargeholder directly; (ii) into an account with the chargeholder bank that the company cannot access; or (iii) into a separate account with a third-party bank which the chargeholder then takes a fixed charge over.**

Stop and think 13.2

Why did the company's preferential creditors question the status of the purported fixed charge? What did they have to gain by the charge being found to be a floating charge?

The conditions required for a fixed charge over book debts to be made are strict. In cases of this type, the courts have usually found the purported fixed charge to be a floating charge.

Test yourself 13.3

1. **Why is it important to be able to distinguish between fixed and floating charges?**
2. **If a charge instrument describes the charge as fixed, does that mean that the charge is a fixed charge?**
3. **What are book debts?**
4. **Can a fixed charge be taken over a company's book debts?**

5.4 Registration of charges

Taking security over the company's property by a creditor can prioritise that creditor's claim over that of other creditors. The creditor will want to know if that asset is already subject to an existing security before lending money to a company and securing the loan over an asset of the company. Prior to reforms introduced in 2013, the law's response was to require companies to keep a register of charges affecting the company's property and to register charges with Companies House. Failure to register a charge was a criminal offence. However, significant dissatisfaction with the system resulted in the system of registration being radically overhauled in April 2013.

The post-2013 system of registration

Under the pre-2013 system of registration, it was not entirely clear what types of charge had to be registered. This is no longer the case as the registration system now applies to all charges (s. 859A(1)), apart from a few specified exceptions (s. 859A(6)) and charges created before the new rules came into effect.

Companies are no longer required to keep a register of charges. They are required to keep a copy of every instrument creating a charge and every instrument effecting any variation or amendment of a charge (s. 859P(1)). These instruments can be inspected by any creditor of the company free of charge, and any other person upon payment of a fee (s. 859Q).

Companies are no longer required to register charges with Companies House, although the company or any person interested in a charge (such as the creditor in whose favour the charge is granted) may register it with Companies House (s. 859A(2)) using Form MR01. In order to register a charge, the following conditions must be complied with:

- The person who wishes to register the charge (usually the creditor in question) must deliver to Companies House a certified copy of the instrument that created the charge along with a statement of particulars (s. 859A(2)) containing the information specified in s. 859D, including:
  - the registered name and number of the company;
  - the date the charge was created and, if applicable, the date of acquisition of the property or undertaking concerned;
  - where the charge is created or evidenced by an instrument, then the information specified in s. 858D(2) must be provided; and
  - where the charge is not created or evidenced by an instrument, then the information specified in s. 858D(3) must be provided.
- The instrument and the statement of particulars must be delivered to Companies House in 'the period allowed for delivery', which is 21 days beginning on the day after the creation of the charge (s. 859A(2) and (4)). If a charge has not been registered within this period then the company, or any person interested in the charge, can apply to the court for an order extending the period allowed for delivery (s. 859F).

If the required documents are delivered to Companies House within the period allowed for delivery, the Registrar must register the charge (s. 859A(2)).

The effects of registration

The registration of a charge has the following effects.

- The information provided will be included in the register of companies (s. 859I(2)), and can be freely accessed online or by visiting Companies House.
- The registrar will provide a certificate of registration to the person who registered the charge (s. 859I(3)). This certificate will provide conclusive evidence that the required documents were delivered within the period allowed for delivery (s. 859I(6)).
- The CA 2006 does not state what notice is provided by registering a charge but the courts have stated that registration provides constructive notice of the charge's existence, but does not provide notice of its terms (*Wilson v Kelland* [1910] 2 Ch 306 (Ch)). It could be argued that, as the charge instrument itself is registered, registration also provides notice of the charge's terms. A definitive ruling is needed.

The effects of non-registration

In practice, most charges will be registered even though there is no requirement to do so placed upon a company or anyone interested in the charge. If a charge is not registered within the period allowed for delivery, then it will be void against a liquidator, administrator or creditor of the company (s. 859H(3)). Note that it is the security, not the debt, that is rendered void. The company will still owe the money to the creditor concerned, but the creditor will lose their secured status. To offset this, if a charge becomes void for non-registration, then the money secured by the charge will become immediately payable (s. 859H(4)).

The rendering of a charge void for non-registration is partial only as s. 859H only renders the charge void if the company is in liquidation or administration (*Smith v Bridgend County Borough Council* [2001] UKHL 58). If the company is still a going concern, then the security will stand and can be enforced (*Re Monolithic Building Company* [1915] 1 Ch 643 (CA).

Test yourself 13.4

1. **Explain how the post-2013 system of registration differs to the pre-2013 system.**
2. **When must a charge be registered in order to be validly registered?**
3. **What are the effects of registering a charge?**
4. **What are the effects of not registering a charge?**

Chapter summary

- The main sources of loan capital are term loans, overdrafts and debt securities.
- A debenture is a document that creates or acknowledges a debt, whether secured or unsecured.
- Companies have a power to borrow, subject to any limitations in statute or the articles. Directors are able to borrow on behalf of the company if they are so authorised.
- Larger creditors will often secure their loans by obtaining a right or interest over an asset of the company. Creditors who do not do this are said to be unsecured.
- Possessory security (a pledge and a lien) occurs where the creditor has physical possession of the secured asset. Non-possessory security (a mortgage and an equitable charge) does not involve the creditor taking possession of the secured asset.
- The most common form of security is the charge, of which there are two types:
  - a fixed charge, which is taken over a specific asset of the company and restricts the company's ability to deal with that asset; and
  - a floating charge, which is usually taken over a class of assets or the entire undertaking and does not restrict the company's ability to use the charged assets until the charge crystallises.
- Certain events will cause a floating charge to crystallise, at which point it becomes a fixed charge. These events include the company's liquidation, its business ceasing, a receiver being appointed or the chargeholder providing notice of crystallisation. The charge instrument may also specify events that will cause the charge to crystallise.
- In *Agnew v Inland Revenue Commissioner*, the court held that a two-stage approach is adopted when the courts determine the status of a charge:
  - the court must construe the instrument of charge and seek to gather the intentions of the parties from the language they have used; and
  - the court will, based on the instrument, determine the type of charge based on the rights and obligations the parties intended to grant each other in respect of the charged assets.
- Assets that are fluctuating (such as book debts and raw materials) are not usually suitable security for a fixed charge. They are better suited to a floating charge.
- The Insolvency Service defines book debts as 'sums of money owed to a bankrupt, partnership or company... usually for goods or service supplied or work carried out'.

- In *Re Spectrum Plus Ltd*, the court stated that is possible to take a fixed charge over book debts, but the chargeholder will need to have sufficient control of the book debts and their proceeds. If this control does not exist, the charge will be a floating charge.
- Companies do not need to keep a register of charges, but they must keep copies of every instrument that creates, varies or amends a charge.
- Companies are not obliged to register charges at Companies House, but Companies House must register charges submitted for registration.
- In order to register a charge, the company or any person interested in the charge (such as the creditor in whose favour the charge has been granted) must submit to Companies House a copy of the charge instrument along with a statement of particulars. In order for registration to be valid, these documents must be submitted within a 21-day period beginning on the day after the charge was created.
- If a charge is not registered within the requisite period, it will be void against a liquidator, administrator or creditor of the company.

Chapter fourteen
Corporate transparency

Contents

1. Introduction

This chapter outlines some of the disclosure obligations placed upon companies, as well as examining the role of the company's auditor. UK company law requires all companies to disclose specified information, with quoted and listed companies being required to disclose much more information than other companies. This disclosure aims to provide several benefits:

- persons considering dealing with the company can do so on an informed basis as a significant amount of information about a company is publicly available;
- disclosure allows shares to be accurately priced, and so enables the markets to operate more efficiently; and
- having access to information on a company's activities allows shareholders to hold the company and its directors to account.

The disclosure obligations placed upon companies are numerous. This chapter focuses on the more significant disclosure obligations, beginning with the requirement to keep specified statutory registers.

2. The statutory registers

Every company is required to keep a series of registers containing specified information. In practice, it is almost always the secretary's role to maintain these registers and ensure the information contained within them is up to date and accurate. The relevant registers (all of which have been discussed elsewhere in the text) include:

- the register of members
- the register of directors
- the register of directors' residential addresses
- the register of secretaries
- the register of interests disclosed
- the register of people with significant control.

These are the registers that must be kept (although, in some cases, specific exceptions apply). There are two other registers that need not be kept, but may be kept if the company so chooses: the register of charges and the register of debentures.

2.1 Election to keep information on the public register

The information contained in the above registers is replicated in the register maintained by Companies House. As the purpose of keeping the various registers is to allow certain persons to inspect them, and as much of the information on the register at Companies House is publicly available (usually online and free of charge), it could be argued that it is rather pointless and burdensome to require companies (especially small companies) to maintain these registers. The Small Business, Enterprise and Employment Act 2015 amended the CA 2006 to allow private companies to make an election as regards each register as follows.

- the company can choose to maintain its own register; or
- the company can choose to keep the relevant information on the register at Companies House, in which case it will not need to maintain the relevant register. It will, however, need to inform Companies House of any changes in the information contained in the relevant register.

3. The annual accounts and reports

The directors of a company must prepare annual accounts and reports for each financial year of the company.

Every company must send a copy of its annual accounts and reports for each financial year to every member, every debenture holder and every person who is entitled to receive notice of general meetings (s. 423(1)). Quoted companies must also publish the annual accounts and reports on their websites (s. 430). The annual accounts and reports must be filed with Companies House (s. 441). Public companies are required to lay their annual accounts and reports before the general meeting (s. 437(1)), which usually involves tabling a resolution at the AGM under which the company will 'receive the reports and accounts'.

3.1 Annual accounts

As companies are required to publish annual accounts, every company is required to keep adequate accounting records (CA 2006, s. 386(1)). These records must include sufficient detail:

- to show and explain the company's transactions;
- to disclose with reasonable accuracy the financial position of the company at any time; and
- to enable the directors to ensure that any prepared accounts comply with the CA 2006 and, where applicable, Article 4 of the International Accounting Standards Regulation (s. 386(2)).

A company's annual accounts will cover its finances over its financial year. The following example explains the default rules for determining what period is covered by a company's financial year. It should be noted that companies can change the period covered by their financial year (s. 392).

Case study 14.1

X-Corp Ltd is incorporated on 1 January 2019. To work out its financial year, we first need to know X-Corp's 'accounting reference date'. This is usually the last day of the month on which the anniversary of its incorporation falls (s. 391(4)). Accordingly, X-Corp's accounting reference date is 31 January of each year. Next, we need to work out when X-Corp's 'accounting reference period' is:

- **A company's first accounting reference period begins on the date of its incorporation and ends on the company's 'accounting reference date' (s. 391(5)). X-Corp's first accounting reference period begins on 1 January 2019 and ends on 31 January 2020.**
- **X-Corp's subsequent accounting reference periods begin the day after the company's accounting reference date and last for 12 months (s. 391(6)). Accordingly, subsequent accounting reference periods will run from 1 February to 31 January.**

X-Corp's first financial year begins on the day of its first accounting reference period and ends with the last day of that period, or some other date not more than seven days before or after that period as the directors may determine (s. 390(2)). X-Corp's first financial year will run from 1 January 2019 to 31 January 2020 (or up to seven days later). Subsequent financial years begin on the day following the end of the previous financial year, and end on the last day of its next accounting reference period, or some other date not more than seven days before or after that period as the directors may determine (s. 390(3)), namely from 1 February to 31 January (or up to seven days later).

A company's annual accounts consist of (i) any individual accounts prepared by the company for that year; and (ii) any group accounts prepared by the company for that year (s. 471(1)).

Individual company accounts
The directors of a company (except a dormant subsidiary) are under a duty to prepare accounts for that company for each of its financial years. These accounts are known as the company's 'individual accounts' (ss. 394 and 394A). Section 396 provides that the individual accounts must state:

- the part of the United Kingdom in which the company is registered;
- the company's registered number;
- whether the company is a public or a private company and whether it is limited by shares or by guarantee;
- the address of the company's registered office;
- where appropriate, the fact that the company is being wound-up;
- a balance sheet as of the last day of the financial year, which must give a true and fair view of the state of affairs of the company as at the end of the financial year; and
- a profit and loss account that provides a fair and true view of the profit or loss of the company for the financial year.

Several pieces of subordinate legislation provide that certain companies need not provide all the information specified in s. 396. For example, small companies may prepare abridged accounts instead of full accounts if all the members so consent (Small Companies and Groups (Accounts and Directors' Report) Regulations 2008, Schedule 1, para 1A).

Group accounts
A parent company (except one that is small, s. 399(2A)) must also prepare group accounts for each financial year (s. 399(2)). The information contained in the group accounts is largely the same as that found in the individual accounts, except that the group accounts need to cover the accounts of the parent and all of its subsidiaries (ss. 404 and 405(1)). Some subsidiaries can be excluded, such as where the inclusion of a subsidiary is not material for giving a true and fair view (s. 405(2)).

3.2 Annual reports

A company must prepare annual reports for each year. What constitutes a company's annual reports will depend on whether the company is quoted or unquoted, and whether it is small or not. Section 471(2) and (3) provides that a company's annual reports consist of:

- the strategic report (small companies excluded);
- the directors' report;
- the auditor's report (small companies excluded); and
- the directors' remuneration report (quoted companies only).

As regards the strategic report, the directors' report, the remuneration report and (if it has one) a separate corporate governance statement, a director of a company will be liable to compensate the company for any loss it has suffered as a result of (i) any untrue or misleading statement; or (ii) the omission from a report of anything required to be in it (CA 2006, s. 463(1) and (2)). However, a director will only be liable if:

- they knew the statement to be untrue or misleading or were reckless as to whether it was untrue or misleading, or:
- they knew the omission to be dishonest concealment of a material fact (s. 463(3)).

Annual reports have evolved in recent years. Historically, annual reports primarily contained financial information, but, in recent years, the passing of several EU directives has resulted in a shift towards the inclusion of much more non-financial information (this is known as 'narrative reporting'). This can be seen most notably in the strategic report.

Strategic report

Section 414A(1) provides that the directors of a company must prepare a strategic report for each financial year of the company. Small companies are not subject to this requirement and need not prepare a strategic report (s. 414A(2)). Section 414C(1) provides that the purpose of the strategic report is to 'inform members of the company and help them assess how the directors have performed their duty under section 172 (duty to promote the success of the company)'. The strategic report must contain a 'section 172(1) statement' which describes how the directors have had regard to the matters set out in s. 172(1)(a)–(f) when performing their duty under s. 172 (s. 414CZA(1)). A company that qualifies as medium-sized need not include a section 172(1) statement in its strategic report (s. 414CZA(2)).

The strategic report must include:

- a fair review of the company's business, which provides a balanced and comprehensive analysis of the development and performance of the company's business during the financial year, and the position of the company's business at the end of that year (s. 414C(2)(a) and (3)); and
- a description of the principal risks and uncertainties facing the company (s. 414C(2)(b)).

If the company is quoted, it must also provide the following additional information:

- details of the main trends and factors likely to affect the future development, performance and position of the company's business (s. 414C(7)(a));
- information about environmental matters, the company's employees and social, community and human rights issues (s. 414C(&)(b));
- a description of a company's strategy and business model (s. 414C(8)(a)–(b)); and

- a breakdown showing at the end of each financial year the number of persons of each sex who were directors, senior managers and employees of the company (s. 414C(8)(c)).

Traded companies must include a 'non-financial information statement' (s. 414CA(1)). Other companies can include this statement if they so wish (s. 414CA(10)). Section 414CB states that this statement contains information regarding:

- environmental matters (including the impact of the company's business on the environment);
- the company's employees;
- social matters;
- respect for human rights; and
- anti-corruption and anti-bribery matters.

Directors' report

The directors of a company (except a company that qualifies as a micro-entity (s. 415(1A)) must prepare a directors' report for each financial year (s. 415(1)) that includes the following information:

- the names of the persons who were, at any time during the financial year, directors of the company (s. 416(1)(a));
- the amount that the directors recommend should be paid by way of dividend (s. 416(3)); and
- a statement providing that (i) so far as each director is aware, there is no relevant audit information of which the company's auditor is unaware; and (ii) each director has taken all the steps that they ought to have taken as a director to make themselves aware of any relevant audit information and to establish that the company's auditor is aware of that information (s. 418(2)).

Schedule 7 of the Large and Medium-Sized Companies and Groups (Accounts and Reports) Regulations 2008 provides that large and medium-sized companies must also include further information, including:

- details of political donations exceeding £2,000 made by the company;
- particulars of important events affecting the company, and an indication of likely future developments in the company's business;
- details regarding the company's acquisition of its own shares;
- a description of the company's policy regarding the employment of disabled persons;
- details of action taken by the company in relation to employee consultation and involvement;
- a statement summarising how the directors have had regard to the need to foster the company's business relationships with suppliers, customers and others; and

- if the company is quoted, it must also provide details concerning the company's greenhouse gas emissions, notably the quantity in tonnes of such emissions.

Certain companies must also provide corporate governance-related information in the directors' report. A company that has more than 2,000 employees, or a turnover of more than £200 million and a balance sheet total of more than £2 billion, must include in its directors' report a 'statement of corporate governance arrangements' which states:

- which corporate governance code, if any, the company applied in that financial year;
- how the company applied the code;
- if the company departed from the code, its reasons for doing so; and
- if the company did not apply a corporate governance code for the financial year, the reasons for that decision and an explanation of what corporate governance arrangements were applied for that year.

A company whose shares are traded on a regulated market must provide a 'corporate governance statement' as part of its directors' report, although it can provide this statement as a separate report if it so wishes (DTR 7.2.1R and 7.2.9R). It must provide specified information, including:

- the corporate governance code to which the company is subject or which the company has voluntarily decided to apply (DTR 7.2.2R);
- if the company has departed from the stated corporate governance code, it must explain which parts it has departed from and the reasons for doing so (DTR 7.2.3(1)R);
- a description of the main feature of the company's internal control and risk management systems (DTR 7.2.5R and 7.2.10R); and
- a description of the composition and operation of the company's administrative, management and supervisory bodies and their committees (DTR 7.2.7R), and a description of the diversity policy that applies to these bodies and how that policy is implemented (DTR 7.2.8A).

Companies that are required to provide a corporate governance statement do not need to provide a statement of corporate governance arrangements. Companies with a premium listing must also provide additional information regarding the UK Corporate Governance Code, namely:

- how the company has applied the Principles of the Code (LR 9.8.6(5)R); and
- a statement as to whether the company has complied with all the relevant Provisions of the Code, or a statement identifying which Provisions were not complied with, the period within which they were not complied with and the reasons for non-compliance (Listing Rules, LR 9.8.6(6)R).

Auditor's report

If the company has appointed an auditor to audit its statutory accounts, then the auditor will produce an auditor's report. The role and powers of the auditor are discussed later in this chapter: this section will focus on the auditor's report. The auditor's report must include the information specified in ss. 495–498 of the CA 2006:

- the name of the company whose accounts are being audited;
- a description of the annual accounts that are the subject of the audit and the period covered by those accounts;
- a description of the financial reporting framework that was used to prepare the accounts;
- a clear statement as to whether, in the auditor's opinion, the annual accounts:
  - give a fair and true view of the company's finances;
  - have been prepared in accordance with the relevant financial reporting framework; and
  - have been prepared in accordance with the requirements of the CA 2006;
- a statement on any material uncertainty relating to events or conditions that may cast significant doubt upon the company's ability to continue to adopt the going concern basis of accounting;
- a statement setting out whether, in the auditor's opinion, the information given in the strategic report and the directors' report is consistent with the accounts, and whether those reports are prepared in accordance with applicable legal requirements;
- a statement setting out whether the auditor has found any material misstatements in the strategic report and the directors' report;
- if applicable, a statement setting out whether the directors' remuneration report and corporate governance statement comply with the CA 2006 and the DTRs respectively;
- if applicable, a statement whether the corporate governance statement complies with the relevant rules of the DTRs, and whether the statement contains any material misstatements; and
- a statement setting out whether adequate accounting records have been kept by the company, and whether those records are in agreement with the individual accounts.

Directors' remuneration report

The directors of a quoted company must prepare a directors' remuneration report for each financial year (CA 2006, s. 420(1)). Schedule 8 of the Large and Medium-Sized Companies and Groups (Accounts and Reports) Regulations 2008 provides that the information that must be provided in the report includes the following:

- a single total figure of remuneration for each director;
- details of each director's pension entitlements;
- details of payments to past directors, including loss of office payments;
- details of directors' shareholdings and share interests;
- a performance graph and table providing details of company performance over the last five years;
- the percentage change in remuneration of the CEO;
- a statement on how the company intends to implement the previous year's remuneration policy; and
- details of the directors' remuneration policy of the company.

Concerns regarding the levels of directors' pay in quoted companies led to calls to give the company's shareholders a greater 'say on pay', which has resulted in the shareholders having the right to vote on pay issues as follows.

- At least every three years, a quoted company must table an ordinary resolution at the accounts meeting (usually the AGM) to decide whether to approve the remuneration policy section of the remuneration report (s. 439A(1)). This vote is binding. If the policy section is rejected by the shareholders, the company must continue to follow its existing policy until such time as a new policy does obtain shareholder approval. A quoted company cannot make a remuneration payment to a director unless it is consistent with the approved remuneration policy of the company, or has been approved by a resolution of the members (s. 226B(1)). Any payment made without such approval or authorisation will have no effect (s. 226E(1)).
- Every year, a quoted company must table a resolution at the accounts meeting (usually the AGM) to approve the remuneration report (except the section on remuneration policy, which is subject to the binding vote above) (s. 439(1)). Unlike the s. 439A vote, this vote is advisory and so does not bind the company (s. 439(5)).

Stop and think 14.1

Do you think the introduction of the binding vote in s. 439A will affect the excessive levels of director pay amongst larger companies? Do you think that the issue of directors' pay should be left for the shareholders to determine, or should Parliament intervene further (for example, by imposing a pay cap upon directors)?

Test yourself 14.1

1. **What constitutes a company's annual accounts and reports?**
2. **Explain the difference between individual accounts and group accounts.**
3. **What is 'narrative reporting'?**
4. **Are all companies required to prepare a strategic report and a directors' remuneration report?**

4. The auditor

A company's annual accounts will be relied upon by a range of persons who are contemplating transacting with the company (e.g. persons thinking of buying shares or creditors who may loan money to the company). Such persons may wish to look at the company's annual accounts before making a decision. Knowing that the accounts may influence such decisions, the directors of a company may be tempted to falsify the accounts or present information in such a way as to indicate the company is more profitable than it really is. To prevent this, the CA 2006 generally requires that a company's annual accounts are subject to verification from an independent third party, namely an auditor.

Before looking at the rules relating to auditors, it is important to distinguish between the different types of audit. The legally mandated auditing of the company's accounts is known as a 'statutory audit' and the auditor performing this audit is known as the 'statutory auditor'. Larger companies will also undertake an 'internal audit', which is essentially an audit of the company's processes and systems that aims to determine how effectively the company manages risk, whether the company's internal control systems are operating well, and whether the company is complying with the relevant laws and best practice recommendations. This section focuses on the statutory audit.

4.1 Appointment

An auditor must be appointed for each financial year of the company, unless the directors reasonably resolve otherwise on the grounds that audited accounts are unlikely to be required (CA 2006, ss. 485(1) and 489(1)). In other words, a company must appoint an auditor unless it does not need to have its accounts audited. Section 475(1) provides that a company's annual accounts must be audited, unless:

- the company is a small company (s. 477);
- the company is a subsidiary and meets the conditions set out in s. 479A(2);
- the company is dormant (s. 480); or
- it is a non-profit-making company that is subject to a public sector audit (s. 482).

Eligibility requirements and prohibitions

Before appointing an auditor, the company must make sure that they are eligible to act as auditor. A person who is not so eligible cannot act as a company's statutory auditor (s. 1213(1)) and will commit a criminal offence (s. 1213(3)). Section 1212(1) of the CA 2006 provides that a person is eligible to act as auditor if they satisfy the following two conditions:

1. the proposed auditor is a member of a recognised supervisory body such as the ICAEW or the Association of Chartered Certified Accountants (ACCA); and
2. the proposed auditor is eligible for appointment under the rules of its supervisory body.

Section 1214 requires that an auditor be independent. Certain persons are prohibited from acting as a company's auditor, including:

(a) an officer or employee of the company or associated undertaking (an 'associated undertaking' is (i) a parent or subsidiary of the company; or (ii) a subsidiary of a parent of the company); or

(b) a partner or employee of a person within (a), or a partnership to which a person within (a) is a partner.

(c) If, at any time during their term of office, an auditor becomes prohibited from acting as auditor due to lack of independence, then they must resign immediately and provide notice to the company that they have resigned due to lack of independence (s. 1215(1)). A failure to do so is a criminal offence (s. 1215(2)).

In addition to the above statutory rules, relevant regulatory and professional bodies have also created their own rules regarding auditor independence. The FRC's Ethical Standard (2016) establishes detailed rules aimed at ensuring auditor independence. This Ethical Standard, which reflects the provisions found in the EU Audit Directive and Regulation, strongly influences other professional standards. For example, the ICAEW has its own Code of Ethics, s. 290 of which requires ICAEW members to comply with the FRC's Ethical Standard.

Appointing an auditor of a private company

The directors can appoint the auditor in a private company's first financial year, providing that the appointment is made within the 'period for appointing auditors'. This is the 28-day period after the end of the time allowed for sending out copies of the company's annual accounts and reports for the previous financial year or, if earlier, the day on which copies of the annual accounts and reports were actually sent out (s. 485(2) and (3)).

In subsequent years, the auditor is appointed by passing an ordinary resolution before the end of the period for appointing auditors (s. 485(4)). If no appointment has been made by the end of this period, then s. 487(2) provides that the auditor in office will be deemed to be reappointed unless:

- they were appointed by the directors;
- the company's articles require reappointment by resolution;

- the deemed reappointment is prevented because members representing at least 5% of the company's voting rights notify the company that they do not want the auditor to be reappointed (s. 488);
- the members have resolved that the auditor should not be reappointed;
- the directors have resolved that no auditor should be appointed for the financial year in question; or
- the company is a public interest entity and the auditor's appointment breaches the maximum engagement period.

Appointing an auditor of a public company

In its first financial year, the directors of a public company appoint the auditor providing that the appointment is made before the first accounts meeting (s. 489(3)).

In subsequent years, the auditor is appointed by passing an ordinary resolution (s. 489(4)) before the end of the accounts meeting at which the company's annual accounts and reports for the previous financial year have been laid (s. 489(2)). There is no automatic reappointment process set out in the CA 2006.

In larger public companies, the process for appointing auditors will be led by an audit committee, with Provision 25 of the UK Corporate Governance Code stating that one of the main roles of this committee is 'making recommendations to the board, in relation to the appointment, reappointment and removal of the external auditor, and approving the remuneration and terms of engagement of the external auditor'.

Remuneration

An auditor will require remuneration for the work undertaken. Remuneration will be fixed by those who appointed the auditor (s. 492(1)–(3)). In larger companies, the issue of auditor remuneration has been a concern for two reasons. First, an auditor's independence may be compromised where the auditor is overly reliant on the fee income that a particular audit generates. Accordingly, Article 4(3) of the EU Audit Regulation provides that where, in each of the previous three consecutive years, the total fees that an auditor received from a public interest entity exceeded 15% of the auditor's total fee income, then the auditor must disclose this to the audit committee who will discuss whether this constitutes a threat to the auditor's independence and what safeguards should be applied. Where the fees continue to exceed 15%, the audit committee shall decide whether the statutory auditor may continue to carry on the statutory audit for an additional period, which shall not exceed two years.

Second, a company's statutory auditor may also provide the company with other services (such as tax advice, management consultancy services). An auditor will likely be keen to continue providing such 'non-audit services' and this desire may affect the auditor's independence when conducting the statutory audit (especially if the value of the non-audit services exceeds those of the audit). Article 5 of the EU Audit Regulation aims to combat this in two ways:

- the auditor of a public interest entity will be prohibited from providing certain non-audit services (including specified tax and legal services); and
- the fees received by the auditor for providing non-audit services cannot exceed 70% of the value of the audit fee.

Provision 25 of the UK Corporate Governance Code provides that the audit committee should develop and implement a policy on the engagement of the external auditor to provide non-audit services. Aspects of audit engagement the policy may tackle include:

- ensuring there is prior approval of non-audit services;
- considering the impact this may have on independence;
- taking into account the relevant regulations and ethical guidance; and
- reporting to the board on any improvement or action required.

4.2 Duties and rights

The principal duty placed upon an auditor is set out in s. 498 of the CA 2006. Section 498(1) states that a company's auditor, in preparing the auditor's report, must carry out such investigations as will enable them to form an opinion as to:

- whether adequate accounting records have been kept by the company and returns adequate for their audit have been received from branches not visited by the auditor;
- whether the company's individual accounts are in agreement with the accounting records and returns; and
- in the case of a quoted company, whether the auditable part of the company's directors' remuneration report is in agreement with the accounting records and returns.

To enable the auditor to undertake these investigations, the CA 2006 grants the auditor significant powers including:

- a right of access, at all times, to the company's books, accounts and vouchers (s. 499(1)(a)); and
- the right to require specified persons (such as officers and employees) to provide such information and explanations as the auditor thinks necessary for the performance of their duties (s. 499(1)(b) and (2)).

The auditor must state in the auditor's report if they are of the opinion that:

- adequate accounting records have not been kept;
- the company's individual accounts are not in agreement with the accounting records and returns; or
- the directors' remuneration report is not in agreement with the accounting records or returns (s. 498(2)).

4.3 Auditor liability

An auditor can face contractual, tortious and criminal liability. In terms of civil liability, an auditor owes a duty to the company in contract (*Berg Sons & Co Ltd v Adams* [1992] BCC 6661 (QB)) and tort (*Henderson v Merrett Syndicates Ltd (No 1)* [1995] 2 AC 145 (HL)). In *Re Kingston Cotton Mill Co (No 2)* [1896] 2 Ch 279 (CA), Lopes LJ stated that:

> 'It is the duty of an auditor to bring to bear on the work he has to perform that skill, care, and caution which a reasonably competent, careful, and cautious auditor would use. What is reasonable skill, care, and caution must depend on the particular circumstances of each case. An auditor is not bound to be a detective, or, as was said, to approach his work with suspicion or with a foregone conclusion that there is something wrong. He is a watchdog, but not a bloodhound. He is justified in believing tried servants of the company in whom confidence is placed by the company. He is entitled to assume that they are honest, and to rely upon their representations, provided he takes reasonable care. If there is anything calculated to excite suspicion he should probe it to the bottom; but in the absence of anything of that kind he is only bound to be reasonably cautious and careful.'

Although this is correct as a basic statement of the auditor's duty, the section regarding the auditor being able to believe the servants of the company is no longer accepted and the auditor must perform its duties 'with an inquiring mind – not suspicious of dishonesty, I agree – but suspecting that someone may have made a mistake somewhere and that a check must be made to ensure that there has been none' (*Fomento (Sterling Area) Ltd v Selsdon Fountain Pen Co Ltd* [1958] 1 WLR 45 (HL) (Lord Denning)).

An auditor might try to avoid civil liability by placing an exclusion or limitation clause in the audit contract. An auditor's ability to do this is extremely limited. Section 532 provides that a provision in the contract will be void if it:

- exempts an auditor from any liability that would attach to them in connection with any negligence, default, breach of duty or breach of trust occurring in the course of auditing a company's accounts; or
- by which a company provides an indemnity for an auditor against any liability attaching to them in connection with any negligence, default, breach of duty or breach of trust occurring in the course of auditing a company's accounts.

This is subject to two exceptions.

1. A company can indemnify an auditor against any liability incurred by them in defending proceedings (civil or criminal) in which the auditor is acquitted or judgment given in its favour, or, in connection with an application under s. 1157 in which relief is granted to them (s. 533).
2. Auditors can limit their liability by entering into a liability limitation agreement with the company, which is 'an agreement that purports to limit the amount of a liability owed to a company by its auditor in respect

of any negligence, default, breach of duty or breach of trust, occurring in the course of the audit of accounts, of which the auditor may be guilty in relation to the company' (s. 534(1)). Such an agreement will only be effective if it complies with a range of requirements set out in ss. 534–538.

Contractual liability

Where a contract exists between the company and the auditor (which will almost always be the case), then the company may sue the auditor if they breach a term of that contract. If the auditor does not perform their duties with reasonable skill and care, then the company can also sue for breach of the implied duty placed upon an auditor to act with reasonable skill and care (Supply of Goods and Services Act 1982, s. 13).

Tortious liability

A company can sue an auditor in tort if the auditor makes a statement they know to be false or, as is more usually the case, the auditor provides a negligent audit. One issue that has generated a notable amount of case law is whether third parties who have suffered loss due to a negligent audit can sue the auditor. The following example sets out why a third party may wish to sue an auditor.

Case study 14.2

X-Corp plc's accounts state that the company has made a profit of £1 million, and the auditor's report states that this is a true and fair view of the company's financial position. Relying on the auditor's verification, Ellen purchases 500 shares in X-Corp. It transpires that the annual accounts were incorrect. X-Corp made no profit and is close to insolvency. The auditor, in failing to discover this, has acted negligently. As a result, Ellen's shares are worthless and she wishes to sue the auditor.

Given the range of persons who may read and rely on the company's accounts, and the fear of imposing indeterminate liability on an auditor, the courts have always imposed strict limitations on a third party's ability to sue an auditor. Originally, the tort of negligence only covered negligent acts, and not negligent statements, but in the case of *Hedley Byrne & Co Ltd v Heller & Partners Ltd* [1964] AC 465 (HL), the courts recognised that a negligent statement could result in liability to a third party. The issue is when will an auditor be liable to a third party, with the following leading case providing the answer.

Case law 14.1

***Caparo Industries plc v Dickman* [1990] 2 AC 605 (HL)**

Caparo Industries plc was considering making a takeover bid of Fidelty plc. It examined Fidelity's accounts which showed that the company was running at a profit. Relying on this, Caparo purchased enough shares

in Fidelity to take it over. Caparo then discovered that the accounts were inaccurate and Fidelity was actually running at a loss. Caparo sued Fidelity's auditor.

The key issue was whether Fidelity's auditor owed Caparo a duty of care, and if there was a sufficiently proximate relationship between Fidelity and the auditor (this is often referred to as a 'special relationship'). Lord Oliver stated that such a relationship would typically arise where:

> **'(1) the advice is required for a purpose, whether particularly specified or generally described, which is made known, either actually or inferentially, to the adviser at the time when the advice is given; (2) the adviser knows, either actually or inferentially, that his advice will be communicated to the advisee, either specifically or as a member of an ascertainable class, in order that it should be used by the advisee for that purpose; (3) it is known either actually or inferentially, that the advice so communicated is likely to be acted upon by the advisee for that purpose without independent inquiry, and (4) it is so acted upon by the advisee to his detriment.'**

Applying this, the House held that Fidelity's auditor did not owe a duty to Caparo because the purpose of an audit is not to help potential investors make investment decisions. If a potential investor is to impose liability on the auditor, a special relationship will need to be established, and Caparo had not done that.

The result of *Caparo* (and subsequent cases) is that an auditor will not usually owe a duty to the company's members or other third parties. Such persons will need to show the existence of a special relationship, although subsequent cases have reframed this as the need to show that the auditor assumed a responsibility to the third party in question. This could occur, for example, where a third party specifically asks an auditor to value a company's shares and the auditor knows that the information he provides will be used by the third party when deciding whether to buy the shares or not (*Morgan Crucible Co plc v Hill Samuel & Co Ltd* [1991] Ch 295 (CA)).

Criminal liability

There are two principal offences that relate to an auditor's conduct. The first is found in s. 507 of the CA 2006, which applies:

- where the auditor knowingly or recklessly causes an auditor's report to include any matter that is misleading, false or deceptive in a material particular; or
- where the auditor knowingly or recklessly causes an auditor's report to omit certain specified statements.

The second offence is found in s. 17 of the Theft Act 1968. It applies where a person dishonestly, with a view to gain for themselves or another or with intent to cause loss to another:

- destroys, defaces, conceals or falsifies any account or any record or document made or required for any accounting purpose; or
- in furnishing information for any purpose, produces or makes use of any account, or any such record or document as aforesaid, which to his knowledge is or may be misleading, false or deceptive in a material particular.

4.4 Vacation of office

An auditor can vacate office by resigning, by being removed, by being replaced, or by retiring by rotation.

Resignation
An auditor of a company may resign by sending a notice to that effect to the company (s. 516(1)). The auditor's term of office will end on the date when the company receives the notice or on such later date as may be specified in the notice (s. 516(3)). The notice of resignation will not be effective unless it is accompanied by a statement setting out the auditor's reasons for resigning (s. 519(2)). Such a statement will not be required if:

- the auditor of a private company is ceasing to hold office at the end of the period for appointing auditors, or the auditor of a public company is ceasing to hold office at the end of an accounts meeting (s. 519(2A)); or
- the auditor's reasons for ceasing to hold office are all exempt reasons (as set out in s. 519A(3)) or there are no matters connected with the auditor ceasing to hold office that they consider need to be brought to the attention of the members or creditors of the company (s. 519(2B)).

Removal
An auditor may be removed from office at any time by the members of the company (s. 510(1)). This power is exercisable by passing an ordinary resolution at a meeting – the written resolution cannot be used – and special notice of the resolution must be provided (ss. 510(2) and 511(1)). The auditor must provide a s. 519 statement (discussed above), unless either of the two noted exceptions apply.

Removal of an auditor will not deprive that auditor of any compensation or damages payable as a result of their removal (s. 510(3)).

Replacement
There are two ways in which a company can replace its auditor.

- Where the term of office of the auditor of a private company expires, and the company decides not to reappoint it, then a replacement auditor can be appointed by the company passing a written resolution (s. 514(1)).
- An auditor can be replaced by passing a resolution at a general meeting (s. 515(1) and (1A)). Special notice of the resolution is required, unless the auditor resigned or was removed.

Rotation

Auditor rotation refers to a system under which a company has to change its auditor after a certain period. The rationale behind requiring companies to periodically change their auditors was set out in the Preamble to the 2014 EU Audit Regulation, which states:

> '[i]n order to address the familiarity threat and therefore reinforce the independence of statutory auditors and audit firms, it is important to establish a maximum duration of the audit engagement of a statutory auditor or an audit firm in a particular audited entity.'

Prior to the EU Audit Regulation and its implementation, the UK did not have a system of mandatory auditor rotation, but instead provided that:

- the Auditing Practices Board's Ethical Standard 3 provided that listed companies had to change their audit partner every seven years; and
- FTSE 350 companies are required to put their audit out to tender at least every ten years (Statutory Audit Services for Large Companies Market Investigation (Mandatory Use of Competitive Tender Processes and Audit Committee Responsibilities) Order 2014, para 4(a)).

Both rules are still in effect but have, to a degree, been overtaken by the mandatory rotation rules introduced by the EU Audit Regulation and implemented by amendments to the CA 2006. The rules relating to mandatory auditor rotation apply only to public interest entities (PIEs). For our purposes, this refers to a company whose transferable securities are admitted to trading on a regulated market within an EU Member State (CA 2006, s. 494A). The rules as implemented under the CA 2006 are as follows.

- An auditor of a PIE has a 'maximum engagement period' of ten years (s. 494ZA(1)). In order words, an auditor can audit a company's accounts for ten years, and then the company must replace that auditor. However, this period can be extended to twenty years if the audit is subject to a qualifying selection procedure (essentially a public tender) after at least ten years (s. 494ZA(1)).
- The FRC can extend the maximum engagement period by up to two years if it believes that exceptional circumstances exist (s. 494ZA(2) and (3)).
- If an auditor reaches the maximum engagement period and is replaced, then the PIE cannot appoint that auditor for a period of four years beginning on the date after the maximum engagement period ended (ss. 485C and 489C).

Test yourself 14.2

1. **Explain the difference between a statutory audit and an internal audit.**
2. **Do all companies need to appoint an auditor?**

3. **Which types of person may not be appointed as a company's auditor?**
4. **Does an auditor owe a duty of care to third parties (for example, members of a company)?**
5. **What are the four ways by which an auditor can vacate office?**

5. Periodic financial reporting

Companies whose securities are traded on a regulated market must periodically report on their financial affairs. Disclosure Guidance and Transparency Rule 4 requires that such companies publish an annual financial report and a half-yearly financial report.

Disclosure Guidance and Transparency Rule 4.1 provides that, within four months of the end of a company's financial year, it must publish an annual financial report. This report must remain publicly available for at least 10 years. The annual financial report must include the following:

- the company's audited financial statements;
- a management report, which contains a fair review of the company's business and a description of the principal risks and uncertainties facing the company; and
- responsibility statements.

In addition to the annual financial report, DTR 4.2 provides that companies must publish a half-yearly financial report covering the first six months of the financial year. The report must contain:

- a condensed set of financial statements;
- an interim management report providing details of important events that affected the company and principal risks and uncertainties; and
- responsibility statements.

This report must be made public as soon as possible, and no later than three months after the end of the period to which the report relates. It must remain available to the public for at least 10 years.

6. The confirmation statement

It used to be the case that every company was required to submit an annual return to Companies House, which involved completion of Form AR01 containing specified information regarding the company. The problem was that much of the information contained in the report did not change and, in such a case, completing the form each year could be viewed as a rather pointless exercise.

The Small Business, Enterprise and Employment Act 2015 amended the CA 2006, abolishing the requirement to submit an annual return. Instead, every company must now deliver an annual confirmation statement to Companies House (CA 2006, s. 853A(1)) on Form CS01. A confirmation statement is simply a statement confirming that all the required information has been delivered or will be delivered at the same time as the confirmation statement (s. 853A(1)(b)). The required information includes:

- notification of specified relevant events, such as a change of the company's registered address (s. 853B);
- notification of a change in the company's principal business activities (s. 853C);
- a statement of capital, but this need only be provided if any information within it has changed since the last confirmation statement was delivered (s. 853D); and
- notification of a change in the trading status of shares (s. 853E).

The information provided in each confirmation statement will relate to a corresponding 'confirmation period', which is calculated as follows:

- the confirmation period for the company's first confirmation statement begins on the date of incorporation and ends on a date specified in the statement (the 'confirmation date') (s. 853A(3)(a)); and
- for subsequent confirmation statements, the confirmation period begins on the day after the last statement's confirmation date and ends with the confirmation date of the statement concerned (s. 853A(3)(b)).

The statement must be delivered to Companies House within a 14-day period following the end of each review period, with a 'review period' being:

- the period of 12 months beginning on the day of the company's incorporation; and
- each period of 12 months beginning on the day after the end of the previous review period (s. 853A(5)).

Failure to deliver a confirmation statement within this period is a criminal offence (s. 853L(1)), although a director or secretary charged with this offence can avoid liability if they can show that they took all reasonable steps to avoid the commission or continuation of the offence (s. 853L(4)).

Chapter summary

- Companies are required to keep a series of statutory registers, although private companies may instead elect to keep the relevant information on the register at Companies House.

- A company's annual accounts and reports consist of the:
  - annual accounts;
  - the strategic report;
  - the directors' report;
  - the auditor's report; and
  - the directors' remuneration report (quoted companies only).
- Companies are required to keep adequate accounting records.
- A company's annual accounts consist of any individual accounts prepared by the company, and any group accounts prepared by the company.
- The directors of a company (except a small company) must prepare a strategic report for each financial year.
- The directors of a company (except a micro-entity) must prepare a directors' report for each financial year.
- If the company is required to have its accounts audited, then the auditor's report will form part of the company's annual reports.
- The directors of a quoted company must prepare a directors' remuneration report, which the members will be given the opportunity to vote on.
- The general rule is that every company must have its accounts audited, although this is subject to certain exceptions (for example, small companies or dormant companies need not have their accounts audited).
- Only eligible persons can act as a statutory auditor, and the CA 2006 prohibits certain persons (such as officers of the company) from acting as auditor due to a lack of independence.
- In a company's first year, the directors can appoint the auditor. In subsequent years, the auditor is usually appointed by passing an ordinary resolution.
- An auditor's remuneration is fixed by the person who appointed them.
- An auditor can face liability in contract, tort and the criminal law.
- A company can sue the auditor if they breach the audit contract or if they commit a tort in the performance of the audit (such as conducting the audit negligently).
- An auditor owes a duty of care to the company that appointed them. Generally, an auditor will not owe a duty of care to third parties (such as members of the company), but a duty may arise if the auditor has specifically assumed a responsibility towards the third party.
- An auditor can vacate office:
  - by resigning;
  - by being removed;
  - by being replaced; or
  - if the company is subject to mandatory rotation and the auditor has served the maximum engagement period.

- Companies whose securities are traded on a regulated market must publish an annual financial report and a half-yearly financial report.
- Every company must provide Companies House with a confirmation statement each year. A confirmation statement is a statement confirming that all the required information has been delivered, or will be delivered at the same time as the confirmation statement.

Chapter fifteen
Market abuse

Contents

1. Introduction

This chapter outlines the UK's regime for combating market abuse. Market abuse can adversely affect the operation of stock exchanges and can result in a loss of confidence in the market.

'Market abuse' is a term that covers a range of prohibited practices, notably insider dealing, the unlawful disclosure of insider information and market manipulation. The law aims to combat such abuses by imposing criminal liability in relation to certain activities (such as insider dealing), and civil liability in relation to others (market manipulation). Some activities (insider dealing) can result in the imposition of both criminal and civil liability. This is unusual, however, as EG 12.3.4 of the Enforcement Guide in the FCA Handbook states that it is the FCA's policy not to bring a civil claim against a person who has been prosecuted for, or convicted or acquitted of, a market misconduct offence.

2. The offence of insider dealing

The criminal offence of insider dealing is established under Part V of the Criminal Justice Act 1993 (CJA 1993).

2.1 The offences

Even though Part V of the CJA 1993 is entitled 'the offence of insider dealing', there are in fact three separate insider dealing offences set out in s. 52:

1. dealing in price-affected securities on the basis of inside information;
2. encouraging another person to deal in price-affected securities on the basis of inside information; and
3. disclosing inside information.

The offences are not mutually exclusive. A person may be found guilty of multiple offences, as the following example demonstrates.

Case study 15.1

Sanjay is the CEO of X-Corp plc, a listed company. He is aware that, in a few days' time, the company is going to issue a profit warning which states that the company's profits are less than half of what it expected to make. This will likely cause the company's share price to drop. Before the announcement is made, Sanjay sells all his shares in X-Corp. He also tells his wife, Claire, of the profit-warning announcement and states 'you had best sell your shares now, as they will be worth much less in a few days'. Claire sells her shares.

In this example, Sanjay has likely engaged in all three forms of insider dealing, in that he has dealt on the basis of inside information, he has disclosed inside information to his wife, and he has encouraged her to deal on the basis of that inside information. Claire, by acting on Sanjay's advice, has also committed the dealing offence.

It should be noted that all three offences can only be committed by an 'individual'. It follows that only natural persons can be convicted of insider dealing, and legal persons (such as companies or LLPs) cannot.

Dealing in price-affected securities

The first offence is found in s. 52(1), which provides that '[a]n individual who has information as an insider is guilty of insider dealing if, in the circumstances mentioned in subsection (3), he deals in securities that are price-affected securities in relation to the information'. A few points should be noted.

- The insider dealing offence relates only to those securities listed in Schedule 2 (s. 54). Shares (Schedule 2, para 1) and debt securities (Schedule 2, para 2) are both listed.
- Securities will be 'price-affected' if, and only if, the information would, if made public, be likely to have a significant effect on their price (s. 56(2)).
- Section 52(3) provides that the dealing: (i) must occur on a 'regulated market'; or (ii) the person dealing is acting as a professional intermediary or relies on such a person. The list of regulated markets is set out in Schedule 1 of the Insider Dealing (Securities and Regulated Markets) Order 1994 (SI 1994/187) and includes the London Stock Exchange. A 'professional intermediary' is defined in s. 59.

The key issue is whether a person 'deals' in securities. Section 55(1) provides that a person deals in securities if any of the following three conditions are met.

- They acquire the securities, whether as principal or agent (s. 55(1)(a)). This will include agreeing to acquire the security and entering into a contract which creates the security (s. 55(2)).
- They dispose of the securities, whether as principal or agent (s. 55(1)(a)). This will include agreeing to dispose of the security or bringing to an end the contract which created the security (s. 55(3)).
- They procure, directly or indirectly, an acquisition or disposal of the securities by any other person (s. 55(1)(b)). A person procures an acquisition or disposal of a security if the security is acquired or disposed of by a person who is their agent, their nominee or a person who is acting at their direction (s. 55(4)). Note that the definition of 'procures' in s. 55(4) is not exhaustive (s. 55(5)).

Encouraging another person to deal

The second offence is found in s. 52(2)(a), which provides that an individual who has insider information is guilty of insider dealing if they 'encourage another person to deal in securities that are (whether or not that other knows it) price-affected securities in relation to the information, knowing or having reasonable cause to believe that the dealing would take place in the circumstances mentioned in subsection (3)...'

Disclosing inside information

The third offence is found in s. 52(2)(b), which provides that an individual who has information as an insider is guilty of insider dealing if they 'disclose the information, otherwise than in the proper performance of the functions of their employment, office or profession, to another person'.

2.2 'Information as an insider'

To obtain a conviction for any of the three insider dealing offences, the prosecution will need to show that the defendant had the 'information as an insider'. Section 57(1) provides that a person has information as an insider if and only if:

- it is, and they know that it is, inside information; and
- they have it, and know that they have it, from an inside source.

mens rea
The 'guilty mind'. The mental element required to convict a defendant of certain offences.

The concept of having information as an insider provides the ***mens rea*** of the insider dealing offences. A person can only be found guilty if they knew the information was inside information and they knew that they obtained it from an inside source. To establish this, we need to know:

- What is 'inside information'?
- What is an 'inside source'?

What is 'inside information'?
Section 56(1) provides that 'inside information' is information which:

1. relates to particular securities, to a particular issuer of securities or particular issuers of securities – not to securities generally or to issuers of securities generally;
2. is specific or precise;
3. has not been made public; and
4. if it were made public would be likely to have a significant effect on the price of any securities.

Section 58 provides non-exhaustive guidance on when information has been made public. Section 58(2) provides that information is made public if:

- it is published in accordance with the rules of a regulated market for the purpose of informing investors and their professional advisers;
- it is contained in records which by virtue of any enactment are open to inspection by the public;
- it can be readily acquired by those likely to deal in any securities to which the information relates, or of an issuer to which the information relates; or
- it is derived from information which has been made public.

Section 58(3) goes on to state that information may be treated as made public even though:

- it can be acquired only by persons exercising diligence or expertise;
- it is communicated to a section of the public and not to the public at large;
- it can be acquired only by observation;
- it is communicated only on payment of a fee; or
- it is published only outside the United Kingdom.

What is an 'inside source'?
Section 57(1) provides that a person has information from an inside source if and only if:

(1) they have it through (i) being a director, employee or shareholder of an issuer of securities; or (ii) having access to the information by virtue of their employment, office or profession; or
(2) the direct or indirect source of the information is a person within (1).

Note that (1) refers to 'a director, employee or shareholder of *an issuer of securities*'. The issuer of securities in question does not need to be the issuer of securities whose price was affected by the inside information in question.

2.3 Defences

Section 53 provides a range of defences for each insider dealing offence (although, it will be seen that certain defences apply to all offences). Section

53(1) provides that individuals will not be guilty of the s. 52(1) dealing offence if they can show:

- that they did not at the time expect the dealing to result in a profit attributable to the fact that the information in question was price-sensitive information in relation to the securities;
- that at the time they believed on reasonable grounds that the information had been disclosed widely enough to ensure that none of those taking part in the dealing would be prejudiced by not having the information; or
- that they would have done what they did even if they had not had the information.

Section 53(2) provides that individuals will not be guilty of the s. 52(2)(a) encouraging offence if they can show:

- that they did not at the time expect the dealing to result in a profit attributable to the fact that the information in question was price-sensitive information in relation to the securities;
- that at the time they believed on reasonable grounds that the information had been or would be disclosed widely enough to ensure that none of those taking part in the dealing would be prejudiced by not having the information; or
- that they would have done what they did even if they had not had the information.

Section 53(3) provides that individuals will not be guilty of the s. 52(2)(b) disclosure offence if they can show:

- that they did not at the time expect any person, because of the disclosure, to deal in securities; or
- that, although they had such an expectation at the time, they did not expect the dealing to result in a profit attributable to the fact that the information was price-sensitive information in relation to the securities.

A 'special defence' is set out in Schedule 1, para 1 of the CJA 1993. This provides that individuals will not be guilty of the dealing offence or the encouraging offence if they can show that they acted in good faith in the course of their business as a market maker or their employment in the business of a market maker. A market maker is a person who holds themself out at all normal times in compliance with the rules of a regulated market or an approved organisation as willing to acquire or dispose of securities, and is recognised as doing so under those rules (Schedule 1, para 1(2)).

2.4 Penalties

Insider dealing is an either-way offence and a person who is guilty of insider dealing is liable:

- on summary conviction, to a fine and/or imprisonment for a term not exceeding six months; or

- on conviction on indictment, to a fine and/or imprisonment for a term not exceeding seven years (s. 61(1)).

Section 61(2) provides that a criminal prosecution for insider dealing cannot be instituted except by, or with the consent of, the Secretary of State or the Director of Public Prosecutions. However, s. 402(1)(a) of the FSMA 2000 provides that the FCA can also institute proceedings for insider dealing.

If a person is convicted of an offence under s. 52, then this will not render void or unenforceable any contract (CJA 1993, s. 63(2)) (including the contract to purchase shares based on inside information).

Test yourself 15.1

1. **What are the three insider dealing offences?**
2. **When will a person have information as an insider?**
3. **What is inside information?**
4. **Who is an insider?**

3. Offences relating to financial services

Part 7 of the Financial Services Act 2012 (FSA 2012) creates several offences relating to financial services. There is some overlap between the Part 7 offences and the civil market abuse regime discussed later in this chapter.

3.1 The offences

Sections 89–91 of FSA 2012 establish three offences in relation to (i) misleading statements; (ii) misleading omissions; and (iii) misleading statements etc. in relation to benchmarks. Like the offence of insider dealing discussed above, the offences in Part 7 are not mutually exclusive (e.g. a misleading statement can also amount to a misleading omission). One notable difference is that, where the insider dealing offences can only be committed by a natural person, both natural persons and companies can be convicted of the Part 7 offences.

Misleading statements

The first offence is found in s. 89 and it applies where a person (*P*) acts in one (or more) of the following three ways:

- *P* makes a statement which *P* knows to be false or misleading in a material respect;
- *P* makes a statement which is false or misleading in a material respect, being reckless as to whether it is; or
- *P* dishonestly conceals any material facts whether in connection with a statement made by *P* or otherwise (s. 89(1)).

Where *P* has engaged in one (or more) of these types of conduct, then an offence will be committed if *P* makes the statement or conceals the facts with the intention of inducing, or is reckless as to whether making it or concealing them may induce, another person (whether or not the person to whom the statement is made):

- to enter into or offer to enter into, or to refrain from entering or offering to enter into, a relevant agreement; or
- to exercise, or refrain from exercising, any rights conferred by a relevant investment (s. 89(2)).

Where *P* makes a statement which *P* knows to be false or misleading in a material respect, then *P* will have a defence if they can show that the statement was made in conformity with price stabilising rules, control of information rules or the exemption for buy-back programmes and stabilisation found in Article 5 of the Market Abuse Regulation (MAR) (s. 89(3)).

Misleading omissions

The second offence is found in s. 90. Section 90(1) provides that a person (P) who does any act or engages in any course of conduct which creates a false or misleading impression as to the market in, or the price or value of, any relevant investments. An offence is committed if *P* intends to create that impression and either of the following two conditions are met:

- *P* intends, by creating the impression, to induce another person to acquire, dispose of, subscribe for or underwrite the investments or to refrain from doing so or to exercise or refrain from exercising any rights conferred by the investments (s. 90(2)); or
- *P* knows that the impression is false or misleading or is reckless as to whether it is, and *P* intends by creating that impression to (i) make a gain for *P* or another or; (ii) cause loss to another person or expose another person to the risk of loss (s. 90(3) and (4)).

Section 90(9) provides that defendants charged under s. 90 can raise a defence if they can show that:

- they reasonably believed that their conduct would not create an impression that was false or misleading (note this only applies where defendants have engaged in the conduct in s. 90(2));
- they acted or engaged in the conduct for the purpose of stabilising the price of investments and in conformity with price stabilisation rules;
- they acted or engaged in the conduct in conformity with control of information rules; or
- they acted or engaged in the conduct in conformity with the exemption for buy-back programmes and stabilisation found in Article 5 of MAR.

Misleading statements etc. in relation to benchmarks

The third offence is found in s. 91, with s. 91 actually creating two separate offences. The first s. 91 offence is found in s. 91(1) and provides that a person (*A*) who makes to another person (*B*) a false or misleading statement commits an offence if:

- *A* makes the statement in the course of arrangements for the setting of a relevant benchmark;
- *A* intends that the statement should be used by *B* for the purpose of the setting of a relevant benchmark; and
- *A* knows that the statement is false or misleading or is reckless as to whether it is.

The second s. 91 offence is found in s. 91(2). This provides that a person (*C*) who does any act, or engages in any course of conduct, which creates a false or misleading impression as to the price or value of any investment, or as to the interest rate appropriate to any transaction, commits an offence if:

- *C* intends to create the impression;
- the impression may affect the setting of a relevant benchmark;
- *C* knows that the impression is false or misleading or is reckless as to whether it is; and
- *C* knows that the impression may affect the setting of a relevant benchmark.

Section 91(4) provides the defendant charged under s. 91 with the following defences:

- the defendant acted or engaged in the conduct for the purpose of stabilising the price of investments and in conformity with price stabilisation rules;
- the defendant acted or engaged in the conduct in conformity with control of information rules; or
- the defendant acted or engaged in the conduct in conformity with the exemption for buy-back programmes and stabilisation found in Article 5 of MAR.

3.2 Penalties and sanctions

The offences in ss. 89–91 are either-way offences. A person who is guilty is liable:

- on summary conviction, to a fine and/or imprisonment for a term not exceeding 12 months; or
- on conviction on indictment, to a fine and/or imprisonment for a term not exceeding seven years (s. 92).

The Secretary of State or the FCA may also apply to the court for various sanctions, notably an injunction or a restitution order, under which the defendant will be ordered to pay to the FCA a sum based on the profit he accrued as a result of the offence, or the loss that was caused to another person as a result of the offence (FSMA 2000, s. 382). The FCA will then pay the sums received to persons to whom the profit should be attributable or who suffered the relevant loss.

4. The market abuse regime

In 2003, the Market Abuse Directive (2003/6/EC) was passed and was implemented by amendments made to Part VIII of FSMA 2000. In 2014, a new Market Abuse Regulation (596/2014/EU) (MAR) was passed. The rationale for this is set out in para 4 of MAR's Preamble:

> '[t]here is a need to establish a more uniform and stronger framework in order to preserve market integrity, to avoid potential regulatory arbitrage, to ensure accountability in the event of attempted manipulation, and to provide more legal certainty and less regulatory complexity for market participants.'

As MAR is directly effective, it automatically forms part of UK domestic law. It is now MAR itself which sets out what constitutes market abuse, with supplementary rules regarding enforcement being found in FSMA 2000. It should be noted here that the market abuse rules in MAR impose civil liability only.

Article 22 of MAR provides that each EU Member State shall designate a 'competent authority' that will be responsible for ensuring that the provisions in MAR are applied in that member state. In the UK, the competent authority is the FCA (Financial Services and Markets Act 2000 (Market Abuse) Regulations 2016 (SI 2016/680), reg. 3). In order to fulfil its role as the competent authority, FSMA 2000 provides the FCA with considerable powers, including:

- the power to require information from issuers for the purposes of:
  - protecting the interests of users of financial markets and exchanges in the UK; or
  - the orderly operation of financial markets and exchanges in the UK (s. 122A);
- the power to require a person to provide specified information or documents (s. 122B);
- the power to enter premises under warrant (s. 122D);
- the power to require an issuer to publish specified information or a corrective statement (s. 122G); and
- the power to suspend trading of a financial instrument (s. 122I).

The activities that constitute market abuse fall into two broad categories: (i) insider dealing; and (ii) market manipulation.

4.1 Insider dealing

The provisions in MAR relating to insider dealing are, in several respects, similar to the insider dealing offence found in the CJA 1993. Consequently, a person who has engaged in insider dealing under MAR may also be found guilty of the insider dealing offence under the CJA 1993. Unlike the insider dealing provisions in the CJA 1993, the insider dealing provisions in MAR apply to both natural and legal persons.

Article 8(1) of MAR provides that insider dealing occurs where:

> '[a] person possesses inside information and uses that information by acquiring or disposing of, for its own account or for the account of a third party, directly or indirectly, financial instruments to which that information relates. The use of inside information by cancelling or amending an order concerning a financial instrument to which the information relates where the order was placed before the person concerned possessed the inside information, shall also be considered to be insider dealing.'

Article 14 provides that insider dealing is prohibited in three circumstances, which mirror closely the three insider dealing offences found in s. 52 of the CJA 1993. Article 14 provides that a person shall not:

- engage or attempt to engage in insider dealing;
- recommend that another person engage in insider dealing or induce another person to engage in insider dealing; or
- unlawfully disclose inside information.

It is important to note that Article 8(4) provides that the prohibition on insider dealing only applies to those persons who possess inside information as a result of:

- being a member of the administrative, management or supervisory bodies of the issuer;
- having a holding in the capital of the issuer;
- having access to the information through the exercise of an employment, profession or duties; or
- being involved in criminal activities.

Inside information

Article 7(1) lists four types of information that constitute inside information, with the principal type being:

> 'information of a precise nature, which has not been made public, relating, directly or indirectly, to one or more issuers or to one or more financial instruments, and which, if it were made public, would be likely to have a significant effect on the prices of those financial instruments or on the price of related derivative financial instruments.'

This definition of inside information is clearly very similar to the definition of inside information set out in s. 56 of the CJA 1993.

Legitimate behaviour

Article 9 establishes what have become known as the 'safe harbours'. These are examples of legitimate behaviour that will not amount to insider dealing, such as where a legal person:

- has established, implemented and maintained adequate and effective internal arrangements and procedures that effectively ensure that neither the natural person who made the decision on its behalf to acquire or dispose of financial instruments to which the information relates, nor another natural person who may have had an influence on that decision, was in possession of the inside information; and
- has not encouraged, made a recommendation to, induced or otherwise influenced the natural person who, on behalf of the legal person, acquired or disposed of financial instruments to which the information relates (Article 9(1)).

4.2 Market manipulation

Article 15 provides that a person shall not engage in market manipulation. Article 12 sets out the types of activities that constitute market manipulation, including:

- entering into a transaction, placing an order to trade or any other behaviour which:
  - gives, or is likely to give, false or misleading signals as to the supply of, demand for, or price of, a financial instrument; or
  - secures, or is likely to secure, the price of one or several financial instruments at an abnormal or artificial level;
- entering into a transaction, placing an order to trade or any other activity or behaviour which affects or is likely to affect the price of one or several financial instruments, which employs a fictitious device or any other form of deception or contrivance;
- disseminating information through the media, including the internet, or by any other means, which gives, or is likely to give, false or misleading signals as to the supply of, demand for, or price of, a financial instrument, or secures, or is likely to secure, the price of one or several financial instruments at an abnormal or artificial level, including the dissemination of rumours, where the person who made the dissemination knew, or ought to have known, that the information was false or misleading;
- transmitting false or misleading information or providing false or misleading inputs in relation to a benchmark where the person who made the transmission or provided the input knew or ought to have known that it was false or misleading, or any other behaviour which manipulates the calculation of a benchmark;
- conduct by a person, or persons acting in collaboration, to secure a dominant position over the supply of or demand for a financial instrument which has, or is likely to have, the effect of fixing, directly or indirectly, purchase or sale prices or creates, or is likely to create, other unfair trading conditions; and

- the buying or selling of financial instruments at the opening or closing of the market, which has or is likely to have the effect of misleading investors acting on the basis of the prices displayed, including the opening or closing prices.

The Article 15 prohibition will not apply to an activity that constitutes an accepted market practice (Article 13(1)). The FCA is empowered to specify which activities amount to an accepted market practice. It has not done so at the time of writing.

4.3 Disclosure requirements

MAR imposes several duties in relation to the disclosure of information. Article 17(1) provides that an issuer shall inform the public as soon as possible of inside information which directly concerns the issuer. The inside information must be made public in a manner which enables fast access and complete, correct and timely assessment of the information by the public. However, an issuer may delay publication in certain situations specified in Article 17(4) (for example, where immediate disclosure would be likely to prejudice the legitimate interests of the issuer).

Article 18(1) provides that an issuer (or a person acting on their behalf) must draw up a list of all persons who (i) have access to inside information and who are working for them under a contract of employment; or (ii) perform tasks through which they have access to inside information (e.g. accountants). This list is known as an 'insider list' with Article 18(3) stating it must contain at least:

- the identity of the person who has access to inside information;
- the reason for that person being on the insider list;
- the date and time at which that person obtained access to inside information; and
- the date on which the insider list was drawn up.

Issuers (or those acting on their behalf) must keep the insider list up to date (Article 18(4)) and the list must be retained for at least five years following the date it is drawn up or updated (Article 18(5)). Upon request, the issuer must provide the insider list to the FCA (Article 18(1)(c)).

Article 19(1) provides that persons discharging managerial responsibilities, as well as those closely associated with them, shall notify the issuer and the FCA of every transaction conducted on their own account relating to shares or debt instruments of that issuer. The issuer must ensure that this information is promptly made public no later than three business days after the transaction (Article 19(3)). Article 18(6) provides that the exact information that must be disclosed includes:

- the name of the person and the name of the issuer;
- the reason for the notification;
- a description of the financial instrument;

- the nature of the transaction (acquisition or disposal) and its date and place; and
- the price and volume of the transaction (how many shares were bought and at what price).

4.4 Administrative sanctions

Where a person (*P*) contravenes a provision of MAR, FSMA 2000 empowers the FCA to impose a range of sanctions upon that person, including:

- imposing upon *P* a penalty of such amount as the FCA considers appropriate (s. 123(1) and (2)) or, instead of imposing a penalty, publishing a statement censuring *P* (s. 123(3));
- temporarily or permanently prohibiting *P* from holding certain positions, such as an office or position involving responsibility for taking decisions about the management of an investment firm (s. 123A(2)(a));
- temporarily prohibiting *P* from acquiring or disposing of financial instruments (s. 123A(2)(b));
- suspending, for such period as the FCA considers appropriate (up to a maximum of 12 months), any permission which *P* has to carry on a regulated activity (s. 123B(2)(a) and (4)); or
- imposing, for such period as the FCA considers appropriate (up to a maximum of 12 months), such limitations or other restrictions in relation to the carrying on of a regulated activity by the person as the FCA considers appropriate (s. 123B(2)(b) and (4)).

A sanction can also be imposed on a person who was knowingly concerned in *P*'s contravention in relation to breaches of MAR other than those involving Articles 14 or 15. The above sanctions are not mutually exclusive and so the FCA may impose any of the above sanctions in relation to the same contravention (s. 123C).

Test yourself 15.2

1. **What piece of EU legislation aims to combat market abuse?**
2. **Which body is the competent authority for applying the EU rules on market abuse?**
3. **Provide five examples of the type of activity that can constitute market manipulation.**
4. **What sanctions can be imposed upon a person who has engaged in market abuse?**

Chapter summary

- Section 52 of the Criminal Justice Act 1993 establishes three insider dealing offences, namely:
  - dealing in price-affected securities on the basis of inside information;
  - encouraging another person to deal in price-affected securities on the basis of inside information; and
  - disclosing inside information.
- A person has information as an insider if and only if:
  - it is, and they know that it is, inside information; and
  - they have it, and know that they have it, from an inside source.
- Inside information is information which:
  - relates to particular securities or to a particular issuer of securities or to particular issuers of securities, and not to securities generally or to issuers of securities generally;
  - is specific or precise;
  - has not been made public; and
  - if it were made public would be likely to have a significant effect on the price of any securities.
- Insider dealing under CJA 1993 is a criminal offence and can result in the imposition of a fine and/or a term of imprisonment of up to seven years.
- Part 7 of the Financial Services Act 2012 establishes three offences relating to financial services that relate to:
  - misleading statements;
  - misleading omissions; and
  - misleading statements etc. in relation to benchmarks.
- The Market Abuse Regulation and Part VIII of FSMA 2000 establish the civil regime for market abuse.
- The FCA is the 'competent authority' as regards MAR in the UK and is responsible for applying it in the UK.
- The Market Abuse Regulation provides that market abuse is classified into two broad activities, namely insider dealing and market manipulation.
- The Market Abuse Regulation imposes several duties of disclosure upon issuers and those persons who discharge managerial responsibilities.
- If a person breaches a provision of MAR, then the FCA has access to a range of sanctions that can be imposed, including:
  - imposing a financial penalty;
  - prohibiting transgressors from holding certain positions;
  - prohibiting transgressors from disposing of financial instruments;
  - suspending a person's permission to carry on a regulated activity; or
  - limiting a person's ability to carry on a regulated activity.

Part five

Chapter 16
Corporate restructuring and takeovers

Chapter 17
Corporate rescue

Chapter 18
Liquidation and dissolution

Corporate restructuring, rescue and liquidation

Overview

Part five looks at the measures designed to restructure a company, rescue a financially struggling company and bring about the end of a company's existence.

Chapter 16 looks at the key procedures for restructuring a company and the takeover rules.

Chapter 17 discusses the legal mechanisms that exist to help financially struggling companies, notably administration and company voluntary arrangements.

Chapter 18 focuses on those procedures designed to bring about the end of a company, namely liquidation and dissolution.

At the end of this Part, students will be able to:

- understand how companies can be restructured;
- understand how takeovers are regulated;

- identify the key rescue procedures and the extent to which the UK has a rescue culture;
- demonstrate an awareness of how administration can help a struggling company;
- consider the effectiveness of company voluntary arrangements as a rescue mechanism;
- identify when a company is insolvent;
- understand the role and powers of the liquidator; and
- understand the processes for dissolving and restoring a company.

Chapter sixteen

Corporate restructuring and takeovers

Contents

1. Introduction

This chapter begins by looking at two methods that companies can use to restructure themselves or the relationships that they have with various stakeholders: the scheme of reconstruction and the scheme of arrangement. A company may also seek to restructure itself by expanding its corporate group structure. One method of doing this will be discussed – taking over other companies.

2. Schemes of reconstruction

At a basic level, a scheme of reconstruction allows a company (the transferor company) to transfer all or part of its business to another company (or companies). The transferor company is then voluntarily wound up. The following example provides a situation in which a scheme of arrangement may be beneficial.

Case study 16.1

X-Corp plc engages in several different lines of business. The directors of X-Corp would like:

- **the liabilities of each line of business to be insulated from the other;**
- **for each line of business to develop and undertake its own strategy; and**
- **for one of the lines of business to be sold off.**

The directors decide to use a scheme of reconstruction to hive-off (or 'demerge') each line of business by transferring it to several new companies. Each company will be legally insulated from the other and will be free to develop its own strategy. It will also be easier to sell off a line of business as it has been segregated into its own company, the shares of which could be sold to a purchaser.

The process for effecting a scheme of reconstruction is found in s. 110 of the IA 1986. Figure 16.1 sets out this process.

The transferor company passes a special resolution resolving to voluntarily wind up the company.

The s. 110 scheme must be sanctioned (s. 110(2)), with the method of sanction depending upon the type of voluntary winding up.

Members' voluntary winding up

The scheme is sanctioned by passing a special resolution that confers authority upon the liquidator to proceed with the scheme (s. 110(3)(a)).

Creditors' voluntary winding up

The scheme is sanctioned by the court or the liquidation committee (s. 110(3)(b)).

Once the scheme has been sanctioned, it will be put into effect and will bind the members of the transferor company (s. 110(5)) as well as its creditors (*Re City & County Investment Co* (1879) 13 ChD 475 (CA)).

The transferor company will be liquidated, and all or part of its business transferred to another company (or companies). In return for the transfer, the members of the transferor company will usually receive shares in the company to which the business has been transferred (s. 110(2)(a)).

Figure 16.1 The s. 110 process

2.1 Dissenting from the scheme

There may be members who oppose the scheme. Where the scheme was sanctioned by a resolution of the members, members who did not vote for the scheme may express their dissent to the liquidator by leaving a written statement to this effect at the company's registered office within seven days of the resolution being passed (s. 111(2)). The liquidator will then be required to either (i) abstain from carrying out the reconstruction; or (ii) purchase the dissenting member's shares at a price to be determined by arbitration or agreement (s. 111(2)). It is the liquidator's choice as to which of these two options is chosen (s. 111(3)).

Creditors who oppose the scheme may protect themselves by inserting a provision into the loan agreement (if one exists). If a creditor who opposes the scheme does not have such protection, their only option is to try and stop the scheme from proceeding by applying to the court for an order winding up the transferor company, usually on the ground that the transferor company cannot pay its debts, or that it is just and equitable for it to be wound up (these grounds for winding up are discussed in Chapters 10 and 18). If the court orders that the transferor company be wound up within a year of the passing of the resolution approving the s. 110 scheme, then this resolution will be regarded as invalid, unless it is approved by the court (s. 110(6)).

Test yourself 16.1

1. **What is a scheme of reconstruction?**
2. **Briefly explain the process for putting a scheme of reconstruction into effect.**
3. **How can a member or creditor dissent from the scheme?**

3. Schemes of arrangement

Part 26 of the CA 2006 (ss. 895–901) allows companies to enter into a scheme of arrangement. A scheme of arrangement is a compromise or arrangement between a company and (i) its creditors, or any class of them; or (ii) its members, or any class of them (CA 2006, s. 895(1)). In other words, it allows a company to amend the rights of its creditors and members, with the important point to note being that it does not need to obtain the unanimous approval of the creditors or members in question. A key benefit of a scheme of arrangement is its versatility – a scheme can be put into operation in order to undertake a wide variety of aims, including:

- to implement a takeover or a merger (as recognised by s. 900(1));
- to restructure a company's debt;
- to attempt to rescue a financially struggling company (for example, an administrator may propose that the company enter into a scheme of arrangement with its creditors);
- to divide or demerge a company; and
- to restructure share capital (e.g. s. 895(2) states that a scheme can be used to consolidate or sub-divide shares).

As a scheme of arrangement involves a 'compromise or arrangement', it follows that a party unilaterally giving up all their rights without receiving anything in return will not constitute a scheme of arrangement, as the following case demonstrates.

Case law 16.1

***Re National Farmers Union Development Trust Ltd* [1972] 1 WLR 1548 (Ch)**

The company's membership of 94,000 was so large that the majority of its income was spent on administration costs, and not on furthering the company's objects. To reduce costs, the company proposed a scheme of arrangement under which all of the members except seven would have their membership terminated and would lose all their rights.

The court refused to sanction the scheme, on the ground that it did not involve a compromise, but would result in the vast majority of members completely surrendering their rights. Brightman J stated:

> **'The word "compromise" implies some element of accommodation on each side. It is not apt to describe total surrender. A claimant who abandons his claim is not compromising it. Similarly, I think that the word "arrangement" in this section implies some element of give and take. Confiscation is not my idea of an arrangement. A member whose rights are expropriated without any compensating advantage is not, in my view, having his rights rearranged in any legitimate sense of that expression.'**

Many schemes will involve an alteration of the rights of the creditors or members but an alteration of rights is not required (*Re T&N Ltd* [2006] EWHC 1447 (Ch)).

3.1 Procedure

A scheme of arrangement is very flexible but its usefulness is hindered by the burdensome procedure that must be followed to put a scheme into effect. Implementing a scheme involves a three-stage process and two court applications. The procedure (which can be complex) must be followed precisely or the court will refuse to sanction the scheme.

Stage one: The application to summon meetings

The first stage involves an application being made to the court. If the application is successful, the court will order that meetings be summoned of the relevant creditors or members who are affected by the proposed scheme (s. 896(1)). Section 896(2) provides that this application can be made by:

- the company;
- any creditor or member of the company;
- the liquidator if the company is in liquidation; or
- the administrator if the company is in administration.

The application will need to identify which members and/or creditors will be affected by the scheme. Stage two meetings need not be convened for members/creditors who are unaffected by the scheme (*Re Bluebrook Ltd* [2009] EWHC 2114 (Ch)). If the scheme does not affect all the creditors/members, it is vital that the application correctly identifies which class of creditors/members will be affected. If the application gets this wrong, then the court will refuse to sanction the scheme in stage three. Unfortunately, determining what amounts to a 'class' of creditor or member is not always easy. The courts have sought to provide guidance, with Bowen LJ in *Sovereign Life Assurance Co v Dodd* [1892] 2 QB 573 (CA) setting out a test to determine a 'class' of creditors or members:

> 'It seems to me that we must give such meaning to the term "class" as will prevent the section being so worked as to result in confiscation and injustice and that it must be confined to those persons whose rights are not so dissimilar as to make it impossible for them to consult together with a view to their common interest.'

Stage two: Approval of the scheme

Stage two involves holding the meetings of affected creditors and members to determine if the scheme is to be approved. Stage two is itself a two-stage process.

1. The affected creditors/members must be provided with notice of the meetings, with the stage one court order setting out the notice requirements for those meetings (how much notice is given, and in what format). Section 897(1)–(2) provides that notice must contain an explanatory statement that:
   - explains the effect of the compromise or arrangement; and
   - states any material interests of the directors of the company, and the effect on those interests of the compromise or arrangement.
2. The meetings will be held to determine if the scheme is approved. Separate meetings must be held for each class of member and creditor affected. Every meeting must approve the scheme in order for it to proceed to stage three. Approval will be obtained if two conditions are satisfied (s. 899(1)):
   - a majority in number of persons present and voting (either in person or by proxy) at the meeting vote in favour of the scheme; and
   - at least 75% in value of the persons present and voting vote in favour of the scheme.

Stage three: Court sanction

If all the meetings approve the scheme, then it can progress onto stage three, which involves an application being made to the court to sanction the scheme (s. 899(1)). The courts' overarching function when determining whether to sanction the scheme was set out by Lindley LJ in *Re English, Scottish, and Australian Chartered Bank* [1893] 3 Ch 385 (CA), who stated:

> 'we are not to register their decisions, but to see that they have been properly convened and have been properly consulted, and have considered the matter from a proper point of view, that is, with a view to the interests

> of the class to which they belong and are empowered to bind, the Court ought to be slow to differ from them. It should do so without hesitation if there is anything wrong; but it ought not to do so, in my judgment, unless something is brought to the attention of the Court to shew that there has been some material oversight or miscarriage.'

More specifically, Chadwick LJ in *Re Hawk Insurance Co Ltd* [2001] EWCA Civ 241 stated that the courts will:

- determine whether the stage two meeting or meetings were summoned and conducted in accordance with the stage one court order;
- determine whether the proposed scheme was approved by the requisite majorities at stage two; and
- consider whether the views and interests of those who did not approve the proposal at stage two should receive impartial consideration.

In *Re Dorman Long & Co Ltd* [1934] Ch 635 (Ch), Maugham J stated that the court will consider whether the proposed scheme 'is such that an intelligent and honest man, a member of the class concerned and acting in respect of his interest, might reasonably approve'.

3.2 The effects of a scheme

If the court decides to sanction the scheme, it will make an order to that effect. This order will not have any effect until a copy of it has been delivered to the registrar of companies (s. 899(4)). The sanctioned scheme will bind the company and all those creditors or members who are affected by it (s. 899(3)). The scheme will not bind third parties, although it can indirectly affect third party rights (see *Re La Seda de Barcelona SA* [2010] EWHC 1364 (Ch)).

Once sanctioned by the court, a scheme of arrangement cannot be amended simply because the members or creditors wish to amend it (*Devi v People's Bank of Northern India Ltd* [1938] 4 All ER 337 (PC)). It may be amended if the scheme itself provides for some form of post-sanction power of amendment, although in *Re Cape plc* [2006] EWHC 1315 (Ch), the court stated that '[t]here are strong reasons why in most cases the court is unlikely to exercise the jurisdiction to sanction a scheme with provisions for future amendments'.

Test yourself 16.2

1. **What is a scheme of arrangement?**
2. **Provide some examples of the types of transactions that a scheme of arrangement can be used for.**
3. **Briefly explain the three stages of putting a scheme of arrangement into effect.**
4. **What are the effects of a scheme of arrangement coming into effect?**

4. Takeovers

A takeover typically occurs where one company acquires sufficient shares in another company to take it over. The company that is seeking to take over another is known as the 'offeror' or 'bidder', whereas the company being taken over is known as the 'offeree' or 'target'. Takeovers operate very differently in different types of company.

- Most private companies have a very small number of shareholders. To take over such a company, the offeror will need to acquire the majority of the company's shares (although offerors will typically wish to acquire all the shares). This is usually done by the offeror entering into a private agreement with the offeree's shareholders to purchase their shares.
- In many public companies (especially quoted companies), the shares are widely dispersed among a large number of shareholders. As many of these shareholders do not exercise the voting rights attached to their shares, it is possible to control the company without controlling a majority of the company's shares. Accordingly, the Takeover Code provides that control of a company is acquired if a person controls an interest in shares carrying 30% or more of the company's voting rights.

Takeovers in large companies tend to be much more complex and a wide-ranging body of rules have evolved to regulate such takeovers. Some of these rules are found in the CA 2006, but the bulk of the rules regulating takeovers are found in the City Code on Takeovers and Mergers. Before looking at the City Code itself, we will first examine the body that created and updates the City Code, namely the Panel on Takeovers and Mergers.

4.1 The Panel on Takeovers and Mergers

Article 4(1) of the Takeover Directive requires Member States to 'designate the authority or authorities competent to supervise bids for the purposes of the rules which they make or introduce pursuant to this Directive'. In the UK, this authority is the Panel on Takeovers and Mergers (CA 2006, s. 942(1)) (commonly known as 'the Takeover Panel').

The Takeover Panel, which is independent of government, consists of up to 36 members – all of whom have some form of expertise in takeovers and most of whom have worked for organisations involved in takeovers (law firms, merchant banks and so on). The day-to-day work of the Takeover Panel is carried out by the Panel Executive which, according to Watkins LJ in *R v Panel on Takeovers and Mergers ex p Guinness plc* (1988) 4 BCC 325 (QB):

> 'takes the lead in examining the circumstances of takeover bids and, if thought necessary, referring them to the Panel for consideration and adjudication according to the Rules. Almost daily it is called upon to give advice and rulings, which are mostly accepted ... The executive and where necessary the Panel monitors, so to speak, take-over bids and mergers as they develop to ensure, as far as possible, that the Code is being observed. It acts as a sort of fire brigade to extinguish quickly the flames of unacceptable and unfair practice.'

The Takeover Panel is empowered to delegate its functions to a committee or sub-committee (CA 2006, s. 942(3)(a)), which has led to the creation of:

- the Hearings Committee, whose function is to review rulings of the Panel Executive (Takeover Code, Introduction, A9); and
- the Code Committee, which is responsible for reviewing and amending the Takeover Code (Takeover Code, Introduction, A9).

Functions of the Takeover Panel

The functions of the Takeover Panel are set out in the CA 2006. The Panel may 'do anything that it considers necessary or expedient for the purpose of, or in connection with, its functions' (CA 2006, s. 942(2)). The Takeover Panel has three broad functions.

1. It must make rules giving effect to certain provisions of the Takeover Directive (CA 2006, s. 943(1)). These rules, namely the City Code on Takeovers on Mergers, are discussed in the next section.
2. The Takeover Panel may give rulings on the interpretation, application or effect of the City Code (s. 945(1)). These rulings are binding (s. 945(2)). A ruling will first be provided by the Panel Executive, and this ruling can be reviewed by the Hearings Committee (s. 951(1)) or by judicial review (*R v Panel on Takeovers and Mergers, ex p Datafin plc* [1987] QB 815 (CA)). Decisions of the Hearings Committee can be appealed to the Takeover Appeal Board (s. 951(3)).
3. The Takeover Panel may provide directions in order (i) to restrain a person from acting, or continuing to act, in breach of the City Code; (ii) to restrain a person from doing, or continuing to do, a particular thing, pending determination of whether that or any other conduct of his is or would be a breach of the City Code; or (iii) otherwise to secure compliance with the City Code (s. 946).

In order to fulfil its functions, the Takeover Panel is granted significant statutory powers. Notably, the Panel can issue a person with a notice requiring that person to provide any specified documents or information (s. 947(1)).

4.2 The City Code on Takeovers and Mergers

As noted, one of the functions of the Takeover Panel is to create and maintain rules that implement the Takeover Directive. These rules are contained in the City Code on Takeovers and Mergers (usually known as the 'Takeover Code'). At the time of writing, the Code in force is the 12th edition, which was last updated in 2016 (although frequent amendments are made between new editions).

The Introduction to the Takeover Code provides that its principal purpose is:

> 'to ensure that shareholders in an offeree company are treated fairly and are not denied an opportunity to decide on the merits of a takeover, and that shareholders in the offeree company of the same class are afforded equivalent treatment by an offeror. The Code also provides an orderly framework within which takeovers are conducted. In addition, it is

> designed to promote, in conjunction with other regulatory regimes, the integrity of the financial markets.'

The Introduction then goes on to point out that the Takeover Code is not concerned with certain matters:

> 'The Code is not concerned with the financial or commercial advantages or disadvantages of a takeover. These are matters for the offeree company and its shareholders. In addition, it is not the purpose of the Code either to facilitate or to impede takeovers. Nor is the Code concerned with those issues, such as competition policy, which are the responsibility of government and other bodies.'

Scope of the Code

The Introduction to the Takeover Code provides that it principally applies to the following companies and transactions:

- to all offers for shares in companies which:
  - have their registered offices in the UK; and
  - have any securities that are admitted to trading on a regulated market in the UK; or
- to all offers for shares in public or private companies which have their registered offices in the UK and their place of central management and control is in the UK.

In relation to private companies, s. 3(a)(ii) of the Code provides that the Code will only apply to private companies in certain cases (such as where any of the company's securities have been traded on a regulated market at any time during the previous 10 years). As a result, the Code will only rarely apply to private companies.

The General Principles

Article 3(1) of the Takeover Directive sets out six General Principles and provides that member states shall ensure that these Principles are complied with. They are repeated in the Takeover Code.

1. All holders of the securities of an offeree company of the same class must be afforded equivalent treatment; moreover, if a person acquires control of a company, the other holders of securities must be protected.
2. The holders of the securities of an offeree company must have sufficient time and information to enable them to reach a properly informed decision on the bid; where it advises the holders of securities, the board of the offeree company must give its views on the effects of implementation of the bid on employment, conditions of employment and the locations of the company's places of business.
3. The board of an offeree company must act in the interests of the company as a whole and must not deny the holders of securities the opportunity to decide on the merits of the bid.
4. False markets must not be created in the securities of the offeree company, of the offeror company or of any other company concerned by the bid

in such a way that the rise or fall of the prices of the securities becomes artificial and the normal functioning of the markets is distorted.

5. An offeror must announce a bid only after ensuring that they can fulfil in full any cash consideration, if such is offered, and after taking all reasonable measures to secure the implementation of any other type of consideration.
6. An offeree company must not be hindered in the conduct of its affairs for longer than is reasonable by a bid for its securities.

The Introduction to the Takeover Code notes that the General Principles are 'expressed in broad general terms and the Code does not define the precise extent of, or the limitations on, their application'. The Introduction also states why the General Principles are so broad, namely so that they can be 'applied in accordance with their spirit in order to achieve their underlying purpose'.

The rules

The Code also contains 38 rules. These are much more detailed than the General Principles and constitute the bulk of the Takeover Code. The Introduction states that both the spirit and the letter of the rules must be observed, but it also acknowledges that the rules must be applied flexibly. Accordingly, the introduction provides that the Panel may derogate or grant a person a waiver from the application of a rule either:

- in the circumstances set out by the rule; or
- in other circumstances where the Panel considers that the particular rule would operate unduly harshly, in an unnecessarily restrictive or burdensome, or otherwise inappropriate manner (in which case a reasoned decision will be given).

A discussion of all 38 rules is beyond the scope of this text, but Table 16.1 sets out the broad topics covered by the rules.

A number of these rules are discussed later in the context of the takeover process and the mandatory offer.

Sanctions and compensation

The Takeover Panel is empowered by statute to create rules that impose sanctions upon persons who breach the Takeover Code or who refuse to comply with the Takeover Panel's directions (CA 2006, s. 952(1)). Sanctions that can be imposed by the Hearings Committee include:

- issuing a public or private statement censuring the offender;
- reporting the offender's conduct to a UK or overseas regulator (notably the FCA), or professional body, and that regulator or body can then decide whether to take action against the offender; and/or
- publishing a statement indicating that the offender is not someone who is likely to comply with the Code. This is known as 'cold-shouldering'. It is, in practice, the most severe sanction available to the Panel as the members of certain professional bodies (such as the FCA) will not act for a cold-shouldered person.

Rules 1–3	The approach, announcements and independent advice
Rules 4–8	Restrictions on dealings
Rule 9	The mandatory offer and its terms
Rules 10–13	The voluntary offer and its terms
Rules 14–18	Rules applicable to all offers
Rules 19–22	Conduct during the offer
Rules 23–27	Documents from the offeror and offeree board
Rule 28	Profit forecasts and quantified financial benefit statements
Rule 29	Asset valuations
Rule 30	Distribution of documentation during an offer
Rules 31–34	Offer timetable and revision
Rule 35	Restrictions following offers
Rule 36	Partial offers
Rule 37	Redemption or purchase by a company of its own securities
Rule 38	Dealings by connected exempt principal traders

Table 16.1 The rules within the Takeover Code

The Takeover Panel can also issue a compensation ruling. This requires the offender to pay, within a specified period, to the holders or former holders of the offeree company's securities such amount as the Panel thinks is just and reasonable so as to ensure that such holders receive what they would have been entitled to receive if the relevant rule had been complied with.

4.3 The takeover process

The Takeover Code provides numerous rules regarding how a takeover offer should proceed, but some of these rules are flexible and can accommodate a wide range of situations and evolving conditions. The basic process of how a public company is taken over under the Code is discussed below and an overview is set out in Figure 16.2.

If the board of a company is considering a takeover bid for another company, the first step is for the potential offeror to engage in due diligence regarding the potential offeree based on publicly available information. In order to ensure that a false market in the offeree's shares is not created (which is prohibited by General Principle 4), rules 1 and 2 of the Takeover Code provide that certain information regarding takeover offers or possible takeover offers is publicly announced in a timely manner. Rule 2.2 provides that an announcement of an offer or a possible offer must be made in certain circumstances, including:

Announcement of an offer or possible offer

In certain circumstances, the offeror must announce an offer or a possible offer (rule 2.2)

↓

Announces firm intention to make an offer

Once the offeror decides to make an offer, it must first notify the offeree's board that it has a firm intention to make an offer (rule 1), and it must then announce this generally (rule 2.2(a))

↓

Publication of the offer document

Within 28 days of this announcement, an offer document must be published (rule 24.1(a))

↓

Day 1

The publication of the offer document represents Day 1 of the offer timetable (rule 24.1)

↓

Day 14

The response circular must be sent within 14 days of the offer document being published, unless the Panel consents to it being sent at a later date (rule 25.1(a))

↓

Day 21 (earliest first closing date)

The offer must remain open for at least 21 days (rule 31.1)

↓

Day 60

Unless the Panel so consents, Day 60 is the maximum period up to which an offer (whether revised or not) can be extended (rule 31.6)

↓

Day 74

If an offer became unconditional as to acceptances on Day 60, it must remain open for a further 14 days (rule 31.4)

↓

Consideration sent to the accepting shareholders

The consideration for the offeree's shares must be sent to accepting shareholders within 14 days of the first closing date, the date the offer became wholly unconditional or the date of receipt of acceptance (whichever is the later) (rule 31.8).

Figure 16.2 The takeover process

- where the offeror notifies the offeree's board that it has a firm intention to make an offer;
- where the offeror acquires sufficient shares to trigger the mandatory offer rules; and
- where the offeree is subject to rumour and speculation (particularly rumours that it will be taken over) or there is untoward movement in its share price.

Where rule 2.2 applies, the offeror must announce an offer. If it is not ready to announce an offer, it can announce a possible offer (rule 2.4). The announcement of an offer or a possible offer commences the 'offer period'. If a possible offer is announced, this leaves the offeree is an uncertain state, as it does not know if it will be subject to a takeover bid or not. Rule 2.6 provides for what is known as a 'put up or shut up' announcement, which provides that, within 28 days of the announcement of a possible offer, the potential offeror must either:

- announce a firm intention to make an offer; or
- announce that it does not intend to make an offer. If it announces that it does not intend to make an offer, then it may not make an offer within a six-month period following the announcement (rule 2.8).

Rule 2.1(a) provides that prior to any announcement being made, all persons privy to confidential information (especially price sensitive information) concerning the offer treat that information as secret. A failure to do so could have legal consequences (e.g. breach of the laws relating to insider dealing or market abuse).

Once the offeror's board decides that it intends to make a takeover offer, it must notify the offeree's board at first instance that it has a firm intention to make an offer (rule 1). It must then make an announcement that it has a firm intention to make an offer (rule 2.2(a)). The firm intention to make an offer announcement must contain the information specified in rule 2.7, including setting out the terms of the offer. An announcement of a firm intention to make an offer effectively requires the offeror to make the offer, unless the offer is subject to pre-conditions (rule 2.7(b)). In practice, most offers are subject to conditions, with a common condition being that the offeror will only be bound by the offer if the offer is accepted by a specified proportion of the offeree's shareholders. Rule 13 regulates pre-conditions and the offeror will need to obtain the Takeover Panel's approval if it wishes to include pre-conditions in the offer (rule 13.3).

Within 28 days of the offer announcement, an offer document containing the terms of the offer must be posted on the offeree's website and sent to all shareholders of the offeree (rule 24.1). The publication of the offer document commences the offer timetable (known as 'Day One'). Within 14 days of the offer document being published, the board of the offeree company must send a response circular to all its shareholders, in which it sets out its opinion of the offer (rules 25.1(a) and 25.2(a)). The offer must remain open for at least 21 days (rule 31.1) and the expiration of this period is known as the 'first closing date' (therefore Day 21 is the earliest first closing date).

If the offer is subject to pre-conditions then the offeror must announce the acceptance level achieved (rule 17.1) on the first business day following the first closing date. If the acceptance condition has not been satisfied, the offer can be extended for up to 60 days following the publication of the offer document (rule 31.6). At the end of Day 60, the offeror must announce whether the acceptance condition has been satisfied. If the acceptance condition is satisfied on Day 60, then the offer must remain open for a further 14 days (rule 31.4). If the acceptance condition has not been satisfied by Day 60, then the offer will lapse, unless the offeror decides to proceed anyway (although the offer will not be allowed to proceed if the offeror has not secured over 50% of the offeree's voting rights). If the offer lapses, the takeover bid will fail and the offeror cannot make a further offer for at least 12 months (rule 35.1).

If the offer is successful, then the consideration for the offeree's shares must be sent to the accepting shareholders within 14 days of the first closing date, the date the offer become wholly unconditional, or the date of receipt of acceptance (whichever is the later) (rule 31.8).

Defensive action

Where the takeover is hostile (i.e. where the offeree's board is opposed to the takeover), the directors may find themselves in a conflicted position insofar as they will likely lose their jobs if the takeover bid succeeds. Such directors may therefore seek to engage in defensive action in order to frustrate the bid. General Principle 3 of the Takeover Code provides that the offeree's board 'must not deny the holders of securities the opportunity to decide on the merits of the bid'. This is backed up by rule 21.1(a) which prohibits the offeree's board from taking any action that could result in the bid being frustrated or in the shareholders being denied the opportunity to decide on the bid's merits, unless the shareholders in general meeting so approve.

The issue that arises is that the offeree's board may honestly believe that a takeover bid is not in the company's interests (or to use the language of s. 172, that it would not promote the success of the company). The question is whether directors acting in such a way are acting in breach of duty, notably the duties found in ss. 171 and 172. To date, the cases have provided limited guidance only and have held that the directors cannot prevent the shareholders from obtaining the best price for their shares (*Heron International Ltd v Lord Grade* [1983] BCLC 244 (CA)). If there are competing bids, the directors are not bound to recommend the highest bid (*Dawson International plc v Coats Paton (No 1)* (1988) 4 BCC 305 (Court of Session)).

Devices used to frustrate takeover bids are often referred to as 'poison pills', but the use of pills is rare in the UK. Sadly, no authoritative case law exists on the use of poison pills in the UK. The case of *Criterion Properties plc v Stratford UK Properties LLC* [2004] UKHL 28 involved a poison pill, but the House did not need to address the validity of the pill in that case as the issue had not been brought up by the lower courts or counsel.

4.4 Minority shareholder protection

Once an offeror acquires control of a company, the remaining shareholders in the offeree may feel powerless and may wish to exit the company. It is a well-established principle of takeover regulation that, where a change in control of a company occurs, that company's shareholders should be given the ability to exit the company. This is implemented in two ways:

- by requiring the offeror to make a mandatory offer in certain cases; and
- by giving shareholders sell-out rights in certain circumstances.

The mandatory offer

Rule 9 of the Takeover Code provides the shareholders of the company with the ability to exit the company by requiring a person who has obtained a controlling interest in a company to make an offer to purchase all the shares in the company. This is known as a mandatory offer. Rule 9.1 provides that a mandatory offer must be made where:

- a person (on his own or acting in concert with others) acquires an interest in shares that carry 30% or more of the company's voting rights; or
- a person (acting on their own or in concert with others) is interested in shares which carry between 30% and 50% of the company's voting rights, and that person (or someone acting in concert with them) acquires an interest in any other shares that increases the percentage of shares carrying voting rights in which they are interested.

A person who acquires the requisite voting rights must offer to purchase the shares of all the other shareholders in the company (rule 9.1). The offer price will be the highest price which the offeror (or any person who acted in concert with them) paid for the shares in the 12-month period prior to the offer (rule 9.5(a)). It is clear that the purpose of rule 9 is to prevent a person obtaining control of a company without having to make a takeover offer for all the shares in the offeree. A person who does not wish to acquire complete control of the offeree should ensure that they do not acquire more than 29.9% of the offeree's shares.

Sell-out rights

Section 983 of the CA 2006 provides the offeree's shareholders with the ability to exit the company by compelling the offeror to purchase their shares. However, an offeree shareholder can only exercise this sell-out right if:

- the shareholder has not accepted the takeover offer;
- the offer period has not expired;
- the offeror has by virtue of acceptances of the offer acquired or unconditionally contracted to acquire some (but not all) of the shares to which the offer relates; and
- those shares amount to not less than 90% in value of all the voting shares in the company and carry not less than 90% of the voting rights in the company (s. 983(2)).

If these conditions have been met, shareholders can exercise their sell-out rights by writing to the offeror and requiring that the offeror acquire their shares (s. 984(1)). The offeror then becomes bound to acquire that shareholder's shares on the terms of the takeover offer or on any other such terms as may be agreed (s. 985(2)).

4.5 Squeeze-out rights

It is important that takeover regulation strikes a balance between the interests of the offeror and the interests of the shareholders of the offeree. The offeree's shareholders are protected by numerous measures in the Takeover Code and by sell-out rights. One way in which the offeror's interests are protected is by granting the offeror with the right to 'squeeze-out' the remaining shareholders by compelling them to sell their shares to the offeror (CA 2006, s. 979). The rationale behind providing offerors with squeeze-out rights is that an offeror may want to acquire the offeree as a wholly-owned subsidiary. This goal should 'not [be] undermined by a small minority or because some shareholders cannot be traced' (*Re Greythorn Ltd* [2002] BCC 559 (Ch)).

An offeree can only exercise squeeze-out rights if it has acquired or unconditionally contracted to acquire:

- not less than 90% in value of the shares to which the offer relates; and
- in a case where the shares to which the offer relates are voting shares, not less than 90% of the voting rights carried by those shares (s. 979(2) and (4)).

An offeror who satisfies these two conditions can give notice to the remaining shareholders that it desires to acquire their shares (s. 979(2) and (4)). A shareholder who receives such a notice can challenge it (s. 986) but, given the significant majority required to exercise squeeze-out rights, such challenges will only succeed if there are very strong grounds for regarding the scheme as unfair (*Re Hoare & Co Ltd* [1933] All ER Rep 105 (Ch)). For an example of a case where unfairness was established, see *Re Bugle Press Ltd* [1961] Ch 270 (CA).

In the absence of a successful challenge, the offeror becomes entitled and bound to acquire the shares to which the notice relates (s. 981(2)).

Test yourself 16.3

1. **What are the three principal functions of the Takeover Panel?**
2. **What is the principal purpose of the Takeover Code?**
3. **Can the Panel ignore a rule in the Takeover Code?**
4. **Provide three examples of sanctions that can be imposed for a breach of the Takeover Code.**
5. **For how long must an offer remain open once the offer document has been published?**
6. **When will an offeror be required to make a mandatory offer?**
7. **What are squeeze-out and sell-out rights?**

Chapter summary

- A scheme of reconstruction allows a company (the transferor company) to transfer all or part of its business to another company (or companies), and the transferor company is then voluntarily wound up.
- A scheme of arrangement is a compromise or arrangement between a company and (i) its creditors, or any class of them; or (ii) its members, or any class of them.
- Implementing a scheme of arrangement is a three-stage process:
  - an application is made to the court to order that meetings of the relevant creditors/members be summoned;
  - the meetings are held to determine if the scheme is to be approved; and
  - an application is made to the court to sanction the scheme.
- A scheme of arrangement, once sanctioned by the court, will bind the company and those creditors/members affected by it.
- A takeover typically occurs where one company acquires sufficient shares in another company to take it over.
- The body responsible for regulating takeovers in the UK is the Panel on Takeovers and Mergers (Takeover Panel). The Panel's functions are:
  - it creates rules that regulate takeovers;
  - it provides rulings on the interpretation and application of the rules; and
  - it gives directions to restrain breaches of the rules.
- The body of rules created by the Takeover Panel is the City Code on Takeovers and Mergers (the Takeover Code).
- The Takeover Code consists of six General Principles and 38 rules.
- Breach of the Takeover Code can result in:
  - the offender being censured;
  - the offending conduct being disclosed to a regulator or professional body; and/or
  - the publication of a statement indicating that the offender is not someone who is likely to comply with the Code.
- Rule 9 of the Takeover Code provides that a person who acquires 30% or more of a company's voting rights must make an offer (known as a 'mandatory offer') to all the other shareholders to purchase their shares.
- If an offeror acquires 90% in value of the offeree's shares, and if those shares carry at least 90% of the offeree's voting rights, then the remaining shareholders of the offeree can require the offeror to purchase their shares.
- Where an offeror acquires 90% in value of the offeree's shares, then if those shares carry at least 90% of the offeree's voting rights, the offeror can compel the remaining shareholders of the offeree to sell their shares to the offeror.

Chapter seventeen
Corporate rescue

Contents

1. Introduction

This chapter outlines how the law seeks to help companies that are struggling financially. Such companies may be able to trade their way out of difficulty but often this is not possible. The UK's legislative framework provides two formal mechanisms that are designed to rescue struggling companies: the company voluntary arrangement (CVA) and administration. The chapter also looks at the concept of receivership.

Before looking at the two recue mechanisms, it is worth briefly looking at why UK company law decided to adopt a rescue culture.

2. The UK's rescue culture

The financial collapse of a company can adversely impact a wide range of persons. The shareholders' shares become worthless. Employees will lose their jobs. The company's creditors might go unpaid. The company's suppliers will lose business. Depending on the size of the company, the local or national economy might even be affected. To try and prevent these adverse effects, the 1982 Cork Committee recommended that the law should adopt a 'rescue culture' that would 'provide means for the preservation of viable commercial enterprises capable of making a useful contribution to the economic life of the country'. This has led to the creation of two rescue mechanisms: administration and the CVA.

As the Cork Committee's quote above indicates, these mechanisms are designed to try and rescue viable companies. They should not be used to try and rescue inefficient companies that are not economically viable. It is also important that these mechanisms strike a balance between the desire to rescue the company and the rights of the company's creditors. A failed rescue attempt could further reduce the pool of assets to which the creditors will look for payment.

2.1 Reform

The government has proposed a number of reforms to the UK's rescue regime (see BEIS, Insolvency and Corporate Governance: Government Response (BEIS 2018)), of which the two most notable are the introduction of a preliminary moratorium and a new restructuring plan. It should be noted that more detailed proposals will follow, which may differ from these current proposals.

A preliminary moratorium

A major advantage of administration is that it provides the company with a moratorium (a period within which a winding up petition cannot be brought and the creditors cannot enforce their security). A more limited moratorium is also available in relation to certain CVAs. A moratorium is not available outside of these instances.

The government has proposed to provide a moratorium to any company that has a legitimate reason for seeking protection. This will be determined based on the financial state of the company, particularly whether the company will become insolvent if action is not taken. There are other conditions that will need to be satisfied (on the balance of probabilities, the rescue should be more likely to succeed than not), and some companies are excluded from obtaining this moratorium (already insolvent companies are excluded).

If the moratorium is granted, it will be supervised by an insolvency practitioner known as the 'monitor'. The moratorium will initially last for 28 days but can be extended for a further 28 days. In certain cases, it may be possible to extend the moratorium further.

A flexible restructuring plan

One notable disadvantage of a CVA is that it cannot affect the rights of secured creditors without their consent. The government has decided that a more flexible restructuring plan is needed (although the CVA will continue to be available) that can bind all creditors – secured and unsecured.

The plan will be available to both solvent and insolvent companies, but some companies will be excluded (for example, those excluded from the small company CVA moratorium). The terms of the plan will be for the company to determine, with the process for entering into the plan being similar to that for a scheme of arrangement (discussed in Chapter 16). In order for the plan to come into effect, it will require the approval of at least 75% in value of the company's creditors within each class. The plan will also need to be confirmed by the court. If the plan is confirmed, it will bind all affected parties.

3. Administration

The Cork Report recommended that, in certain circumstances, a person should be able to appoint someone who could effectively take over the company's management and seek to rescue a financially struggling company. This led to the establishment of administration, the rules for which can be found in Part II and Schedules B1 and 1 of the IA 1986. Understanding the purpose of administration is key to understanding the role of the administrator.

3.1 The purpose of administration

Schedule B1, para 3(1) provides that the administrator of a company must perform his functions with the objective of:

(1) rescuing the company as a going concern;

(2) achieving a better result for the company's creditors as a whole than would be likely if the company were wound up (without first being in administration); or

(3) realising property in order to make a distribution to one or more secured or preferential creditors.

These three objectives are collectively referred to as 'the purpose of administration'. It is important to understand the relationship between them.

- Administrators are required to perform their functions in order to achieve objective (1) unless they think (i) it is not reasonably practicable to achieve that objective; or (ii) objective (2) would achieve a better result for the company's creditors as a whole (Schedule B1, para 3(3)). In either case, the administrator can perform his functions in order to achieve objective (2).
- Administrators may only perform their functions in order to achieve objective (3) if they think it is not reasonably practicable to achieve objectives (1) and (2), and they do not unnecessarily harm the interests of the company's creditors as a whole (Schedule B1, para 3(4)).

In practice, administrators have considerable discretion as to which objective to pursue, as the decision is based on what they 'think'. As a result, objective (1) is rarely pursued. The most common outcome of administration is that the business of the company is sold and the company is dissolved.

3.2 Entering administration

A company enters administration when the appointment of its administrator takes effect (Schedule B1, para 1(2)(b)). There are three limitations on who can be appointed as an administrator:

1. an administrator must be a qualified insolvency practitioner (Schedule B1, para 6);
2. a person cannot generally be appointed as administrator of a company that is already in administration (Schedule B1, para 7); and

3. a person cannot generally be appointed as administrator of a company that is in liquidation (Schedule B1, para 8(1)), although several exceptions are contained in Schedule B1, paras 37 and 38.

There are three ways to appoint an administrator. The first two methods tend to be the most popular as they are out of court procedures.

Appointment by the company or its directors

An administrator can be appointed by:

- the company (Schedule B1, para 22(1)): this power of appointment is exercised by the members passing an ordinary resolution, unless the company's articles provide that the board may appoint an administrator on behalf of the company; or
- the directors (Schedule B1, para 22(2)), providing that the majority of the directors agree to the appointment (Schedule B1, para 105).

Neither the company nor its directors can appoint an administrator:

- within 12 months of the ending of a previous administration initiated under para 22 (Schedule B1, para 23(2));
- within 12 months of the ending of a moratorium under Schedule A1 which failed to result in a CVA being in force (Schedule B1, para 24); or
- if (i) a petition to wind up the company has been presented and has not yet been disposed of; (ii) an administrative application has been made and is not yet disposed of; or (iii) an administrative receiver of the company is in office (Schedule B1, para 25).

The procedure for the company or its directors to appoint an administrator is as follows. The company or its directors must provide at least five business days' notice of their intention to appoint an administrator to:

- any person who could appoint an administrative receiver; or
- any person who could appoint an administrator by virtue of being a qualifying floating chargeholder (Schedule B1, para 26(1)).

This notice must be filed with the court, along with other specified documentation (Schedule B1, para 27). The person appointing the administrator must also file with the court a notice of appointment (Schedule B1, para 29). Once these relevant notices have been filed, the appointment of the administrator will take effect (Schedule B1, para 31).

Appointment by a qualifying floating chargeholder

The holder of a 'qualifying' floating charge over the company's property can appoint an administrator (Schedule B1, para 14(1)). A floating charge will qualify if:

- the instrument that created the charge states that para 14 applies to the charge, or that the chargeholder can appoint an administrator or administrative receiver (Schedule B1, para 14(2)); and

- the charge, on its own or together with other security held by the chargeholder, covers the whole, or substantially the whole, of the company's property (Schedule B1, para 14(3)).

A qualifying floating chargeholder will not be able to appoint an administrator if:

- the floating charge in question is not enforceable (Schedule B1, para 16); or
- a provisional liquidator has been appointed or an administrative receiver is in office (Schedule B1, para 17).

A qualifying floating chargeholder must provide at least two business days' written notice to any prior holder of a qualifying floating charge, unless the prior holder has consented in writing to the administrator being appointed (Schedule B1, para 15(1)).

The qualifying floating chargeholder must file a notice of appointment with the court (Schedule B1, para 18). The appointment of the administrator will take effect once this notice has been filed (Schedule B1, para 19).

Appointment by court order

The court can make an administration order to appoint a person as administrator of the company (Schedule B1, para 10). The court can only make an administration order following an application to the court which can only be made by specified persons, including:

- the company, the directors of the company, one or more creditors of the company, or a combination of these persons (Schedule B1, para 12(1));
- the supervisor of a CVA (s. 7(4)(b));
- the liquidator of the company (Schedule B1, para 38(1)); or
- the FCA (FSMA 2000, s. 359(1)).

The court will only make an administration order if two conditions are satisfied (even if they are satisfied, the court is not bound to make an order):

1. the company is unlikely to be able to pay its debts (note that this condition need not be satisfied if the applicant is able to appoint an administrator by virtue of being a qualifying floating chargeholder (Schedule B1, para 35)); and
2. the administration order is reasonably likely to achieve the purpose of administration (Schedule B1, para 11).

If the court decides to make the administration order, then the order takes effect at the time stated in the order. Where no time is stated in the order, the order takes effect when it is made (Schedule B1, para 13(2)).

3.3 The effects of entering administration

The reason why administration is the most popular rescue mechanism is because a number of beneficial effects occur once a company enters administration. These effects are designed to give administrators breathing space so they can attempt to fulfil the purpose of administration.

Dismissal of winding up petitions

The winding up of a company would frustrate the administrator's ability to fulfil the purpose of administration. Accordingly, a petition to wind up a company will be:

- dismissed if an administration order is made; and
- suspended if an administrator is appointed by a qualifying floating chargeholder (Schedule B1, para 40(1)).

The petition will not be dismissed or suspended if it is made on public interest grounds under s. 124A (Schedule B1, para 40(2)). The following example demonstrates how useful a dismissal or suspension can be.

Case study 17.1

Portsmouth Football Club, a Premier League club relegated to the Championship League at the end of the 2009–10 season, can be used to illustrate the interplay between administration, CVAs and compulsory winding up, including the effect of the appointment of an administrator on a winding up petition. The club has had the misfortune to see three companies that have owned it go into administration – in 1998, 2010 and again in 2012.

Portsmouth City Football Club Limited (Pompey)
Winding up and Administration Timeline

	Pompey failed to make scheduled payments to HMRC as they fell due.
23 December 2009	**HMRC filed a winding up petition in the High Court.**
	Ongoing negotiations between HMRC and Pompey to arrive at a settlement in relation to £7.5 million in unpaid taxes (unpaid Pay As You Earn (PAYE) deductions from wages, National Insurance (NI) contributions and Value Added Tax (VAT)).
19 January 2010	**High Court dismissed an application from Pompey for the winding up petition to be struck out.** **Pompey had seven days to lodge an appeal against the order.**

10 February 2010	**Winding up petition hearing.** **Court granted Pompey a nine-day adjournment requiring them to present a detailed financial breakdown of the state of the company (a 'statement of affairs'), within seven days with HMRC to have two days to examine the document.** **Winding up petition to be heard on the first available date after 19 February 2010.**
	Provisional date for hearing winding up petition fixed for 1 March 2010.
26 February 2010	**Pompey entered into administration when Portpin Ltd, a British Virgin Island company believed to have connections with Pompey's owner, appointed an administrator (in fact, three individuals were appointed to be joint administrator) pursuant to two charges held over Pompey assets.** **The appointment of the joint administrator suspended the winding up petition.**
2 March 2010	**High Court hearing of HMRC application for the court to consider the validity of the appointment of the joint administrator.** **Court ordered a hearing of the validity of the appointment of the joint administrator and ordered the production of documentary evidence of the charges.**
11 March 2010	**Having received documentation (including two debentures) proving the validity of the appointment of the joint administrator, HMRC withdrew its winding up petition and signed a consent order conditional upon the holding of a provisional creditors' meeting.**
25 March 2010	**Provisional creditors' meeting held.**
19 April 2010	**Joint administrator publishes a letter to all known creditors, together with:** ◆ **Formal notice of a creditors' meeting pursuant to para. 51 of the IA 1986 to be held on 6 May 2010.** ◆ **Statement setting out the proposals of the joint administrator to achieve the purpose of the administration pursuant to IA 1986, Sch. B1, para. 49.** ◆ **Proof of debt form.** ◆ **Proxy form.** **Resolutions to be voted on at the meeting were summarised as:** ◆ **Administrator to be authorised to draft a CVA proposal to be circulated to creditors.** ◆ **Creditors committee to be constituted.**

	◆ Joint administrator to be discharged from liability. ◆ Joint administration to be closed by the purpose being sufficiently achieved in accordance with Sch. B1, para. 80 by the company being placed into CVA. ◆ If CVA not approved, joint administrator to be able to exit via a creditors' voluntary liquidation (CVL), compulsory liquidation or dissolution as appropriate. ◆ Joint administrator to be authorised to achieve a sale of the business assets of the company in any manner they deem fit.
6 May 2010	Creditors' meeting held lasting five hours pursuant to IA 1986, Sch. B1, para. 51. Pompey debts disclosed to stand at £135 million. Resolutions approved (with modifications) by a majority of creditors, including resolution that the club should move from administration to liquidation via a CVA.
	Meeting to be convened to approve the CVA. Approval must be supported by 75% in value of the creditors. HMRC may have more than 25% of the debt.
17 June 2010	CVA approved by 81% by value of creditors. HMRC not allowed votes for c. £13 million debt and CVA provided for 100% payment of 'football creditors' but 20 pence in the pound for other creditors.
	HMRC lodged an appeal against the amount allowed as its debt on the vote and applied for the approval to be revoked or suspended based on unfair prejudice and material irregularity, under s. 6 of the IA 1986 and r. 1.17 of the Insolvency Rules1986 (SI 1986/1925).
5 August 2010	*HMRC v Portsmouth City Football Club Ltd (in administration) and others* [2010] EWHC 2013 (Ch): The High Court dismissed HMRC's claim.
24 October 2010	The business and assets (principally the Club) are sold to a new company, Portsmouth Football Club (2010) Ltd.
18 January 2011	Creditors' meeting resolved that Pompey move from administration to compulsory liquidation.
10 February 2011	Order of the court granted for Pompey to move to compulsory liquidation.
24 February 2011	Completion of the Pompey's CVA and exit from administration. Liquidation commences.
1 June 2011	Liquidators sells all of the shares in Portsmouth Football Club (2010) Ltd to Convers Sports Intiatives plc.

24 January 2012	**HMRC issue a winding up petition against Portsmouth Football Club (2010) Ltd for £1.6 million in unpaid taxes.**
13 February 2012	**Portsmouth Football Club (2010) Ltd goes into administration and HMRC's winding up petition was withdrawn.**
19 April 2013	**The assets of Portsmouth Football Club (2010) Ltd are transferred to a new company, Portsmouth Community Football Club Ltd, which is primarily owned by the Pompey Supporters' Trust.**
29 September 2014	**Pompey Supporters' Trust announces that the Club is debt-free after paying off all its creditors.**

Dismissal of receivers

When a company enters administration by virtue of an administration order, then any administrative receivers will vacate office (Schedule B1, para 41(1)). Where a company is in administration (irrespective of how the administrator was appointed), any receiver of part of the company's property shall vacate office if required by the administrator (Schedule B1, para 41(2)).

Moratorium on insolvency proceedings

Schedule B1, para 42 provides that no resolution may be passed for the winding up of the company, as long as a company is in administration, and no order may be made for the winding up of the company (except a public interest petition, Schedule B1, para 42(4)(a)).

Moratorium on other legal processes

Schedule B1, para 43 provides that as long as a company is in administration, then unless the consent of the administrator or the permission of the court is obtained:

- no step can be taken to enforce security over the company's property;
- no step can be taken to repossess goods in the company's possession under a hire-purchase agreement;
- a landlord cannot exercise a right of forfeiture by re-entry; and
- no legal process may be commenced or continued against the company or its property.

Interim moratorium

The moratoriums discussed above only come into effect when a company enters administration. Prior to a company entering administration, a company can be wound up or the above legal processes may be instigated (for example, a creditor may enforce his security). This could serve to frustrate the purpose of administration. To combat this, the IA 1986 provides for an interim moratorium, which applies:

- where an administration application has been made and the application has not yet been granted or dismissed, or the application has been granted but has not yet taken effect (Schedule B1, para 44(1)); or
- in the time between a qualifying floating chargeholder filing a notice of appointment with the court up until:
  - the date of the appointment of the administrator taking effect; or
  - five business days following the filing and no administrator has been appointed (Schedule B1, para 44(2)).

An interim moratorium has the same effects as a standard moratorium (Schedule B1, para 44(5)).

Exercise of managerial powers by the directors

The directors do not automatically vacate office when a company enters administration (although the administrator can remove directors). In practice, the powers of the directors are suspended as the IA 1986 provides that the company and any officer of the company cannot exercise a management power without the consent of the administrator (Schedule B1, para 64(1)).

Publicity

The effects of administration clearly impact upon persons who have dealt with and deal with the company. For example, a prospective creditor might decide not to lend to a company in administration as it may not be able to enforce any security it might have. It is important that persons who deal with a company in administration are made aware of this. While a company is in administration, every business document issued by or on behalf of the company or the administrator, and all the company's websites, must state the name of the administrator and that the affairs, business and property of the company are being managed by the administrator (Schedule B1, para 45(1)).

3.4 The role of an administrator

The administrator's role is to attempt to achieve the purpose of administration. Accordingly, within eight weeks of being appointed, the administrator must make a statement setting out proposals for achieving the purpose of administration (Schedule B1, para 49(1)). This statement must be sent to the registrar of companies, every creditor, and every member (Schedule B1, para 49(4)).

Within 10 weeks of the company entering administration, the administrator must seek a decision from the company's creditors as to whether they approve the proposals (Schedule B1, para 51(1)–(2)), although Schedule B1, para 52 provides that the creditors' decision need not be sought if:

- the company has sufficient property to pay each creditor in full;
- the company has insufficient property to enable a distribution to be made to the unsecured creditors (other than the prescribed part); or
- the first two purposes of administration (See Schedule B1, para 3(1)(a) and (b)) cannot be achieved.

If a creditors' decision is required, then two methods exist to determine whether they approve the administrator's proposals. The administrator can choose whether to use:

- the qualifying decision procedure, with the details of this procedure (how the result of the decision is determined, whether the decision is taken by correspondence, physical meeting or electronic meeting) to be decided by the administrator (s. 246ZA(2)); or
- the 'deemed consent procedure', under which the proposal will be approved unless 10% of the creditors in value object to the proposal (s. 246ZF). If such a percentage does object, then the decision will be deemed not to have been made and, if a decision on the same matter is sought again, it must be sought using a qualifying decision procedure (s. 246ZF(5)).

If the creditors approve the administrator's proposals, the administrator must manage the company in accordance with those proposals (Schedule B1, para 68(1)(a)). If the creditors do not approve the proposals, then the court may:

- terminate the administrator's appointment;
- adjourn the hearing conditionally or unconditionally;
- make an interim order;
- make an order on a petition for winding up; or
- make any other order that it thinks appropriate (Schedule B1, para 55(2)).

3.5 The powers of an administrator

The administrator is given extremely broad powers to achieve the purposes of administration, being able to 'do anything necessary or expedient for the management of the affairs, business and property of the company' (Schedule B1, para 59(1)). Schedule 1 provides a list of 23 more specific powers, including the power to:

- take possession of, collect and get in the property of the company, and, for that purpose, to take such proceedings as may seem to him expedient;
- sell or otherwise dispose of the property of the company by public auction or private contract;
- raise or borrow money and grant security over the company's property;
- bring or defend any action or other legal proceedings in the name and on behalf of the company;
- appoint agents and appoint and dismiss employees;
- make any payment that is necessary or incidental to the performance of his functions;
- carry on the business of the company and establish subsidiaries of the company; and
- present or defend a petition for the winding up of the company.

Further specific powers are listed in Schedule B1, paras 61–63, including the power to:

- appoint or remove a director;
- call a meeting of the company's members or seek a decision from the company's creditors; and
- apply to the court for directions in connection with his functions.

In addition to these specific powers, the administrator will be empowered to engage in certain acts on behalf of the company by virtue of his status as an officer (Schedule B1, para 5) and agent (Schedule B1, para 69) of the company.

Pre-packs

The administrator's power to sell the company's property has led to an interesting development. Administrators can exercise their powers as soon as they are appointed, which includes the ability to sell the company's property. This has led to the development of pre-packaged administrations (or 'pre-packs'), which tend to operate as follows.

Case study 17.2

X-Corp plc is experiencing financial difficulties and is unable to pay its debts. The board is considering appointing an administrator. Y-Corp plc approaches the board of X-Corp and indicates that it is willing to purchase X-Corp's assets. Prior to X-Corp entering administration, X-Corp appoints a qualified insolvency practitioner to negotiate a draft agreement between X-Corp and Y-Corp, under which Y-Corp will acquire all the assets and business of X-Corp. The directors of X-Corp appoint the insolvency practitioner as its administrator, and the next day the agreement is entered into for the sale of X-Corp's assets and business.

Paragraph 1 of Statement of Insolvency Practice 16 defines a pre-pack as 'an arrangement under which the sale of all or part of a company's business or assets is negotiated with a purchaser prior to the appointment of an administrator and the administrator effects the sale immediately on, or shortly after, appointment'.

The problem with pre-packs is that, as the above example demonstrates, the creditors of X-Corp have not had the chance to approve the sale. It may be that it will hinder their chances of being repaid. The courts have sought to remedy this concern by strongly stating that a pre-pack should only be implemented if it is in the interests of the company's creditors (*Re Transbus International Ltd* [2004] EWHC 932 (Ch); *DKLL Solicitors v Revenue and Customs Commissioners* [2007] EWHC 2067 (Ch)).

Statement of Insolvency Practice 16 also requires the administrator to provide the creditors with a 'SIP 16 statement' that sets out how the administrator has acted with due regard for the creditors' interests and justifies why the pre-pack was entered into.

3.6 Ending administration

A company ceases to be in administration when the administrator's appointment ceases (Schedule B1, para 1(2)(c)). This can occur in a number of ways. As administration adversely affects the company's creditors (by preventing them from enforcing their security), it is vital that a company does not remain in administration for an excessive period for time. Schedule B1, para 4 therefore provides that administrators must perform their functions as quickly and efficiently as is reasonably practicable. This is backed up by Schedule B1, para 76(1), which provides that an administrator's appointment will cease one year after it takes effect. This can be extended in two ways.

1. The administrator can apply to the court for an order extending their appointment for a specified period (Schedule B1, para 76(2)(a)). The court can grant as many extensions as it wishes. However, an extension cannot be granted after the administrator's term of office has expired (Schedule B1, para 77(1)(b)).
2. The administrator's appointment can be extended once, for up to one year, by obtaining the consent of each secured creditor and, if the company has any, the unsecured creditors (Schedule B1, paras 76(2)(b) and 78).

An administrator's appointment can also cease in a number of other ways.

- The administrator can apply to the court if they think that: (i) the purpose of administration cannot be achieved; (ii) the company should not have entered administration; or (iii) the company's creditors make an application under Schedule B1, para 79. The court can then provide that the administrator's appointment will cease from a specified time (Schedule B1, para 79).
- If the administrator thinks that the purpose of administration has been sufficiently achieved, they can file a notice with the court and the Registrar of Companies (Schedule B1, para 80(2)). Once these filings have been made, the administrator's appointment ceases (Schedule B1, para 80(3)).
- A creditor may apply to the court for an order ending the appointment of the administrator if they can show that the motive for appointing the administrator was improper (Schedule B1, para 81).
- Where a company in administration is the subject of a winding up petition in the public interest, then the court shall either order:
  - that the administrator's appointment will cease (which is usually the case); or
  - that the administrator's appointment shall continue to have effect (Schedule B1, para 82).
- Where the administrator thinks that the total amount which each secured creditor of the company is likely to receive has been paid or set aside, and that a distribution will be made to unsecured creditors (other than the prescribed part), then the administrator may file a notice with the registrar of companies (Schedule B1, para 83(1) and (3)). The registrar will register the notice, at which point the appointment of the administrator will

cease, and the administration will be converted to a creditors' voluntary winding up (Schedule B1, para 83(4) and (6)). If the company's creditors have not nominated a liquidator, the administrator will act as the liquidator (Schedule B1, para 7).

- If the administrator of a company thinks that the company has no property to distribute to its creditors, they should send a notice to that effect to the registrar of companies (Schedule B1, para 84(1)). The registrar will register the notice and, three months later, the company is deemed to be dissolved (Schedule B1, para 84(3) and (6)).

Test yourself 17.1

1. **What is the purpose of administration?**
2. **What are the three methods of appointing an administrator?**
3. **Briefly outline the effects of administration.**
4. **What is a pre-pack?**
5. **When will a company cease to be in administration?**

4. Company voluntary arrangements

Part I (ss. 1–7B) and Schedule A1 of the IA 1986 allow a company to enter into a binding arrangement with its creditors that is known as a company voluntary arrangement (CVA). A CVA is an insolvency procedure and so is used by insolvent companies to try to rescue the business. CVAs are considerably less popular than administration but, in recent months, a notable number of high street companies (e.g. Mothercare, House of Fraser, Toys 'R' Us) have implemented CVAs in an attempt to rescue their businesses.

Stop and think 17.1

In 2018, 356 companies entered into a CVA, compared to 1,464 companies that entered administration. Why do you think CVAs are so much less popular compared to administration?

4.1 Implementing a CVA

The process of implementing a CVA begins with a proposed arrangement between the company and its creditors. A proposal for a CVA may come from:

- the company's directors, providing that the company is not in administration or liquidation (s. 1(1));

- the company's administrator, if the company is in administration (s. 1(3)(a)); or
- the company's liquidator, if the company is in liquidation (s. 1(3)(b)).

The nominee

The CVA will need to be supervised by a qualified insolvency practitioner (s. 1(2)) known as a 'nominee'. The rules relating to nominees depend upon the status of the company. If the company is in administration, then the administrator can act as nominee. If the company is in liquidation, the liquidator can act as nominee. In either case, the nominee shall summon a meeting of the company and seek a decision from the company's creditors as to whether they approve the proposal (s. 3(2)).

Where the nominee is not an administrator or liquidator (which occurs where the directors propose the CVA or the administrator/liquidator decides not to act as nominee) and the directors are not seeking a moratorium, a nominee will have to be appointed. That nominee must, within 28 days of being given notice of the proposed CVA, submit a report to the court stating whether:

- the proposed CVA has a reasonable prospect of being approved and implemented;
- the proposal should be considered by a meeting of the company and by the company's creditors; and
- the date on which, and time and place at which, he proposes a meeting of the company should be held if necessary (s. 2(2)).

If the nominee states that the proposal should be considered by the company and its creditors, he will summon a meeting of the company and seek a decision from the company's creditors (s. 3(1)).

Approval of the proposal

The proposed CVA will need to be approved by the company and its creditors.

- The nominee must invite the company's members to a meeting to consider the proposed CVA to obtain the company's approval (IR 2016, r 2.25(1)). The members, who must be provided with at least 14 days' notice of the meeting, will approve the proposal if a majority of them (in value) vote in favour of the proposal (IR 2016, r 2.36(1)).
- The creditors will approve the proposal by way of a qualifying decision procedure (IA 1986, s. 3(3)). The details of this procedure (e.g. venue, how the decision is to be decided) will be determined by the nominee (IA 1986, s. 246ZE(2)). Alternatively, the 'deemed consent procedure' can be used, under which the proposal will be approved unless 10% of the creditors in value object to the proposal (IA 1986, s. 246ZF).

Both the company and creditors can approve the proposal as is or they can approve it with modifications (IA 1986, s. 4(1)). However, a proposal or modification cannot be approved if:

- it affects the right of a secured creditor of the company to enforce his security, except with the concurrence of the creditor concerned (IA 1986, s. 4(3)); or
- it affects the priority of any preferential debt, unless the preferential creditor concerned concurs (IA1986, s. 4(4)).

The decisions of the company and the creditors must be reported to the court (IA 1986, s. 4(6) and (6A)). If the decisions of the company and the creditors conflict, the decision of the creditors prevails (IA 1986, s. 4A(2)(b)). However, a member can apply to the court within 28 days of the decisions. The court may:

- order that the decision of the meeting of the company shall have effect; or
- make any other order that it sees fit (IA 1986, s. 4A(3) and (6)).

If the proposal is approved by both the company and its creditors, it will come into effect at the time when the creditors approved it (IA 1986, s. 5(2)(a)). The nominee will supervise the CVA and will become known as the 'supervisor' (IA 1986, s. 7(2)). The CVA will bind every person who was entitled to vote in the qualifying decision procedure by which the creditors' decision was made, or would have been so entitled if they had notice of it (IA 1986, s. 5(2)(b)).

If the company is in administration or being liquidated, the court can:

- stay the winding up or terminate the administrator's appointment; or
- give such directions with respect to the winding up or administration as it thinks appropriate for facilitating the implementation of the CVA (IA 1986, s. 5(3)).

Challenging the CVA

Within 28 days of the report of the meeting being given to the court, a nominee, liquidator, administrator or anyone who had a right to vote as a member or creditor, can apply to the court on the ground that:

- the CVA unfairly prejudices the interests of a creditor, member or contributory of the company; and/or
- there has been some material irregularity at or in relation to the meeting of the company, or in relation to the decision procedure in which the creditors decided to approve the CVA (IA 1986, s. 6(1)–(3)).

If the court agrees with the applicant, it can:

- revoke or suspend any decision approving the CVA;
- give directions for a further meeting of the company to be convened to consider a revised proposal; or
- direct any person to seek a decision from the creditors as to whether they approve the revised proposal (IA 1986, s. 6(4)).

During the implementation of the CVA, if any creditor or any other person is dissatisfied by any act, omission or decision of the supervisor, they may apply to the court and the court may:

- confirm, reverse or modify any act or decision of the supervisor;
- give the supervisor directions; or
- make such other order as it thinks fit (IA 1986, s. 7(3)).

4.2 The small company moratorium

One reason why administration is more popular than a CVA is because administration comes with a statutory moratorium, whereas a CVA generally does not. As a result, a CVA is rather fragile: it can be frustrated by the appointment of a receiver or by petitioning the court for a winding up order. The Insolvency Act 2000 amended the IA 1986 to provide a form of CVA with a moratorium. However, a CVA with a moratorium is only available to 'eligible companies' (IA 1986, s. 1A), namely those companies that are classified as 'small companies' under s. 382(3) of the CA 2006 (IA 1986, Schedule A1, para 3(2)(a)). A company will be small if it satisfies two of the following three conditions:

1. it has a turnover of not more than £10.2 million;
2. it has a balance sheet total of not more than £5.1 million; or
3. it has no more than 50 employees.

Schedule A1, paras 4–4C provide that certain companies will not be eligible for the moratorium, including:

- a company in administration;
- a company that is being wound up;
- a company that is already subject to a CVA; or
- a company that has had a moratorium in force at any time during the previous 12 months.

If the directors of an eligible company wish to obtain a moratorium, they must submit to the nominee a document setting out the terms of the proposed CVA and a statement of the company's affairs (Schedule A1, para 6(1)). The nominee will then submit to the directors a statement indicating, whether or not:

- the proposed CVA has a reasonable prospect of being approved and implemented;
- if the company is likely to have sufficient funds available to it during the proposed moratorium to enable it to carry on its business; and
- the proposed CVA should be considered by a meeting of the company and the company's creditors (Schedule A1, para 6(2)).

The directors of the company must then file specified documents with the court, including the terms of the proposed CVA, a statement of the company's affairs, a statement from the nominee consenting to act, and a statement from the nominee that the proposed CVA has a reasonable prospect of being approved and implemented (Schedule A1, para 7(1)). As soon as these documents are filed, the moratorium comes into effect (Schedule A1, para 8(1)) and the directors must notify the nominee of this (Schedule A1, para 9(1)).

While the moratorium is in effect:

- no petition may be presented to wind up the company, and no resolution may be passed to wind up the company;
- no meeting of the company can be called, except with the consent of the nominee or leave of the court;
- no administrator can be appointed by the company, its directors or by a qualifying floating chargeholder, nor can an administrative receiver be appointed; and
- no other steps may be taken to enforce any security over the company's property, or to repossess goods in the company's possession under any hire-purchase agreement, except with the leave of the court and subject to such terms as the court may impose (Schedule A1, para 12(1)).

The moratorium ends on the day on which the meeting of the company is first held or the day on which the company's creditors decide to approve the CVA (whichever is the later) (Schedule A1, para 8(2)). If neither of these events have occurred within 28 days of the moratorium commencing, then the moratorium will end at the end of day 28 unless an extension to the moratorium is sought (Schedule A1, para 8(2)–(4)). The members or creditors may decide to extend the moratorium by up to two months (Schedule A1, para 32). Once the moratorium comes to an end, the nominee must advertise this fact. The nominee must also notify the court, the registrar of companies, the company and any creditor of the company (Schedule A1, para 11(1)).

Test yourself 17.2

1. **What is a CVA?**
2. **Who can propose, and act as nominee for, a CVA?**
3. **How is a CVA approved?**
4. **When will a company be eligible for a CVA with a moratorium?**
5. **What are the effects of the moratorium?**

5. Receivership

Receivership is not a rescue mechanism. It is instead a mechanism that allows a secured creditor to recover what is owed to them. Although receivership is rarely used, it is worth briefly discussing.

A secured creditor can appoint a receiver in one of two ways.

1. The loan agreement or charge instrument between the creditor and the company might give the creditor the right to appoint a receiver.

The receiver's duty is to the creditor who appointed him, and his client's interests will trump those of the company or other creditors.

2. The creditor can apply to the court, and the court can then appoint a receiver (IA 1986, s. 32). In this situation, the receiver's duty is to the court and he does not need to follow the creditor's instructions.

The receiver's principal role is to seize the secured assets, sell them and then use the proceeds to satisfy the debt of the creditor who appointed him. It may be the case that the loan agreement provides that the receiver will also be appointed as an agent of the company, in which case the receiver will be able to enter into certain acts on the company's behalf and may even have powers of management akin to those of the directors.

5.1 Administrative receivership

Brief mention should be made of administrative receivership. An administrative receiver is a receiver or manager of the whole (or substantially the whole) of a company's property. They are appointed by or on behalf of the holders of any debentures of the company secured by floating charge (IA 1986, s. 29(2)(a)). As floating charges tend to be taken over the entire company's business, administrative receivers have considerable powers that often displace those of the directors.

The concept of administrative receivership was largely abolished by the Enterprise Act 2002, but floating chargeholders whose charges were registered before 15 September 2003 will still have the power to appoint an administrative receiver (IA 1986, s. 72A; Insolvency Act 1986, Section 72A (Appointed Date) Order 2003, SI 2003/2095, article 2).

Chapter summary

- The purpose of administration is:
  - to rescue the company as a going concern;
  - achieve a better result for the company's creditors as a whole than would be likely if the company were wound up (without first being in administration); or
  - realise property in order to make a distribution to one or more secured or preferential creditors.
- A company enters administration once an administrator is appointed. An administrator can be appointed by the company, its directors, a qualifying floating chargeholder or by the court.
- Once a company enters administration, winding up petitions and receivers are dismissed, and there is a moratorium on insolvency proceedings and other legal processes (e.g. creditors cannot enforce their security).
- The administrator must set out proposals for fulfilling the purpose of administration and, generally, these proposals must be put for approval to the company's creditors.

- A company ceases to be in administration when the administrator's appointment ceases. This can happen automatically (for example, the administrator's appointment will automatically cease after one year unless it is extended) or through the action of certain persons (for example, the administrator can apply to the court to end the administrator's appointment in certain cases).
- A CVA is a binding arrangement between a company and its creditors.
- A CVA can be proposed by:
  - the directors;
  - an administrator (if the company is in administration); or
  - a liquidator (if the company is in liquidation).
- The CVA will need to be supervised by a qualified insolvency practitioner who is initially known as the 'nominee'. Once the CVA comes into effect, the nominee will become known as the 'supervisor'.
- The proposed CVA will need to be approved by the company and its creditors.
- A CVA does not normally come with a moratorium, but a CVA with a moratorium is available to small companies.
- Receivership is a mechanism that allows a secured creditor to recover what is owed.

Chapter eighteen
Liquidation and dissolution

Contents

1. Introduction

This chapter outlines the processes for liquidating a company and bringing its existence to an end. The bulk of this chapter will focus on the different types of liquidation, the role and powers of the liquidator and the imposition of liability on persons who engage in certain conduct prior to or while a company is in liquidation. It then concludes by looking at how a company's existence can be ended and how a dissolved company can be resurrected.

2. When is a company insolvent?

A company does not need to be insolvent to be liquidated or dissolved. Even so, the focus of this chapter is on insolvent liquidations. A company is insolvent when it cannot pay its debts. Section 123(1) of the IA 1986 provides that a company is unable to pay its debts:

- if a creditor, who is owed more than £750, leaves at the company's office a statutory demand requiring the company to pay the sum due and the company has not paid the sum within three weeks;
- if a judgment has been executed against the company in the UK, and the company fails to satisfy that judgment; or

- if it is proved to the satisfaction of the court that the company is unable to pay its debts as they fall due.

Section 123(2) goes on to provide that a company is deemed unable to pay its debts if it is proved to the satisfaction of the court that the value of the company's assets is less than the amount of its liabilities, taking into account its contingent and prospective liabilities.

3. Liquidation

Before a company's existence can come to an end, its affairs need to be brought to a close. The company's assets must be collected and used to pay off the company's debts and liabilities, with the remainder being distributed to persons so entitled. This resolving of the company's affairs prior to it being dissolved is known as 'liquidation' or 'winding up'. It should be noted that not all companies are liquidated prior to being dissolved (indeed, most companies that are dissolved are not liquidated, as discussed on page 371). A company can be liquidated irrespective of whether it is solvent or insolvent.

A company in liquidation is required to state that it is being wound up:

- on every invoice, order for goods, business letter or order form issued by or on behalf the company or the liquidator; and
- on all the company's websites (s. 188(1)).

There are two types of liquidation:

1. voluntary winding up
2. winding up by the court.

3.1 Voluntary winding up

The Cork Committee (whose recommendations ultimately led to the IA 1986) stated that '[t]he purpose of voluntary winding up is to avoid involving the courts and to allow the company and its creditors to settle affairs between themselves with, however, recourse to the court in the case of difficulty or dispute'. It is therefore unsurprising that the vast majority of liquidations are voluntary as they are usually faster and less costly than a winding up by the court.

A voluntary winding up is commenced by the company passing a special resolution stating that it be wound up voluntarily (IA 1986, s. 84(1)(b)). The winding up is deemed to have commenced as soon as this resolution is passed (s. 86), which results in the following consequences:

- the company shall cease to carry on its business, except so far as may be required for its beneficial winding up (s. 87(1)); and
- any transfer of shares (except a transfer made to or with the sanction of the liquidator), and any alteration in the status of the company's members is void (s. 88).

Members' and creditors' voluntary winding up

There are two types of voluntary winding up:

- a members' voluntary winding up
- a creditors' voluntary winding up.

The difference between them is based on whether the directors make a declaration of solvency. This declares that:

- the directors have made a full inquiry into the company's affairs; and
- they have formed the opinion that the company will be able to pay its debts in full within such a period as specified in the declaration (this period cannot exceed 12 months from the date of the commencement of the winding up) (s. 89(1)).

If this declaration is made in the five-week period before the special resolution is passed, the winding up will be a members' voluntary winding up (ss. 89(2)(a) and 90). The winding up will be a creditors' voluntary winding up if no declaration is made (s. 90) or if the liquidator disagrees with the opinion of the directors that the company will be able to pay its debts (ss. 95 and 96).

A members' voluntary winding up is only available to solvent companies, whereas a creditors' winding up is available to both solvent and insolvent companies (although most will be insolvent).

3.2 Winding up by the court

Certain persons may apply to the court for an order winding up a company (this is almost always known as a 'compulsory winding up'). Under s. 124(1) of the IA 1986, the following persons can apply to the court:

- the company (such applications are rare, as the company would likely prefer a voluntary winding up);
- the directors of the company;
- any creditor or creditors of the company, including any contingent or prospective creditor or creditors (most applications are brought by creditors of the company);
- a contributory or contributories (s. 79(1) provides that a 'contributory' is a person liable to contribute to the assets of the company upon it being wound up (e.g. a shareholder whose shares are not fully paid for);
- a liquidator within the meaning of Article 3(1) of the EU Regulation on Insolvency Proceedings; and
- the designated officer in a magistrates' court.

The Secretary of State can also apply to the court on specified grounds (s. 124(4)).

Grounds for a winding up petition

Section 122(1) provides that a company may be wound up by the court if:

- the company has, by special resolution, resolved that the company be wound up by the court;
- being a public company which was registered as such on its original incorporation, the company has not been issued with a trading certificate and more than a year has expired since it was registered;
- it is an old public company, within the meaning of Schedule 3 to the Companies Act 2006 (Consequential Amendments, Transitional Provisions and Savings) Order 2009;
- the company does not commence its business within a year from its incorporation or suspends its business for a whole year;
- the company is unable to pay its debts (this is, by far, the most popular ground for winding up);
- at the time at which a moratorium for the company under s. 1A comes to an end, no CVA has effect in relation to the company; or
- the court is of the opinion that it is just and equitable that the company should be wound up.

In addition, s. 124A provides that the Secretary of State may apply for a winding up order where it is expedient in the public interest that a company should be wound up.

The effects of winding up

In the majority of cases, a compulsory winding up will be deemed to commence at the time when the winding up application is presented to the court (s. 129(2)). The court may appoint a provisional liquidator at any time between the winding up petition being presented and the winding up order being made (s. 135(1) and (2)). A provisional liquidator cannot wind up the company – only the liquidator can do that. Instead, the role of the provisional liquidator is 'to keep things in status quo and to prevent anybody from getting priority' (*Re Dry Docks Corporation of London* (1888) 39 ChD 306 (Ch) (Kay J)).

A compulsory winding up has the following effects.

- A liquidator will need to be appointed. Once the winding up order is made, the **official receiver** attached to the court will become the company's liquidator, until such time as another person is appointed (s. 136(2)). The company's creditors and contributories can nominate another person to act as liquidator (s. 139(2)) if they so wish. If the creditors nominate a person to act as liquidator, and the contributories nominate another person, the person nominated by the creditors shall be the liquidator (s. 139(3)). If the creditors have not made such a nomination, the person nominated by the contributories will become the liquidator (s. 139(3)). Alternatively, the official receiver himself can apply to the Secretary of State to have someone appointed in his place (s. 137(1)).

official receiver
A civil servant and officer of the court, who can act as provisional liquidator or liquidator of a company.

- Once a winding up order is made or a provisional liquidator has been appointed, no action or proceeding shall be proceeded with or commenced against the company or its property, except by leave of the court and subject to such terms as the court may impose (s. 130(2)).
- The liquidator or provisional liquidator (as the case may be) shall take into his custody or under his control all the property to which the company is, or appears to be, entitled (s. 144(1)).
- The directors will cease to hold office and the liquidator takes over the directors' powers (*Measures Bros Ltd v Measures* [1910] 2 Ch 248 (CA)).
- Any disposition of the company's property, and any transfer of shares, or alteration in the status of the company's members, made after the commencement of the winding up is void, unless the court orders otherwise (s. 127(1)).

Test yourself 18.1

1. **What is liquidation?**
2. **When is liquidation deemed to commence?**
3. **What are the two types of voluntary winding up, and what are the differences between them?**
4. **Name five types of person who can petition the court for a winding up order.**
5. **On what grounds can a compulsory winding up order be made?**

4. The role of the liquidator

Section 143(1) of the IA 1986 (which applies to compulsory windings up) states that the functions of the liquidator are 'to secure that the assets of the company are got in, realised and distributed to the company's creditors and, if there is a surplus, to the persons entitled to it' (a similar provision can be found in s. 107 in relation to voluntary windings up). When undertaking these functions, the liquidator acts as an agent of, and owes his duties to, the company (*Knowles v Scott* [1981] 1 Ch 717 (Ch)).

In order to undertake these functions, the IA 1986 empowers the liquidator to:

- swell the company's assets by commencing legal proceedings against certain persons who have engaged in specified forms of malpractice (discussed on page 358);
- adjust certain transactions that occurred prior to the company entering liquidation (discussed on page 364);
- exercise the powers in Schedule 4 (ss. 165–167), which include paying off a class of creditor, and entering into arrangements with the creditors;

- disclaim onerous property (s. 178), such as any unprofitable contract and other property of the company which is unsaleable or not readily saleable or is such that it may give rise to a liability to pay money or perform any other onerous act;
- require a person to deliver to the liquidator certain property, books, papers or records (s. 234);
- provide the liquidator with such information as the liquidator may reasonably require (s. 235); and
- the court can, upon an application from the liquidator, summon certain persons (such as officers of the company) to appear before it, and require them to submit an account of their dealings with the company or produce any books, papers or other records relating to the company (s. 236).

In some cases, the official receiver or liquidator will be under a duty to investigate and report on certain matters:

- where a company enters insolvent liquidation or administration, the liquidator or administrator must send a report to the Secretary of State that describes any conduct of a director occurring in the previous three years that may assist the Secretary of State in deciding whether to seek a disqualification order under s. 6 of the CDDA 1986 or accept a disqualification undertaking (CDDA 1986, s. 7A);
- where a winding up order is made by the court, the official receiver is under a duty to investigate:
  - the causes of the company's failure (if it did fail); and
  - the promotion, formation, business dealings and affairs of the company (IA 1986, s. 132(1)).

The official receiver may report to the court on these issues.

4.1 The distribution of assets

Once the liquidator has got in and realised the company's assets, their job is to apply those assets 'in satisfaction of the company's liabilities pari passu …' (s. 107, which applies to compulsory windings up – a similar rule relating to voluntary windings up is found in r 14.12 of the IR 2016). The ***pari passu*** principle states that the liquidator will distribute the assets to the creditors in proportion to the size of their claim against the company (each creditor will receive an equal proportion of the debt owed to it). The following example demonstrates this in action.

pari passu
'With equal step.'

Case study 18.1

X-Corp Ltd is in the process of being liquidated. The liquidator gathers in the assets and, after deducting the liquidation expenses, £1,000 remains. The company has no other preferential creditors or secured creditors, but it owes £2,000 to four unsecured creditors:

- **X-Corp borrowed £1,000 from BigBank plc;**
- **X-Corp's bank account with SmallBank Ltd is overdrawn by £500;**
- **X-Corp owes £250 each to two suppliers, BuildTech Ltd and Toolbox Ltd.**

The following table sets out how much each creditor is owed and, under the *pari passu* principle, how the £1,000 is distributed among them.

Creditor	Is Owed	Receives
BigBank plc	£1,000	£500
SmallBank Ltd	£500	£250
BuildTech Ltd	£250	£125
Toolbox Ltd	£250	£125

Each creditor is said to receive '50 pence in the pound' (i.e. each creditor receives 50% of the debt that is owed to it).

In practice, it may not be the case that every creditor will be paid *pari passu*, as certain types of debt are prioritised or subordinated to other types of debt:

- statute provides that certain types of debt must be paid ahead of, or rank behind, other types of debt; and
- a creditor can prioritise their claim over certain other claims by taking security over the company's assets.

The order of distribution

Figure 18.1 sets out the order in which the liquidator must distribute the company's assets.

As the liquidator pays each debt in turn, higher-ranking debts have a better chance of being paid than lower-ranking debts. If there are not enough assets to pay of a class of creditor in full, they are generally paid *pari passu* (subject to some exceptions noted below), and creditors who rank below that class will not receive anything.

It will be noted that certain types of creditor do not appear in Fig. 18.1 and this is because their claims will be over property that is not available to the liquidator for distribution.

Property or assets of the company that are subject to a fixed charge do not fall within the order of distribution set out in Fig. 18.1. The fixed chargeholder can simply take possession of the charged property, sell it and use the proceeds to satisfy his debt. If the proceeds exceed the debt owed, the chargeholder must return the excess to the liquidator. If the proceeds do not satisfy the chargeholder's debt, the outstanding debt will rank as unsecured (unless the chargeholder has additional security over the property).

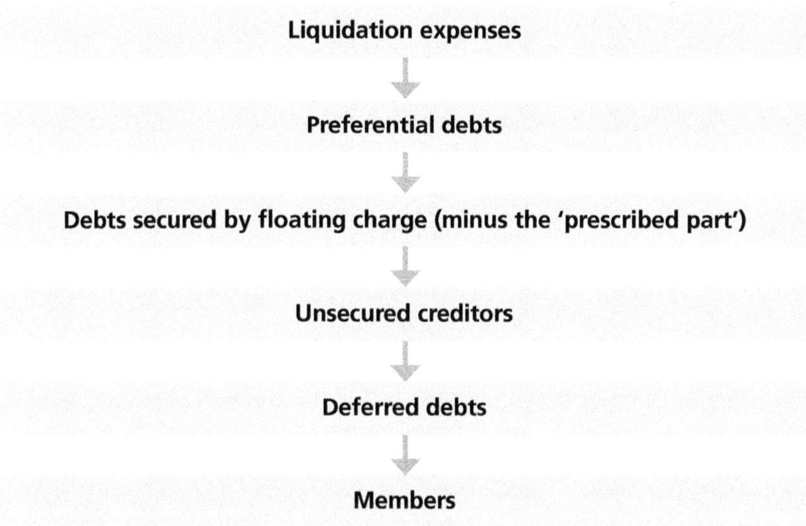

Figure 18.1 The order of distribution

A seller may sell goods to the company subject to a retention of title clause, which will provide that the goods remain the property of the seller until they are fully paid for. If the company goes into liquidation at a time when the goods have not been fully paid for, the seller can recover the goods.

Liquidation expenses

The liquidator will first pay off the liquidation expenses (IA 1986, ss. 115 and 175(1)–(1A)). What is covered here are the *liquidation* expenses, and not merely the *liquidator's* expenses. This is made clear by r 7.108(1) of the Insolvency (England and Wales) Rules 2016 (IR 2016) which provides that '[a]ll fees, costs, charges and other expenses incurred in the course of the winding up are to be treated as expenses of the winding up'. Liquidation expenses can take a number of different forms, with r 7.108(4) identifying 18 types of liquidation expenses. These types of liquidation expenses are not paid *pari passu*, but are instead paid off in the order as set out in r 7.108(4).

Preferential debts

Once the liquidation expenses have been paid and if any funds remain, the liquidator will pay off the company's preferential debts as identified in Schedule 6 of the IA 1986 (IA 1986, s. 365). Preferential debts include:

- contributions to occupational pension schemes; and
- certain remuneration owed to employees (but only the first £800 ranks as preferential).

Crown debts (such as sums owed to HMRC) used to rank as preferential, but this is no longer the case. They will rank as unsecured debts.

The various types of preferential debts are classified as either 'ordinary' or 'secondary' preferential debts (IA 1986, s. 386(1A) and (1B)). The ordinary preferential debts will be paid first, followed by the secondary preferential debts (s. 175(1A) and (1B)).

Debts secured by floating charge

Once the preferential debts have been paid, the liquidator will pay off those creditors whose debts have been secured by a floating charge (if any assets remain). Floating charges are often taken over all the business and assets of the company. They often consume all the remaining assets, leaving lower-ranking creditors (notably unsecured creditors) with nothing.

Parliament decided that the position of the unsecured creditors needed to be strengthened. This was done in two ways. First, the proceeds of certain claims brought by the liquidator (such as fraudulent trading or wrongful trading) cannot be used to satisfy the debts of floating chargeholders (s. 176ZB). Second, and more importantly, s. 176A, which applies to floating charges created on or after the 15 September 2003, provides that the liquidator must set aside a portion of the assets subject to a floating charge:

- where the company's net property does not exceed £10,000 in value, 50% of that property; and
- where the company's net property does exceed £10,000 in value, 50% of the first £10,000 in value, and 20% of that part of the company's net property that exceeds £10,000 (Insolvency Act 1986 (Prescribed Part) Order 2003, article 3(1)).

The sum that is set aside is known as the 'prescribed part' and it cannot exceed £600,000 (although the government has stated that it plans to increase this cap). This prescribed part is set aside to be used to satisfy the claims of the unsecured creditors, as the following example demonstrates.

Case study 18.2

X-Corp Ltd is in the process of being liquidated. The liquidator has gathered in all the company's assets, realised them and has raised £100,000. The company's creditors are:

- **the liquidation expenses amount to £20,000;**
- **the company's preferential creditors are owed £30,000;**
- **£50,000 is owed to BigBank plc, secured by a floating charge taken over all the assets and business of X-Corp; and**
- **£20,000 is owed to various unsecured creditors.**

The liquidation expenses will be paid first, leaving £80,000. The preferential creditors will then be paid next, leaving £50,000. BigBank is the next creditor to be paid, but as it is a floating chargeholder, the prescribed part must be set aside:

- **50% of the first £10,000 = £5,000**
- **20% of the remainder = £8,000 (20% of £40,000).**

BigBank will receive £37,000. The prescribed part will amount to £13,000 and will be distributed to the X-Corp's unsecured creditors. As there is not enough to fully pay off all the unsecured creditors, the £13,000 will be distributed *pari passu*.

It should be noted that the prescribed part cannot be used by any fixed or floating chargeholder in respect of an unsecured part of their debt (for example, if a shortfall meant that a part of their debt became unsecured) (*Re Airbase (UK) Ltd* [2008] EWHC 124 (Ch)). However, a fixed or floating chargeholder will be able to participate in the prescribed part if they wholly surrender their security, thereby becoming an unsecured creditor (*Kelly v Inflexion Fund 2 Ltd* [2010] EWHC 2850 (Ch)).

Unsecured debts
The prescribed part (if there is one) and any remaining funds will then be used to pay the unsecured creditors. There may not be enough left to pay off all the unsecured creditors: if so, the remaining funds will be distributed *pari passu*.

Deferred debts
Statute provides that certain deferred debts (e.g. sums due to a member by way of dividend, IA 1986, s. 74(2)(f)) rank below the claims of unsecured creditors. The deferred creditors will receive less than their due if insufficient assets remain after payment of other creditors.

Members
If the company was solvent when it entered into winding up, then sums may remain once all the creditors have been paid. If so, any remaining sums will be distributed to the company's members.

Test yourself 18.2

1. **What is the role of a liquidator?**
2. **What does the *pari passu* principle state?**
3. **Set out the order in which the assets of the company are distributed.**
4. **What is a preferential debt?**
5. **How is the prescribed part calculated?**
6. **What is a deferred debt?**

5. Malpractice before and during liquidation

Sections 206–219 of the IA 1986 impose liability on certain persons who engage in specified forms of malpractice before and during liquidation. In most cases, these provisions allow the liquidator to increase the assets of the company by requiring wrongdoers to contribute to the company's assets. The first set of rules discussed impose criminal liability on certain persons.

5.1 Offences of fraud, deception and so on

Sections 206–211 create a range of offences that impose criminal liability on certain persons (usually past and present officers of the company) who have engaged in specified conduct:

- fraud in anticipation of the company being wound up (s. 206) (e.g. falsifying book entries, disposing of property obtained on credit which has not been fully paid for);
- transactions in fraud of creditors (s. 207) (e.g. gifting company property, concealing company property);
- misconduct in the course of winding up (s. 208) (e.g. concealing information from the liquidator);
- falsification of company books (s. 209);
- material omissions from statements relating to the company's affairs (s. 210); and
- false representations to creditors (s. 211).

5.2 Summary remedy

misfeasance
The improper or unlawful performance of a lawful act.

Section 212 applies where, in the course of a winding up, it appears that a liquidator or current/former officer of the company has misapplied or retained, or become accountable for, any money or other property of the company, or been guilty of any **misfeasance** or breach of any fiduciary or other duty in relation to the company (s. 212(1)).

It is important to note that s. 212 does not create a new legal wrong – it simply provides a procedurally simple remedy for breaches of existing company law rules (notably breach of directors' duties). Effectively, it allows certain persons (namely an official receiver, a liquidator or any creditor or contributory) to bring a claim in situations where normally the claim would have to be brought by the company itself. Such persons can apply to the court. Following an examination of the conduct of the defendant, the court can compel the defendant:

- to repay, restore or account for the money or property or any part of it, with interest at such rate as the court thinks fit; or
- to contribute such sum to the company's assets by way of compensation in respect of the misfeasance or breach of duty as the court thinks fit (s. 212(3)).

5.3 Fraudulent trading

Sections 213 (which applies to companies in liquidation) and 246ZA (which applies to companies in administration) apply where, in the course of a winding up or while a company is in administration, it appears that any business of the company has been carried on with intent to defraud creditors of the company, creditors of any other person or for any fraudulent purpose (ss. 213(1) and 246ZA(1)). In *Morris v Bank of India* [2003] EWHC 1868 (Ch), Patten J stated that this requires three elements to be proven.

First, it must be established the business of the company has been carried on:

- with intent to defraud creditors of the company;
- with intent to defraud creditors of any other person; or
- for any fraudulent purpose.

Statute does not define 'intent to defraud' or 'fraudulent purpose', but the courts have stated that these phrases relate to 'actual dishonesty involving, according to current notions of fair trading among commercial men, real moral blame' (*Re Patrick and Lyon Ltd* [1933] Ch 786 (Ch) (Maugham J)).

Second, it must be established that the defendant participated in the business being carried on in a fraudulent manner. The key term is 'participated in' and, in *Re Maidstone Building Provisions Ltd* [1971] 1 WLR 1085 (Ch), Pennycuick VC stated that this requires:

> 'some positive steps of some nature. I do not think it can be said that someone is party to carrying on a business if he takes no positive steps at all. So, in order to bring a person within the section, you must show that he is taking some positive steps in the carrying on of the company's business in a fraudulent manner.'

Third, it must be shown that the defendant knowingly participated in the fraudulent conduct. According to Patten J in *Morris v Bank of India*, the word 'knowingly' requires 'actual realisation' that fraudulent conduct occurred or was likely to occur, but the defendant would not need to know 'every detail of the fraud or the precise mechanics of how it would be carried out' in order for liability to be imposed.

Only a liquidator or administrator may apply to the court (ss. 213(2) and 246ZA(2)). If the court is of the opinion that the defendant has engaged in fraudulent conduct, it can order the defendant to make such contributions to the company's assets as the court thinks proper (ss. 213(2) and 246ZA(2)). If the defendant is a director, they can also be disqualified for up to 15 years (CDDA 1986, s. 10).

Fraudulent trading under the Companies Act 2006

The concept of fraudulent trading also exists under s. 993 of the CA 2006. The conduct that can constitute fraudulent trading under s. 993 is largely the same as that under IA 1986, but there are two key differences:

- the IA 1986 provisions only apply where the company is in liquidation or administration, whereas s. 993 can apply at any time; and
- the IA 1986 provisions impose civil liability, whereas s. 993 imposes criminal liability.

If fraudulent trading has occurred in relation to a company in liquidation or administration, then both sets of provisions can apply. This means civil and criminal liability can be imposed.

5.4 Wrongful trading

Sections 214 (which applies to companies in liquidation) and 246ZB (which applies to companies in administration) provide that a person will have engaged in wrongful trading if three conditions are satisfied:

1. the company has gone into insolvent liquidation or insolvent administration;
2. at some time before the commencement of the winding up of the company or before the company entered administration, that person knew or ought to have concluded that there was no reasonable prospect that the company would avoid going into insolvent liquidation or entering insolvent administration; and
3. that person was a director or shadow director of the company at that time (ss. 214(2) and 246ZB(2)).

The second condition can prove tricky to apply in practice as it is based on what the defendant knew or ought to have known. Guidance on how the court can determine this is found in ss. 214(4) and 246ZB(4). These state that the facts which a director of a company ought to know or ascertain, and the conclusions which he ought to reach, are those which would be known, ascertained or taken by a reasonably diligent person having both:

1. the general knowledge, skill and experience that may reasonably be expected of a person carrying out the same functions as are carried out by that director in relation to the company; and
2. the general knowledge, skill and experience that that director has.

The standard in (1) is objective in that it is based on 'the general knowledge, skill and experience that may reasonably be expected' from the director. Conversely, the standard in (2) is subjective as it based on the general knowledge, skill and experience that that director actually has. The following case demonstrates the application of this objective/subjective standard in practice.

Case law 18.1

Re Produce Marketing Consortium Ltd (No 2) **[1989] 5 BCC 569 (Ch)**

A company, incorporated in 1964, was profitable until 1980, after which time its performance decreased. By 1984, it had built up an overdraft of over £90,000, and the company's decline was clearly evidenced in

its audited accounts. The annual accounts for 1984/85, which were delayed from July 1986 to January 1987, showed that the company was insolvent. Despite this, the company continued trading until October 1987 when it was liquidated with debts of over £300,000. The liquidator alleged that the directors had engaged in wrongful trading.

Knox J stated that the directors' knowledge was based 'not only what was actually there but what, given reasonable diligence and an appropriate level of general knowledge, skill and experience, was ascertainable'. Although the annual accounts were delayed, the directors would have known of the company's financial position by July 1986. Based on this, they ought to have concluded that the company was in 'irreversible decline', and that the company should not have continued trading. Accordingly, the directors had engaged in wrongful trading and they were ordered to contribute £75,000 to the company's assets.

Another potentially tricky issue is determining when the directors started engaging in wrongful trading. This moment occurs when the directors knew or ought to have known that there was no reasonable prospect that the company would avoid going into insolvent liquidation or entering insolvent administration. Chadwick J in *Secretary of State for Trade and Industry v Taylor* [1997] 1 WLR 407 (Ch) provided guidance:

> 'The companies legislation does not impose on directors a statutory duty to ensure that their company does not trade while insolvent; nor does that legislation impose an obligation to ensure that the company does not trade at a loss... Directors may properly take the view that it is in the interests of the company and of its creditors that, although insolvent, the company should continue to trade out of its difficulties. They may properly take the view that it is in the interests of the company and its creditors that some loss-making trade should be accepted in anticipation of future profitability. They are not to be criticised if they give effect to such views, properly held.'

Accordingly, a company may justifiably continue to trade even though it is insolvent. For example, in *Re Cubelock Ltd* [2001] BCC 523 (Ch), Park J stated that it is common for a company to trade while insolvent 'particularly in a company's early months when it is seeking to get itself established and may have anticipated an initial period of losses before turning the corner and moving into profit'.

Another example of a company justifiably trading while insolvent could be where the company has taken advantage of a formal rescue procedure and the directors have reasonable cause to believe that the rescue will succeed. It should, however, be noted that attempting to trade out of insolvency is risky and frequently fails. Company secretaries would be advised to recommend that the board calls in an insolvency practitioner at the earliest opportunity to provide advice.

Minimising the potential loss

The court will not make a declaration against a director if it is satisfied that the director 'took every step with a view to minimising the potential loss to the company's creditors as… he ought to have taken' (ss. 214(3) and 246ZB(3)). It is the directors who must prove, on the balance of probabilities, that they took every step to minimise the loss for all the company's creditors (*Brooks v Armstrong* [2015] EWHC 2289 (Ch)). The type of steps the directors should take will be based on the facts, but could include:

- keeping themselves informed of the company's financial position;
- reviewing the company's financial position with professional assistance;
- raising concerns with the board and suggesting solutions;
- minuting board discussions and recording board decisions; or
- advising creditors of the risks of advancing further credit.

Remedies

A liquidator or administrator may apply to the court if they feel wrongful trading has occurred. If the application is successful, the court may declare that the defendant is liable to make such contribution to the company's assets as the court thinks proper (ss. 214(1) and 246ZB(1)). When determining the amount of the contribution, Knox J in *Re Produce Marketing Consortium Ltd (No 2)* stated the wrongful trading provisions are 'primarily compensatory rather than penal. *Prima facie,* the appropriate amount that a director is declared to be liable to contribute is the amount by which the company's assets can be discerned to have been depleted by the director's conduct.'

A director who has engaged in wrongful trading can also be disqualified for up to 15 years (CDDA 1986, s. 10).

5.5 Restriction on re-use of company names

The Cork Report was extremely concerned at:

> 'the ease with which a person trading [through a company] can allow such a company to become insolvent, form a new company, and then carry on trading much as before, leaving behind him a trail of unpaid creditors, and often repeating the process several times. The dissatisfaction is greatest where the director of an insolvent company has set up business again, using a similar name for the new company, and trades with assets purchased at a discount from the liquidator of the old company.'

Section 216 aims to combat the use of these so-called 'Phoenix companies'. Section 216 applies to a person where a company (known as the 'liquidating company') has gone into insolvent liquidation and that person was a director or shadow director of that company at any time in the 12-month period leading up to the date of liquidation (s. 216(1)). Unless that person obtains the leave of the court, they cannot, for a period of five years beginning on the date of the company's liquidation:

- be a director of any other company that is known by a prohibited name;
- in any way, whether directly or indirectly, be concerned or take part in the promotion, formation or management of a company with a prohibited name; or

- in any way, whether directly or indirectly, be concerned or take part in the carrying on of a business carried on (otherwise by a company) under a prohibited name (s. 216(3)).

A 'prohibited name' is:

(1) a name by which the liquidating company was known at any time in the 12-month period prior to its liquidation; or

(2) a name which is so similar to a name falling within (1) as to suggest an association with that company (s. 216(2)).

Note that s. 216(3) provides that a person will be permitted to use a prohibited name in two instances:

- where that person obtains the leave of the court to use the prohibited name; or
- in such circumstances as may be prescribed, with r. 22 of IR 2016 prescribing several such circumstances (such as where the business, or substantially the whole of it, is to be acquired from the insolvent company under arrangements made by its liquidator).

Liability

A person who breaches s. 216 commits a criminal offence (s. 216(4)).They can be made personally liable for the debt and liabilities of the new company incurred while they were involved in its management in contravention of s. 216 (s. 217). This personal liability is **joint and several** with that of the company (s. 217(2)).

The following case demonstrates ss. 216 and 217 in practice.

joint and several liability
Where two or more persons (the 'wrongdoers') commit a legal wrong that can result in joint and several liability, then the victim of the wrong can sue any wrongdoer for the loss sustained or all the wrongdoers.

Case law 18.2

Ricketts v Ad Valorem Factors Ltd **[2003] EWCA Civ 1706**

Ricketts had been a director of the Air Component Company Ltd, which had gone into liquidation and been dissolved. He had subsequently been a director of the Air Equipment Company Ltd, which had also gone into liquidation, leaving several of its creditors unpaid. Ad Valorem Factors Ltd was one such creditor and it argued that 'Air Equipment Company Ltd' was a prohibited name under s. 216, and therefore Ricketts should be liable for that company's debts.

The court stated that this was not a true 'Phoenix syndrome' case in that there was no transfer of assets between the two companies run by Ricketts, nor was there any evidence to indicate that the company had been used to avoid debts or that anyone has been misled by the similarity in the companies' names. However, the court rejected a purposive approach and stated that if Air Equipment was a prohibited name, then s. 216 would be breached. Mummery LJ stated that the name 'Air Component' was so similar to 'Air Equipment' as to suggest an

association with it. Accordingly, it was a prohibited name and Ricketts had breached s. 216. He was found criminally liable and was held personally liable for the debt that Air Equipment Co Ltd owed to Ad Valorem.

Stop and think 18.1

Do you agree with the decision in *Ricketts*? Do you think that the courts should take a purposive approach and confine s. 216 to cases involving true Phoenix companies? Mummery LJ did state that the imposition of criminal liability on Ricketts seemed harsh, but felt that the legal position required him to find Ricketts guilty.

Test yourself 18.3

1. **Provide six examples of the type of conduct that can result in liability under ss. 206–211.**
2. **How does fraudulent trading under IA 1986 differ from fraudulent trading under the CA 2006?**
3. **When will a person have engaged in wrongful trading?**
4. **How can a director avoid liability for wrongful trading?**
5. **What is a prohibited name?**
6. **What are the consequences of breaching s. 216?**

6. Adjustment of prior transactions

Sections 238–246 of the IA 1986 allow a liquidator (or administrator) to adjust certain pre-liquidation transactions if these transactions harm the creditors' interests or undermine the *pari passu* principle. These include:

- transactions at an undervalue
- preferences
- extortionate credit transactions
- invalid floating charges.

The provisions either invalidate the transaction or require those who engaged in the transaction to contribute to the company's assets.

6.1 Transactions at an undervalue

Case study 18.3

X-Corp has significant debts that it is unable to pay. The directors realise that the company will need to be liquidated. Before they place the company in liquidation, the directors sell off the company's registered office to John for about a quarter of its market value. John is married to Rebecca, a director of X-Corp. X-Corp is placed in liquidation, but the liquidator cannot sell the office as it no longer belongs to X-Corp. As a result, most of X-Corp's creditors go unpaid. A few months later, the former directors of X-Corp form a new company, and this company acquires the office from John.

The directors of X-Corp have clearly sold the office in order to place it outside the control of the liquidator. To combat this, s. 238 of the IA 1986 provides that a liquidator or administrator may apply to the court for an order where the company has, at the relevant time, entered into a transaction at an undervalue. A company enters into a transaction at an undervalue if:

- the company makes a gift to a person or otherwise enters into a transaction with a person on terms that provide for the company to receive no consideration; or
- the company enters into a transaction with a person for a consideration the value of which, in money or money's worth, is significantly less than the value, in money or money's worth, of the consideration provided by the company (s. 238(4)).

Where the company gifts an asset to a person or receives no consideration, then little difficulty arises. The issue is slightly more complex where the company does receive consideration, but it is significantly less than the consideration it provides. In order to determine whether such a transaction is at an undervalue, Millet J in *Re MC Bacon Ltd (No 1)* [1990] BCC 78 (Ch) stated:

> [it requires] 'a comparison to be made between the value obtained by the company for the transaction and the value of consideration provided by the company. Both values must be measurable in money or money's worth and both must be considered from the company's point of view.'

The question is when will the consideration received be 'significantly less than the value' of the consideration provided by the company. There is little case law on the issue, but in *Phillips v Brewin Dolphin Bell Lawrie Ltd* [2001] UKHL 2, Lord Scott stated that a transaction would not be at an undervalue if the value of the asset sold by the company is '*prima facie*, not less than the amount that a reasonably well informed purchaser is prepared, in arms' length negotiations, to pay for it'. In *Brewin Dolphin* itself, the consideration received by the company was around 60% of the consideration provided by the company. This amounted to a transaction at an undervalue.

The 'relevant time' and 'connected persons'

Not all transactions at an undervalue will fall within s. 238. In order to obtain a remedy under s. 238, the transaction must have been entered into at the 'relevant time', which requires the following two conditions to be satisfied:

(1) the transaction was entered into within a two-year period ending on the onset of the company's insolvency (s. 240(1)(a)); and

(2) when the company entered into the transaction, it was unable to pay its debts or it became unable to pay its debts as a consequence of the transaction (s. 240(2)).

The condition in (2) will, unless the contrary is shown, be presumed to be satisfied if the company enters into a transaction at an undervalue with a person connected with the company (s. 240(2)). The concept of a person 'connected with the company' applies to all the transactions mentioned on page 364. Section 249 provides that a person is connected with a company if:

- they are a director or shadow director of the company;
- they are an associate of a director or shadow director of the company; or
- they are an associate of the company.

Section 435 sets out in detail who is an associate.

- A person (*A*) is an associate of an individual (*B*) if *A* is (i) *B*'s husband, wife or civil partner; (ii) a relative of *B* or *B*'s husband, wife or civil partner; or (iii) the husband, wife or civil partner of a relative of *B* or *B*'s husband, wife or civil partner. A 'relative' is defined in s. 435(8) and includes brothers, sisters, uncles, aunts, nephews, nieces, lineal ancestors or lineal descendants.
- A person (*A*) is an associate of another person (*B*) if they are in partnership with *B*.
- A person is an associate of any person whom they employ or by whom they are employed (for this purpose, a director or other officer of the company is to be treated as an employee).
- A company is an associate of another company if (i) the same person controls both companies; or (ii) a person has control of one company and persons who are their associates control the other company.
- A company is an associate of another company if a group of two or more persons have control of each company, and the groups consist of the same persons.
- A company is an associate of another person if (i) that person has control of the company; or (ii) if that person and his associates together have control of the company.

The definition of associate is complex and covers a wide array of persons, but there are some surprising loopholes.

Stop and think 18.2

Tom and David are directors of X-Corp Ltd. They also both own 25% of the shares in Y-Corp Ltd. Are X-Corp and Y-Corp connected? Surprisingly, the answer is no. Tom and David are not associates of each other simply because they are directors of X-Corp. Consequently, X-Corp and Y-Corp are not connected. However, if Tom and David controlled X-Corp, then both companies would be controlled by the same persons. They would be associates and would be connected.

Remedies

If a company does enter into a transaction at an undervalue at the relevant time, the liquidator or administrator may apply to the court for an order (s. 238(2)). The court may then make an order as it thinks fit for restoring the position to what it would have been if the company had not entered into that transaction (s. 238(3)). The court cannot make an order if it is satisfied that:

- the company entered into the transaction in good faith and for the purpose of carrying on its business; and
- at the time it entered into the transaction, there were reasonable grounds for believing that the transaction would benefit the company (s. 238(5)).

Section 241(1) provides a non-exhaustive list of how the position could be restored, including requiring that any property transferred from the company be transferred back.

6.2 Preferences

Case study 18.4

X-Corp plc is struggling financially and the directors know that the company is close to insolvency. The company borrows £10,000 from BigBank plc secured by a floating charge over all the business and assets of X-Corp. This loan is insufficient to help the company get back on track and BigBank refuses to lend any more money.

Joanne, one of X-Corp's directors, lends the company £5,000 on an unsecured basis. This also does not help and the directors realise that the company will have to be put into liquidation. A few days before the company is placed into liquidation, X-Corp repays Joanne the £5,000 it owes her. As a result of this, there are insufficient assets for the liquidator to repay BigBank.

By repaying Joanne prior to liquidation, her claim against X-Corp has effectively been preferred over that of BigBank, even though BigBank's claim should rank first due to the security it has. To combat this, s. 239 provides that an administrator or liquidator can apply to the court for an order where the company has, at the relevant time, given a person a preference (s. 239(2)). A company gives a preference to a person if:

- that person is one of the company's creditors or a surety or guarantor for any of the company's debts or other liabilities; and
- the company does anything or suffers anything to be done which (in either case) has the effect of putting that person into a position which, in the event of the company going into insolvent liquidation, will be better than the position he would have been in if that thing had not been done (s 239(4)).

Relevant time

A preference will only fall within s. 239 if it was given at the 'relevant time':

- in the case of a preference which is given to a person connected with the company, within a period of two years ending on the date of the onset of insolvency (s. 240(1)(a)); or
- in the case of a preference which is not also a transaction at an undervalue and which is not given to a connected person, within a period of six months ending on the date of the onset of insolvency (s. 240(1)(b)).

Even if a preference is given at the times stated in s. 240(1)(a) or (b) it will not be regarded as being given at the relevant time, unless the company was unable to pay its debts or it became unable to pay its debts as a consequence of the transaction. This condition will be presumed to be satisfied if the company enters into a transaction at an undervalue with a person connected with the company (s. 240(2)), unless the contrary can be shown.

Desire to prefer

The court will not make an order in respect of a preference given to a person unless the company desired to give the person a preference. This means the company was influenced by a desire to put that person into a position which, in the event of the company going into insolvent liquidation, will be better than the position they would have been in otherwise (s. 239(5)).

Case law 18.3

Re MC Bacon Ltd (No 1) **[1990] BCC 78 (Ch)**

MC Bacon Ltd (Bacon) was near its overdraft limit when it lost its principal customer. Bacon's bank was only willing to offer Bacon continued support in relation to the overdraft facility if Bacon granted the bank security for its overdraft liabilities. Bacon agreed and granted the bank a debenture. Bacon was eventually placed into liquidation, owing the bank £235,530 and owing £329,435 to a group of unsecured creditors. The granting of the debenture meant that the bank's claim ranked above that of the unsecured creditors. Bacon's liquidator alleged that this amounted to a preference.

Millett J stated that 'there must have been a desire to... improve the creditor's position in the event of an insolvent liquidation'. However, 'the mere presence of the requisite desire will not be sufficient by itself. It must have influenced the decision to enter into the transaction... It need not have been the only factor or even the decisive one.'

The court held that Bacon had not desired to prefer the bank. Bacon's choice was to either grant the bank the security it sought or be forced into liquidation by the bank calling in the overdraft. Granting the debenture was 'the unavoidable price of obtaining the desired advantages'. The desire behind granting the debenture was not to prefer the bank, but to enable Bacon to continue trading.

Where a preference is given to a person who, at the time it is given, is connected with the company, then it will be presumed that a desire to prefer exists, unless the contrary can be shown (s. 239(6)).

Remedies

Where a company has given a person a preference at the relevant time, the liquidator or administrator may apply to the court (s. 239(2)). The court may make an order as it thinks fit to restore the position to what it would have been if the company had not given the preference (s. 239(3)). This will depend upon the nature of the preference and could include:

- where the preference involves repayment of a loan, the court may order the creditor to return the repaid sum to the company;
- where the preference involves releasing a creditor from an obligation (such as a guarantee), the court may renew the obligation; or
- where the preference involves the granting of security to a creditor, the court may set aside the security.

6.3 Extortionate credit transactions

Section 244 provides that a liquidator or administrator may apply to the court for an order where the company has entered into an extortionate credit transaction (s. 244(2)). The following conditions must be satisfied:

- the company is, or has been, a party to a transaction for, or involving the provision of, credit to the company (s. 244(1));
- the credit transaction is extortionate – meaning that, having regard to the risk accepted by the person providing the credit:
  - the terms of the transaction are or were such as to require grossly exorbitant payments to be made (whether unconditionally or in certain contingencies) in respect of the provision of the credit; or
  - the transaction otherwise grossly contravened ordinary principles of fair dealing (s. 244(3)); and

- the transaction was entered into within a three-year period prior to the day on which the company entered administration or went into liquidation (s. 244(2)).

The burden of proof here is reversed. It need not be proved that the transaction was extortionate – instead, it will be presumed that the transaction is extortionate unless the contrary is shown (s. 244(3)).

Remedies
If a credit transaction meets the above conditions, the court can make an order which may contain one or more of the following:

- a provision setting the transaction aside (in full or in part);
- a provision varying the terms of the transaction;
- a provision requiring a party to the transaction to pay to the liquidator or administrator any sums paid by the company; or
- a provision requiring any person to surrender any property held as security for the purposes of the transaction (s. 244(4)).

6.4 Avoidance of certain floating charges

Section 245 allows a liquidator or administrator to invalidate certain floating charges made prior to insolvency. Unlike other transactions, no application to the court is required. A floating charge can be invalidated if it was made at the relevant time, as follows:

- in the case of a charge which is created in favour of a person connected with the company, within a period of two years ending on the date of the onset of insolvency; and
- in the case of a charge which is created in favour of any other person, within a period of 12 months ending on the date of the onset of insolvency (s. 245(3)).

A charge will not be made at the relevant time unless the company was unable to pay its debts at the time the company created the charge or it became unable to pay its debts due to the transaction under which the charge was created (s. 245(4)).

Stop and think 18.3

Why does s. 245 only apply to floating charges, not fixed charges? The Cork Report provided the answer:

> **'The floating charge is an excessive security because, unlike a fixed charge, it extends to future assets not paid for by the company. It is one thing to permit a prudent creditor, fearing for the solvency of his debtor, to insist either upon payment of the debt due to him or a fixed charge upon existing assets of his debtor instead...**

It is quite another matter to permit a creditor, concerned for the solvency of his debtor, to take a security which will allow the debtor to trade and acquire further assets on credit with which to swell the security at the expense of the unpaid vendors.'

In certain circumstances, an invalidated charge will remain valid in part. Section 245(2) provides that a charge will remain valid, but only to the extent of the aggregate of the value of so much of the consideration for the creation of the charge as consists of money paid, or goods or services supplied. This must have been paid or supplied to the company at the same time as or after the creation of the charge.

Invalidating a floating charge does not invalidate the debt – the debt will simply lose its secured status and will become unsecured.

Test yourself 18.4

1. **When will a transaction be at an undervalue?**
2. **When will a person be connected with the company?**
3. **What is a preference?**
4. **When will a credit transaction be extortionate?**
5. **When can a liquidator or administrator invalidate a floating charge?**

7. Dissolution

The process for ending a company's existence is called dissolution. A company is dissolved when it is removed from the register at Companies House. The dissolution of a company terminates the company's separate personality and also ends any legal relationships between the company and other persons. If, at the point of dissolution, the company still owns any property, then this property will be deemed ***bona vacantia*** and will pass to the Crown (CA 2006, s. 1012(1)). Assets which go to the Crown under the *bona vacantia* principle can be purchased from the *bona vacantia* office.

bona vacantia
'Ownerless goods.' Such goods usually pass to the Crown but can then be bought back by others.

Three months after the registrar of companies has been notified that the winding up of a company is complete, the company will be deemed to be dissolved (IA 1986, ss. 201 and 205). A company can also be dissolved without it first being liquidated in a range of circumstances.

- Companies House's decision to register a company can be judicially reviewed. The company will be dissolved if the judicial review is granted. This could occur, for example, where the company's objects are illegal and unenforceable (*R v Registrar of Companies ex parte Attorney General* [1991] BCLC 476 (DC)).

- If the administrator of a company thinks that the company has no property to distribute to creditors, he will notify Companies House of this. Three months after the notice is filed, the company will be deemed to be dissolved (IA 1986, Schedule B1, para 84).
- Section 1000 of the CA 2006 provides that, if the registrar of companies believes that a company is not carrying on any business, he can send that company a communication enquiring if it is carrying on business. If no reply is received within 14 days, a second communication will be sent. If no reply is received to this second communication, or if the company replies to confirm it is not carrying on business, the registrar will place an advertisement in *The Gazette*, and the company will be dissolved two months later.
- A company can have itself dissolved by applying to the registrar of companies using Form DS01. Following the application, an advertisement will be published in *The Gazette* and the company will be dissolved two months later (CA 2006, s. 1003).
- An Act of Parliament may state that a company is to be dissolved. For example, HSBC Investment Bank plc was dissolved by the HSBC Investment Banking Act 2000.

8 Restoration

A dissolved company may be restored and placed back in the register of companies. A company that has been restored will be regarded as if it was never dissolved or struck off the register (CA 2006, ss. 1028(1) and 1032(1)). There are two ways in which a dissolved company can be restored.

The first method is called administrative restoration. It applies where a company was dissolved on the ground that it was not carrying on any business (CA 2006, s. 1024(1)). In such a case, a former director or former member can apply to the registrar of companies (using Form RT01) to have the dissolved company restored (s. 1024(3)). This application must be made within six years of the date of the company's dissolution (s. 1024(4)). The registrar will restore the company only if the following conditions are met:

- the company was carrying on business at the time it was dissolved;
- if any property or right vested in the company was deemed *bona vacantia*, the Crown representative has consented in writing to the company being restored; and
- the applicant has delivered specified documentation to the registrar (s. 1025).

The second method of restoration involves an application being made to the court to restore a dissolved company (s. 1029(1)). Under s. 1029(2), a number of persons are empowered to bring such an application, including:

- the Secretary of State;
- any former director, member or liquidator of the company;

- any person who, but for the company's dissolution, would have a contractual relationship with it;
- any person with a potential legal claim against the company; and
- any person who was a creditor of the company at the time it was dissolved.

If the court orders that the company be restored, the restoration takes effect when a copy of the court order is delivered to the registrar of companies (s. 1031(2)). The registrar will then publish in *The Gazette* a notice stating that the company has been restored (s. 1031(3)).

Chapter summary

- A company will be insolvent when it is unable to pay its debts.
- There are two types of liquidation:
  - voluntary winding up; and
  - winding up by the court (usually known as 'compulsory winding up').
- A voluntary winding up occurs where the company decides to wind itself up by passing a special resolution. If the directors make a declaration of solvency, it will be a members' voluntary winding up. If no such declaration is made, it will be a creditors' voluntary winding up.
- A compulsory winding up occurs where specified persons petition the court on specified grounds for an order winding up the company.
- The liquidator's role is to secure that the assets of the company are collected, realised and distributed to the company's creditors. If there is a surplus the liquidator will distribute it to the persons entitled to it.
- The *pari passu* principle provides that the liquidator will distribute the assets to the creditors in proportion to the size of their claim against the company (i.e. each creditor will receive an equal proportion of the debt owed to it).
- As creditors can obtain security and as statute prioritises and subordinates certain types of debt, the liquidator must distribute the company's assets to the creditors in a specified order.
- Liability can be imposed on certain persons who engage in malpractice before and during liquidation, which includes:
  - where a person has engaged in offences relating to fraud and deception;
  - where a person, in the course of a winding up, misapplied or retained, or become accountable for, any money or other property of the company, or has been guilty of any misfeasance or breach of any fiduciary or other duty in relation to the company;
  - where a person has engaged in fraudulent or wrongful trading; or
  - where a person has used a prohibited name.

- The liquidator has the power to adjust certain transactions, namely:
  - transactions at an undervalue;
  - preferences;
  - extortionate credit transactions; and
  - certain floating charges can be invalidated.
- The process for ending a company's existence is called dissolution. A company is dissolved when it is removed from the register at Companies House.
- A dissolved company can, in certain circumstances, be restored and placed back in the register of members.

Test yourself answers

Chapter 1

Test yourself 1.1

1. Name the principal piece of UK company law legislation.
The principal piece of UK company law legislation is the Companies Act 2006 (CA 2006).

2. Why is subordinate legislation such an important source of company law?
Subordinate legislation serves a number of useful purposes:

- it expands upon the basic rules found within an Act of Parliament;
- it is used to bring parts of Acts of Parliament into force in the form of Commencement Orders;
- it can be used to amend existing legislation, including (controversially) amending Acts of Parliament;
- it is often used to implement EU law; and
- it can empower certain persons (e.g. the Secretary of State) or bodies to create law.

3. What role does BEIS have in relation to company law?
BEIS is the governmental department that is responsible for (amongst other things) 'leading the government's relationship with business'. To that end, it is the government department that is most closely involved in company law and corporate governance reform.

4. Provide three examples of company law rules that have legislative backing.
Examples of non-statutory rules that have legislative backing include:

- the FCA Handbook
- the City Code on Takeovers and Mergers
- standards imposed by the FRC in relation to the conduct of audits.

Test yourself 1.2

1. Name the principal corporate governance codes that operate in the UK.
The principal corporate governance codes are:

- the UK Corporate Governance Code
- the UK Stewardship Code
- the Wates Corporate Governance Principles for Large Private Companies.

2. Explain how the 'comply or explain' approach operates, and how it differs to the 'apply and explain' approach.
The 'comply or explain' approach requires companies with a premium listing to (i) apply the Principles of the UK Corporate Governance Code; and (ii) comply with the Code's Provisions or explain why they were not complied with. The Wates Corporate Governance Principles adopt an 'apply and explain' approach, under which large private companies are expected to apply the Principles fully and explain how they have applied them.

3. What type of company is subject to the UK Corporate Governance Code?
The UK Corporate Governance Code applies to companies with a premium listing, although other companies may comply with the Code's Principles and Provisions if they wish to do so.

Test yourself 1.3

1. What are the two major sources of European company law?
The two major sources of EU law are regulations and directives.

2. What is the 'right of establishment'?
The right of establishment prohibits restrictions on the freedom to set up and manage undertakings, including companies.

3. Why has the EU process of company law harmonisation been largely carried out via directives?
The process of EU company law harmonisation has been conducted via directives because they provide member states with considerable flexibility. This is because directives set out the goals or aims of the directive and then allow member states discretion in terms of how those aims are implemented.

4. Name five areas of UK company law that have been heavily influenced by EU law.
Examples of areas of UK company law that have been influenced by EU law include:

- cross-border mergers and insolvencies
- the Listing Regime
- the regulation and independence of auditors
- the market abuse regime

- the capital maintenance regime
- shareholders' rights
- corporate transparency.

Chapter 2

Test yourself 2.1

1. What is a sole proprietorship?
A sole proprietor is a sole individual carrying on some form of business activity on their own account (such individuals are also known as 'self-employed' or as 'independent contractors').

2. What is the difference between a sole practitioner and a sole trader?
A sole trader is a sole proprietor who is not a professional. A sole proprietor who is a professional (such as a lawyer or accountant) is known as a sole practitioner.

3. Explain the advantages and disadvantages of running a business through a sole proprietorship.
The advantages of a sole proprietorship are:

- it is easy to set up;
- it is subject to much less regulation than other forms of business;
- it is required to disclose much less information than other business, so can be run with more privacy; and
- it is easy to dissolve.

The disadvantages of a sole proprietorship are:

- sole proprietors may find it difficult to raise finance, and so may have to use their own money; and
- the liability of the sole proprietor is personal and unlimited.

4. How can a sole proprietor raise finance?
A sole proprietor has several ways to raise finance:

- they could invest their own money in the business
- they could obtain a loan
- they could seek investment from outside parties.

Test yourself 2.2

1. What are the three types of partnership that can be created?
The principal types of partnership that can be created are:

- the partnership (often known as the 'ordinary' or 'general' partnership)
- the limited partnership
- the limited liability partnership.

2. Explain what ss. 5 and 10 of PA 1890 state.
Section 5 of PA 1890 states that every partner is an agent of the firm and his other partners for the purpose of the business of the partnership. In other words, a partner can bind the firms and his co-partners to an agreement with a third party.

Section 10 of PA 1890 states that each partner is vicariously liable for the wrongful acts or omissions of another partner, as long as the partner was acting within the ordinary business of the partnership or within his authority.

3. How does a limited partnership differ to an ordinary partnership?
An ordinary partnership and a limited partnership differ in two ways. First, an ordinary partnership is created and governed by PA 1890, whereas a limited partnership is created and governed by the Limited Partnerships Act 1907.

Second, in an ordinary partnership, each partner's liability is personal and unlimited, as well as being joint and several. Conversely, a limited partnership can have limited partners, whose liability will be limited to an amount as specified in the registration document. Note, however, that a limited partnership must have one partner (known as a general partner) whose liability will be unlimited.

4. Explain the differences between an LLP and an ordinary partnership.
The differences between an ordinary partnership and an LLP are set out in the following table.

	Ordinary partnership	**Limited liability partnership**
Regulating legislation	PA 1890	LLPA 2000 and accompanying subordinate legislation
Governed by which area of law	Partnership law	Company law, unless LLPA 2000 states otherwise
Formation	Formed via an agreement between the partners	Formed by registering specified documents with Companies House
Has corporate personality	No	Yes
Partners known as	Partners	Members
Liability of the partners	Personal and unlimited	The LLP is liable for its debts and liabilities, and the members' liability is limited

Test yourself 2.3

1. What are the five types of company that can be created under the CA 2006?

The five types of company that can be created under the CA 2006 are:

- a public company limited by shares;
- a private company limited by shares;
- a private company limited by guarantee;
- a private unlimited company with a share capital; and
- a private unlimited company without a share capital.

2. What are the differences between a public and private company?

The differences between a public company and a private company are set out in the following table.

	Public company	Private company
Required to have a share capital	Yes	No
Liability of members	Must be limited	Limited or unlimited
Can offer to sell securities to the public at large	Yes	No
Can trade securities on a stock exchange	Yes	No
Minimum capital requirement	Yes (£50,000)	No minimum capital requirement
Minimum number of directors	Two	One
Suffix	'plc' or 'public limited company'	'Ltd' or 'Limited'
Required to appoint a company secretary	Yes	No (unless the articles provide otherwise)
Can be classified as micro-entity, small or medium-sized	No	Yes

3. In a limited company, to what extent is the members' liability limited?

In a limited company, the method by which the members' liability is limited will depend on whether the company is a company limited by guarantee or a company limited by shares.

- In a company limited by shares, the liability of the members of such companies is limited to the amount that is unpaid on their shares.

- In a company limited by guarantee, the liability of the members is limited to the amount they have undertaken to contribute in the event of its being wound up. This amount will be stated in the statement of guarantee that was submitted to Companies House when the company was incorporated (and may also be stated in the company's articles).

4. What is the difference between a quoted company and a listed company?

The difference between a listed company and a quoted company is as follows.

- A listed company is a company that has a class of its securities listed on the UK's official list.
- A quoted company is a company whose share capital (i) has been included on the official list; (ii) is officially listed in an EEA state; or (iii) is admitted to dealing on the New York Stock Exchange or NASDAQ.

5. How does the CA 2006 classify companies in terms of size?

The Companies Act 2006 determines company size by reference to (i) turnover; (ii) balance sheet total; and (iii) number of employees, as set out in the following table.

	Micro-entity (s. 384A)	Small (s. 382(3))	Medium-sized (s. 465(3))	Large
Turnover	Not more than £623,000	Not more than £10.2 million	Not more than £36 million	Any company that is not a micro-entity, small or medium-sized
Balance sheet total	Not more than £316,000	Not more than £5.1 million	Not more than £18 million	
Number of employees	Not more than 10	Not more than 50	Not more than 250	

In a company's first financial year, it need only satisfy at least two criteria out of three. In subsequent years, a company that is classified as a certain size will continue to be classified as that size unless it fails to satisfy at least two criteria in two consecutive financial years.

6. How can a private company re-register as public, and vice versa?

A private company can re-register as public by passing a special resolution, delivering specified documents to Companies House and complying with certain conditions placed upon public companies. A public company can re-register as private by passing a special resolution and delivering specified documents to Companies House.

Chapter 3

Test yourself 3.1

1. What is a promoter?
Neither statute nor the courts have sought to provide a specific, precise definition of what a promoter is, but instead have provided broad guidance. Bowen J in *Whaley Bridge Calico Printing Co v Green* (1880) LR 5 QBD 109 (QB), stated that a promoter is someone who engages in those 'business operations familiar to the commercial world by which a company is generally brought into existence'.

2. How does s. 51 of the CA 2006 differ to the common law rules relating to pre-incorporation contracts?
Under the common law rules, whether a promoter was bound by a pre-incorporation contract would depend upon the intention of the parties as evidenced in the contract. Section 51 changes this so that a promoter who enters into a pre-incorporation contract with a third party will be bound by that contract.

3. How can a company be bound by a pre-incorporation contract?
There are two ways in which a company can become bound by a pre-incorporation contract:

- the pre-incorporation contract could contain a term which provides that, upon incorporation, the promoter will cease to be liable under the contract if the company enters into a contract with the third party on the same terms as the pre-incorporation contract; or
- following incorporation, the company, the promoter and the third party could enter into an agreement which provides that the pre-incorporation contract will be discharged, and a new agreement will be entered into between the company and the third party (this is known as 'novation').

4. When will a pre-incorporation contract not be subject to s. 51 of the CA 2006?
Section 51 will not apply where (i) a company was bought off the shelf after the contract was entered into but was in existence at the time the contract was entered into; or (ii) where the company once existed but has since been dissolved (*Cotronic (UK) Ltd v Dezonie* [1991] BCC 200 (CA)).

Test yourself 3.2

1. What documentation must be submitted to Companies House to incorporate a company by registration?
In order to incorporate a company by registration, the promoters must provide to Companies House the specified registration documents under s. 9 of the CA 2006. These consist of (i) the memorandum of association; (ii) the application for registration and accompanying documentation; and (iii) the statement of compliance.

2. What information does Form IN01 require?

Form IN01 (or the application for registration) requires a substantial amount of information:

- whether the company will be public or private;
- whether the liability of the members will be limited or unlimited (and, if liability is to be limited, whether it will be limited by shares or guarantee);
- the proposed name of the company;
- the intended address of the company's registered office;
- if the proposed company is to have a share capital, a statement of capital and initial shareholdings must be provided;
- if the proposed company is to be limited by guarantee, the application must contain a statement of guarantee;
- a statement of the company's proposed officers;
- a statement of significant control;
- a copy of the proposed articles of association (unless the company wishes to use the model articles); and
- a statement of the type of company it is to be and its intended business activities.

3. What limitations and restrictions exist in relation to a company's name?

There are numerous restrictions and limitations on the names that companies can have:

- a company cannot choose for its name the same name as another company listed on the index maintained by Companies House;
- a company can only use certain letters, numbers and punctuation marks etc. in its name;
- a name must not be registered if, in the opinion of the Secretary of State, the use of that name would constitute an offence;
- a company name must not be registered if, in the opinion of the Secretary of State, it is offensive; and
- certain words and phrases will require approval from certain governmental and non-governmental bodies (for example, a company that wishes to use the word 'insurance' in its name must obtain a letter of non-objection from the FCA).

4. Explain the differences between a certificate of incorporation and a trading certificate.

A certificate of incorporation is issued to a company upon its incorporation. Trading certificates are only issued to public companies. A public company cannot commence any business or exercise any borrowing powers until it has also been issued with a trading certificate. This certificate will only be issued if Companies House is satisfied that the additional registration requirements for public companies have been complied with (chiefly the requirements as to minimum share capital).

5. What is an 'off-the-shelf' company, and what are the advantages and disadvantages of such companies?
'Incorporation agents', or 'company formation agents' specialise in creating and selling companies. They will register the necessary documents with Companies House and then leave the company dormant and 'on the shelf' until it is purchased. Upon purchase, the incorporation agent will notify Companies House of the relevant changes (such as change of directors, registered office and so on).

The advantages of buying a company off the shelf is that the promoter does not need to incorporate the company. This can be useful if the promoter lacks the necessary knowledge, or simply wishes to avoid the effort of incorporating a company. Purchasing such a company is often inexpensive and can be done very quickly.

The disadvantage of buying a company off the shelf is that it will not be tailored to the needs of the promoter and their business. Accordingly, the promoter may need to engage in work to tailor the new company to their needs (such as changing the company's name, amending the share structure, amending the articles and so on).

Test yourself 3.3

1. What is the difference between a person and an individual?
In law, the word 'individual' tends to refer to a natural person, whereas the word 'person' can be used to refer to natural persons and legal persons (e.g. companies, LLPs).

2. Explain the key consequences of a company having a corporate personality.
There are numerous consequences of a company having corporate personality, including:

- a company has a nationality, a domicile and a residence;
- a company can continue to exist indefinitely;
- a company has the capacity to enter into contracts;
- a company can own assets;
- a company undertakes its own business;
- a company can sue and be sued;
- a company can create, and participate in, other business structures; and
- a company has some 'human' rights.

3. In Salomon, *how did the House of Lords disagree with the High Court and Court of Appeal?*
In *Salomon*, the High Court held that the company was Salomon's agent and so Salomon was liable for its debts. The Court of Appeal also held that Salomon was liable for the company's debts on the grounds that the company was not formed in accordance with the Companies Act, and the other members were not genuine active members.

The House of Lords disagreed with both the High Court and the Court of Appeal. It held that generally a relationship of agency will not exist between a company and its members. The House also stated that there was nothing in the Companies Act 1862 which stated that the members had to be unconnected or active, and so the company had been formed in accordance with the Act. The House held that Salomon was not liable for the company's debts.

4. Why is Salomon *considered to be such a seminal case?*
Salomon is regarded by many as the most important case in company law for three reasons:

- The House of Lords clearly stated that a validly incorporated company could legitimately be used to shield its members from liability (although this had been recognised previously).
- It implicitly recognised the validity of the 'one-person company' (that is, a company run only by one person, with several dormant nominee shareholders) almost a century before it was possible to formally create a one-person company in 1992.
- It recognised the fact that a person holding shares in a company (even all the shares) is not enough to establish a relationship of agency or trusteeship.

5. When will the courts disregard a company's corporate personality?
The courts will pierce the veil where (i) statute provides that a company's corporate personality is to be disregarded; or (ii) where a person is under an existing legal obligation or liability, or subject to an existing legal restriction, which they deliberately evade or whose enforcement they deliberately frustrate by interposing a company under their control, and all other, more conventional, remedies have proved to be no assistance.

6. What are the three conditions required for the evasion principle to apply?
The evasion principle will apply where:

- an existing legal obligation is placed upon a person (*X*);
- *X* interposes a company in order to evade or frustrate the obligation or liability in question; and
- the company being interposed is under *X*'s control.

Chapter 4

Test yourself 4.1

1. What are the three ways in which a company can enter into a contract?
According to ss. 43 and 44 of the CA 2006, a company can enter into a contract in three ways:

- by affixing its common seal to a document;
- by a person who has authority (express or implied) to contract on behalf of the company; and
- by complying with the rules in s. 44(2)–(8).

2. What is a 'common seal' and is a company required to have one?
A common seal is effectively a stamp that can be used to 'sign' or execute a document by embossing the company's name onto the document in question. Companies are not legally required to have a common seal, and most do not.

3. Who is an authorised signatory for the purpose of executing a document on behalf of the company?
Every director of the company is an authorised signatory, as is the company secretary (if the company has one).

Test yourself 4.2

1. What forms part of a company's constitution?
A company's constitution is not found in a single document. Instead, s. 17 of the CA 2006 provides that a company's constitution will include:

- the company's articles; and
- resolutions and agreements affecting the company's constitution, which are listed in s. 29(1).

2. Is a company required to register a set of articles when it is incorporated?
A company is not required to register its own set of articles when it submits its application for incorporation.

3. How can the articles be amended?
A company may amend its articles either by (i) passing a special resolution (CA 2006, s. 21(1)); or (ii) if all of the members so agree (*Cane v Jones* [1980] 1 WLR 1451 (Ch)).

4. What does s. 33(1) of the CA 2006 state?
Section 33(1) of the CA 2006 provides that '[t]he provisions of a company's constitution bind the company and its members to the same extent as if there were covenants on the part of the company and of each member to observe those provisions'. What this means is that the constitution of a company forms a contract (often known as a 'statutory contract') that imposes obligations on:

- the company when dealing with its members;
- the members when dealing with the company; and
- the members when dealing with each other.

5. Can all the terms of the constitution be enforced by the company or a member?
No, members cannot sue to enforce outsider rights (rights granted to them in their capacity other than as a member).

Test yourself 4.3

1. What is the objects clause and are companies required to have such a clause in their constitution?
An objects clause is a clause in the company's articles which states the objects or purposes for which the company was set up. Companies incorporated under the CA 2006 are not required to have an objects clause in their articles but may do so if they wish.

2. What does s. 39(1) of the CA 2006 state?
Section 39(1) of the CA 2006 provides that '[t]he validity of an act done by a company shall not be called into question on the ground of lack of capacity by reason of anything in the company's constitution'. Accordingly, a contract entered into by a company cannot be invalidated on the ground that the contract is outside the scope of the company's contractual capacity.

Test yourself 4.4

1. What is a relationship of agency?
A relationship of agency arises where one person (the principal) appoints another (the agent) to engage in or act on behalf of the principal. This act is usually to bring about a contract between the principal and a third party.

2. What is actual authority?
In *Freeman & Lockyer v Buckhurst Park Properties (Mangal) Ltd* [1964] 2 QB 480 (CA), Diplock LJ defined actual authority as:

> 'a legal relationship between the principal and agent created by a consensual agreement to which they alone are parties. Its scope is to be ascertained by applying ordinary principles of construction of contracts, including any proper implications from the express words used, the usages of the trade, or the course of business between the parties.'

3. How does express actual authority differ from implied actual authority?
Express actual authority refers to authority that has been expressly conferred upon the agent (for example, by the articles). Implied actual authority is authority that has been conferred upon the agent as a result of the conduct of the parties (such as by appointing the agent to a particular position) or the relationship between them.

4. When will an agent have apparent authority?
In order to establish that an agent has apparent authority, three requirements will need to be satisfied, namely:

- there must be a representation;
- this representation must be relied on; and
- the person relying on the representation must alter their position in reliance on that representation.

Test yourself 4.5

1. What does s. 40(1) of the CA 2006 state?
Section 40(1) provides that '[i]n favour of a person dealing with a company in good faith, the power of the directors to bind the company, or authorise others to do so, is deemed to be free of any limitation under the company's constitution'

2. Who can rely on s. 40?
Section 40 can only be relied on by persons dealing with the company. It cannot be used by the company itself. In order to rely on s. 40, the person dealing with the company must also deal with the company in good faith.

3. What does the 'indoor management' rule state?
The 'indoor management rule' states that when persons deal with the company, they can assume that the company's internal rules (such as its articles) have been complied with.

Chapter 5

Test yourself 5.1

1. How does s. 250 of the CA 2006 define a director?
Section 250 of the CA 2006 states that '[i]n the Companies Acts "director" includes any person occupying the position of director, by whatever name called'.

2. What is the difference between a de jure *and a* de facto *director?*
A *de jure* director is a person who has been validly appointed as a director (in accordance with the articles), whereas a *de facto* director is a person who acts as a director but has not been validly appointed.

3. Define the following: (i) shadow director; (ii) alternate director; and (iii) nominee director.
A 'shadow director' is 'a person in accordance with whose directions or instructions the directors of the company are accustomed to act'.

An alternate director is someone who is appointed to act as director on behalf of another director (for example, because that director is ill).

A nominee director is a person who has been appointed to the board to act on behalf of another person (such as a major creditor or shareholder).

Test yourself 5.2

1. Provide examples of persons who are ineligible to act as director.
The following persons are ineligible to act as the company's director:

- when s. 156A of the CA 2006 comes into force, a legal person (such as a company) will not be able to act as director, unless regulations provide for exceptions;
- a person under the age of 16 cannot act as director (CA 2006, s. 157);
- a company's statutory auditor cannot act as its director (CA 2006, s 1214);
- a person subject to a disqualification order/undertaking commits a criminal offence if they act as a director (CDDA 1986, ss. 1 and 13), unless they obtain leave to act; and
- an undischarged bankrupt cannot act as director, unless they obtain the leave of the court (CDDA 1986, s. 11(1)).

2. Who has the power to appoint a director?
A company's first directors will be appointed upon the company's incorporation (CA 2006, s. 16(6)). After that, the appointment of directors is a matter for the company's articles. If the company's articles say nothing about the appointment of directors, then the model articles will apply and provide that a director can be appointed by an ordinary resolution or by a decision of the directors (model articles for private companies, article 17(1); model articles for public companies, article 20). If such a company has excluded the model articles, then the power to appoint a director is exercised by the members passing an ordinary resolution (*Worcester Corsetry Ltd v Witting* [1936] Ch 640 (CA)).

3. What does s. 161(1) of the CA 2006 state? Give three examples of when s. 161 will not apply.
Section 161(1) of the CA 2006 provides that the acts of a person acting as a director are valid notwithstanding that it is afterwards discovered:

- that there was a defect in their appointment;
- that they were disqualified from holding office;
- that they had ceased to hold office; or
- that they were not entitled to vote on the matter in question.

However, s. 161 will not apply in three situations:

- where the person seeking to rely on s. 161 has not acted in good faith (*Channel Collieries Trust Ltd v Dover, St Margaret's and Martin Mill Light Railway Co* [1914] 2 Ch 506 (CA));
- where the person seeking to rely on s. 161 knew, at the time of the appointment, of the defect in the appointment and of the legal effect of the defect (*British Asbestos Co Ltd v Boyd* [1903] 2 Ch 439 (Ch)); and
- where there was no purported appointment in the first place (*Morris v Kanssen and Others* [1946] AC 459 (HL)).

Test yourself 5.3

1. Are directors entitled to be paid for their services?
A director is *prima facie* an office holder and so is not entitled to be paid, unless the payment is authorised (such as by the articles or the director's service contract).

2. Who determines how much a director will be paid?
Who determines a director's pay is a matter for the company's articles. If the articles say nothing on this, the directors' remuneration can be determined by the company in general meeting (*Re George Newman & Co* [1895] 1 Ch 674 (CA)). The model articles provide that the directors themselves can determine their remuneration for their services to the company as directors, and for any other service which they undertake to the company (model articles for private companies, article 19(2); model articles for public companies, article 23(2)). The boards of larger companies will delegate the role of remuneration setting to a remuneration committee.

Test yourself 5.4

1. What are four ways in which a director can vacate office?
The four methods by which a director can vacate office are (i) resignation; (ii) vacation in accordance with the articles; (iii) removal; and (iv) disqualification.

2. How can a director be removed from office?
A director can be removed from office in two ways:

- by passing an ordinary resolution at a meeting (CA 2006, s. 168(1)); or
- by exercising a power of removal in the articles (if the articles contain such a power).

3. Identify five grounds for the disqualification of a director.
The grounds for disqualifying a director as set out in the CDDA 1986 are:

- where they are convicted of an indictable offence in connection with the promotion, formation, management, liquidation or striking off of a company, or with the receivership of a company's property, or with their being an administrative receiver of a company (s. 2);
- where it appears that they have been persistently in default in relation to provisions of the companies legislation requiring any return, account or other document to be filed with, delivered or sent, or notice of any matter to be given, to the registrar of companies (s. 3);
- where they have been found guilty of fraudulent trading under s. 993 of the CA 2006 or other fraud in relation to the company (s. 4);
- where they have been convicted of a specified summary offence and they have, during the five-year period prior to the conviction, been convicted of similar offences at least three times (s. 5);
- where they have been convicted of certain indictable offences overseas that involve (i) the promotion, formation, management, liquidation or

striking off of a company; (ii) the receivership of a company's property; or (iii) a person being an administrative receiver of the company (s. 5A);

- where they are or have been a director or shadow director of a company which has at any time become insolvent (whether while they were a director or subsequently), and their conduct as a director of that company (either taken alone or taken together with their conduct as a director/ shadow director of other companies) makes them unfit to be concerned in the management of a company (s. 6);
- where, in the opinion of the Secretary of State, it is expedient in the public interest that a person who is, or has been, a director or shadow director should be disqualified (s. 8);
- where they have exercised the requisite influence over a person disqualified under s. 6 (s. 8ZA) or s. 8 (s. 8ZD);
- where they have breached competition law and their conduct makes them unfit to be concerned in the management of a company (s. 9A);
- where they have been found liable for fraudulent trading or wrongful trading under IA 1986 (s. 10); and
- where a person is an undischarged bankrupt (s. 11).

4. Explain the distinction between a disqualification order and a disqualification undertaking.
A disqualification order is an order of the court providing that a person is to be disqualified. A disqualification undertaking is an undertaking from the director stating that he will not, for a specified period, act as director of a company and so on.

Chapter 6

Test yourself 6.1

1. In whom is managerial power vested?
The power to manage the company is initially vested in the members but, in all but the smallest companies, it is impractical for the members to manage the company. It is common for the members to delegate managerial power to the directors.

2. What does article 3 of the model articles state?
Article 3 of the model articles states that '[s]ubject to the articles, the directors are responsible for the management of the company's business, for which purpose they may exercise all the powers of the company'.

3. To what extent can the members interfere in management?
If the articles contain a provision vesting general managerial power in the directors (which is usually the case), then the members cannot interfere in management, unless the articles so provide. For example, article 4(1) of the model articles provides that the members may 'by special resolution, direct the directors to take, or refrain from taking, specified action'.

4. Can the directors delegate their managerial powers to others?
By default, the board does not have the power to delegate its managerial powers to others – such delegation is only permissible if the articles allow for it (which they usually do). For example, article 5(1) of the model articles provides the directors with wide powers of delegation, stating that '[s]ubject to the articles, the directors may delegate any of the powers which are conferred on them under the articles:

- to such person or committee;
- by such means (including by power of attorney);
- to such an extent;
- in relation to such matters or territories; and
- on such terms and conditions; as they think fit'.

Test yourself 6.2

1. Who has the power to call a board meeting?
The power to call a board meeting is a matter for the company's articles, with the model articles providing that any director may call a board meeting. Such a meeting is called by providing notice of it to the other directors (model articles for private companies, article 9(1); model articles for public companies, article 8(1)–(3)).

2. In relation to board meetings, what constitutes a quorum?
What constitutes a quorum is a matter for the company's articles. If the articles are silent, a majority of directors will be required to attend (*York Tramways Co Ltd v Willow* (1882) 2 QBD 685 (CA)). The model articles provide that the quorum for a board meeting can be determined by a decision of the directors, but it must not be less than two. If the directors have not decided what constitutes a quorum, it will be two (model articles for private companies, article 11(2); model articles for public companies, article 10(2)).

3. How are board decisions taken in private companies and public companies?
How the board makes decisions at a meeting is a matter for the company's articles, with the model articles specifying different rules for private and public companies.

- Article 7(1) of the model articles for private companies provides that any decision of the directors must either be (i) a majority decision at a meeting; or (ii) a decision taken in accordance with article 8. Article 8(1) and (3) provides that a decision of the directors can be taken without a board meeting if all the directors eligible to vote on the matter indicate to each other by any means that they share a common view on the matter.
- Article 13 of the model articles for public companies provides that, subject to the articles a decision is taken at a board meeting by a majority of the votes of participating directors, and each director participating in a board meeting has one vote. Decisions may also be taken without a meeting via a directors' written resolution.

4. For how long must a company keep minutes of its board meetings?
The Companies Act 2006 provides that every company must record all minutes of proceedings at directors' meetings (s. 248(1)) and must keep these records for at least 10 years from the date of the meeting (s. 248(2)).

Test yourself 6.3

1. Is a company required to appoint a company secretary?
A public company must appoint a company secretary (CA 2006, s. 271), and may have more than one secretary (who will be known as 'joint secretaries'). A private company is not required to appoint a company secretary (CA 2006, s. 270(1)) (unless its articles state otherwise) but it may do so if it wishes.

2. What is the role of a company secretary?
The role of the secretary is not set out in the law, nor are there any activities that the secretary must carry out under the CA 2006. The precise role of the secretary will vary from company to company but, in many companies, the secretary will be 'the chief administrative officer of the company' (*Panorama Developments (Guildford) Ltd v Fidelis Furnishing Fabrics Ltd* [1971] 2 QB 711 (CA)). They will engage in tasks such as:

- ensuring that the company's filing and disclosure requirements are complied with;
- preparing the agenda and minutes of board meetings and general meetings;
- ensuring that board meetings and general meetings are conducted in accordance with the law and the company's articles;
- maintaining the company's books and statutory registers;
- advising on the preparation and publication of annual reports and accounts, and other financial disclosures; and
- advising on compliance with legal requirements and best practice recommendations.

3. What authority does a company secretary have as an agent?
An agent may be given express authority to engage in certain acts and a secretary also has apparent authority to bind the company in relation to administrative matters (*Panorama Developments (Guildford) Ltd v Fidelis Furnishing Fabrics Ltd* [1971] 2 QB 711 (CA)).

Chapter 7

Test yourself 7.1

1. Is the s. 172 duty subjective or objective?
Section 172(1) provides that a director must act *in a way he considers, in good faith, would be most likely to promote the success of the company*. The italicised words here indicate that the duty is subjective, meaning that 'the question is whether the director honestly believed that his act or omission was

in the interests of the company' (*Regentcrest plc v Cohen* [2001] BCC 494 (Ch)). A subjective approach is, however, only of use if directors actually consider whether their actions promoted the success of the company. If a director did not even consider this, then the approach to determining if s. 172 has been breached will cease to be subjective and an objective approach will be used.

2. Can the directors prioritise the interests of the company over the interests of its members?

The courts have held that where the interests of the company conflict with the interests of part of the company's membership, then the directors will not breach s. 172 if they favour the company's interests (*Mutual Life Insurance Co of New York v Rank Organisation Ltd* [1985] BCLC 11 (Ch)). No authority exists on whether the directors can prioritise the interests of the company over all of its members.

3. Identify the six factors listed in s. 172(1) that the directors must have regard to.

The six factors listed in s. 172(1) are:

- the likely consequences of any decision in the long term;
- the interests of the company's employees;
- the need to foster the company's business relationships with suppliers, customers and others;
- the impact of the company's operations on the community and the environment;
- the desirability of the company maintaining a reputation for high standards of business conduct; and
- the need to act fairly as between members of the company.

4. What are the remedies for a breach of the s. 172 duty?

An agreement in breach of the s. 172 duty is voidable at the company's instance. If a breach of the s. 172 duty causes the company loss, the director in breach may be required to compensate the company (*Extrasure Travel Insurances Ltd v Scattergood* [2003] 1 BCLC 598 (Ch)).

Test yourself 7.2

1. How does the standard of care in s. 174 differ from its common law predecessor?

Under the common law, the standard of care was subjective, and was based on the skill and knowledge that the director actually had. Under s. 174, the standard of care has an objective and a subjective component, and is based on:

- the general knowledge, skill and experience that may reasonably be expected of a person carrying out the functions carried out by the director in relation to the company; and
- the general knowledge, skill and experience of the director.

2. When will the subjective element of the s. 174 duty apply?
Section 174(2)(a) imposes a subjective standard based on the actual knowledge, skill and experience of the director. It will only apply where the director has some skill, qualification or experience that merits raising the standard expected of him (for example, a financial director will be expected to have a higher degree of skill and knowledge in relation to financial matters).

3. If a director delegates one of his functions to another person, and that person does not perform with the requisite skill and care, will the director be in breach of the s. 174 duty?
Generally, a director will not breach s. 174 if they delegate a function to another person and that person performs that function unlawfully or with a lack of skill and care (*Dovey v Corey* [1901] AC 477 (HL)). This is subject to several exceptions:

- The directors must exercise reasonable skill and care when deciding to whom their functions are delegated. If they fail to do so, and the delegated functions are performed unlawfully or without due skill and care, the directors could be in breach of the s. 174 duty.
- The directors are required to supervise those persons to whom they have delegated their powers. A failure to supervise such persons can result in a breach of the s. 174 duty.

4. What is the remedy for a breach of the s. 174 duty?
Directors will be required to compensate the company for any loss it sustains due to their breach of the s. 174 duty.

Test yourself 7.3

1. What types of situation do not amount to a conflict under s. 175?
The s. 175 duty will not apply in relation to a transaction or arrangement with the company itself (s. 175(3)), or where the situation cannot reasonably be regarded as likely to give rise to a conflict of interest (s. 175(4)(a)).

2. Are directors able to sit on the boards of competing companies?
There is no rigid rule preventing a director from sitting on the board of a rival company, and so a director is generally free to sit on the board of a rival company (*London and Mashonaland Exploration Co Ltd v New Mashonaland Exploration Co Ltd* [1891] WN 165), unless prohibited from doing so (by the articles or his service contract, for example). However, whether sitting on the board of a rival company is a breach of duty will depend strongly on the facts of the case.

3. Does the s. 175 duty apply to former directors of a company?
Section 175 can apply to a former director of a company where the former director exploits any property, information or opportunity of which he became aware at a time when he was a director of the company (s. 170(2)(a)).

4. When will a director in a position of conflict not be in breach of the s. 175 duty?
The s. 175 duty will not be infringed where the conflict has been authorised by the company (s. 180(4)(a)) or by the directors (s. 175(4)(b)).

5. Can directors authorise a s. 175 conflict?
The directors' ability to authorise a s. 175 conflict is as follows.

- The directors cannot authorise a conflict where statute requires member approval to be provided (e.g. a third-party benefit under s. 176).
- In the case of a private company, the directors may authorise the conflict providing that the company's constitution does not invalidate such authorisation (s. 175(5)(a)). The model articles for private companies do not invalidate the directors' ability to authorise a conflict.
- In the case of a public company, the directors may only authorise a conflict if there is a provision in the articles enabling them to do so (s. 175(5)(b)). The model articles for public companies do not contain such a provision.

Test yourself 7.4

1. Explain the various differences between the duties in ss. 177 and 182.
The differences between the ss. 177 and 182 duties are as follows.

- The s. 177 duty applies to proposed transactions or arrangements, whereas s. 182 applies to transactions or arrangements that the company has entered into.
- Under s. 177, the declaration must be made before the transaction/ arrangement is entered into. Under s. 182, the declaration must be made as soon as is reasonably practicable (s. 182(4)).
- A breach of s. 177 results in civil consequences only. Conversely, a breach of s. 182 is a criminal offence (s. 183).

2. How can a director with an interest in a proposed transaction with the company avoid a breach of the s. 177 duty?
In order to avoid a breach of s. 177, a director will need to declare the nature and extent of their interest to the other directors before the transaction or arrangement is entered into (s. 177(4)). Obviously, this will not apply where the company only has one director.

3. Does a breach of ss. 177 or 182 result in criminal liability?
A breach of s. 177 results in civil consequences only. Conversely, a breach of s. 182 is a criminal offence (s. 183).

Test yourself 7.5

1. Can a director avoid liability for breach of duty by including a provision in the articles excluding such liability?
A director who is liable for breach of duty may try to obtain protection from liability via a provision in the articles. A director's ability to do this is heavily limited by s. 232 of the CA 2006, which provides that any provision that

purports to exempt a director of a company (to any extent) from any liability that would otherwise attach to them in connection with any negligence, default, breach of duty or breach of trust in relation to the company is void (s. 232(1)).

2. Explain the two ways by which a director can obtain relief from liability.
A director can attempt to obtain relief from liability in two ways.

- The company can ratify a breach of duty by passing a resolution of the members (s. 239)).
- The court can relieve a director from liability for breach of duty (s. 1157)).

3. When will a court grant relief under s. 1157?
The court may, under s. 1157, relieve a director from liability if it appears to the court that they acted honestly and reasonably, and that having regard to all the circumstances of the case, they ought fairly to be excused.

Test yourself 7.6

1. What four transactions require member approval?
Part 10, Chapter 4 of the CA 2006 provides that the following four transactions require member approval:

- long-term service contracts;
- substantial property transactions;
- loans, quasi-loans and other credit transactions; and
- remuneration and payments for loss of office.

2. What are the consequences of a director not obtaining member approval for a long-term service contract?
If a director's service contract contains a provision guaranteeing them a term of employment of over two years, then member approval is required. If member approval is not obtained, then the provision in question is void, to the extent of the contravention (s. 189(a)). The remainder of the contract will remain valid, but it will be deemed to contain a term entitling the company to terminate it at any time by giving reasonable notice (s. 189(b)).

3. What is a substantial property transaction?
A substantial property transaction is an arrangement under which:

- a director of a company or its holding company, or a person connected with such a director, acquires or is to acquire from the company (directly or indirectly) a substantial non-cash asset; or
- the company acquires or is to acquire a substantial non-cash asset (directly or indirectly) from such a director or a person so connected (s. 190(1)).

A 'non-cash asset' is defined broadly as 'any property or interest in property, other than cash' (s. 1163(1)). A non-cash asset will be 'substantial' if it is over £100,000 or exceeds 10% of the company's asset value and is more than £5,000 (s. 191(2)).

4. What is a quasi-loan?
A 'quasi-loan' is a transaction under which one party (the creditor) agrees to pay a sum for another person (the borrower) or agrees to reimburse expenditure incurred by another party for another (the borrower):

- on terms that the borrower (or a person on their behalf) will reimburse the creditor; or
- in circumstances giving rise to a liability on the borrower to reimburse the creditor (s. 199(1)).

5. Does a loss of office payment made to a director of a quoted company require member approval?
Sections 226B(1) and 226C(1) provide that a quoted company may not make a remuneration payment or a loss of office payment to a person who is, or is to be or has been, a director of the company unless:

- the payment is consistent with the approved directors' remuneration policy; or
- the payment is approved by a resolution of the members.

Member approval is not required where the loss of office payment is consistent with the approved directors' remuneration policy.

Chapter 8

Test yourself 8.1

1. Are all shareholders in a company also members of that company?
Being a member and being a shareholder are two different things (although, in practice, almost all shareholders will also be members). There may be occasions where a person will acquire shares in a company, but the company should not accept that person as a member (for example, an unincorporated body should not be accepted as a member).

2. What are the two ways by which a person can become a member under s. 112 of the CA 2006?
Section 112 of the CA 2006 provides that are two methods by which a person can become a member:

- the subscribers of a company's memorandum are deemed to have agreed to become members of the company: upon the company's registration, they become members and their names must be entered as such in the register of members (s. 112(1)); or
- every other person who agrees to become a member of the company and whose name is entered in its register of members is a member of the company (s. 112(2)).

3. Does a person need to have their name entered into the register of members in order to become a member?
When the company is first incorporated, the subscribers to the memorandum are deemed to have agreed to become members even if their names are not entered into the register of members (although the company is required to enter their names into the register of members).

4. Provide an example of a situation where the directors should refuse to enter someone's name into the register of members.
It is the directors who decide whether a person's name should be entered into the register of members, and there are several instances where the directors may validly decide to refuse to enter a person's name into the register.

- Unincorporated associations (such as partnerships) have no legal personality and so they should not be accepted as members. In the case of a sole proprietorship, the name of the sole proprietor should be entered into the register. In the case of an ordinary partnership, the names of the partners should instead be entered into the register.
- Companies are generally able to become members of other companies, but there are limits to this. For example, a company cannot generally be a member of itself (*Trevor v Whitworth* (1887) 12 App Cas 409 (HL)).

Test yourself 8.2

1. What information must be included in the register of members?
Section 113(2) and (3) provides that the information that must be included in the register includes:

- the names and addresses of each member;
- the date on which each person was registered as a member;
- the date on which any person ceased to be a member;
- if the company has a share capital, then the register must contain a statement of the shares of each member, setting out (i) the number of shares the member holds and, if applicable, the class of shares; and (ii) the amount paid or agreed to be considered as paid on the shares; and
- if the company does not have a share capital, but it does have more than one class of member, then the register must identify to which class each member belongs.

2. Can the company rectify an error in the register of members?
The company cannot rectify an error in the register (*Gardiner v Victoria Estates Co Ltd* (1885) 12 R 1356). The company must apply to the court for a rectification order.

3. Who has the right to inspect the register of members, and what procedure must they follow?
Any member of the company has a right to inspect the register of members free of charge and anyone else may inspect the register upon paying a fee (s. 116(1)). The process for inspecting the register is that the person wishing to

inspect the register must send a request to the company to inspect the register, in which they must provide certain information (including their name and address) and must state their reason for wanting to inspect the register. The company will either comply with the request, or it may apply to the court for an order refusing the request on the ground that the request was not made for a proper purpose. If the court makes such an order, the company will be directed not to comply with the request.

Test yourself 8.3

1. What is a 'nominee'?
When a person buys shares in a company, they can have those shares registered in the register of members in the name of someone else (this other person is known as the 'nominee').

2. What information is found in the register of interests disclosed?
The register of interests disclosed contains information disclosed to the company under s. 793 (namely information relating to a person's interest in the company's shares).

3. What is a person with significant control?
Schedule 1A, Part 1 of the CA 2006 provides that a person will have significant control if any one of the following conditions are satisfied:

- a person holds, directly or indirectly, more than 25% of the company's shares or voting rights;
- a person holds the right, directly or indirectly, to appoint or remove a majority of the company's directors;
- a person has the right to exercise, or actually exercises, significant influence or control over the company; or
- the trustees of a trust or the members of the firm that is not a legal person (i) meet any of the conditions above in relation to the company or would do so if they were individuals; and (ii) have the right to exercise, or actually exercise significant influence or control over the activities of that trust or firm.

Chapter 9

Test yourself 9.1

1. Explain the difference in the ways that votes are calculated at a meeting and by using the written resolution procedure.
Votes are calculated differently based on whether a resolution is at a meeting or if the written resolution procedure is used.

- Where the resolution is tabled at a meeting, the requisite majority is calculated based on the votes cast by those eligible to vote (ss.282(3) and (4) and 283(4) and (5)). In other words, the votes are calculated based only on those who actually vote.

- Where a written resolution is used, the requisite majority is calculated based on the voting rights of the total number of members eligible to vote (ss. 282(2) and 283(2)), not just those who actually do vote.

2. Explain the difference between an ordinary resolution, a special resolution and a resolution.
The three resolution types are:

- an ordinary resolution is a resolution that is passed by a simple majority (i.e. over 50%) (s. 282(1));
- a special resolution is a resolution that is passed by a majority of not less than 75% (s. 283(1)); and
- a resolution (i.e. one that is not specified as ordinary or special) will be classed as an ordinary resolution (and so will require a simple majority), unless the company's articles specify a higher majority or unanimity (s. 281(3)).

3. What does the unanimous assent rule state?
The unanimous assent rule provides that if all of the members agree on a matter, the decision will be validly made even if no meeting takes place and no resolution is passed.

4. What types of decisions cannot be taken by unanimous assent?
The courts have limited the ability to use the unanimous assent rule in several ways, including:

- the unanimous assent rule will not apply where statute requires that a decision be taken at a meeting (*Re Oceanrose Investments Ltd* [2008] EWHC 3475 (Ch));
- in *EIC Services Ltd v Phipps* [2003] EWHC 1507 (Ch), the court stated that the unanimous assent rule can only be used in cases where (i) the members who assented had appropriate or full knowledge of the matter in question; and (ii) all the members gave their actual assent (if a member's assent is not sought, the rule will not apply even if the member would likely have assented); and
- the rule cannot be used to make a decision that could not have been made by a resolution (e.g. to declare an unlawful dividend. *Secretary of State for Business, Innovation and Skills v Doffman* [2010] EWHC 3175 (Ch)).

Test yourself 9.2

1. Identify three possible limitations on a member's ability to vote.
A member's ability to vote can be taken away or restricted in several ways, including:

- a member may be unable to vote if his shares have no voting rights;
- a company's articles may place restrictions upon a member's ability to vote; and

- statute may limit a member's ability to vote (e.g. a director who is also a member cannot vote on a resolution to ratify his negligence or breach of duty (s. 239(3) and (4)).

2. What are the two methods of voting on a resolution and how do they differ?
There are two different ways to pass resolutions at a meeting:

- The first method is a show of hands, under which the members attending raise their hands to signify support for, or opposition to, a resolution. Each member will have one vote, unless the articles state otherwise (s. 284(2) and (4)).
- The second method is a poll vote, under which each member has one vote per share, unless the company has no share capital, in which case, each member has one vote (s. 284(3) and (4)).

3. What is a proxy?
A member is entitled to appoint another person (known as a 'proxy') to exercise all or any of their rights to attend, speak and vote at a meeting of the company (s. 324(1)).

4. What is a corporate representative?
A corporate representative is a person who has been authorised by a resolution of the directors of a company (*A*) to represent *A* at a meeting of another company (*B*) in which *A* is a member (s. 323(1)). The representative will be entitled to exercise *A*'s powers as a member at the meeting.

Test yourself 9.3

1. What types of company must hold an AGM?
The requirements placed upon companies to hold an AGM are as follows.

- A private company does not need to hold an annual general meeting, but it can do if it so wishes. A private company will be required to hold an AGM if it is a traded company (s. 336(1A)) or if its articles require that an AGM be held.
- A public company must hold an AGM every year within a six-month period beginning with the day following its accounting reference date (s. 336(1)). This period is increased to nine months in the case of a traded company (s. 336(1A)).

2. Identify five items of business that typically arise at an AGM.
The business that is typically dealt with at an AGM includes:

- laying the accounts and the various reports before the meeting;
- a resolution providing that the members agree to receive and adopt the accounts and reports;
- approving the remuneration report (if the company is quoted);
- approving the appointment/re-appointment of directors and the auditor;
- declaration of a final dividend; and

- providing directors of the company with authorisation to engage in certain acts (such as allot shares, disapply pre-emption rights, authorise the company to purchase its own shares and so on).

3. Under the model articles, when can a chair adjourn a meeting of the company?
The model articles (model articles for private companies, article 41(2) and (3); model articles for public companies, article 33(2) and (3)) provide that a chair can adjourn a meeting in the following circumstances:

- if a meeting is not quorate within half an hour of the time it was due to start, or if it starts quorate but then becomes inquorate, then the chair must adjourn the meeting;
- the chair may adjourn the meeting if the meeting consents to an adjournment;
- the chair may adjourn the meeting if it appears to them that an adjournment is necessary to protect the safety of any person attending the meeting or ensure that the business of the meeting is conducted in an orderly manner; or
- the chair must adjourn a general meeting if directed to do so by the general meeting.

4. What records of meetings and resolutions must the company keep, and for how long must they be kept?
Specified records must be kept by a company for at least 10 years (s. 355(2)) and any member can inspect these records free of charge (s. 358(3)). The records that must be kept are:

- copies of all resolutions of members passed otherwise than at general meetings (such as written resolutions);
- minutes of all proceedings of general meetings; and
- details of decisions taken by a sole member (ss. 355(1) and 357).

Chapter 10

Test yourself 10.1

1. If a third party causes loss to both the company and its members, can both sue to recover their loss?
A third party may cause loss to both the company and its members. In such a case, the general rule is that both the company and its members have a personal right to sue the wrongdoer (*Pender v Lushington* (1877) 6 ChD 70 (Ch)).

2. What is the no-reflective loss principle?
The no-reflective loss principle basically states that where the members' losses are reflective of the loss sustained by the company, then it is the company that should recover the loss and the member will not be able to claim. An obvious example of such a situation is where a person causes loss to the company, which in turn causes the company's share price to drop. Both the company and

its shareholders have suffered a loss, but the loss suffered by the shareholders is merely reflective of that suffered by the company.

3. In what situation will the no-reflective loss principle not apply?
The no-reflective loss principle will not apply where the actions of a person have caused a member loss and that loss is reflective of that of the company, but the company is unable to claim due to the loss it has sustained (*Giles v Rhind* [2002] EWCA Civ 1428).

4. What is the difference between a representative action and a group litigation order?
Where more than one person has the same interest in a claim, then a representative action may be commenced by one or more of the persons who have the same interest as representatives of any other persons who have that interest (CPR, r 19.6(1)). Under a representative action, all the affected members will obtain the same remedy. If differing members wish to obtain differing remedies, then a group litigation order will be preferable.

Test yourself 10.2

1. What two principles form the rule in* Foss v Harbottle*?
The two principles in *Foss v Harbottle* are:

- the 'proper claimant principle', which provides that if a wrong is committed against a company, then only the company can sue for redress and its members cannot sue on the company's behalf; and
- the 'irregularity principle', which provides that a member cannot bring a claim in relation to an irregularity that could be remedied or ratified by a simple majority of the members.

2. In what situations could a common law derivative action be brought?
In *Edwards v Halliwell* [1950] 2 All ER 1064 (CA), Jenkins LJ stated that there were four instances where a derivative action could be brought, namely:

- where the act complained of was illegal or *ultra vires*;
- where the act complained of infringed the personal rights of a member;
- where the act complained of could only be done or sanctioned by the passing of a special resolution; and
- where the act complained of constituted a 'fraud on the minority'.

3. What is a derivative claim and what causes of action can form the basis of a derivative claim?
A derivative claim is a claim brought by a member of a company in respect of a cause of action vested in the company, which seeks relief on behalf of the company (CA 2006, s. 260(1)). A derivative claim can only derive from an actual or proposed act or omission involving negligence, default, breach of duty or breach of trust by a director of the company.

4. Briefly explain the process used by the court to determine whether a derivative claim should be permitted to continue.

The court uses a two-stage procedure in order to determine if a derivative claim should be given permission to continue.

- In stage 1, the court will determine if, based on the evidence provided, there is a *prima facie* case for granting permission to continue the claim (s. 261(2)).
- In stage 2, the court will decide whether permission to continue should actually be granted. Section 263(2) sets out certain circumstances in which permission must be refused. Section 263(3) and (4) sets out factors that must be taken into account by the court when deciding whether to grant permission for the claim to continue.

Test yourself 10.3

1. A s. 994 petition can be made by which parties?

Section 994(1) provides that a petition may be made by 'a member of a company', so any person who is a member within s. 112 may petition the court. In two situations, non-members may also petition the court.

- A person who is not a member may petition the court if shares have been transferred or transmitted to them by the operation of law (s. 994(2)).
- The Secretary of State may bring a petition in certain circumstances (s. 995), although such petitions are extremely rare (see e.g. *Re Scitec Group Ltd* [2012] EWHC 661 (Ch)).

2. A s. 994 petition can be brought against which parties?

This will depend upon whether s. 994(1)(a) or (b) is applicable.

- Section 994(1)(a) does not identify whose conduct must be unfairly prejudicial, and so a claim can be based on the actions of a wide variety of persons, including the company, the directors, other members or third parties.
- As s. 994(1)(b) refers to an actual or proposed omission of the company, the courts have held that 'the petitioner must identify something which the company does or fails to do' (*Graham v Every* [2014] EWCA Civ 191 (Arden LJ)).

3. Provide eight examples of conduct that has been held to amount to unfairly prejudicial conduct.

Examples of conduct that have been held to amount to unfairly prejudicial conduct include the following.

- Abuse of a controlling position can amount to unfair prejudice, with examples including the directors (i) selling company assets at an undervalue to another company they control (*Re Little Olympian Each Ways Ltd (No 3)* [1995] 1 BCLC 636 (Ch)); (ii) transferring business to another company they control (*Re London School of Electronics Ltd* [1986] Ch 211 (Ch)); or (iii) paying themselves excessive remuneration (*Re Cumana Ltd* [1986] BCLC 430 (CA)).

- Serious mismanagement of a company (*Re Macro (Ipswich) Ltd* [1994] 2 BCLC 354 (Ch)).
- A breach of directors' duties (see e.g. *Re Cumana Ltd* [1986] BCLC 430 (CA)).
- A breach of the company's constitution, or statutory rights (see e.g. *Re a Company (No 00789 of 1987)* [1990] BCLC 384 (Ch)).
- Criminal conduct (*Bermuda Cablevision Ltd v Colica Trust Co Ltd* [1998] AC 198 (PC)).
- Exclusion from management of a quasi-partnership company (*Re Ghyll Beck Driving Range Ltd* [1993] BCLC 1126 (Ch)).
- A failure to consider paying dividends (*Re McCarthy Surfacing Ltd* [2008] EWHC 2279 (Ch)), the payment of derisory dividends (*Re Sam Weller & Sons Ltd* [1990] Ch 682 (Ch)), or refusing to pay a declared dividend (*Grace v Biagioli* [2005] EWCA Civ 1222).

4. Give five examples of the types of remedy that the court can order under s. 996.

Although the court can make any order that it thinks fit, s. 996(2) provides a non-exhaustive list of remedies that the court can award, including:

- an order regulating the conduct of the company's affairs in the future (e.g. where the defendant is a director, the court may strip that director of certain powers);
- an order requiring the company to refrain from doing an act complained of, or to perform an act that it has failed to perform;
- an order authorising civil proceedings to be brought in the name and on behalf of the company by such persons and on such terms as the court may direct;
- an order requiring the company not to make any, or any specified, alterations in its articles without the leave of the court;
- an order providing for the purchase of the shares of any members of the company by other members or by the company itself and, in the case of a purchase by the company itself, a reduction of the company's capital accordingly.

5. When determining the value of shares, when will the court discount the price of the shares?

The court will normally apply a discount where the claimant is a minority shareholder in order to reflect the minority shareholder's lack of control.

6. Can the court wind up a company under s. 996?

The issue is not entirely clear. In *Apex Global Management Ltd v FI Call Ltd* [2015] EWHC 3269 (Ch), Hildyard J implied that winding up was available by stating that 'the court should not ordinarily make a winding-up order pursuant to section 996, given the specific provisions for such a remedy …' However, the Law Commission has argued that winding up is not available based on the judgment of Ferris J in *Re Full Cup International Trading Ltd* [1995] BCC 682 (Ch).

Test yourself 10.4

1. What is a contributory?
A 'contributory' is a 'person liable to contribute to the assets of a company in the event of its being wound up' (IA 1986, s. 79(1)). An obvious example of a contributory would be shareholder who had not fully paid for their shares.

2. Provide five examples of the type of conduct that may result in the company being wound up.
The types of conduct that may, on the facts, result in a company being wound up under s. 122(1)(g) include the following.

- If a company is formed for a particular purpose (this is known as its 'substratum') and this purpose is stated in its objects clause, then a company may be wound up if it becomes impossible to fulfil this purpose.
- A company may be wound up where it becomes deadlocked.
- A company may be wound up if it was set up for an unlawful purpose.
- A company may be wound up if it was set up for a fraudulent purpose.
- In *Loch v John Blackwood Ltd* [1924] AC 783 (PC), Lord Shaw stated that a company may be wound up where there is a 'justifiable lack of confidence in the management of the company's affairs'.

3. What are three characteristics of a quasi-partnership?
In *Ebrahimi v Westbourne Galleries Ltd* [1973] AC 360 (HL), Lord Wilberforce stated that the characteristics of a quasi-partnership company are:

- there will be an association formed or continued on the basis of a personal relationship, involving mutual confidence – this element will often be found where a pre-existing partnership has been converted into a limited company;
- there will be an agreement, or understanding, that all, or some (for there may be 'sleeping' members), of the shareholders shall participate in the conduct of the business; or
- there will be restrictions upon the transfer of the members' interest in the company – so that if confidence is lost, or one member is removed from management, they cannot take out their stake and go elsewhere.

4. Can a claimant bring a winding up petition and an unfair prejudice petition in relation to the same conduct?
It is possible for a claimant to bring a winding up petition and an unfair prejudice petition in relation to the same conduct, but the court has issued a Practice Direction stating that a winding up petition should only accompany an unfair prejudice petition if winding up 'is the relief which the petitioner prefers or if it is considered that it may be the only relief to which he is entitled' (*Practice Direction (Companies Court: Contributory's Petition)* [1990] 1 WLR 490 (Ch)).

Chapter 11

Test yourself 11.1

1. Explain the distinction between a share's nominal value and the share premium.
Section 542(1) of the CA 2006 provides that shares in a limited company must each have a fixed nominal value attached to them. Shares are often allotted for more than their nominal value, and the excess is known as the share premium.

2. Explain the distinction between a company's allotted share capital and its issued share capital.
The total nominal value of shares that have actually been allotted is known as the allotted share capital. Once shares have been allotted to a person and that person's name has been entered into the register of members in respect of those shares, those shares have been issued (*National Westminster Bank plc v Inland Revenue Commissioners* [1995] 1 AC 119 (HL)). The total nominal value of shares that have been issued is called the issued share capital (s. 546(1)(a)).

3. Explain the distinction between a company's paid-up share capital and its called-up share capital.
A company's paid-up share capital represents the combined total of the nominal value of shares that has actually been paid. A company's called-up share capital represents the paid-up share capital plus the amount called for/instalment amount due (irrespective of whether this payment is actually made).

Test yourself 11.2

1. What is the difference between allotting and issuing shares?
The distinction between when shares are allotted and when they are issued is:

- shares are allotted 'when a person acquires the unconditional right to be included in the company's register of members in respect of the shares' (CA 2006, s. 558); and
- shares are issued when the person's name is actually entered into the register of members (*National Westminster Bank v Inland Revenue Commissioners* [1995] 1 AC 119 (HL)).

2. A private company that has allotted ordinary shares wishes to allot preference shares. Do the directors have the authority to allot these shares?
Where a private company that has allotted ordinary shares wishes to allot preference shares, then the directors will only have the authority to allot shares on behalf of the company if they are authorised to do so by the company's articles or by a resolution of the company (s. 551(1)).

3. Explain the concept of a minimum share capital.
A public company must not conduct any business until it has been issued with a trading certificate (CA 2006, s. 761(1)). The Registrar should not issue a public company with a trading certificate unless the nominal value of the company's

allotted share capital is not less than the authorised minimum (s. 761(2)). This authorised minimum is £50,000 or the prescribed euro equivalent (s. 763(1)).

4. What are pre-emption rights?
Where pre-emption rights apply, the company cannot allot equity securities unless it has first offered them to existing shareholders in a manner that allows them to maintain their existing shareholding.

5. Explain the distinction between fully paid, partly-paid and nil-paid shares.
A company can allot shares that are:

- fully paid (i.e. the full purchase price is payable on allotment);
- partly paid (i.e. part of the purchase price is due on allotment, with the remainder at a later date); or
- nil paid (nothing is due on allotment, with the full price to be paid at some point in the future).

6. What limitations are placed upon a public company's ability to accept non-cash consideration as payment for shares?
A public company's ability to accept non-cash consideration as payment for shares is limited in several ways:

- A public company must not accept, in payment for its shares or any premium on them, an undertaking from a person that he or someone else will do work or perform services for the company (s. 585(1)).
- A public company cannot accept as payment an undertaking which is to be performed more than five years after the date of the allotment (s. 587(2)).
- A public company cannot generally accept non-cash consideration as payment for shares, unless the non-cash consideration has been independently valued and a copy of the valuation report made available to the company and the proposed allottee (s. 593(1)).

7. What two functions does a share certificate fulfil?
A share certificate fulfils two functions. First, it provides basic information about the shares to which it relates (what information is contained in a share certificate is a matter for the company's articles). Second, the share certificate provides evidence that the person named on it holds legal title to the shares related to the certificate.

Test yourself 11.3

1. What three sets of rules within the FCA Handbook are relevant to the public offering of shares?
The key rules within the FCA Handbook relating to a public offering of shares are:

- the Listing Rules, which set out the rules for listing shares and the rules that listed companies must comply with;

- the Prospectus Rules, which set out rules regarding the preparation and publication of prospectuses; and
- the Disclosure Guidance and Transparency Rules, which impose a range of disclosure obligations on listed companies.

2. Identify the four main types of public offering of shares.
There are four main types of public offer.

- An offer for subscription involves the company offering to the public a certain amount of shares.
- An offer for sale involves an investment bank subscribing for all the shares being offered by the company, and the bank then offering those shares to the public.
- A placing usually involves an investment bank 'placing' its shares with selected purchasers (normally institutional investors selected by the bank), rather than the public at large. The bank is essentially identifying which persons may wish to purchase the shares. Once the placing is made, those persons can then decide whether to purchase the shares or not.
- A rights issue is an offer made to existing shareholders of the company, under which each shareholder is offered shares in proportion to their existing shareholding. It is often the case that shareholders who choose not to take up the rights offer can sell the right to purchase the shares to another person (if the shareholder does not have this right, it is known as an 'open offer').

3. Explain the distinction between a standard listing and a premium listing.
Companies with a standard listing are required to comply with certain base obligations. Companies with a premium listing are subject to greater regulation and the UK Corporate Governance Code applies to companies with a premium listing.

4. When will a company be required to prepare and publish a prospectus?
Section 85(1) and (2) of FSMA 2000 provides that it is unlawful for transferable securities to be offered to the public, or request that shares be admitted to trading on a UK regulated market, unless an approved prospectus has been made available before the offer/request is made.

5. If a company decides to divide a prospectus up into separate documents, what are these documents? Briefly explain what they cover.
If a prospectus is drawn up as separate documents, then three separate documents are required (PR 2.2.2(1)):

- the registration document, which contains information about the company issuing the shares in question;
- the securities note, which contains information about the shares to which the prospectus relates; and

- the summary, which must convey concisely, in non-technical language and in an appropriate structure, the key information relevant to the securities which are the subject of the prospectus. When read with the rest of the prospectus, it must be an aid to investors considering whether to invest in the securities (FSMA 2000, s. 87A(6)).

6. What is underwriting?
An underwriting agreement typically involves the company entering into an agreement with an underwriter (usually an investment bank), under which the underwriter agrees to subscribe for or purchase any shares that are not taken up by the public.

Test yourself 11.4

1. What are class rights?
Most companies with a share capital will have only one class of share, and most companies without a share capital will only have one class of member. However, as long as the articles so permit, companies may have multiple classes of share or member, with each class having different rights.

2. What approach have the courts adopted in order to determine if an alteration of class rights amounts to a variation?
The approach adopted by the courts was set out in *White v Bristol Aeroplane Co Ltd* [1953] Ch 65 (CA), where Evershed MR stated that 'there is to my mind a distinction, and a sensible distinction, between an affecting of the rights and an affecting of the enjoyment of the rights, or of the stockholders' capacity to turn them to account'. In other words, a distinction is drawn between an alteration that affects a class right and an alteration that affects the enjoyment of a class right, with only the former being capable of amounting to a variation.

3. What are the two methods for varying class rights?
Sections 630 and 631 provide that there are only two ways to vary class rights.

- First, where the company's articles contain a provision stating how class rights are to be varied, class rights can be varied by complying with that provision (s.s 630(2)(a) and 631(2)(a)).
- Second, where the articles contain no provision for the variation of class rights, then class rights can be varied as follows:
  - In order to vary rights attached to a class of shares, the consent of the holders of shares of that class will need to be obtained (s. 630(2)(b)).
  - In order to vary the rights of a class of member in a company without a share capital, the consent of members of that class will need to be obtained (s. 631(2)(b)).

Test yourself 11.5

1. Explain the difference between the transfer and transmission of shares.
Transmission of shares occurs where a person acquires shares by operation of the law. Shares are transferred where they pass from one person to another and this is not by the operation of law.

2. What document is required to transfer certificated shares?
A company will not register a transfer of certificated shares unless a proper instrument of transfer has been delivered (CA 2006, s. 770(1)). A company's articles may specify what amounts to a 'proper instrument of transfer', but this usually refers to the 'stock transfer form' found in Schedule 1 of the Stock Transfer Act 1963.

3. In what three situations will the transmission of shares occur?
The transmission of shares occurs in three situations:

- The death of a shareholder will cause their shares to be transmitted to their personal representative.
- The shares of a shareholder who has been declared bankrupt will be transmitted to their trustee in bankruptcy (IA 1986, ss. 283(1) and 306).
- The shares of a shareholder who becomes a patient under the Mental Health Act 1983 will be transmitted to a receiver appointed by the Court of Protection.

Chapter 12

Test yourself 12.1

1. What are the two methods by which a company can reduce its share capital?
The courts have long held that a company may only reduce its share capital in a manner permitted by the Companies Act (*Trevor v Whitworth* (1887) 12 App Cas 409 (HL)), with the CA 2006 providing for two methods to reduce capital:

- special resolution followed by court confirmation; and
- special resolution followed by solvency statement.

2. What two limitations are placed on a company's ability to reduce its share capital?
A company's ability to reduce its share capital is limited as follows:

- a company that seeks to reduce its capital by special resolution supported by solvency statement cannot do so if the result of the reduction is that there would be no members of the company holding shares other than redeemable shares (s. 641(2)); and
- a company may not reduce its share capital by either method if the reduction is part of a scheme under which a person is to acquire all the

shares in the company or all the shares in one or more classes, other than those they already hold (s. 641(2A)).

3. When deciding whether to confirm a reduction, what is the court's principal concern?
When deciding whether to confirm the reduction, the primary concern of the court is the interests of the company creditors.

4. What does a solvency statement state?
The solvency statement is a statement that each of the directors has formed the opinion that:

- as regards the company's situation at the date of the statement, there is no ground on which the company could then be found to be unable to pay (or otherwise discharge) its debts; and
- the company will be able to pay (or otherwise discharge) its debts as they fall due during the year immediately following the date of the statement.

Test yourself 12.2

1. Why are companies generally prohibited from acquiring their own shares?
Companies are generally prohibited from acquiring their own shares for various reasons:

- such an acquisition would return capital to the shareholders, which is generally prohibited under the capital maintenance rules;
- a company could purchase its own shares in an attempt to manipulate its own share price; and
- such an acquisition would reduce the company's share capital, and could therefore allow a company to avoid the procedures for reducing share capital discussed in the previous section.

2. What are redeemable shares?
Redeemable shares are shares issued by the company on the condition that they will be redeemed (bought back) by the company if the company or the shareholder so requires.

3. Does a company require authorisation in its articles in order to issue redeemable shares?
A public company may only issue redeemable shares if authorised to do so by its articles (s. 684(3)). A private company does not require authorisation from its articles, but its articles may exclude or restrict the company's ability to issue redeemable shares (s. 684(2)).

4. If a company wishes to redeem or purchase its own shares, where must the payment come from?
The payment for redeemable shares must come from the company's distributable profits or from the proceeds of a fresh issue of shares made for the purpose of the redemption (s. 687(2)).

5. What happens to a company's shares when it redeems or purchases them?
When redeemable shares are redeemed, they are cancelled and the company's share capital must be reduced by the nominal value of the shares redeemed (s. 688).

Test yourself 12.3

1. Why was the prohibition on providing financial assistance introduced?
The prohibition on a company providing financial assistance to acquire its own shares was introduced to:

- prevent a company from being able to manipulate its share price; and
- to prevent a company (*A*) from providing financial assistance to another company (*B*), and *B* then using that money to purchase shares in *A* and take it over.

2. What types of company are prohibited from providing financial assistance to acquire their shares?
The prohibition on providing financial assistance only applies to public companies.

3. What is 'financial assistance'? Provide three examples of such assistance.
Section 677(1) of the CA 2006 provides that 'financial assistance' means financial assistance given by way of gift, guarantee, security, indemnity, release or waiver, or loan, and any other financial assistance given by a company where the net assets of the company are reduced to a material extent by the giving of the assistance or the company has no assets. Examples of financial assistance include:

- where a company lends money to a person and that person uses that money to buy shares in the company;
- where a company guarantees a loan made by a bank to another person (*A*) and *A* uses that money to buy shares in the company; and
- where a person (*X*) borrows money from a bank and uses it to buy enough shares to control a company. *X* then uses the resources of the company to repay the money loaned by the bank.

4. Explain the 'principal purpose' and 'incidental part' exceptions.
Financial assistance will not be prohibited where:

- the assistance is given in good faith in the interests of the company; and
- the company's principal purpose in giving the assistance is not for the purpose of acquiring the shares, or the giving of assistance is for the purpose of acquiring shares but this is only an incidental part of some larger purpose of the company (ss. 678(2) and (4) and 679(2) and (4)).

5. What are the consequences of a company providing prohibited financial assistance?

The CA 2006 only states one consequence of a company engaging in prohibited financial assistance – that the company and every officer in default commits a criminal offence (s. 680(1)). However, a number of civil consequences have been established by the courts, including:

- an agreement to provide unlawful financial assistance is unenforceable in its entirety (*Heald v O'Connor* [1971] 1 WLR 497 (QB));
- a director who is party to a transaction that amounts to prohibited financial assistance may be held in breach of duty (see e.g. *Re In a Flap Envelope Co Ltd* [2003] EWHC 3047 (Ch)), or disqualified (*Re Continental Assurance Co of London plc (No 1)* [1996] BCC 888 (Ch)).
- the court in *Belmont Finance Corp v Williams Furniture Ltd (No 2)* [1980] 1 All ER 393 (CA) held that (i) a recipient of prohibited financial assistance will be liable to account for the sum received if they knew or ought to have known of the impropriety of the transaction; and (ii) a person who knowingly assists the directors to cause the company to provide prohibited financial assistance can be personally liable to the company.

Test yourself 12.4

1. How does the CA 2006 define a 'distribution'?

The definition of 'distribution' in the CA 2006 is extremely wide and means 'every description of distribution of a company's assets to its members, whether in cash or otherwise' (s. 829(1)).

2. What is a dividend? Explain the differences between a final dividend and an interim dividend.

A dividend is simply a distribution of part or all of the company's profits to its members, with each member usually getting *X* pence for each share they own. There are two types of dividend payment:

- A final dividend, which is a dividend paid out once the company's final accounts have been prepared (i.e. it is paid following the end of relevant financial year).
- An interim dividend, which is a dividend paid out before the company's final accounts have been prepared (i.e. it is paid during the relevant financial year).

3. A distribution must be paid out of what assets of the company?

Section 830(1) of the CA 2006 states that '[a] company may only make a distribution out of profits available for the purpose', which are defined by s. 830(2) as the company's 'accumulated, realised profits, so far as not previously utilised by distribution or capitalisation, less its accumulated, realised losses, so far as not previously written off in a reduction or reorganisation of capital duly made'.

4. What is the usual three-stage process for paying a final dividend?
The usual three-stage process for paying a final dividend is:

- the directors will recommend an amount of distributable profit to be distributed by way of dividend;
- the company will 'declare' the dividend by the members passing a resolution;
- the dividend will be paid out based on the rights of the members.

5. Do dividends have to be paid in cash?
Dividends must generally be paid in cash (*Wood v Odessa Waterworks Co* (1889) 42 ChD 636 (Ch)), unless the company's articles provide for some other form of payment

6. If an unlawful dividend is paid, to what extent will the company's directors and members be liable?
If an unlawful dividend is paid, then:

- a director who authorises the payment of an unlawful distribution is jointly and severally liable to repay the amount of the distribution to the company (*Re Exchange Banking Co, Flitcroft's Case* (1882) 21 ChD 519 (CA));
- if, at the time of the distribution, a member knows or has reasonable grounds for believing that it was made unlawfully, the member is liable:
  - to repay the distribution (or part of it, as the case may be) to the company; or
  - in the case of a distribution not made in cash, to repay the company a sum equal to the value of the distribution (or part) at the time (s. 847).

Chapter 13

Test yourself 13.1

1. Explain the difference between secured and unsecured borrowing.
It is common for creditors to take steps to ensure that repayment is made. The most common way to do this is to obtain a right or interest over an asset or the business of the company. Where such a right or interest is obtained, the loan is said to have been 'secured' as the creditor has sought to secure his chances of being repaid. Where the creditor does not secure the loan, the loan is said to be unsecured.

2. What are the advantages of taking security over a company's assets?
The advantages of taking security over a company's assets are:

- if the company breaches the loan agreement, the lender will have rights over the company's assets that have been secured (for example, selling the asset and recovering the proceeds);

- if the company is liquidated, secured debts are paid ahead of unsecured debts, meaning that secured creditors have a better chance of being repaid; and
- a secured creditor may be able to negotiate other benefits that unsecured creditors do not have (such as the right to consult with the board in certain cases).

3. Explain the differences between, and types of, possessory and non-possessory security.
Possessory security involves the creditor taking physical possession of the secured asset. Where security is non-possessory, the borrower will retain possession of the secured asset.

Test yourself 13.2

1. What is a fixed charge and why do they provide such a powerful form of security?
A fixed charge is a charge taken over a specific asset of the company (such as a building or piece of equipment). Depending upon the terms of the charge, it will provide the chargeholder with certain rights and impose upon the chargor certain restrictions. The exact rights contained within a fixed charge will depend upon its terms, but typically fixed charges will provide the following advantages.

- Should the company default on the loan or if it enters liquidation, then the chargeholder will typically be able to appropriate the charged asset, and sell it to recover the money owed.
- The company will be unable to sell or deal with the charged asset, unless it first repays the chargeholder or obtains the chargeholder's consent to sell or deal with the charged asset (*Agnew v Inland Revenue Commissioner* [2001] UKPC 28).
- The charge instrument usually provides that no subsequent fixed charges can be granted over the charged assets, unless the chargeholder so agrees.
- Assets secured by the fixed charge are not available to the liquidator if the company enters liquidation. This effectively means that debts secured by fixed charge rank ahead of all other debts.

2. What are the three key characteristics of a floating charge?
In *Re Yorkshire Woolcombers Association Ltd* [1903] 2 Ch 284 (CA), Romer LJ identified the three key characteristics of a floating charge:

- the charge is taken over a class of assets present or future (in practice, it is common for a floating charge to be taken over all the assets and business of the company);
- that class of assets is one which, in the ordinary course of the company's business, would be changing from time to time (such as stock in trade); and
- until some future step is taken by the chargeholder, the company is free to use the charged assets.

3. What does 'crystallisation' mean and when will a floating charge crystallise?
A floating charge floats over the charged assets until some specified event occurs, at which point it becomes a fixed charge over the charged assets (although it will not rank as a fixed charge for the purposes of liquidation). The chargor is then no longer free to dispose or deal with the charged assets, unless the chargeholder consents. The process by which a floating charge becomes fixed is known as 'crystallisation'.

The charge instrument may specify which events will cause crystallisation. It is common for the instrument to specify that the charge will crystallise if the company defaults on the loan, or if the chargeholder gives notice of crystallisation. It is implied that crystallisation will occur upon the following events (although the charge instrument can provide that they will not cause the charge to crystallise):

- the company goes into liquidation (*Re Panama New Zealand and Australian Royal Mail Co* (1870) LR 5 Ch App 318 (CA));
- the company's business ceases (*Re Woodroffes (Musical Instruments) Ltd* [1986] Ch 366 (Ch)); or
- a receiver is appointed (*Re Carshalton Park Estate Ltd* [1908] 2 Ch 62 (Ch)).

Test yourself 13.3

1. Why is it important to be able to distinguish between fixed and floating charges?
It is vital to be able to distinguish between fixed and floating charges for several reasons:

- In the event of a company being liquidated, assets secured by fixed charge are not available to the liquidator, meaning that fixed chargeholders effectively rank ahead of other creditors.
- In the event of a liquidation, a portion of the debt owed to floating chargeholders is set aside to pay off the unsecured creditors. This does not occur in relation to a debt owed to a fixed chargeholder.
- Certain floating charges are vulnerable to being set aside by the liquidator, whereas fixed charges cannot be set aside by a liquidator.

2. If a charge instrument describes the charge as fixed, does that mean that the charge is a fixed charge?
The charge instrument's classification of the charge is relevant, but not conclusive (*Street v Mountford* [1985] AC 809 (HL)). The court may conclude that a charge that is described as floating is actually a fixed charge, or vice versa.

3. What are book debts?
The Insolvency Service defines book debts as 'sums of money owed to a bankrupt, partnership or company … usually for goods or service supplied or work carried out'.

4. Can a fixed charge be taken over a company's book debts?
It is possible to take a fixed charge over book debts. Lord Hope in *Re Spectrum Plus Ltd* [2005] UKHL 41, stated that in order to take a fixed charge over book debts, either of the following would need to occur:

- the charge should prevent the company from dealing with the book debts in any way, so they are preserved for the benefit of the chargeholder's security; or
- the charge should prevent all dealings with the book debts other than their collection, and to require the proceeds when collected to be paid:
  - to the chargeholder directly;
  - into an account with the chargeholder bank that the company cannot access; or
  - into a separate account with a third-party bank, which the chargeholder then takes a fixed charge over.

Test yourself 13.4

1. Explain how the post-2013 system of registration differs to the pre-2013 system.
Before 2013, companies were required to keep a register of charges. A failure to do so was a criminal offence. The post-2013 system of registration is different. Companies are no longer required to keep a register of charges, and companies are not required to register charges. However, if a charge is not registered, then it will be void against a liquidator, administrator or creditor.

2. When must a charge be registered in order to be validly registered?
In order to register a charge, a statement of particulars and a copy of the charge instrument must be delivered to Companies House within a 21-day period beginning after the day the charge was created (s. 859A).

3. What are the effects of registering a charge?
The registration of a charge has the following effects:

- the information provided will be included in the register of companies (s. 859I(2)), and can be freely accessed online or by visiting Companies House;
- the Registrar will provide a certificate of registration to the person who registered the charge (s. 859I(3)) and this certificate will provide conclusive evidence that the required documents were delivered within the period allowed for delivery (s. 859I(6)); and
- although the CA 2006 does not state what notice is provided by registering a charge, the courts have stated that registration provides constructive notice of the charge's existence but does not provide notice of its terms (*Wilson v Kelland* [1910] 2 Ch 306 (Ch)). It is unclear whether this is still the case under the new system of registration.

4. What are the effects of not registering a charge?
If a charge is not registered, then it will be void against a liquidator, administrator or creditor of the company (s. 859H(3)). Note that it is the security and not the debt that is rendered void. Accordingly, the company will still owe the money to the creditor concerned, but the creditor will lose their secured status. To offset this, if a charge becomes void for non-registration, then the money secured by the charge will become immediately payable (s. 859H(4)).

Chapter 14

Test yourself 14.1

1. What constitutes a company's annual accounts and reports?
Section 471 of the CA 2006 provides that a company's annual accounts and reports consist of:

- the annual accounts;
- the strategic report;
- the directors' report;
- the auditor's report; and
- the directors' remuneration report (only quoted companies need prepare this report).

Not all companies need prepare all the above reports (e.g. a small company need not prepare a strategic report).

2. Explain the difference between individual accounts and group accounts.
The directors of a company (except a dormant subsidiary) are under a duty to prepare accounts for that company for each of its financial years. These are referred to as the company's individual accounts (ss. 394 and 394A).

A parent company (except one that is small, s. 399(2A)) must also prepare group accounts for each financial year (s. 399(2)). The information contained in the group accounts is largely the same as that found in the individual accounts, except that the group accounts need to cover the accounts of the parent and all of its subsidiaries (ss. 404 and 405(1)).

3. What is 'narrative reporting'?
Narrative reporting refers to the inclusion of non-financial information in a company's annual reports and other reports (except financial reports).

4. Are all companies required to prepare a strategic report and a directors' remuneration report?
All companies, except small companies, are required to prepare a strategic report. Only quoted companies are required to prepare a directors' remuneration report.

Test yourself 14.2

1. Explain the difference between a statutory audit and an internal audit.
The legally mandated auditing of the company's accounts is known as a 'statutory audit' and the auditor performing this audit is known as the 'statutory auditor'. Companies may also undertake an 'internal audit', which is essentially an audit of the company's processes and systems that aims to determine how effectively the company manages risk, whether the company's internal control systems are operating well, and whether the company is complying with the relevant laws and best practice recommendations.

2. Do all companies need to appoint an auditor?
An auditor must be appointed for each financial year of the company, unless the directors reasonably resolve otherwise on the ground that audited accounts are unlikely to be required (CA 2006, ss. 485(1) and 489(1)). In other words, a company must appoint an auditor unless it does not need to have its accounts audited.

3. Which types of person may not be appointed as a company's auditor?
Before appointing an auditor, the company must make sure that they are eligible to act as auditor, because a person who is not so eligible cannot act as a company's statutory auditor (s. 1213(1)) and will commit a criminal offence (s. 1213(3)). Section 1212(1) of the CA 2006 provides that a person is eligible to act as auditor if they satisfy the following two conditions:

- the proposed auditor is a member of a recognised supervisory body (e.g. the Institute of Charted Accountants in England and Wales, or the Association of Chartered Certified Accountants); and
- the proposed auditor is eligible for appointment under the rules of the supervisory body to which they belong.

4. Does an auditor owe a duty of care to third parties (for example, members of a company)?
An auditor will only owe a duty to third parties if the third party can show that the auditor assumed a responsibility to them (such as where a third party specifically asks an auditor to value a company's shares and the auditor knows that the information they provide will be used by the third party when deciding whether to buy the shares or not).

5. What are the four ways by which an auditor can vacate office?
The four ways that an auditor can vacate office are

- resignation;
- removal;
- replacement; and
- rotation.

Chapter 15

Test yourself 15.1

1. What are the three insider dealing offences?
Section 52 of CJA 1993 sets out the three insider dealing offences:

- dealing in price-affected securities on the basis of inside information;
- encouraging another person to deal in price-affected securities on the basis of inside information; and
- disclosing inside information.

2. When will a person have information as an insider?
Section 57(1) provides that a person has information as an insider if and only if:

- it is, and they know that it is, inside information; and
- they have it, and know that they have it, from an inside source.

3. What is inside information?
Section 56(1) provides that 'inside information' is information which:

- relates to particular securities, to a particular issuer of securities or to particular issuers of securities – not to securities generally or to issuers of securities generally;
- is specific or precise;
- has not been made public; and
- if it were made public would be likely to have a significant effect on the price of any securities.

4. Who is an insider?
Section 57(1) provides that a person has information from an inside source if and only if they have it through:

(a) being a director, employee or shareholder of an issuer of securities;
(b) having access to the information by virtue of their employment, office, or profession; or
(c) the direct or indirect source of the information is a person within (a).

Test yourself 15.2

1. What piece of EU legislation aims to combat market abuse?
The piece of EU legislation that seeks to combat market abuse is the 2014 Market Abuse Regulation (596/2014/EU) (MAR).

2. Which body is the competent authority for applying the EU rules on market abuse?
In the UK, the competent authority for applying the EU rules on market abuse is the Financial Conduct Authority.

3. Provide five examples of the type of activity that can constitute market manipulation.

Article 12 of MAR sets out the types of activities that constitute market manipulation, including:

- entering into a transaction, placing an order to trade or any other behaviour which:
  - gives, or is likely to give, false or misleading signals as to the supply of, demand for, or price of, a financial instrument; or
  - secures, or is likely to secure, the price of one or several financial instruments at an abnormal or artificial level;
- entering into a transaction, placing an order to trade or any other activity or behaviour which affects or is likely to affect the price of one or several financial instruments, which employs a fictitious device or any other form of deception or contrivance;
- disseminating information through the media, including the internet, or by any other means, which gives (or is likely to give) false or misleading signals as to the supply of, demand for, or price of, a financial instrument, or secures (or is likely to secure) the price of one or several financial instruments at an abnormal or artificial level. This includes the dissemination of rumours where the person who made the dissemination knew, or ought to have known, that the information was false or misleading;
- transmitting false or misleading information or providing false or misleading inputs in relation to a benchmark where the person who made the transmission or provided the input knew or ought to have known that it was false or misleading, or any other behaviour which manipulates the calculation of a benchmark;
- conduct by a person, or persons acting in collaboration, to secure a dominant position over the supply of or demand for a financial instrument, which has, or is likely to have, the effect of fixing, directly or indirectly, purchase or sale prices or creates, or is likely to create, other unfair trading conditions; or
- the buying or selling of financial instruments at the opening or closing of the market, which has or is likely to have the effect of misleading investors acting on the basis of the prices displayed, including the opening or closing prices.

4. What sanctions can be imposed upon a person who has engaged in market abuse?

Where a person (*P*) engages in prohibited insider dealing or prohibited market manipulation, then FSMA 2000 empowers the FCA to impose a range of sanctions upon that person, including:

- imposing upon *P* a penalty of such amount as the FCA considers appropriate (s. 123(1) and (2)) or, instead of imposing a penalty, publishing a statement censuring *P* (s. 123(3));

- temporarily or permanently prohibiting *P* from holding certain positions, such as an office or position involving responsibility for taking decisions about the management of an investment firm (s. 123A(2)(a));
- temporarily prohibiting *P* from acquiring or disposing of financial instruments (s. 123A(2)(b));
- suspending, for such period as the FCA considers appropriate (up to a maximum of 12 months), any permission which *P* has to carry on a regulated activity (s. 123B(2)(a) and (4));
- imposing, for such period as the FCA considers appropriate (up to a maximum of 12 months), such limitations or other restrictions in relation to the carrying on of a regulated activity by the person as the FCA considers appropriate (s. 123B(2)(b) and (4)).

Chapter 16

Test yourself 16.1

1. What is a scheme of reconstruction?
A scheme of reconstruction allows a company (the transferor company) to transfer all or part of its business to another company (or companies), and the transferor company is then voluntarily wound up.

2. Briefly explain the process for putting a scheme of reconstruction into effect.
The process for putting a scheme of reconstruction into effect is as follows:

- the transferor company passes a special resolution to voluntarily wind itself up;
- the scheme of reconstruction must be sanctioned;
- the scheme, once sanctioned, will be put into effect and will bind the members and creditors of the transferor company;
- the transferor company is liquidated and all or part of its business transferred to another company or companies; and
- the members of the transferor company will usually receive shares in the company to which the business has been transferred.

3. How can a member or creditor dissent from the scheme?
Members can dissent from the scheme by leaving a written statement to this effect at the company's registered office within seven days of the resolution being passed (IA 1986, s. 111(2)). The liquidator will then be required to either:

- abstain from carrying out the reconstruction; or
- purchase the dissenting member's shares at a price to be determined by arbitration or agreement (s. 111(2)).

Creditors have no right of dissent under the IA 1986, but can try to stop the scheme by petitioning the court for a winding up order.

Test yourself 16.2

1. What is a scheme of arrangement?
A scheme of arrangement is a compromise or arrangement between a company and (i) its creditors, or any class of them; or (ii) its members, or any class of them (CA 2006, s. 895(1)).

2. Provide some examples of the types of transactions that a scheme of arrangement can be used for.
A scheme can be put into operation in order to undertake a wide variety of aims, including:

- to implement a takeover or a merger (as recognised by s. 900(1));
- to restructure a company's debt;
- to attempt to rescue a financially struggling company (e.g. an administrator may propose that the company enter into a scheme of arrangement with its creditors);
- to divide or demerge a company; or
- to restructure share capital.

3. Briefly explain the three stages of putting a scheme of arrangement into effect.
The three stages of putting a scheme of arrangement into effect are:

- an application is made to the court and, if this application is successful, the court will summon meetings of the relevant creditors/members;
- approval of the scheme is sought from the relevant members/creditors; and
- an application is made to the court to sanction the scheme.

4. What are the effects of a scheme of arrangement coming into effect?
The sanctioned scheme will bind the company and those creditors or members who are affected by it (s. 899(3)). The scheme will not bind third parties, although it can indirectly affect third party rights (see e.g. *Re La Seda de Barcelona SA* [2010] EWHC 1364 (Ch)).

Test yourself 16.3

1. What are the three principal functions of the Takeover Panel?
The Takeover Panel has three broad functions:

- It must make rules giving effect to certain provisions of the Takeover Directive (CA 2006, s. 943(1)), namely the City Code on Takeovers on Mergers.
- The Takeover Panel may give rulings on the interpretation, application or effect of the City Code (s. 945(1)). These rulings are binding (s. 945(2)).
- The Takeover Panel may provide directions in order:
  - to restrain a person from acting, or continuing to act, in breach of the City Code;
  - to restrain a person from doing, or continuing to do, a particular

thing, pending determination of whether that or any other conduct of his is or would be a breach of the City Code; or

- otherwise to secure compliance with the City Code (s. 946).

2. What is the principal purpose of the Takeover Code?

The Introduction to the Takeover Code provides that its principal purpose is:

> 'to ensure that shareholders in an offeree company are treated fairly and are not denied an opportunity to decide on the merits of a takeover and that shareholders in the offeree company of the same class are afforded equivalent treatment by an offeror. The Code also provides an orderly framework within which takeovers are conducted. In addition, it is designed to promote, in conjunction with other regulatory regimes, the integrity of the financial markets.'

3. Can the Panel ignore a rule in the Takeover Code?

The Panel may derogate or grant a person a waiver from the application of a rule either:

- in the circumstances set out by the rule; or
- in other circumstances where the Panel considers that the particular rule would operate unduly harshly or in an unnecessarily restrictive or burdensome or otherwise inappropriate manner (in which case a reasoned decision will be given).

4. Provide three examples of sanctions that can be imposed for a breach of the Takeover Code.

Sanctions that can be imposed include:

- issuing a public or private statement censuring the offender;
- reporting the offender's conduct to a UK or overseas regulator, or professional body (notably the FCA), and that regulator or body can then decide whether to take action against the offender; and
- publishing a statement indicating that the offender is not someone who is likely to comply with the Code (this is known as 'cold-shouldering').

5. For how long must an offer remain open once the offer document has been published?

The offer must remain open for at least 21 days (rule 31.1).

6. When will an offeror be required to make a mandatory offer?

Rule 9.1 provides that this 'mandatory offer' must be made where:

- a person (on their own or acting in concert with others) acquires an interest in shares that carry 30% or more of the company's voting rights; or
- a person (acting on their own or in concert with others) is interested in shares which carry between 30% and 50% of the company's voting rights, and that person (or someone acting in concert with them) acquires an interest in any other shares that increases the percentage of shares carrying voting rights in which he is interested.

7. What are squeeze-out and sell-out rights?
Sell-out rights provide the shareholders of an offeree company with the ability to compel the offeror to purchase their shares once certain conditions are met. Squeeze-out rights empower an offeror to compel the offeree's shareholders to sell their shares once certain conditions have been met.

Chapter 17

Test yourself 17.1

1. What is the purpose of administration?
Schedule B1, para 3(1) of the IA 1986 provides that the administrator of a company must perform their functions with the objective of:

- rescuing the company as a going concern; or
- achieving a better result for the company's creditors as a whole than would be likely if the company were wound up (without first being in administration); or
- realising property in order to make a distribution to one or more secured or preferential creditors.

These three objectives are collectively referred to as 'the purpose of administration'.

2. What are the three methods of appointing an administrator?
An administrator can be appointed in three ways:

- by the company or its directors
- by a qualifying floating chargeholder
- by court order.

3. Briefly outline the effects of administration.
The effects of administration are:

- depending on the method of appointment, any pending winding up petition will be dismissed or suspended;
- any administrative receivers will vacate office;
- there is a moratorium of insolvency proceedings and certain other legal processes;
- the powers of the directors are effectively suspended; and
- the business documents and websites of the company must state that it is in administration.

4. What is a pre-pack?
Paragraph 1 of Statement of Insolvency Practice 16 defines a pre-pack as 'an arrangement under which the sale of all or part of a company's business or assets is negotiated with a purchaser prior to the appointment of an administrator and the administrator effects the sale immediately on, or shortly after, appointment'.

5. When will a company cease to be in administration?
A company ceases to be in administration when the administrator's appointment ceases (Schedule B1, para 1(2)(c)), which can occur in a number of ways.

Test yourself 17.2

1. What is a CVA?
A company voluntary arrangement (CVA) is an insolvency procedure that allows a company to enter into a binding arrangement with its creditors.

2. Who can propose, and act as nominee for, a CVA?
The process of implementing a CVA begins with a proposed arrangement between the company and its creditors. A proposed CVA comes from:

- the company's directors, providing that the company is not in administration or liquidation (s. 1(1));
- the company's administrator, if the company is in administration (s. 1(3)(a)); or
- the company's liquidator, if the company is in liquidation (s. 1(3)(b)).

3. How is a CVA approved?
The proposed CVA will need to be approved by the company and its creditors.

- As regards obtaining the company's approval, the nominee must invite the company's members to a meeting to consider the proposed CVA (IR 2016, r 2.25(1)). The members, who must be provided with at least 14 days' notice of the meeting, will approve the proposal if a majority of them (in value) vote in favour of the proposal (IR 2016, r 2.36(1)).
- The creditors will approve the proposal by way of a qualifying decision procedure (IA 1986, s. 3(3)), and the details of this procedure (e.g. venue, how the decision is to be decided) will be determined by the nominee (IA 1986, s. 246ZE(2)). Alternatively, the 'deemed consent procedure' can be used, under which the proposal will be approved unless 10% of the creditors in value object to the proposal (IA 1986, s. 246ZF).

4. When will a company be eligible for a CVA with a moratorium?
A CVA with a moratorium is currently available to small companies (although the government has stated that it plans to abolish this moratorium).

5. What are the effects of the moratorium?
While the moratorium is in effect:

- no petition may be presented to wind up the company, and no resolution may be passed to wind up the company;
- no meeting of the company can be called, except with the consent of the nominee or leave of the court;

- no administrator can be appointed by the company, its directors or by a qualifying floating chargeholder, nor can an administrative receiver be appointed; and
- no other steps may be taken to enforce any security over the company's property, or to repossess goods in the company's possession under any hire-purchase agreement, except with the leave of the court and subject to such terms as the court may impose (Schedule A1, para 12(1)).

Chapter 18

Test yourself 18.1

1. What is liquidation?
Liquidation is the process by which the company's assets are collected and distributed to persons so entitled. The company will then be dissolved.

2. When is liquidation deemed to commence?
The commencement of winding up will depend upon the type of winding up:

- a voluntary winding up is deemed to commence when the special resolution is passed resolving to wind the company up;
- a compulsory winding up usually commences when the winding up application is presented to the court.

3. What are the two types of voluntary winding up, and what are the differences between them?
There are two types of voluntary winding up: a members' voluntary winding up and a creditors' voluntary winding up. The difference between them is based on whether the directors make a declaration of solvency. If such a declaration is made, it will be a members' voluntary winding up. If no declaration is made, it will be a creditors voluntary winding up.

4. Name five types of person who can petition the court for a winding up order.
Under s. 124(1) of the IA 1986, the following persons can apply to the court for a winding up order:

- the company (such applications are rare, as the company would likely prefer a voluntary winding up);
- the directors of the company;
- any creditor or creditors of the company, including any contingent or prospective creditor or creditors (most applications are brought by creditors of the company);
- a contributory or contributories (s. 79(1) provides that a 'contributory' is a person liable to contribute to the assets of the company upon it being wound up, e.g. a shareholder whose shares are not fully paid for);

- a liquidator within the meaning of Article 3(1) of the EU Regulation on Insolvency Proceedings; and
- the designated officer in a magistrates' court.

5. On what grounds can a compulsory winding up order be made?
Section 122(1) provides that a company may be wound up by the court if:

- the company has by special resolution resolved that the company be wound up by the court;
- being a public company which was registered as such on its original incorporation, the company has not been issued with a trading certificate and more than a year has expired since it was so registered;
- it is an old public company;
- the company does not commence its business within a year from its incorporation or suspends its business for a whole year;
- the company is unable to pay its debts;
- at the time at which a moratorium for the company under s. 1A comes to an end, no CVA has effect in relation to the company; or
- the court is of the opinion that it is just and equitable that the company should be wound up.

Test yourself 18.2

1. What is the role of a liquidator?
Section 143(1) of the IA 1986 (which applies to compulsory windings up) states that the functions of the liquidator are 'to secure that the assets of the company are got in, realised and distributed to the company's creditors and, if there is a surplus, to the persons entitled to it' (a similar provision can be found in s. 107 in relation to voluntary windings up).

2. What does the* pari passu *principle state?
The *pari passu* principle states that the liquidator will distribute the assets to the creditors in proportion to the size of their claim against the company (each creditor will receive an equal proportion of the debt owed to it).

3. Set out the order in which the assets of the company are distributed.
The order of distribution of assets upon liquidation is as follows:

- liquidation expenses
- preferential debts
- debts secured by floating charge (minus the 'prescribed part')
- unsecured debts
- deferred debts
- any remaining assets are distributed to the members.

4. What is a preferential debt?
Preferential debts include:

- contributions to occupational pension schemes; and
- certain remuneration owed to employees (but only the first £800 ranks as preferential).

5. How is the prescribed part calculated?
The liquidator must set aside a portion of the assets subject to a floating charge:

- where the company's net property does not exceed £10,000 in value, 50% of that property; or
- where the company's net property does exceed £10,000 in value, 50% of the first £10,000 in value, and 20% of that part of the company's net property that exceeds £10,000 (Insolvency Act 1986 (Prescribed Part) Order 2003, Art. 3(1)).

The sum that is set aside is known as the 'prescribed part' and it cannot exceed £600,000 (although the government plans to increase this cap).

6. What is a deferred debt?
Statute provides that certain deferred debts (e.g. sums due to a member by way of dividend, IA 1986, s. 74(2)(f)) rank below the claims of unsecured creditors.

Test yourself 18.3

1. Provide six examples of the type of conduct that can result in liability under ss. 206–211.
Sections 206–211 create a range of offences that impose criminal liability on certain persons (usually past and present officers of the company) who have engaged in specified conduct:

- fraud in anticipation of the company being wound up (s. 206) (e.g. falsifying book entries, disposing of property obtained on credit which has not been fully paid for);
- transactions in fraud of creditors (s. 207) (e.g. gifting company property, concealing company property);
- misconduct in the course of winding up (s. 208) (e.g. concealing information from the liquidator);
- falsification of company books (s. 209);
- material omissions from statements relating to the company's affairs (s. 210); and
- false representations to creditors (s. 211).

2. How does fraudulent trading under the IA 1986 differ from fraudulent trading under the CA 2006?
The two key differences between fraudulent trading under the IA 1986 and fraudulent trading under the CA 2006 are:

- the IA 1986 provisions only apply where the company is in liquidation or administration, whereas s. 993 of the CA 2006 can apply at any time; and
- the IA 1986 provisions impose civil liability, whereas s. 993 of the CA 2006 imposes criminal liability.

3. When will a person have engaged in wrongful trading?
Sections 214 (which applies to companies in liquidation) and 246ZB (which applies to companies in administration) provide that a person will have engaged in wrongful trading if three conditions are satisfied, namely:

- the company has gone into insolvent liquidation or insolvent administration;
- at some time before the commencement of the winding up of the company or before the company entered administration, that person knew or ought to have concluded that there was no reasonable prospect that the company would avoid going into insolvent liquidation or entering insolvent administration; and
- that person was a director or shadow director of the company at that time (ss. 214(2) and 246ZB(2)).

4. How can a director avoid liability for wrongful trading?
A director will not be liable for wrongful trading if the court is satisfied that the director 'took every step with a view to minimising the potential loss to the company's creditors as … he ought to have taken' (ss. 214(3) and 246ZB(3)).

5. What is a prohibited name?
A 'prohibited name' is:

- a name by which the liquidating company was known at any time in the 12-month period prior to its liquidation; or
- a name which is so similar to a name falling within (a) as to suggest an association with that company (s. 216(2)).

6. What are the consequences of breaching s. 216?
A person who breaches s. 216 commits a criminal offence (s. 216(4)) and can be made personally liable for the debt and liabilities of the new company incurred while they were involved in its management in contravention of s. 216 (s. 217). This personal liability is joint and several with that of the company (s. 217(2)).

Test yourself 18.4

1. When will a transaction be at an undervalue?
A company enters into a transaction at an undervalue if:

- the company makes a gift to a person or otherwise enters into a transaction with a person on terms that provide for the company to receive no consideration; or
- the company enters into a transaction with a person for a consideration the value of which, in money or money's worth, is significantly less than

the value, in money or money's worth, of the consideration provided by the company (s. 238(4)).

2. When will a person be connected with the company?
Section 249 provides that a person is connected with a company if:

- they are a director or shadow director of the company;
- they are an associate of a director or shadow director of the company; or
- they are an associate of the company.

3. What is a preference?
A company gives a preference to a person if:

- that person is one of the company's creditors or a surety or guarantor for any of the company's debts or other liabilities; and
- the company does anything or suffers anything to be done which (in either case) has the effect of putting that person into a position which, in the event of the company going into insolvent liquidation, will be better than the position they would have been in if that thing had not been done (s. 239(4)).

4. When will a credit transaction be extortionate?
A credit transaction is extortionate if:

- the terms of the transaction are or were such as to require grossly exorbitant payments to be made (whether unconditionally or in certain contingencies) in respect of the provision of the credit; or
- the transaction otherwise grossly contravened ordinary principles of fair dealing (s. 244(3)).

5. When can a liquidator or administrator invalidate a floating charge?
A floating charge can be invalidated by a liquidator or administrator if it was made at the relevant time:

- in the case of a charge which is created in favour of a person connected with the company, within a period of two years ending on the date of the onset of insolvency; or
- in the case of a charge which is created in favour of any other person, within a period of 12 months ending on the date of the onset of insolvency (s. 245(3)).

Directory of Resources

Further reading

- Armour, *The Company Secretary's Handbook* (11th edn, ICSA 2016).
- Davies & Worthington, *Gower's Principles of Modern Company Law* (10th edn, Sweet & Maxwell 2016).
- French, *Mayson, French & Ryan on Company Law* (35th edn, OUP 2018).
- Hannigan, *Company Law* (5th edn, OUP 2018).
- Kershaw, *Company Law in Context* (2nd edn, OUP 2012).
- Mallin, *Corporate Governance* (6th edn, OUP 2018).
- Morse, *Palmer's Company Law* (Swet & Maxwell 2018).
- Roach, *Company Law* (OUP 2019).
- Worthington, *Sealy & Worthington's Text, Cases & Materials in Company Law* (11th edn, OUP 2016).

Web resources

Companies House
https://www.gov.uk/government/organisations/companies-house

Companies House Service
https://beta.companieshouse.gov.uk

Competition & Markets Authority
https://www.gov.uk/government/organisations/competition-and-markets-authority

Department for Business, Energy & Industrial Strategy
https://www.gov.uk/government/organisations/department-for-business-energy-and-industrial-strategy

Financial Conduct Authority
https://www.fca.org.uk

FCA Handbook
https://www.handbook.fca.org.uk

Financial Reporting Council
https://www.frc.org.uk

Governance & Compliance Magazine
https://www.icsa.org.uk/knowledge/governance-and-compliance

Insolvency Service
https://www.gov.uk/government/organisations/insolvency-service

Institute of Directors
https://www.iod.com

London Stock Exchange
https://www.londonstockexchange.com/home/homepage.htm

Model articles
http://www.legislation.gov.uk/uksi/2008/3229/contents/made

Office of the Regulator of Community Interest Companies
https://www.gov.uk/government/organisations/office-of-the-regulator-of-community-interest-companies

Panel on Takeovers and Mergers
http://www.thetakeoverpanel.org.uk

Serious Fraud Office
https://www.sfo.gov.uk

Takeover Appeal Board
http://www.thetakeoverappealboard.org.uk

Takeover Code
http://www.thetakeoverpanel.org.uk/wp-content/uploads/2008/11/code.pdf?v=8Jan2018

UK Corporate Governance Code
https://www.frc.org.uk/directors/corporate-governance-and-stewardship/uk-corporate-governance-code

UK Stewardship Code
https://www.frc.org.uk/investors/uk-stewardship-code

Wates Corporate Governance Principles for Large Private Companies
https://www.frc.org.uk/directors/corporate-governance-and-stewardship/governance-of-large-private-companies

Glossary

Allotted share capital – The total nominal value of shares that a company has allotted.

Articles of association – The internal constitutional rules that regulate a company.

Authorised share capital – The maximum total nominal value of shares that a company may issue.

Beneficial owner – The beneficial owner of shares is the person who ultimately controls those shares.

Bona vacantia – 'Ownerless goods.' Such goods usually pass to the Crown but can then be bought back by others.

Bonus shares – Shares that are issued fully paid up to existing shareholders in proportion to their existing holdings.

Called-up share capital – The paid-up share capital plus any payment called for or any instalment due.

Codification – The placing of law into statute.

Contractual capacity – The ability to enter into contracts.

Debenture – A document which acknowledges or creates a debt.

Debt capital – Capital obtained by borrowing from others (also known as loan capital).

Default – A failure to perform a legally obligated act.

Derivative claim – An action brought by a member on behalf of the company to enforce a right belonging to the company.

Fiduciary – A person who occupies a position of trust in relation to another and owes certain duties to that other person.

Forfeiture – Where the company or directors exercise a power (e.g. in the articles) to take away a person's shares.

Form IN01 – The application for registration that provides details regarding the company to be incorporated.

Institutional investors – Powerful shareholders such as banks, pension funds and insurance companies that invest significant sums in the stock market on their own behalf and on behalf of their customers/clients.

Issued share capital – The total nominal value of shares that a company has issued.

Joint and several liability – Where two or more persons (the 'wrongdoers') commit a legal wrong that can result in joint and several liability, then the victim of the wrong can sue any wrongdoer for the loss sustained or all the wrongdoers.

Legal owner – The legal owner of shares is the person whose name is entered into the register of members in respect of those shares.

Memorandum of association – A document that provides details of a company at the time of its incorporation.

mens rea **–** The 'guilty mind.' The mental element required to convict a defendant of certain offences.

Minutes – A written account providing records of a meeting.

Misfeasance – The improper or unlawful performance of a lawful act.

Model articles – A set of default articles provided by the Companies (Model Articles) Regulations 2008.

Money laundering – The process by which the source of illegally obtained money is concealed, usually by passing the money through a series of legitimate businesses.

Negligent misstatement – A statement negligently made where the statement maker owes a duty to another person and that person has suffered loss due to the statement.

Nominal value – A fixed value that must be attached to all the shares in a limited company.

Novation – A tripartite agreement which involves discharging a contract between two parties, then creating a new contract between one of those parties and a third party.

Obiter dictum – 'A thing said by the way.' A statement made by a judge in a judgment which is not directly relevant to the case, and so is merely of persuasive authority.

Official List – The FCA-maintained list of companies that have securities listed on a UK-regulated market.

Official receiver – A civil servant and officer of the court, who can act as provisional liquidator or liquidator of a company.

Paid-up share capital – The combined total of the nominal value of shares that has actually been paid.

Pari passu – 'With equal step.'

Passporting – The right of a company registered in an EEA state to do business in another EEA state without obtaining further authorisation.

Pre-incorporation contract – A contract entered into with a company prior to that company being fully incorporated.

Premium listing – A company whose shares have a premium listing is subject to additional rules and is expected to meet the highest standards of regulation and governance.

Private Act – An Act of Parliament that affects specified persons, groups of persons, organisations or localities.

Promoter – A person involved in the creation of a company, other than through providing professional services.

Public Act – An Act of Parliament that deals with matters of public interest and usually affects the general population.

Qua – 'In the capacity of.'

Quorum – A minimum number of qualifying persons required to be present in order to conduct business.

Right of establishment – The right afforded to EU persons to establish a business in another EU member state.

Royal charter – A formal document issued by the Crown or certain persons empowered to act on her behalf.

Securities – Shares or debentures (note, this is the CA 2006 definition – other legislation may define the term differently).

Severed – Where part of a transaction (e.g. a term of a contract) can be discarded while leaving the remainder of the transaction intact.

Share premium – The amount paid for a share that is over the nominal value.

Single alternative inspection location – The location other than the company's registered office, where documents may be kept available for inspection.

Stayed – The suspension of proceedings.

Surrendered – Where shares are given up by a member.

Thing in action – A 'thing' is an asset other than land, with a 'thing in action' being an intangible thing.

Traded company – A company with any shares that (i) carry rights to vote at general meetings; and (ii) are admitted to trading on a regulated market in an EEA state by or with the consent of the company.

Ultra vires – 'Beyond one's powers.'

Uncalled share capital – The amount that a company can call on before the shares are fully paid for.

Vicarious liability – Liability imposed upon a person for the acts or omissions of another person.

Index

www.ingramcontent.com/pod-product-compliance
Ingram Content Group UK Ltd.
Pitfield, Milton Keynes, MK11 3LW, UK
UKHW051928100926
8556IPUK00022B/1440

9 781860 7274